# Women & Change
# in the Caribbean

Photograph on jacket and cover
Edna Manley, *The Message*, 1977
(Climent fondu, height 45")
Collection of: Commonwealth
Secretariat, London, used with
permission of the
Commonwealth Secretariat
Photographer: Maria La Yacona

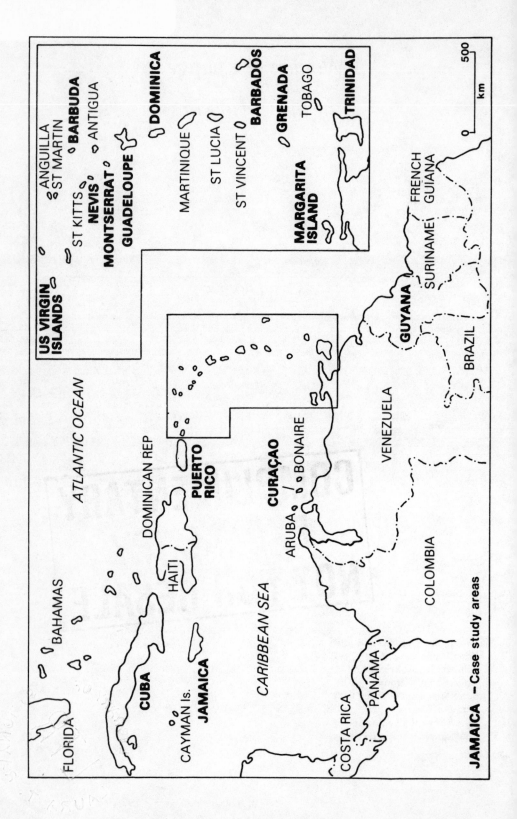

# Women & Change in the Caribbean

A PAN-CARIBBEAN
PERSPECTIVE

EDITED BY
**JANET MOMSEN**

IAN RANDLE
KINGSTON

INDIANA UNIVERSITY PRESS
BLOOMINGTON & INDIANAPOLIS

JAMES CURREY
LONDON

James Currey Ltd
54b Thornhill Square, Islington, London, N1 1BE

Ian Randle Publishers
206 Old Hope Road, Kingston 6, Jamaica

Indiana University Press
601 North Morton Street
Bloomington 47404-3797, USA

**British Library Cataloguing in Publication Data**

Women and Change in the Caribbean:
Pan-Caribbean
Perspective
     I. Momsen, Janet Henshall
     305. 4209729


    ISBN    0-85255-403-6 (Paper)
             0-85255-404-4 (Cloth)

**Library of Congress Cataloging-in-Publication Data**

Women and change in the Caribbean / edited by Janet Momsen.
    p.      cm.
    Includes bibliographical references and index.
    ISBN 0-253-33897-2 (cloth). — ISBN 0-253-33896-4 (paper)
     1. Women in development — Caribbean Area. 2. Women — Caribbean
Area — Social conditions. I. Momsen. Janet Henshall.
HQ1240.5.C27W66 1993
305.42'09729—dc20                                     93–422


1 2 3 4 5 97 96 95 94 93


Typeset in 9/10 pt Palatino by
Selro Publishing Services, Oxford
Printed by Villiers Publications, London

# Contents

SECTION TWO
## *Economic Roles*
## *of Caribbean Women*                                      179

# Preface

The Caribbean is one of the key areas in the development of world capitalism. Here the first plantations were established by European entrepreneurs using the forced labour of women and men from Africa and Asia. Within the consequent regional diversity of race, class, language and religion, new social forms developed. The unifying theme of the book, which all 21 contributors have taken as their focus, is this process of change and its impact on gender roles and gender relations.

The contributors come from the academic disciplines of agriculture, anthropology, economics, geography, history, sociology and women's studies. They are based in universities in the Caribbean, Europe, Canada and the United States and are all active field research workers.

The aim of the book is to examine a number of critical issues concerning women and development by bringing together research on one particular small but complex region. Over the last decade many projects have been undertaken on Caribbean women. However, this is the first to include studies of the English, French, Spanish and Dutch speaking Caribbean and so provides a benchmark in Caribbean gender research.

The gestation period of this book has been unusually long because of the difficulties of bringing together such a wide ranging corpus of work. I thank all the contributors for their patience, support, and friendship and, above all, for encouraging me to put together this collection despite being an outsider.

# Contributors

**Eva Abraham-Van der Mark**, Ph.D. (Amsterdam) is a research officer with the Anthropological-Sociological Centre of the University of Amsterdam, the Netherlands. She has done extensive research in the Netherlands Antilles and in the Netherlands.

**Charles S. Alexander** (1916-87), Ph.D. (Berkeley), was Professor of Geography at the University of Illinois at Champaign-Urbana. He wrote his doctoral thesis on the geography of Margarita Island and also did research on Puerto Rico.

**Christine Barrow**, D. Phil. (Sussex). An anthropologist, she has been at the University of the West Indies in Barbados since 1970 and is currently Senior Lecturer and Head of the Department of Sociology and Government. She was a Research Fellow on the Women in the Caribbean Project and has worked in Barbados, St Lucia, St Kitts-Nevis, Antigua and Montserrat.

**Riva Berleant-Schiller**, Ph.D. (State University of New York at Stony Brook) is Professor of Anthropology at the University of Connecticut. She is the author of *Montserrat: A Critical Bibliography* (Clio 1991) and co-author of *The Keeping of Animals: Ecology and Social Organization in Livestock Producing Communities* (Allenheld-Rowman 1984). She has published many papers based on her field and archival research in Barbuda, Montserrat and Nevis.

**Jean Besson**, Ph.D. (Edinburgh), Senior Lecturer in Anthropology, Goldsmiths' College, University of London. A Jamaican, Dr Besson taught Social Anthropology at the University of Edinburgh, Scotland from 1974-6. She subsequently lectured in Anthropology at the University of Aberdeen (1976-90); was Chair of the Society for Caribbean Studies in the UK (1987-9); and Visiting Associate Professor in Anthropology at the Johns Hopkins University (1989-90). Dr Besson has conducted extensive fieldwork in rural Jamaica and published widely on Caribbean peasantries. She is co-editor of *Land and Development in the Caribbean* (Macmillan 1987) and editor of *Caribbean Reflections: The Life and Times of a Trinidad Scholar (1901-1986). An Oral History Narrated by William W. Besson* (Karia Press 1989).

**Rosemary Brana-Shute**, Ph.D. (Florida) is Associate Professor in the Department of History at the College of Charleston, South Carolina. She has done extensive fieldwork in Suriname and the Eastern Caribbean. She is co-editor of *Crime and Punishment in the Caribbean* (University of Florida Press 1980) and editor of *A Bibliography of Caribbean Migration and Caribbean Immigrant Communities* (University of Florida Press 1983).

**John Brierley**, Ph.D. (Edinburgh) is Professor in the Geography Department at the University of Manitoba, Winnipeg. His Caribbean research has focused on Grenada and he is author of *Small Farming in Grenada, WI* (Manitoba 1974) and co-editor of *Small Farming and Peasant Resources* (Manitoba 1988).

**Huguette Dagenais**, Doctorat (Paris), is Professor in the Department of Anthropology at Laval University, Quebec. She is Director of the journal *Recherches féministes* and has published extensively on feminist methodology and on Guadeloupe and has also carried out field research in Haiti and Trinidad.

**Indra S. Harry**, Ph.D. (University of Calgary, Canada), is a Trinidadian. She is presently working at the University of Calgary as a Research Associate and Laboratory Manager in Plant Biotechnology. Her research interests include gender, Caribbean agriculture, economic botany and biotechnology.

**Bill Maurer** (Ph.D. candidate, Stanford University) is doing research in Tortola on the mutual construction of national and ethnic immigrant identities. His paper 'Caribbean Dance: "Resistance", Colonial Discourse and Subjugated Knowledges' appeared in the *Nieuwe West-Indische Gids/New West Indian Guide* in 1991.

**Lesley McKay**, M.Litt. (Aberdeen). She received her undergraduate and graduate training in Sociology and Social Anthropology at the University of Aberdeen, Scotland. She carried out fieldwork in Jamaica in 1985, studying the impact of tourism on the small community of Negril, and is author of 'Tourism and Changing Attitudes to Land in Negril, Jamaica', in Jean Besson and Janet Momsen (eds) *Land and Development in the Caribbean* (Macmillan 1987).

**Janet Momsen**, Ph.D. (London) is currently Senior Lecturer in Geography at the University of Newcastle upon Tyne and Acting Professor, University of California, Davis. Her Caribbean field experience includes research in Barbados, St Vincent, Grenada, St Lucia, Martinique, Dominica, Nevis and Montserrat. She was Chair of the Society for Caribbean Studies (1989-92) and is Chair of the International Geographical Union Commission on Gender and Geography. She is co-author of *A Geography of Brazilian Development* (Bell & Hyman 1974), co-editor of *Geography and Gender in the Third World* (Hutchinson 1987) and of *Land and Development in the Caribbean* (Macmillan 1987) and author of *Women and Development in the Third World* (Routledge 1991).

**Janice Monk**, Ph.D. (Illinois) is Executive Director of the South-West Institute for Research on Women and Adjunct Professor in the Department of Geography, University of Arizona, Tucson. She has done field research in Margarita Island and Puerto Rico and is Vice-Chair of the International Geographical Union Commission on Gender and Geography. She is co-editor of *The Desert is no Lady* (Yale University Press 1987) and of *Western Women: Their Land, Their Lives* (University of New Mexico Press 1988).

**Karen Olwig**, Ph.D. (Copenhagen), is a Lecturer in the Institute of Anthropology at the University of Copenhagen. Her Caribbean research has focused on St John, US Virgin Islands and Nevis. She has published extensively and is the author of *Cultural Adaptation and Resistance on St John: Three Centuries of Afro-Caribbean Life* (University of Florida Press 1985).

**Linda Peake**, Ph.D. (Reading) has taught in the School of Development Studies, University of East Anglia and in the Department of Geography at Kingston Polytechnic and is currently in Urban Studies at York University, Canada. She has spent several field periods in Jamaica and Guyana and is particularly interested in developing feminist perspectives in urban and political geography. She is co-editor of *Women, Human Settlements and Housing* (Tavistock 1987).

**Ruth Pearson**, D. Phil. (Sussex), is a lecturer in economics and gender analysis in the School of Development Studies at the University of East Anglia. She has written extensively on the internationalization of production and the sexual division of labour and has worked in Jamaica, Mexico, Argentine and Nigeria. She is co-editor of *Multinational Companies and Women's Employment in Europe* (Macmillan 1989).

**Lydia Mihelic Pulsipher**, Ph.D. (Southern Illinois) is Associate Professor in the Department of Geography at the University of Tennessee. She has been doing research on the cultural/historical geography and historical archaeology of the Eastern Caribbean since 1970 and since 1980 has directed the interdisciplinary study of Galways Plantation on Montserrat. This research was featured in the Smithsonian Museum of Natural History Exhibition, *Seeds of Change* (1991) which commemorated the changes wrought in New and Old World human geography by Columbus's voyages of exploration. Her publications include *Seventeenth Century Montserrat* (Geo Books 1986).

**Rhoda Reddock**, Ph.D. (The Hague) is Trinidadian. She was formerly an Associate Lecturer in the Women and Development programme at the Institute of Social Studies at The Hague . She is presently a Research Fellow at the Institute of Social and Economic Studies, University of the West Indies, St Augustine, Trinidad and is a founder member of the Caribbean Association for Feminist Research and Action (CAFRA). Her publications include *National Liberation and Women's Liberation* (edited with Maria Mies) and *Elma Francois, the NWSCA and the Workers Struggle for Change in the Caribbean* (New Beacon Books 1988).

**Jean Stubbs**, Ph.D. (London) lived in Cuba for 19 years where she researched Cuban history and contemporary development, with a special focus on gender and socialism. She has taught at the Institute of Development Studies of the University of Sussex and, in 1989-90, was Visiting Associate Professor under the CUNY Caribbean Exchange Programme at Hunter College, New York. She is currently Coordinator for the University of London's Institute of Commonwealth Studies and Institute of Latin American Studies Joint Caribbean Studies Programme and Senior Lecturer in Caribbean Studies and Latin American History at the University of North London. Her publications include *Tobacco on the Periphery: A Case Study in Cuban Labour History, 1860-1958* (Cambridge University Press 1985) and *Cuba: The Test of Time* (Latin America Bureau/Monthly Review Press 1989).

**Kevin A. Yelvington**, Ph.D. (University of Sussex) is an assistant professor in the Department of Sociology and anthropology at Florida International University. He is the editor of *Trinidad Ethnicity* (University of Tennessee Press and Macmillan 1992) and the author of *Producing Power on the Factory Floor: Ethnicity, Class and Gender in a Caribbean Workplace* (Temple University Press 1993). His research interests include ethnicity, class and gender relations, labour studies, development studies and Latin American and Caribbean history and popular culture.

# I Introduction*

JANET HENSHALL MOMSEN

*The Caribbean is the oldest area of European colonisation in the world. The indigenous Amerindian populations were virtually exterminated by European settlers and small-scale subsistence agriculture was replaced by the archetypal sugar plantation. A plantocracy from several European nations created some of the most profitable and advanced industrial enterprises of the seventeenth and eighteenth-century Western world, using African slave labour and later indentured workers from India, Indonesia and elsewhere. Hart (1989) identifies the region as the site of a precocious experiment in social engineering and a major crucible from which modern social organizations have evolved. Thus Caribbean social institutions are potentially of wide significance.*

*Within the Caribbean regional diversity of ethnicity, class, language and religion there is an ideological unity of patriarchy, of female subordination and dependence.[1] Yet there is also a vibrant living tradition of female economic autonomy, of female-headed households and of a family structure in which men are often marginal. So Caribbean gender relations are a double paradox: of patriarchy within a system of matrifocal and matrilocal families; and of domestic ideology coexisting with the economic independence of women. The roots of this contemporary paradoxical situation lie in colonialism. This book examines these contradictions within a trans-imperial framework.*

## Historical Context

The transhipment of Africans under slavery and the bonded or indentured migration of Asian workers offered many women, for a time, unplanned release from the patriarchal control of individual men within their own households. Instead they were, like men, subordinated to the dictates of capital and the ruling class. Women slaves were seen as equal to men in the eyes of the master as long as they worked as hard and were of equal strength (Patterson 1967) although, in addition, women were expected to provide sexual services on demand. Women resisted slavery both by limiting their fertility and by active rebellion (Mair 1974). Most women migrants came to the Caribbean to be plantation workers not housewives, as field workers not household servants, and their labour contributed to the development of European industrial capitalism. These experiences bestowed on Caribbean women a degree of social and economic independence which, in the

* An earlier version of this chapter was presented at a joint meeting of the University of London, Institute of Commonwealth Studies Postgraduate Seminar on Women, Colonialism and Commonwealth and of the Seminar on Caribbean Societies. I am grateful for the constructive comments of the participants in that seminar.

1

post-emancipation period, colonial and neo-colonial agencies such as the Church and the education system sought to destroy.

In the nineteenth century slavery was abolished and women were taught that marriage was both prestigious and morally superior. Yet many women continued to resist it for fear of violence within marriage or of losing parental rights, as well as because of a preference for economic autonomy. Single women in towns were arrested for unbecoming behaviour and many were punished for involvement in the anti-colonial struggles of the early twentieth century (Rodney 1981). Despite these pressures to conform to a Victorian ideology and retreat into the domestic sphere, Caribbean women's participation in the labour force continued to be very high (see Chapter 15). This societal conflict is reflected in ambivalent attitudes to women workers, for 'while the planters criticized mothers for neglecting their offspring, they preferred to hire females, whom they considered more regular than males in their work habits' (Levy 1980: 113).

In Trinidad, under indenture, planters sought only male workers but the colonial government insisted on a small proportion of female indentured workers on the grounds that this would prevent immoral behaviour and prostitution (Tikasingh 1973). The contradiction between the planters' short-term preference for adult male labourers and their long-term need for a self-reproducing cheap and plentiful labour force illustrates the paradoxes inherent in the perceptions of women's role in Caribbean society. Both Reddock (1985) and Emmer (1986) have shown, for Trinidad and Suriname respectively, that the women who left India to work in the Caribbean were more independent than most of their compatriots. Indenture was an escape route for Brahmin widows and child-widows, offering the opportunity for both remarriage and economic improvement. Only about one-third of the women who arrived from India were accompanied by husbands. Indian women indentured workers did not easily accept the prevailing male orthodoxy of the colonial view of women as 'housewives' or the Indian insistence on the seclusion of women of higher castes. The supply constraints on Indian women enabled them to resist the subordination of traditional arranged marriages and to develop the independence both to leave unsatisfactory marriages and to claim autonomy over their own lives. In 1880 in Trinidad, Indian men, with the help of Presbyterian ministers, petitioned the colonial government to control the mobility of women and force them to return to their husbands. In this way Church and State combined to reconstruct the Indian patriarchal family. The feminist movement emerging in the Caribbean today is seen by Rhoda Reddock (1990) as rooted in this long tradition of resistance to oppression and struggle for individual and collective autonomy.

A further paradox is that the contemporary patriarchy of Caribbean societies is often a patriarchy *in absentia*. This arises as a consequence of gender specific patterns of social behaviour (see Chapters 17 and 18) and of migration (see Chapters 9 and 10), which has become institutionalized in the region (Richardson 1983). The plantation workers torn from their native African communities created a population which after emancipation formed an international diaspora of migrants and settlers. At first this involved predominantly male migrants to Central America, where they played a major role in developing banana plantations and building the Panama Canal. After the Second World War both sexes migrated, separately and in families. The women who went to North America and Britain were often forced to leave their children behind in the care of grandmothers. Today every Caribbean territory is linked by complex movements of people, goods, money and information to settler communities in the industrialized countries of the north. Through this diaspora the influence of Caribbean social forms has spread widely. Although Caribbean nations may be tiny in world terms, their peoples have cosmopolitan attitudes with spatial perceptions which extend their territorial boundaries to disjunct corners of New York, London, Amsterdam, Paris and Toronto.

During the 1980s real wages in the Caribbean fell and unemployment in some islands reached 30 per cent. Harder times have led to accelerated migration from the region and provided fertile ground for crime, especially drug smuggling, and for domestic violence. In most territories the level of female unemployment is higher than male, yet women are also expected to cope with the extra care-giving necessitated by cutbacks in public services such as health and education and the effect on the family of social disruption (Deere et al. 1990). Most governments in the region are trying to save foreign exchange by substituting home grown food for imported items and it is often women, as the traditional producers and distributors of domestic foodstuffs, who are expected to respond to these policy initiatives. This has been made more difficult by the degradation of the fragile ecosystems of these small countries through long-term soil erosion, deforestation and water pollution and catastrophic events such as hurricanes, which appear to be increasing in intensity, possibly in response to global warming. Perceptions of and responses to such natural hazards also have gender dimensions (Momsen 1992).

Caribbean women are giving higher priority to economic autonomy as they seek more education and reduce their fertility. Today the Caribbean region has one of the highest levels of female economic activity rates and education in the so-called developing world, while the birth-rate in many territories has fallen to a level similar to that of the industrialized north (see Table 1.1).[2] These changes have occurred rapidly and a study of the processes involved has international relevance.

## Caribbean Feminist Research

Over the last few years Caribbean feminist research has developed a distinctive voice and an alternative vision (Antrobus 1989). Most of the major recent research projects on Caribbean women, notably the Women in the Caribbean Project 1979-82 (WICP), coordinated by Joycelin Massiah (Massiah 1986), the work of the Women and Development Unit (WAND) under the leadership of Peggy Antrobus (Ellis 1986) and the Women and Development Studies Project coordinated by Lucille Mathurin Mair and Rhoda Reddock (Mohammed and Shepherd 1988; Mohammed 1989) have been carried out under the auspices of the University of the West Indies. This work has basically focused on women of the Commonwealth Caribbean, and within those territories on Afro-Caribbean women, particularly the poor. Other research on Caribbean women has been within broadly the same locational parameter, even when focused on a particular historical period (Bush 1990; Morrissey 1989) or on a single economic sector (FAO 1989). Despite the enormous importance of this work in extending our understanding of gender relations and gender roles in Caribbean society, it has provided a somewhat unidimensional view of the women of a multi-faceted complex region.

Although Afro-Caribbean people are the largest ethnic group in the region, they are not a majority in every territory, particularly in those colonized by Spain. Other racial and religious groups, such as Amerindians, East Indian Hindus, Muslim East Indians and Indonesians, and Sephardic Jews play major cultural roles in certain territories. Different colonial traditions and the legacy of a variety of European languages creolized by the addition of African or Asian structures and vocabulary, or so intermingled that they become a separate language as in the Papiamento of the Dutch Antilles, have both divided and enriched the region. The greatest Caribbean poets and writers, such as Aimé Césaire, C.L.R. James and Derek Walcott, are those who have been able to interpret the conflict between colonial and Creole cultures, the Old World and the New. Yet language remains a barrier to the transmission of ideas within the region.

For English-speaking Caribbean feminists, theory development has been strongly influenced by American and British white middle-class ideas mediated through the close links between the Institute of Social Studies at The Hague, the Institute of Development Studies at the University of Sussex and the University of the West Indies, and by the training of West Indians at various universities in Britain, the US and Canada. There is great resistance to feminism in French scholarship and so work on gender in the French Caribbean *départements* has been isolated from both the European and the regional mainstream (Chapter 6). Gender relations in Spanish-speaking Caribbean territories have often been seen in Latin American rather than Caribbean terms. Intellectually their extra-territorial links have been strongly reinforced by politics, with Cuba following strict Marxist views on economic equality and Puerto Rico recreating American capitalist society. Both these approaches have sat uneasily on societies dominated by strong Latin traditions of *machismo*.

Yet individuals within the region have played major roles internationally: Lucille Mathurin Mair, currently Jamaica's Ambassador to the United Nations, was a leading figure throughout the United Nations Decade for Women and Peggy Antrobus of Barbados was a founder member of the Development Alternatives with Women for a New Era (DAWN) movement. They continue to bring a strong Caribbean voice to international feminist critiques of development theory. As Lucille Mair (1988: 9) has said, 'The challenge to a new and growing generation of Caribbean women scholars and activists is even more exciting. Located as they are within a diverse and dynamic global network, their individual interests and convictions show promise of coalescing, and thereby creating a historic vanguard.'

## Distinctiveness of the Caribbean

Such a coalescence was perhaps detected by Boserup (1970) in her trail-blazing study of *Women's Role in Economic Development*. Here she identifies the Caribbean as an anomalous region in terms of women's roles in agriculture, suggesting it is more like Africa than Latin America according to her continental-scale classification. Boserup explains this distinctiveness in terms of the dominance of a population of African origin. This approach appears to contradict her basic materialist thesis in which gender roles are seen to be principally determined by the system of production, primarily through the workings of the labour market and the level of technology. More recent studies show that commonalities among Caribbean women are based on more than ethnicity.

If the Caribbean is to be seen as more than a geographical expression, we need to explore the common ground for a feminist understanding of its culture and society. As Jean Franco (1989: xii) has stated for Mexico, 'the intervention of modern feminism in the sphere of public debate demands critical reflection on the differences between cultures and on the diverse configurations of the struggle for interpretative power.' This is especially so because, 'in studying the very different articulations of gender and subjectivity in societies formed by conquest and colonization, we confront a problem which has seldom been posed in modern theories of ideology — that is, the violent incorporation of a population into "forms of life" which they can never perceive as organic or natural' (Dews 1986: 209-10). This distinctive complexity has posed great problems for academic researchers. As Mintz and Price (1985: 8) argue:

> To date, literary works by Caribbean authors seem to have captured the special nature of women's experiences in the region more successfully than have academic analyses, and this is not altogether surprising. For gender seems to be an aspect of life where it is particularly difficult for observers to shed their own perspectives (whether sexist, feminist or somewhere in between) in order to explore with an open mind the complex ensembles of goals and expectations concerning men and women that have developed over time in particular cultural settings.

Women in the Caribbean exhibit higher levels of economic autonomy than are found in most parts of the south. This situation may be attributed to three factors. Firstly, under slavery women 'more fully encountered the impact of expropriation and growing labor exploitation than did slave men' (Morrissey 1989: 79) and, after emancipation, male out-migration left many women alone to carry the burden of supporting their children (Momsen 1988). The restrictions on marriage enforced by slave owners weakened the conjugal ties while often leaving the mother/child bond intact. This has led to the paradoxical view of Caribbean women as overburdened superwomen castrating and evicting men from the family (Dagenais 1988). Sex-specific migration further encouraged the development of female-headed households. In the Eastern Caribbean, 35 per cent of rural households are headed by women and some two-thirds of children are born out of wedlock. Marriage is often only entered into after the reproductive life stage is complete and it is seen as providing respectability for older women rather than economic support and legal status for children.

A second enabling factor for women in the Anglophone Caribbean has been their legal equality with male siblings in access to land (Safa 1986). In the Hispanic and Francophone Caribbean, however, patriarchal inheritance laws have limited women's ownership of land (Poirier and Dagenais 1986). Although in some areas land is now less important for its agricultural productivity, it remains an important symbol of status, security and autonomy (Besson 1987). Land reform has benefited women less than men in the Anglophone Caribbean (Andaiye and Antrobus 1991), and Jean Stubbs (Chapter 15) argues that it has had both negative and positive effects in Cuba, while in the Francophone Caribbean Dagenais (Chapter 6) shows that such changes have displaced women by ending sharecropping. In most parts of the region, farms run by women tend to be smaller, less accessible and to have fewer resources than male-operated farms (Henshall (Momsen) 1981).

Thirdly, this region is characterized by a highly educated population. Women value education and often struggle to maximize it for their children as the best means of ensuring upward economic mobility. There are clear age differences in educational attainment. Older women rarely have more than primary education, but younger women are not only better educated than their mothers[3] but are becoming more qualified than men (see Chapter 6). Where men have sought economic opportunity through migration, women have achieved it through education. This is particularly true in those islands, such as Montserrat and Nevis, which have had high levels of male out-migration.

## Organization of the Book

This volume offers a feminist interpretation of a multi-cultural society emerging from colonialism and experiencing rapid change and restructuring. It provides a trans-imperial and pan-Caribbean regional perspective by means of case studies of 15 different Caribbean territories, with Jamaica, Trinidad, Barbados, Nevis and Montserrat represented more than once. The book is divided into two sections: the first looks at women's status and gender relations in the private and public spheres; the second looks at women's economic activity. The collection is distinctive in that it takes a broad comparative view with contributions on territories with American, British, Dutch, Danish, French and Spanish colonial traditions and current political links. As Berleant-Schiller notes in her chapter, 'one of the great challenges of Caribbean research is reconciling the unmistakable individuality of each island with equally unmistakable pan-Caribbean commonalities' (see Table 1.1).

Although the contributors come from a range of disciplinary backgrounds, including agriculture, anthropology, economics, geography, history, sociology and women's studies, they have in common a strong basis in fieldwork. The unifying theme of the book, which all contributors have taken as their focus, is the process of change and development and its impact on gender roles and gender relations. It is hoped that our common belief in intensive field research and the focus on change will overcome the problems of the division of reality by individual social sciences and the use of partial methodologies for the study of social phenomena noted by Chhachhi (1989). The book's multi-disciplinary and pan-Caribbean coverage allows the extraction of new insights from this rare integration of wide-ranging yet similarly focused research. Secondly, by concentrating on a region with such a complex history and multi-cultural society, it provides an example which has relevance far beyond the Caribbean region.

Much of the recent discussion of post-modern culture has been expressed in terms of a movement from centre to periphery, and privileging cultures that were formerly marginalized. The subaltern voices of women who are marginalized by both gender and race in societies of a region such as the Caribbean, which is itself seen as increasingly marginalized in global terms (Manley 1990), are central to these issues.

## Main Themes

Several major themes run through the various chapters. The first is the concept of resistance to dominant patriarchal colonial policies[4] (see especially Chapters 2, 6, 7, 8, 16, and 17). Secondly, several contributors question the notion of a public/private dichotomy underlying gender roles (see Chapters 5, 9, 12, 18) and the focus in Caribbean research on women and the family (Chapters 2, 6).[5] The third master narrative considers the interaction of race, class and gender differentials (Chapters 3, 6, 7, 8, 9 and 17). A fourth overriding theme is the multiplicity of women's work (see especially Chapters 6, 10, 11, 14, 15 and 18). Feminist critiques of traditional paradigms provide themes which may be traced through several chapters.

Four contributors (Besson, McKay, Brana-Shute and Yelvington) present critiques of the model of respectability and reputation put forward by Wilson (1969), who saw Caribbean society as organized on the basis of a dialectic between these two opposed principles. Respectability is supposedly rooted in Eurocentric culture and based on class, wealth and education, while reputation offers an indigenous counter-culture based on equality and personal, as opposed to social, worth. Wilson argues that women are the bearers of respectability because of their closer association with the master class during slavery and that this role is reflected in their supposed restriction to the home and the emphasis they put on church affairs and the institution of marriage. He sees a man's virility as forming the basis of his reputation.

Besson (Chapter 2) criticizes Wilson's model by pointing out that women also gain status from their fertility and that men acquire more respectability as they age. Furthermore, she demonstrates that reputations, constructed in the context of male peer groups, are not based on the principle of equality since they are partly dependent on tarnishing female respectability. Besson concludes that Wilson himself fell into the trap of a preoccupation with and a Eurocentric interpretation of Caribbean family structure. She sees the cultures of Afro-Caribbean peasantries as dynamic outcomes of the class conflict in the capitalist world system. She further argues that the subcultures of subordinate classes, including women, may represent active modes of a resistant response to their 'violent incorporation' into the dominant culture.

The public/private dichotomy is also criticized by several contributors. The contradiction between economic autonomy and an ideology that restricts women to domestic activities is seen by Olwig (Chapter 9) as leading to conflict between the spheres of activity. Berleant-Schiller (Chapter 5) also questions the separation of the domestic and public realms and, with Olwig, believes that overlapping the domestic and community-based spheres makes the dichotomy useless for under-standing gender roles and ideology in the region. Christine Barrow (Chapter 11), too, in her study of Barbadian women small farmers, found that they did not perceive a demarcation of domains into public and private, but saw social repro-duction as including productive money-making activities. According to Dagenais (Chapter 6), Guadeloupean women also link the two spheres through a multiplic-ity of activities, combining paid work and home duties by taking on part-time work or home-based paid work.

Even where the domestic ideology is especially strong, the links with female economic autonomy are close. In Curaçao, Abraham-Van der Mark (Chapter 3) found that among the rich Sephardic Jewish families, where slaves and later servants were responsible for all household chores and child care, the domestic ideology was very marked. Arranged marriages, dowries and the very strict relegation of women to the domestic sphere because of the link between marriage and family resources paradoxically eventually gave women greater control over their own lives. This was also because under the Napoleonic Code they were able to inherit wealth in their own right. The widening of the economic base of the island in the twentieth century, making jobs available for both women and black men, undermined the institution of concubinage as well as that of marriage among the white élite.

In Jamaica, the domestic ideology encourages male support of women who act as landladies for tourists in Negril, for this activity is seen as a continuation of their mothering role. Thus men are willing to provide capital for these ventures, but McKay (Chapter 18) describes how women often resent male control and influ-ence over such enterprises and for this reason sometimes reject this work. On the other hand, Pearson (Chapter 19) shows that even among young, educated Jamaican women working in data processing, many aim only for careers in stereotyped female jobs as secretaries.

The cross-cutting of class, gender and age is seen in migration, which encourages increased flexibility in social relations. Using Margarita Island and Puerto Rico as case studies, Monk and Alexander (Chapter 10) show how development has differential gender and class effects, which lead to gender specific migration patterns and their consequent impact on social relations. Where fewer women than men migrate they become the guardians of tradition and culture, as noted by Brierley for rural Grenada (Chapter 12). Migrant women, according to Olwig (Chapter 9), tend to retain their links with their native island and send back remittances to a much greater extent than male migrants. In these cases they see their domestic sphere remaining in their natal source area and it is often many years before they recreate a family structure at the migration destination. Nevisian women view the household not as a residential unit but rather as a tight network of exchanges of support in which migration is just one strategy. As Olwig concludes, 'West Indians are the hunters and gatherers of the modern world economy, always on the look out for new economic opportunities'.

The multiplicity of women's roles is facilitated by the distinctive locus of the domestic sphere in the Caribbean, the yard, which can be traced back to slave days. The yard and its internal articulation allows Caribbean women to combine productive and reproductive roles. Both Besson and McKay note the importance of the yard for women's lives in Jamaica. Using field data from Montserrat, Lydia Pulsipher (Chapter 4) sees the houseyard as providing a coping strategy whereby women can both fulfil their reproductive imperative and achieve economic auton-omy by having a full-time paid job either at home or abroad. This is achieved by sharing child care and domestic duties among the inhabitants of the yard, both men and women. Most yards surveyed were matrifocal and matrilocal, with only 15 per cent of residents in nuclear families. Houseyards are female space and young girls are confined to these areas while boys are allowed to roam. House-yards also instil the value of personal autonomy and economic independence. The authority of the head of the yard increases with age and, with the support of their kin, women can retain their independence in the yard despite the growing infir-mities of old age.

For most Caribbean women, the stage in one's life cycle is an important determi-nant of one's status. Brana-Shute's work in Suriname, Abraham-Van der Mark's in Curaçao and Berleant-Schiller's in Barbuda show that women are accorded greater status, influence and spatial freedom as they move beyond child-bearing age. Age also brings status to the small-scale women farmers of Grenada (Brierley) and to East Indian women farmers in Trinidad (Harry). Older women are also allowed greater social freedom (Berleant-Schiller and Maurer). Stubbs noted that in Cuba women were happy to leave field labour when their household pressures eased as their children grew up, but that the new stress being laid on local food production is forcing them back into farming. Work on the division of labour (Momsen, Pearson, Brierley, McKay) illustrates how certain tasks and occupations are associated with women of specific age groups. Young women are most likely to work in export-oriented assembly industries (Monk, Momsen, Pearson and Yelvington), while older women turn to farming, higglering (Momsen, Brierley) and keeping guesthouses (McKay).

Several contributors focus on the importance of women's formal and informal networks in providing financial, emotional and child care support to individual women (Pulsipher), in spreading news and information (Berleant-Schiller and Maurer) and in organizing grassroots political action (Reddock, Brana-Shute, Peake). These last three contributors also emphasize the failure of women to gain political power at the national level, as does Jean Stubbs in her study of Cuban agriculture.

## Conclusion

Basically, the contributors to this volume see male-female relations in the Caribbean as a series of paradoxes (Besson 1987; and Chapters 3 and 6). During a period of increasing economic stress these paradoxes are becoming more acute among all ethnic groups. Consciousness of gender subordination is growing and national and regional women's organizations in the Caribbean are building alliances which are 'transcending some of the boundaries of language, culture, class, race and political affiliation in the region' (Safa and Antrobus 1991). Such pan-Caribbean links have a vital role to play at a time when the next decade in the Caribbean is seen (Jessop 1991) as one of intense marginalization and severe recession, followed by the restructuring of economies and the formation of new regional groupings cross-cutting the old colonial patterns (Andaiye and Antrobus 1991).

## Notes

1  We need to unpack patriarchy in the Caribbean in order to reveal its many paradoxes. Economic autonomy does not give women power nor does spatial separation of the sexes. McKay notes that in Negril men lead quite separate social lives but often control women's economic activities. Because of the maintenance of close links with migrants, men often retain decision-making power even when living for long periods in a different country. Jean Stubbs notes that in Cuba, although there is official democratization of the family, there is still state patriarchy. Although Caribbean women may have power in the family, especially when older, and may be economically independent, this does not negate patriarchy. Huguette Dagenais (Chapter 6) indicates that women's position in the labour market rarely provides economic security and in Guadeloupe men see the introduction by the state of an allowance for single mothers as threatening male control over women.
2  Dagenais sees the acceptance of family planning in Guadeloupe as a major break with tradition.
3  Brierley did not find this generational change in levels of education among rural women in Grenada, but both Harry and Yelvington noted it in Trinidad and Stubbs observed it in Cuba.
4  In her innovative doctoral thesis Lucille Mathurin Mair provided a model for the integration of gender, class and race in Caribbean research. She also considers the important role played by women in slave resistance and elaborates this concept in her keynote address in 1988 (Mair 1988a).
5  Barrow (1988: 156-69) discusses the major theoretical approaches to the Caribbean family, while Ellis (1986: 7) also briefly describes family structure.

## References

Andaiye, A. and Peggy Antrobus (1991) 'Towards a Vision of the Future: Gender Issues in Regional Integration'. Paper commissioned by the West Indian Commission, Barbados, WAND, University of the West Indies

Antrobus, Peggy (1989) 'Women and Planning: The Need for an Alternative Analysis'. Paper presented at the University of the West Indies Second Disciplinary Seminar in the Social Sciences on Women, Development Policy and the Management of Change, Barbados, April

Barrow, Christine (1988) 'Anthropology, the Family and Women in the Caribbean'. In Mohammed and Shepherd, q.v., 156-69

Besson, Jean (1987) 'A Paradox in Caribbean Attitudes to Land'. In Jean Besson and Janet Momsen (eds) Land and Development in the Caribbean. London: Macmillan, 13-45

Boserup, Ester (1970) *Women's Role in Economic Development*. London: George Allen & Unwin

Bush, Barbara (1990) *Slave Women in Caribbean Society 1650-1838*. London: James Currey; Kingston, Jamaica: Heinemann; Bloomington: Indiana University Press

Chhachhi, Amrita (1989) 'Women, Development Policy and the Management of Change: A Critique of the Social Sciences'. Keynote address at the University of the West Indies Second Disciplinary Seminar in the Social Sciences, Barbados, April

Dagenais, Huguette (1988) 'Du point de vue des dominants—Reflexions théorisés et méthodologiques à partir d'une recherche en Guadeloupe'. In *Les rapports sociaux de sexe: Problématique, méthodologies champs d'analyse*, Proceedings of the International Round Table, 24-26 November 1987. Paris: CNRS Atelier/ Production/Reproduction, 106-13

Deere, Carmen Diana (coordinator) with Peggy Antrobus, Lynne Bolles, Edwin Melendez, Peter Philips, Marcia Rivera and Helen Safa (1990) *In the Shadows of the Sun: Caribbean Development Alternatives and US Policy*. Boulder: Westview Press

Dews, Peter (ed.) (1986) *Habermas: Autonomy and Solidarity: Interviews with Jurgen Habermas*. London: Verso

Ellis, Pat (ed.) (1986) *Women of the Caribbean*. London and New Jersey: Zed Books

Emmer, M.R. (1986) 'The Great Escape: The Migration of Female Indentured Servants from British India to Suriname 1873-1916'. In David Richardson (ed.) *Abolition and its Aftermath: The Historical Context 1790-1916*. London: Frank Cass, 245-66

FAO (Food and Agriculture Organization of the United Nations) (1989) *Women in Caribbean Agriculture*. Rome: FAO

Franco, Jean (1989) *Plotting Women: Gender and Representation in Mexico*. London: Verso

Hart, Keith (1989) 'Introduction'. In Keith Hart (ed.) *Women and the Sexual Division of Labour in the Caribbean*. Kingston, Jamaica: The Consortium Graduate School of Social Sciences, 1-8

Henshall [Momsen], J.D. (1981) 'Women and Small-scale Farming in the Caribbean'. In Oscar Horst (ed.) *Papers in Latin American Geography in Honor of Lucia C. Harrison*, Muncie Indiana: CLAG, 28-43

Jessop, David A. (1991) 'The Nineties: A Time of Crisis for the Caribbean'. Paper presented to the Conference on Alternatives for the 1990s Caribbean, Institute of Commonwealth Studies, London, 9-11 January

Levy, C. (1980) *Emancipation, Sugar and Federalism: Barbados and the West Indies 1833-1876*. Gainesville: University of Florida Press

Mair, Lucille Mathurin (1974) 'A Historical Study of Women in Jamaica, 1655-1844'. Unpublished doctoral dissertation, University of the West Indies, Jamaica

—— (1988) 'Women's Studies in an International Context'. In Mohammed and Shepherd, *q.v.*, 1-9

—— (1988a) 'Recollections of a Journey into a Rebel Past'. Keynote address of the First International Conference on Women Writers of the English-speaking Caribbean, Wellesley College, Boston, US, April 1988

Manley, Michael (1990) Speech to West India Committee Conference on Europe/Caribbean, 29 November 1990

Massiah, Joycelin (ed.) (1986) 'Women in the Caribbean'. Special numbers of *Social and Economic Studies*, 35 (2 & 3)

Mintz, Sidney W. and Sally Price (1985) 'Introduction'. In S.W. Mintz and S. Price (eds) *Caribbean Contours*. Baltimore: Johns Hopkins Press, 3-13

Mohammed, Patricia (ed.) (1989) *Report on the Second Disciplinary Seminar, Social Studies*. Trinidad and Tobago: University of the West Indies, Women and Development Studies Project

Mohammed, Patricia and Catherine Shepherd (eds) (1988) *Gender in Caribbean Development*. Trinidad and Tobago: University of the West Indies, Women and Development Studies Project

Momsen, Janet (1988) 'Changing Gender Roles in Caribbean Peasant Agriculture'. In J.S. Brierley and H. Rubenstein (eds), *Small Farming and Peasant Resources in the Caribbean*. Winnipeg: University of Manitoba, Manitoba Geographical Studies No. 10, 83-100

—— (1992) 'Gender and Environmental Perception in the Eastern Caribbean'. In David Drakakis-Smith and G. Lockhart (eds) *The Development Process in Small Island States*, London: Routledge, 75-91

Morrissey, Marietta (1989) *Slave Women in the New World: Gender Stratification in the Caribbean*. Lawrence: University Press of Kansas

Patterson, Orlando (1967) *The Sociology of Slavery*. London: McGibbon & Kee

Poirier, Jean and Huguette Dagenais (1986) 'En Marge, la Situation des Femmes dans l'Agriculture en Guadeloupe: Situation actuelle, Questions méthodologiques', *Environnement caraïbe*, 151-86

Reddock, Rhoda (1985) 'Freedoms Denied: Indian Women and Indentureship in Trinidad and Tobago, 1845-1917'. *Economic and Political Weekly*, 20 (43) 26 October, 79-87

—— (1990) 'The Caribbean Feminist Tradition.' *Women Speak!* 26/27, 12-24

Richardson, Bonham C. (1983) *Caribbean Migrants*. Knoxville: University of Tennessee Press

Rodney, Walter (1981) *History of the Guyanese Working People, 1881-1905*. London: Johns Hopkins University Press

Safa, Helen I. (1986) 'Economic Autonomy and Sexual Equality in Caribbean Society', *Social and Economic Studies*, 35 (3) 1-22

Safa, Helen I. and Peggy Antrobus (1991) 'Women and the Economic Crisis in the Caribbean'. Paper presented to the Conference on Alternatives for the 1990s Caribbean, Institute of Commonwealth Studies, London, 9-11 January

Tikasingh, G. (1973) 'The Establishment of the Indians in Trinidad, 1870-1900'. Unpublished Ph.D. thesis, University of the West Indies, Trinidad

Wilson, P.J. (1969) 'Reputation and Respectability: A Suggestion for Caribbean Ethnology'. *Man*, 4 (1) 70-84

## Table 1.1: Caribbean Statistics with Special Reference to Women

| State | Area Kms² | GDP per capita $US 1987 | Population 1989 '000 | Female popul. (%) | % economically active population female | Caloric daily per capita intake | Fertility rate |
|---|---|---|---|---|---|---|---|
| Anguilla | 91 | +2900 | 7.3 | 50.90 | 40.5 | n/a | 1. |
| Antigua & Barbuda | 442 | 2570 | 78.4 | 52.00 | 40.1 | 2089 | 1. |
| Aruba | 193 | +6810 | 61.3 | 51.62 | 36.7 | 2925 | 1. |
| Bahamas | 13939 | 10320 | 249.0 | 50.20 | 44.5 | 2699 | 2. |
| Barbados | 430 | 5330 | 255.0 | 52.15 | 47.2 | 3181 | 1. |
| Belize | 22965 | 1250 | 18.5 | 49.34 | 32.5 | 2585 | 5. |
| Bermuda | 54 | 23100 | 58.8 | 51.28 | 46.8 | 2545 | 1. |
| British Virgin Is. | 153 | +9490 | 12.5 | 49.9 | 38.8 | n/a | 2. |
| Cayman Is. | 264 | +17390 | 25.3 | 51.4 | 43.8 | n/a | 1. |
| Cuba | 110861 | 2690 | 10540.0 | 49.65 | 35.8 | 3107 | 1. |
| Dominica | 750 | 1440 | 82.8 | 50.19 | 34.1 | 2649 | 3. |
| Dominican Republic | 48443 | 730 | 7012.4 | 49.18 | 28.9 | 2464 | 3. |
| French Guiana | 86504 | 2130 | 95.0 | 47.34 | 45.5 | 2747 | 3. |
| Grenada | 345 | 1340 | 96.6 | 51.80 | n/a | 2409 | 3. |
| Guadeloupe | 1780 | +*3490 | 341.0 | 51.20 | 46.6 | 2674 | 2. |
| Guyana | 215083 | 380 | 754.0 | 49.84 | 29.9 | 2456 | 2. |
| Haiti | 27400 | 360 | 5520.0 | 51.52 | 40.9 | 1902 | 4. |
| Jamaica | 10991 | 960 | 2376.0 | 50.25 | 45.3 | 2581 | 2. |
| Martinique | 1091 | +*4280 | 337.0 | 51.52 | 50.6 | 2780 | 2. |
| Montserrat | 102 | *2530 | 12.0 | 51.90 | 42.7 | n/a | 1. |
| Netherlands Antilles | 800 | *6810 | 183.0 | 51.32 | 41.8 | 2925 | 3 |
| Nevis | 93 | 1700 | 9.7 | 49.66 | 41.0 | 2349 | 3 |
| Puerto Rico | 9104 | 5520 | 3308.0 | 51.32 | 37.5 | n/a | 2. |
| St Kitts | 176 | 1700 | 34.4 | 49.66 | 41.0 | 2349 | 3. |
| St Lucia | 617 | 1370 | 150.0 | 51.46 | 39.1 | 2776 | 3. |
| St Vincent | 389 | 1070 | 114.0 | 51.56 | 36.1 | 2499 | 3 |
| Suriname | 163820 | 2360 | 405.0 | 50.40 | 27.2 | 2713 | 3. |
| Trinidad & Tobago | 5128 | 4220 | 1285.0 | 49.95 | 33.8 | 3058 | 2. |
| Turks & Caicos Is. | 500 | +4780 | 13.5 | 51.7 | 42.8 | n/a | 3. |
| US Virgin Islands | 352 | 10050 | 107.0 | 52.15 | 45.5 | n/a | 2. |
| UK | 244110 | 10430 | 57218.0 | 51.23 | 41.4 | 3218 | 1 |
| US | 9529063 | 19860 | 248777.0 | 51.29 | 44.3 | 3642 | 1. |
| USSR | 22403000 | 8160 | 287800.0 | 52.74 | 49.9 | 3205 | 2. |

* 1985 data; + GNP. *Source: Encyclopaedia Britannica* (1990) Book of the Year, Chicago

# SECTION ONE

## Private & Public Spheres of Women's Lives

---

# PART 1

## The Domestic Domain & the Community

---

Women's formal and informal networks link the community and act as conduits for information. Through interrelational and transnational links they organize family survival strategies, religious leadership and exchange of goods and services.

The houseyard provides a distinctive West Indian domestic domain. It offers both a protected location and a locus of intergenerational interaction. However, modernization and the growth of nuclear families is destroying this traditional spatial grouping. In Montserrat, the rebuilding after Hurricane Hugo has ignored the traditional pattern of houseyards and so is breaking up the social groups which were based on yards and which provided assistance with child care and household chores.

Life cycle determines the role played by women both within the family and the community. Women have less spatial freedom than men when young and during their reproductive years, often being restricted to the yard. Older women have status in the community and are able to play a wider role.

Forms of male-female relations also vary with age and with ethnic group. Among Afro-Caribbean working-class families, marriage is not usually entered into until after most of the children have been born. However, in Indo-Caribbean and Jewish groups women were given into arranged marriages at a very early age and were largely restricted to the domestic domain. Increased gender equality of educational and employment opportunities has brought greater autonomy to these women.

# II  Reputation & Respectability Reconsidered: A New Perspective on Afro-Caribbean Peasant Women

JEAN BESSON

For many decades social scientists have sought to identify, through various theoretical perspectives, the essence of Caribbean societies; societies regarded as unique in the modern world because they were artificially created to serve the needs of European capitalism (cf. Besson 1986; Cross 1979). Such theories have been wide-ranging and have mainly drawn on sociological and anthropological perspectives from beyond the Caribbean region. These have included Parsonian functionalism (Braithwaite 1975; Henriques 1968; Rodman 1971; Smith 1956); Furnivall's pluralism (Smith 1965; 1965a; 1984); Weberian and neo-Marxist frameworks (Cross 1979; Stone 1973); and dependency theory (Beckford 1972; 1975).

Particularly resilient in the Caribbean context has been the functionalist-pluralist debate. In an attempt to come to terms with the complexities of colour, class and culture in Caribbean societies, functionalists have focused on a 'white bias' integrating different 'colour-classes' through common adherence to a Eurocentric value system; while pluralists have sought to portray culturally distinctive value systems and the theme of power.

Some theorists have attempted to dissolve this deadlock of functionalists and pluralists by rejecting the centrality of class in Caribbean society (for example, Kuper 1976), or to resolve it through simple combinations of functionalist and pluralist perspectives (Beckford 1972; Lowenthal 1972). A more intriguing synthesis has been advanced by Wilson (1969; 1973) through the concepts of 'reputation' and 'respectability'. This approach offers a uniquely Caribbean perspective, although it also has some parallels with the Mediterranean concepts of 'honour' and 'shame' (Peristiany 1966) and the analysis of ideology and conflict in 'complex' societies (Jayawardena 1968). Wilson's theory seeks to resolve the opposing views of shared or separate value systems. It also aims to shift the preoccupation of Caribbean social anthropology from the study of the Afro-Caribbean family and household, with its emphasis on women, to a focus on the total social system and an understanding of the behaviour of the so-called 'marginal' Afro-Caribbean male.

However, as I will argue in this chapter, while Wilson has undoubtedly elucidated the behaviour of Afro-Caribbean men, he has obscured our understanding of Afro-Caribbean women. I will first outline Wilson's theory of reputation and respectability, highlighting both its strengths and weaknesses. I will then show, through both a case study of a Jamaican peasant community and a synthesis of comparative evidence from the Caribbean regional literature, how this theory may be critically reinterpreted and developed to elucidate the lives of Afro-Caribbean peasant women. Finally, I will argue that this reinterpretation advances our understanding of Caribbean communities, shifting attention from the functionalist-pluralist debate on value systems to an analysis of class related cultural resistance in which women play a central role.[1]

## Reputation & Respectability

Wilson's theory of reputation and respectability aims to provide an analysis of Caribbean societies as total social systems, by isolating 'the principles of thought and sentiment that produce not only actual behaviour but also the groupings and segments' (1973: 7) of these societies. He is especially concerned to correct the preoccupation of Caribbeanists with domestic organization and the matrifocal family, and to uncover the informal groupings and internal differentiation of Caribbean communities, highlighting the principles structuring their moral and social systems. His theory is rooted in the ethnography of the tiny island of Providencia, but is developed to provide a social anthropology of the English-speaking Negro societies of the Caribbean region. Five miles by three, with 14 villages, Providencia is seen by Wilson as comparable to the rural communities studied by anthropologists elsewhere in the Anglophone Caribbean. Though politically tied to Catholic Spanish-speaking Colombia, having been settled in the late eighteenth century by Euro-Jamaican planters and their Negro slaves, Providencia has a primarily Protestant Anglophone Caribbean culture.

Wilson argues that the essence of Providencian society is a dialectic between the two opposed principles of respectability and reputation. Respectability is rooted in the metropolitan-oriented colonial system of social stratification based on class, colour, wealth and Eurocentric culture, life style and education. It is perpetuated especially by the white churches, the European institution of marriage and Eurocentric educational systems. Reputation, by contrast, is an indigenous counter-culture based on the ethos of equality and rooted in personal, as opposed to social, worth. It is a response to colonial dependence and a solution to the scarcity of respectability. In Providencia, island identity and equality and the associated indigenous value system of reputation are particularly rooted in the symbolism of land. This is especially reflected in the ideology of equal inheritance by siblings of house-spots and gardens, and in the institution of undivided family land. Another important basis of island equality is common kinship, which is based on the solidarity of being 'all one family' rather than discriminating among classes of kin. In its more literal sense, reputation is also based on verbal skills and anti-establishment activities.

Reputation and respectability are, Wilson argues, differentially subscribed to in terms of the variables of class, sex and age. Wilson identifies two classes in Providencia: a small 'high class' and a larger, poorer 'other class'. Respectability is especially the concern of the 'high class', which sees its respectable life style as a rationale for its élite status and wealth. Claims to respectability are validated publicly by invitation parties, which only those of suitable status may attend. While the 'other class' also shares this value system of respectability, it is more fully oriented to the principle of reputation with its egalitarian ethos.

Secondly, men and women vary in their orientation to reputation and respectability. Wilson sees women in particular, even those of the 'other class', as the bearers and perpetuators of Eurocentric respectability. For Afro-Caribbean women, this orientation is explained with reference to their closer association with the master class during slavery as concubines and domestic slaves. Women are also more involved in the white churches, with their secular concern for the propriety of domestic life and the European institution of marriage. Church affairs are therefore seen as 'women's business', as is the household and domestic domain. For Wilson, Afro-Caribbean women's concern with respectability is especially underlined by the custom of shaming an unmarried girl on her first pregnancy, which culminates in her being made a temporary outcast from her mother's house (Wilson 1973: 128-9).

Men by contrast, argues Wilson, particularly those of the 'other class', subscribe especially to the egalitarian value system of reputation. Land, the symbol of island identity and equality, is essentially controlled by men in Providencia, despite the ideology of equal inheritance. Some 71 per cent of landholders are male, for the sons tend to buy out the daughters' shares of village and garden land, and 95 per cent of Providencian men own land. Most house-spots, which form the basic units of named family sections in the villages, are therefore in male hands and brotherhood provides a model for kinship solidarity. Men's concern with kinship is, however, confined to the politico-legal sphere and, as elsewhere in the Caribbean, they are peripheral to the essentially female domestic domain.

It is here that Wilson's main theoretical contribution emerges, with his pursuit of the question of the existential focus of the so-called marginal Afro-Caribbean male. Wilson locates this in the small informal groupings of men of similar status and generation called 'crews', who have often sailed, fished or worked together, and who meet regularly beyond the household. Crews meet especially in rum-shops and it is in this context that the dynamics of reputation, in the more literal sense of informal ranking based on personal worth, may be observed. The basis of a man's reputation is his virility, manifested in sexual conquests and the fathering of many children — 'poor man's riches' — and established by boasting in this public domain. Virility is, however, only one of a wider class of expressive skills that also contribute to a man's reputation. These include 'sweet talk', musical ability, prowess in slanging matches and 'arguments' displaying 'learning' and 'erudition' — based, for example, on travel and lore of the sea. Certain occupations embodying 'the skills of strength and knowledge' reinforce a man's reputation, such as sea-captain and obeahman (Wilson 1973: 106), and a man's reputation is recognized and validated in the bestowing of titles or nick-names. Wilson hypothesizes that reputation throughout the Anglophone Caribbean is also rooted in Afro-Christian cults which, in contrast to the female-focused secular white churches with their interest in the morality of the domestic domain, are male-oriented and more concerned with power and the sacred. He cites the Jamaican Rastafari cult as an extreme example of the general case.

Finally, the variable of age also influences the differential orientation to respectability and reputation; for as men age they become less interested in the dynamics of reputation and more concerned with respectability. This is evidenced by less frequent visits to the rum-shop, more interest in the Church and a greater commitment to legal marriage.

In Providencia, the dialectic between reputation and respectability is manifested in 'crab antics', behaviour designed to level claims to superior status.[2] A major context for such crab antics is the inheritance of land; for as Wilson notes land is not only a source of equality, but also of differentiation and prestige. Thus, despite the ideology of equal inheritance, co-heirs manoeuvre to secure a greater share of land and, therefore, of island identity. This is manifested in two island attitudes towards land, namely 'covetousness and contentiousness' (Wilson 1973: 58) and in land disputes, which occur especially among men. Common kinship, another source of island identity, is also manipulated in crab antics. Claims to common kinship serve as a status leveller, and also as a lever to pressure richer high status kinsmen into providing their poorer relatives with loans.

Crab antics are also manifested in certain sanctions against the Providencian 'high class'. Unlike the poorer 'other class' they are not allowed to grow their food, but are expected to purchase it from poorer folk — an expectation sanctioned by vandalism of crops and praedial larceny. Nor are they permitted to establish regular channels of supply from the 'other class', and therefore have to 'almost fall over themselves to buy' (Wilson 1973: 116). A similar situation pertains with fishing, the well-off being 'dependent on "others" for their supply' (Wilson 1973: 116). Likewise, those with most land are expected to provide work for the poorer class and at the latter's convenience. Other levelling mechanisms are ridicule and gossip, and both reputation and respectability may be destroyed by words.

Wilson generalizes the themes of reputation, respectability and crab antics to other Anglophone Afro-Caribbean societies by synthesizing hints of these themes in the literature on both the contemporary era and the slavery past, arguing that 'the onus is on others to prove otherwise or to offer alternatives' (Wilson 1973: 215). Wilson is also concerned with even wider generalizations, and with the inter- face between social anthropology and political action. He argues (Wilson 1973: 219) that the Caribbean social system, with its tension between reputation and respectability, 'is possibly the clearest instance in history of a dialectical social system' and that this conclusion resolves the deadlock between functionalists and pluralists on the question of shared or separate value systems. Wilson contends, however, that while the essence of colonial Caribbean societies lay in this dialectic between reputation and respectability, political independence now provides the possibility for the triumph of the indigenous counter-culture of reputation. There- fore, for true independence to be achieved, respectability must be destroyed or changed and realigned with reputation.

Wilson maps out various strategies to realize this future Afro-Caribbean auton- omy. To begin with, Caribbean control of land must be ensured, for, until a new history can be written to replace the region's Eurocentric history, the burden of Caribbean identity lies with Caribbean land. Educational systems, traditionally rooted in colonial values and perpetuating Eurocentric respectability, must also be transformed and rooted in the ethos of egalitarian reputation. In addition, indige- nous cults and sects must be given sufficient validity to replace the white churches with their emphasis on Euro-American respectability. Furthermore, as 'we really know next to nothing about the relations between them [these cults] and the community', Wilson (1973: 233) urges 'the necessary research'. He argues (Wilson 1973: 234) that Caribbean women must also change, reorienting from the Euro- centric value system of respectability to that of indigenous reputation, for:

> women are one of the strongest forces for respectability. ... By and large ... it is women who think and act in terms of respectability, it is women, far more than men, who conceive of the future as respectability. If they themselves cannot become respectable, then perhaps their children will. There is a constant tacit approval of respectability and a deliberate working on its behalf.

Wilson (1973: 236) concludes that concern for change and development in the Caribbean should not only focus on economic themes, but also on 'the equally fundamental matters of social and moral values' in achieving true independence.

Wilson's study is in many ways a major contribution to the social anthropology of Anglophone Afro-Caribbean societies, with wider implications for Third World development and change. In particular, it identifies an indigenous counter-culture of resistance to colonialism and uncovers the existential focus of the Afro- Caribbean male. It also challenges the widespread assumption that Caribbean communities are 'weakly' or 'loosely' organized because they lack formalized groupings (for example, see Beckford 1972: 76-7; Wagley 1960: 8) and shifts the

focus of analysis to the underlying principles of thought and sentiment that artic-
ulate the total social system. Furthermore, the potential of Wilson's perspective for
a comparative theory of Caribbean social systems has already been realized by
studies in Barbados (Barrow 1976), Barbuda (Berleant-Schiller 1977), the British
Virgin Islands (Dirks 1972), and Suriname (Brana-Shute 1976; 1979). It has also
been extended to explore the themes of cultural continuity and social change
among Afro-Caribbean migrants overseas (Wright 1984).

However, despite the comparative utility of Wilson's theory and its elucidation of
the social life of Afro-Caribbean men, it has certain weaknesses when considered
from the perspective of Afro-Caribbean women. Firstly, the male value system of
reputation, which Wilson advances as a model for development, is partially based
on unequal and exploitative gender relations (cf. Keesing 1981: 413). Secondly, in
Wilson's theory cultural resistance against colonial culture is seen as essentially
the preserve of Afro-Caribbean men; while Afro-Caribbean women are regarded
as bearers and perpetuators of the Eurocentric colonial value system. Thirdly,
Wilson's analysis of reputation as primarily male-oriented also overlooks the fact
that women, too, compete for status, both among themselves and with men. This
view of Afro-Caribbean women as passive imitators of colonial culture is reflected
in other studies of gender relations in the region, such as Dirks's study of the
British Virgin Island of Rum Bay (1972: 579-80):

> In Rum Bay and the Afro-Caribbean generally, the behaviour appropriate to the male
> category is explicitly stereotyped. Wilson (1969) has provided an excellent description of
> this stereotype. ... Achievement is not based on conformity to outside standards but on a
> man's reputation among men. ... A woman's behaviour is typically very different from that
> of most men. Ideally, the woman is passive and enduring. Her world is restricted; her place
> is home. ... A woman's domain is one of formalized morality and codified legality. Church
> membership is important to her and marriage is her fulfilment. The woman does not seek
> to build a reputation on the basis of personal exploits. She seeks rather to fashion a mantle
> of respectability.

At first sight the ethnography of Martha Brae, a peasant community in the
Jamaican parish of Trelawny at the heart of Anglophone Afro-Caribbean society
(Besson 1974; 1984; 1984a; 1987a; 1988), appears to support Wilson's analysis of
reputation and respectability. The separation of the sexes is a significant theme in
certain aspects of village life. Whereas females emphasize the domestic domain
and Christian Church, male work focuses on the provision ground and the men
meet in rum-shop crews for dominoes and drinking. Long-term fieldwork in
Martha Brae has, however, uncovered a more complex scenario which, in many
respects, departs from Wilson's theory as the next two sections show.


## Eurocentric Respectability?

The two interrelated contexts of so-called Eurocentric respectability analysed by
Wilson can indeed be identified in Martha Brae. These are the domestic domain,
with its spatial dimension in the house and yard and its existential focus in the
household, family and marriage; and the 'secular' Christian Church, with its
emphasis on the domestic domain and legal marriage. However, within these
contexts, female cultural values in Martha Brae are not a mirror image of the
Eurocentric value system of respectability, but a transformation of this system
within an Afro-Caribbean peasant culture of resistance in which women play a
central role (cf. Mintz 1974: 131-250).

*The Baptist Church*

Women in Martha Brae do indeed play a significant part in the Christian Church, but this is the Nonconformist Baptist Church, which is the peasant community's formal symbol of resistance to the Established Anglican Church of the plantocracy and the plantation system. This symbol of resistance is rooted in Martha Brae's history as an Afro-Caribbean peasant village, established within the context of the Jamaican Nonconformist church-founded free village system. This post-slavery village movement was especially pronounced in the parish of Trelawny under the sponsorship of William Knibb, the Baptist missionary stationed in the parochial capital of Falmouth around the time of emancipation. The free villages drew on the traditions of slave resistance and Nonconformist anti-slavery struggle. These were highly developed in Trelawny, which was at the centre of Caribbean slave society and subsequently became the heart of the region's plantation-peasant interface (Besson 1984: 64-5; 1984a; 1987a; 1988; Mintz 1974: 157-79; Paget 1964).[3]

Martha Brae's contemporary villagers, the core of whom are descended from the ex-slave settlers of the free village — which remains hemmed in by surroundinge plantations — are still strongly Baptist in formal faith and regularly attend the William Knibb Memorial Baptist Church in Falmouth.[4] There is also a Baptist Prayer House in Martha Brae, 'Class 5' of the Falmouth Baptist circuit, which the oldest villagers remember as always having been there. This Class House, which had recently fallen into disrepair, was refurbished by the Falmouth Baptist Church from 1984-6 and reopened in November 1986 at a large function in Martha Brae. Attended by members of the Falmouth Baptist Church and the vice-president of the Jamaica Baptist Union, the function was especially well supported by the women of Martha Brae. For, after over 150 years of freedom, Martha Brae's women remain at the forefront of the Baptist Church's stand against colonial Christianity and the plantation system (Besson 1987a: 123).

*The Domestic Domain*

Like the Baptist Church, the house and yard in Martha Brae — the spatial dimension of the domestic domain — are a symbol of resistance to imposed colonial culture and the plantation system. The primarily female sphere of house and yard is the basic social unit of the peasant community and the nucleus of its peasant economy, established and maintained in the face of the plantations which still surround contemporary Martha Brae. The significance of the house and yard within these contexts, complementing the predominantly male sphere of the provision ground beyond the village, is rooted in Martha Brae's history as a post-slavery peasant community whose origins lie in proto-peasant slave resistance. The yards in the Jamaican slave plantation villages, reinforced by the provision grounds in the plantation backlands, were the core of the proto-peasant economy elaborated by plantation slaves in resistant response to the plantation system. House and yard in the slave village also symbolized a degree of freedom from the plantation regime and were the basis of Afro-Caribbean identity, kinship and community. This proto-peasant adaptation was highly developed in Trelawny and directly forged the peasant economy and community of post-emancipation Martha Brae (Besson 1987a; 1992; Genovese 1975: 536-7; Mintz 1974: 131-250; Patterson 1973: 216-30).

In Wilson's model of respectability, the house and yard and Christian Church are linked through the common theme of the domestic domain and a focus on European legal marriage. The link between the Christian Church and domestic domain can also be identified in Martha Brae, where village women sometimes remark that the Baptist Church condemns 'sinful living' and baptises illegitimate children on special days. This does not, however, reflect a commitment to European marriage among the women of Martha Brae, who value their conjugal freedom in younger years, bear most of their children out of wedlock and enter legal marriage only in middle or old age. Those women particularly concerned with this aspect of the Christian Church interpret 'sinful living' literally, confining non-legal childbearing to extra-residential conjugal relations rather than consensual cohabitation. Moreover, childbearing is rarely limited to one conjugal relationship, and multiple sequential conjugal unions typify both men and women.

Household structures in Martha Brae therefore manifest features common to Afro-Caribbean households: varying conjugal statuses, a range of household forms, male or female headship, foster children, 'outside' children and a high incidence of half-siblingship and so-called illegitimacy. This household structure has traditionally been regarded as evidence of a 'disorganized' family system and has received much anthropological attention explaining it as a deviation from Eurocentric norms (cf. Besson 1974 (I): 36-107; Mintz 1975: 484). These explanations do not, however, elucidate family structure in Martha Brae, where domestic groups and conjugal relations are generated, dissolved and integrated by an ordered family system rooted in Afro-Caribbean culture building. This family system comprises three interrelated themes: a dynamic conjugal complex, bilateral kinship networks and cognatic family lines. Each is a continuance of proto-peasant cultural resistance.

Following the destruction of African marriage traditions on the Jamaican slave plantations, a new conjugal complex was created in resistance to the dehumanizing slavery regime. Conjugality reflected an internal status system based on age: short-lived extra-residential unions typified the younger slaves, while older slaves lived in consensual cohabitation. In the nineteenth century when slaves were allowed to enter legal Christian marriage, they transformed this European institution to symbolize proven conjugal commitment among the oldest slaves (cf. Patterson 1973: 159-70). This conjugal complex and internal status system persist in Martha Brae as Creole transformations of European legal marriage and social stratification based on Eurocentric respectability.

The bilateral kinship system was also forged on the Jamaican slave plantations, where the Creole conjugal complex generated extensive kinship networks of exchange and mutual aid on both parental sides. These networks were crucial in forging slave communities (Mintz and Price 1976; Patterson 1973: 167-70) and still serve as bases for community, exchange and mutual aid in Martha Brae today.

The cognatic family lines are rooted in the customary system of land use, tenure and transmission that evolved in the slave communities and became more firmly established in post-slavery villages with the purchasing of land (Besson 1984a; 1987a; 1989; 1992). This aspect of Martha Brae's family system which, like the conjugal complex and bilateral kinship networks, represents a mode of cultural resistance to the plantation system incorporating both men and women, is explored more fully in the following section on reputation under the theme of 'family land'.

## Reputation: A Male Domain?

The Christian Church and domestic domain do not exhaust the themes of women's lives in Martha Brae. For village women participate in all the main dimensions of reputation identified by Wilson as male-oriented, namely landholding, indigenous cults, entrepreneurial skills, titles and procreation. Women also compete for status, in the sense of personal worth, both among themselves and with men as this section also shows.

### Landholding

Land, especially family land, is identified by Wilson as a prime basis for Providencia's indigenous value system of reputation. In Providencia family land lies mainly outside the villages in the interior of the island, while village land and gardens are subdivided and concentrated in male hands despite the ideology of equal inheritance. In Martha Brae, however, family land is in the village itself and forms the central theme of Martha Brae's history as a post-slavery village; a theme reflected in both the villagers' oral tradition and the continuity of their peasant community (Besson 1984a: 8-10, 1987a). Family land is also a prime basis for village internal differentiation (Besson 1984: 57-8).[5]

Family land in Martha Brae is rooted in the usufructory system of land tenure and transmission that evolved as an aspect of proto-peasant cultural resistance, and was consolidated in the post-slavery era through the purchasing of land (Besson 1984a; 1987a; 1989; 1992). Within the latter context the ex-slave settlers of Martha Brae transformed such purchased land to family land for their descendants, in a situation of persisting plantation hegemony, to ensure them perpetual freehold rights to land. Such land rights were not only of economic significance, providing some independence from the plantations and a bargaining position for higher wages when working on them, but also symbolized freedom, personhood and prestige among the descendants of former slaves.

The system of unrestricted cognatic descent at the heart of family land, which includes all children and their descendants regardless of sex, birth order, residence or legitimacy, in contrast to colonial male primogeniture, maximizes the transmission of these customary freehold rights to land. The unrestricted system also maximizes descent ties, generating ever-increasing overlapping landholding family lines (Besson 1979; 1984a; 1988). These family lines and their estates have been central in perpetuating the post-slavery peasant community of Martha Brae in the face of the surrounding plantations. Family land therefore emerged and persists as a resistant response to the plantation regime (Besson 1984; 1987). Moreover, in the context of the continuing plantation system and new forms of land monopoly by the mining and tourist industries, the Martha Brae villagers still create family estates from purchased land.[6]

The cognatic descent system at the heart of family land in Martha Brae is not an ideology, as Wilson argues for Providencia, for women feature prominently in this customary institution of cultural resistance. For example, many of the trustees of the old family estates are women, including the trustee of Martha Brae's largest post-slavery landholding family line. Women also play a significant role in creating new family estates from purchased land and engage in the crab antics sometimes surrounding such family land. One example illustrates these themes.

Mrs J's paternal grandparents were former slaves, who purchased one square chain of land in Martha Brae after emancipation and transformed it into family land for their descendants.[7] These descendants, who are dispersed in several village households and beyond the village, comprise the largest landholding family line in Martha Brae. Mrs J, who entered legal marriage late in life after having several children and died aged 83 in 1980, was for many years the trustee of the family estate where she lived in her old age with her recently acquired husband. With one square chain of land and an ever-increasing landholding family line, complexities of land use typified this family estate. These included both the positively sanctioned strategy of voluntary non-use by co-heirs with alternative options, and elements of the negatively sanctioned strategy of crab antics (cf. Besson 1987; 1988). A comment by a younger kinswoman of the trustee, Miss U, who lives elsewhere in Martha Brae, highlights the latter theme: 'She [the trustee] crave for everything, and she taken it [the family land] over, and nobody fight her; she just keep it. The reason? Just to crave. You know some people want everything.' (Besson 1988: 50.) In addition, Mrs J's reputation as a powerful family land trustee was so pronounced that, in the escalation of crab antics following her death, her spirit was reputed to have caused her widower's illness when he broke the rules of cognatic descent and interfered with the transmission of the family estate (Besson 1988: 51). While Mrs J's widower languished from this illness and consulted the revival Zion cult for healing, her younger kinswoman, Miss U, was living independently on purchased land which she was transforming into family land for her own descendants.

*Revival and Reputation*
As noted previously, Wilson sees the black indigenous Afro-Caribbean cults as a major dimension of the egalitarian counter-culture of reputation but, as with landholding, regards these cults as essentially male-oriented. While this is true to some extent of the Rastafarian movement now spreading through Trelawny's villages, it is not so of the older revival Zion cult which coexists with the Baptist Church in Martha Brae (Besson 1987a; 1989b).

This coexistence of church and cult, both female-oriented in Martha Brae, is rooted in the proto-peasant adaptation of the Jamaican plantation slaves. Until the arrival of Nonconformist missionaries in Jamaica in the late eighteenth century, the slaves were untouched by Christianity (Patterson 1973: 207). Following the destruction of their traditional African religions by slavery, however, the proto-peasants created new rituals and cosmologies. Drawing on the African baseline beliefs of witchcraft, medicine, ancestral cults and a pantheon of gods and spirits, they forged the new Afro-Jamaican magico-religious cults of obeah and myalism (Patterson 1973: 182-207). The former, involving clients and an obeahman, was practised at an individual level for purposes of protection or revenge. The latter was centred around community rituals including spirit possession and the Myal dance. These united the slaves in resistant response to slavery and European values, and protected their communities from both internal and external harm (Patterson 1973: 190-5; Schuler 1980: 32-3).

From the late eighteenth century these African-derived Creole beliefs became merged with Christianity, as the Nonconformist missionaries took advantage of the slaves' neglect by the planters' Established Anglican Church (Patterson 1973: 207-15). Of particular significance was the teaching of the black Baptists, George Liele and Moses Baker from the US, and the subsequent arrival, in the early nineteenth century, of British Baptist missionaries. The slaves formally embraced the Baptist faith, attending the Baptist churches which provided an added dimension to plantation life, while still remaining committed to their myalist traditions. As a result, two variants of Baptist faith emerged among the slaves: the 'orthodox' form, taught by the missionaries and practised by the slave congregations in the churches; and the 'native' or 'black' Baptist variant, incorporating myalism, taught by Negro class leaders in the plantation villages (Patterson 1973: 211-12; Schuler 1980: 34-7). This latter variant played a prominent role in the 'Baptist War', the 1831 slave rebellion in Jamaica's western parishes which hastened the abolition of slavery in the British colonies.

After emancipation, this parallel commitment continued among the former slaves. Orthodox Baptist faith provided the formal framework of free village life while the native Baptist variant, rooted in myalism, formed 'the core of a strong, self-confident counter-culture' (Schuler 1980: 44) and the basis of a black ethnicity (Robotham 1988: 35-6) in the face of the persisting plantation system. In the 1860s native Baptist beliefs, reinforced by the myalist revival of the 1840s and 1850s and the religion of post-emancipation African indentured immigrants, gave rise to the great evangelical revival (Patterson 1973: 187-8, 214-15; Schuler 1980: 40-1, 44, 104-5). This produced a new Afro-Christian variant revival, which is the basis of Jamaica's contemporary revival cults, revival Zion and pocomania, today.[8]

Women play a central role in Martha Brae's revival Zion cult, and two of the village's three revival 'bands' are led by women (cf. Seaga 1982: 5).[9] Visiting revival leaders to the village also include both men and women. Oral skills and spirit possession provide both sexes with a basis for building reputations in the cult and my own participant-observation in 1983, with follow-up research to 1990, uncovered competing factions within the cult in which the reputations of both men and women rose and declined. An outline of these events illustrates these themes.

Mrs K is 'leadress' of the oldest revival bands in Martha Brae, founded by her many years ago when she and her husband came to the village from the neighbouring parish of St James. The Ks have managed to obtain a few square chains of cliff-side land, where they have built a wooden cottage and a simple corrugated-iron cult house with an earthen floor. This is furnished with wooden benches, an altar with bottles of holy water and other ritual symbols, and several goat-skinned drums — symbols of resistance from the slavery past (Campbell 1985: 25).

As a young woman Mrs K could neither read nor write, but she has great oral skill and is now literate in middle age. She leads her cult meetings three times a week, choosing her text by divine inspiration and elaborating its theme for hours. In addition, she prophesies and heals through spirit possession, which also occurs among members of her bands in varying degrees. Mrs K's 'leadress' role is complemented by her husband's role as chaplain, pastor or preacher; male deacons; and a secretary and drummers who are female. Her reputation as leadress, prophetess and healer draws a regular congregation from within the village. In addition, she diverted the following of a male revival leader in the neighbouring village of Granville. Gossip of doctrinal impurity in his preaching[10] surrounds the defection of his followers to Mrs K.

Mrs K's reputation was, however, itself challenged by a former member of her congregation, Mrs G, a woman in middle age. A few years earlier, Mrs G had a vision instructing her to build her own revival Zion cult house and break away from Mrs K. Following this dream, Mrs G built an elaborate bamboo cult house in her yard which, in architectural design, quite overshadowed that of Mrs K. Mrs G, however, has no permanent congregation as she lacks Mrs K's verbal skill.

With her reputation as leadress, prophetess and healer, Mrs K has a network of alliances with other Zion bands throughout Jamaica, especially in the neighbouring parishes of St Ann and St James. This results in visits between bands and leaders in such communities, and in the summer of 1983 there was a spate of such visits to Martha Brae. These included meetings in Mrs K's own cult house and one at the central village crossroads. The latter, the largest held in Martha Brae that summer, was led by 'Mother D', a revival Zion leader from St Ann who used to live in Martha Brae. At her crossroads meeting, she prophesied impending doom for Martha Brae resulting from an incident that would soon come to pass.[11] With such specific prophecy she put her reputation on the line, and it was both

challenged and validated by whispered words among the crossroads congregation. Whatever the pros and cons, however, Mother D so excelled in oral skill that
she held the crowd spellbound for many hours.

In a final bid for rival leadership to Mrs K, Mrs G assisted Mother D in her rituals
at the village crossroads. Mrs G also invited another visiting revival leader, Pastor
E, to lead a week of nightly meetings in the bamboo cult house in her yard. After
an initial plan to boycott these rival meetings, Mrs K decided to attend them in a
gesture of *noblesse oblige*. This strengthened Mrs K's own reputation for her oral
skill in testimony outshone that of Mrs G and, after Pastor E's departure, Mrs G's
temporary congregation melted entirely away.

Two years later, Pastor E returned to Martha Brae, where he took up residence,
built a revival cult house in his yard and established a rival faction to Mrs K. Mrs
K did not, however, see this as a serious challenge and shrugged off his reputation
by alluding to doctrinal impurities within his rival bands.[12] By 1990 Pastor E had
left the village, apparently due to gossip, and Mrs G's bamboo cult house had
entirely decayed. Mrs K, however, still retained her reputation; and her cult house,
which remained the centre of revival Zionism in Martha Brae, had been given a
new coat of turquoise paint.

### Entrepreneurship

In addition to participating in the Afro-Caribbean system of reputation, as defined
by Wilson, through landholding and an indigenous cult, Martha Brae's women
also establish reputations through entrepreneurial roles. The most significant is
that of market higgler in the Falmouth peasant market. Miss F, now a woman
advanced in years, is an outstanding example of this theme. Starting with a capital
investment equivalent to a few Jamaican dollars, she built up her tiny higglering
business over several decades and has now established a considerable reputation
in the Falmouth market where she has a regular stall. Miss F lives on family land
in Martha Brae and sometimes cultivates a kitchen garden there, as well as corn in
her provision ground on 'free land' beyond the village.[13] She has, however,
seldom cultivated sufficient food for sale and, therefore, buys vegetables and
ground provisions from other villagers for resale in the market. Miss F also higgles
in dry goods, especially clothes, on a tiny scale. At first she used to ask another
higgler to buy clothes for her in Kingston, but now she herself makes these trips as
a higgler of established reputation. Other women from Martha Brae also higgle in
food, fish and clothes.

This marketing system — like the Baptist Church, the house and yard, the family
system, the revival cult and family land — is rooted in the proto-peasant adaptation of the Trelawny plantation slaves, established in resistant response to the
slave plantation system (Besson 1987a: 120; cf. Mintz 1974: 180-224). The Falmouth
market, used by the villagers of Martha Brae, originated in the late eighteenth
century as a Sunday market held by plantation slaves (Ogilvie 1954: 43-4; Wright
1973: 56).[14] By 1990, the Falmouth market was regarded as Jamaica's leading rural
market, especially on Ben' Down market days.[15]

In addition to participating in this expanding marketing system, some Martha
Brae women also engage in other entrepreneurial activities, such as selling cooked
food at the Jamaica Tourist Board river rafting project near Martha Brae. Other
women keep small grocery shops, and one a rum-shop, all of which compete for
custom with each other and with similar establishments kept by village men.

*Titles and Procreation*

A fourth dimension of so-called male-oriented reputation identified by Wilson is the validation of reputations by titles and nicknames, and this can also be identified among the men of Martha Brae. For example 'Captain', 'Prof' and 'Sam Isaacs' refer to reputations built on seafaring skills, 'professing science' and 'icing bodies' respectively.[16] In Martha Brae, women also have a variation on this theme in their feminist use of the title 'Miss' combined with the Christian name, regardless of conjugal status, for women of established reputation such as revival leaders, market higglers, landholders and shopkeepers. Women also often have pet names.[17]

Motherhood is another basis of reputation independent of conjugal status among the women of Martha Brae, which parallels the virility of men identified by Wilson as a central dimension of reputation. As elsewhere in Jamaica and the Caribbean region, the children of Trelawny's slave women were not legally their own. In post-slavery Martha Brae, however, children are 'poor man's riches' for women as well as men; being a significant basis of a woman's status, a symbol of her womanhood and, potentially, the beginning and continuance of her landholding family line. The theme of motherhood as a basis for reputation is also reflected in the title 'Mother', sometimes used for female revival leaders among the villagers of Martha Brae (cf. Seaga 1982: 8). Thus for both women and men titles and procreation are aspects of an internal status system based on personal, rather than social, worth within the peasant village — a system established in the face of the external Eurocentric system of social stratification and respectability.

## Cultural Resistance

The two preceding sections show that the case of Martha Brae, at the heart of Anglophone Afro-Caribbean society, challenges Wilson's theory that Afro-Caribbean women perpetuate the Eurocentric value system of respectability and that reputation is male-oriented. Instead, women's lives are seen to be a central part of an Afro-Caribbean peasant culture of resistance, established in the face of the plantation system and rooted in the proto-peasant past. Moreover, comparative evidence from the regional literature suggests that women in Afro-Caribbean rural communities in general depart from Wilson's theory and more closely resemble that advanced for Martha Brae. This section briefly reviews some of this evidence, showing that the allegiance of Afro-Caribbean peasant women to the Christian Church and their role in the domestic domain are aspects of cultural resistance; that such women also participate in the main dimensions of Wilson's model of reputation, namely, landholding, indigenous cults, entrepreneurial activities, titles and procreation; and that Afro-Caribbean women's cultural resistance is rooted in the slavery past.

*Domestic Domain and Christian Church*

The contexts of Afro-Caribbean women's so-called respectability identified by Wilson — the 'secular' white Church and domestic domain — have indeed been widely documented in the regional literature. Closer scrutiny, however, shows that these represent aspects of Afro-Caribbean cultural resistance rather than Eurocentric respectability. Thus, for example, Mintz (1974: 225-50) has shown that the house and yard (the spatial dimension of the domestic domain) are the nucleus of the Afro-Caribbean peasant culture of resistance, established and maintained in the face of the plantation system. Likewise, the female sphere of the kitchen garden in the yard is both the training ground and embryo of the Afro-Caribbean peasant economy (Brierley 1988: 11; cf. Pulsipher, Chapter 4 of this volume).

The existential focus of the domestic domain — the household, family and marriage — may also be widely seen to be an aspect of Afro-Caribbean cultural resistance. For example, Horowitz (1967) argues that conjugal patterns among the peasantry in Martinique are a strategy for maximizing the values of the peasant economy, an analysis that he extends to Anglophone Caribbean peasant communities. Bilateral kinship networks of exchange are also a significant aspect of Afro-Caribbean cultural resistance, rooted in the proto-peasant past (Olwig 1981; 1981a; 1985). Unrestricted landholding cognatic family lines are likewise a central theme in Afro-Caribbean peasant cultures of resistance (Besson 1979; 1984a; 1987; 1989; 1992).

While Afro-Caribbean women do widely support white Christian churches, as Wilson argues, these are primarily the Nonconformist churches, which played a prominent role in the anti-slavery struggle and post-emancipation village movement (see, for example, Besson 1984a; Mintz 1974: 157-9; Paget 1964). Such churches therefore represent a rejection of colonial orthodoxy (Cross 1979: 96-7).

*Dimensions of Reputation*
With respect to Wilson's thesis of reputation as a male-oriented indigenous counter-culture of resistance, much evidence exists of Afro-Caribbean female cultural resistance paralleling that of Martha Brae.

Regarding landholding, Clarke's (1953; 1957) pioneering studies of Jamaican family land highlight the role of women and matrilocal residence in this customary peasant tenurial institution; a point further underlined by Ford-Smith's (1981) discussion of Afro-Jamaican women after emancipation (cited in Besson 1984: 69):

Women in the labouring poor became higglers, domestic servants, farmers and artisans. The mother, who appears in Brathwaite's 'Mother Poem', is a figure whose power base is a plot of land in the country — a few acres, usually less than five. In a sense this plot became an institution of resistance. Many aspects of domestic organization were in direct opposition to ruling class concepts of sex and legitimacy. The plot, or what Edith Clarke calls family land, passed from generation to generation, regardless of sex or legitimacy. It was shared between kin regardless of age. On the other hand, British law in the nineteenth century held that married women could not own land, that the inheritances of illegitimate children should be limited and that the eldest male had the first right to the land.

As I have also shown both for Trelawny and on a pan-Caribbean scale, family land with its unrestricted cognatic descent system incorporating both men and women is not a passive cultural survival from Africa or Europe, as others argue (or from Jamaica, as Wilson contends for Providencia), but a dynamic cultural creation by Caribbean peasantries themselves in resistant response to the plantation system (Besson 1979; 1984; 1984a; 1987; 1987a; 1988; 1992).

Two overviews of Afro-Caribbean women (since Peter Wilson's study) have also highlighted their entrepreneurial roles (Henry and Wilson 1975; Powell 1984); while a more specialist literature has long demonstrated their significance as market women and higglers (for example, Durant-Gonzalez 1983; Katzin 1959; 1960; Mintz 1960; 1974: 214-24). Mintz (1974: 223) also draws a parallel between land ownership and higglering as bases for Afro-Caribbean cultural resistance. That higglering can usefully be considered within Wilson's framework of reputation is further underlined by his observation on the inability of the Providencian 'high class' to establish regular channels of food supply with sellers from the 'other class' — a sanction he interprets as one aspect of the levelling behaviour of crab antics (Wilson 1973: 115-16). Among Afro-Caribbean peasants, by contrast, stabilizing such channels of supply is institutionalized through 'customer' or 'pratik' relations (Katzin 1959; 1960; Mintz 1961). Wilson himself also mentions, but does not develop, the point that 'when women are engaged in trading, they must organize their lives and their standards around their occupation, which demands a sense of competition, often with men' (Wilson 1973: 234). He also briefly refers (Wilson 1973: 161) to the success of female small-scale traders in Providencia.

Turning to Afro-Christian cults, which Wilson hypothesizes are a major dimension of reputation, it has been shown that women play a central role in indigenous religions (such as the Jamaican revival cult and Trinidadian Shango) and that such participation coexists with membership of white Christian churches (Henry and Wilson 1975: 189-90). In these black cults women derive considerable prestige from leadership roles, spirit possession, prophecy and healing (Henry and Wilson 1975: 189-90). It is also becoming clear that the male bias in Rastafari, which Wilson cites as his prime example, has been over-emphasized as a result of both unequal gender relations within the movement and male-biased reporting (Barrett 1977; Campbell 1980; Rowe 1980).

Afro-Caribbean women's oral skills have also received attention in other contexts. Ford-Smith (1986: 2, 4), writing about the women in the working-class Sistren Theatre Collective in Jamaica who, 'from the beginning, saw themselves as representatives of working class women' and who 'analyse and comment on the role of women in Jamaican society through theatre', observes that: 'The women in the group were part of a tradition of story-telling, songs, and ritual imagery. Not only had these forms developed out of attempts to struggle with a powerful colonial system; they also contained the voices of women in strong protest and complaint.' Sistren's tale-telling in *Lionheart Gal* also charts 'the terms of resistance in women's daily lives and illustrates ways in which women can move from the apparent powerlessness of exploitation to the creative power of rebel consciousness' (Ford-Smith 1986a: xiii).[18] Tanna's (1984) study of Jamaican folk tales and oral histories likewise provides extensive evidence of women's verbal skills (cf. Brodber 1983).

There is also comparative evidence of conferring titles in recognition of reputation among Afro-Caribbean women. Such titles include 'Nanny', Jamaica's rebel maroon leader and first national heroine (Mathurin 1975: 35-7); and 'Queenie' and 'Mother', titles of female leaders in the Kumina and revival Zion cults respectively (Ford-Smith 1986: 4, 7; cf. Besson 1984a: 14).

Finally, the significance of motherhood in conferring personal status among Afro-Caribbean women, paralleling the central significance of virility in establishing men's reputations, is widely indicated in the regional literature. In a recent essay MacCormack and Draper (1987: 143) underline this for the Jamaican case:

> In Jamaica ... sexuality is usually conceptually linked with the desire to create children. For both men and women, perceptions of self-identity and social power are contingent upon the expression of sexual potency which is confirmed by the birth of children. Jamaican art, music, and theatre express the vitality of a society in which women, as well as men, achieve social status through their own activity.

Elsewhere in their essay MacCormack and Draper (1987: 146, 147) highlight a tradition of achieving personal status through procreation, among both men and women disadvantaged by the societal system of economic stratification:

> Where there are few rewarding economic roles for men and women, sex, birth and the rearing of children provide an important alternative way to seek adult status and enhanced self-identity. ... Seeking social power through procreation is not a recent Jamaican social pattern. Nearly 30 years ago Clarke described gatherings of men in a sugar plantation talking of their sexual prowess in terms of the number of children they had fathered (1957:

91). For women, too, sexuality was 'natural', and it was 'unnatural' not to have a child. A childless woman was an object of pity, contempt or derision (Clarke 1957: 95).

Within this context the shaming ritual on an unmarried girl's first pregnancy, which parallels that described by Wilson for Providencia, may be seen as a 'ritual of reversal' (see Besson 1989a: 164-5) establishing Afro-Caribbean female reputation rather than reflecting a concern with Eurocentric respectability.

*The Tradition of Female Slave Resistance*
The role of Afro-Caribbean peasant women as resisters has a long history (overlooked by Wilson) rooted in the slavery and proto-peasant past. Thus, as Mathurin (1975) has shown, British Caribbean slave women participated in many modes of slave resistance: some similar to those of men, others peculiar to women. The former included withholding labour and malingering, which were especially damaging to the slave regime towards the end of slavery, when most field slaves were female. Women also plotted with men against the masters' property and persons, and engaged in *marronage*. Resistance particularly typical of women included poisoning the master's food and the 'tongues of women'. The latter included answering back, complaining, ridicule and satire. These feminine modes of resistance were an outgrowth of the closer relationship of slave women to the masters as domestic slaves and concubines, which Wilson (1973) himself identifies. Women's dominant role in resistance based on words was reflected in the fact that female slaves were more often regarded as 'deserving' punishment than men and in the arguments against abolishing flogging, especially for women. As Mathurin (1975: 18) notes, slave women's words not only took up their masters' time and disrupted work, but also forced on them the consciousness of the humanity of the slave:

By refusing to accept slavery like dumb animals, by regularly raising their voices, women in their way, forced their presence on the consciousness of many: this was the thin end of the wedge in undermining the system of slavery. For once the slave is seen or heard, as a human being, it becomes increasingly difficult to justify his or her existence as a chattel.

In Martha Brae today, villagers, especially women, refer to animals as 'dumb things', thus underlining their own humanity based on words.

Bush's (1985) account of slave women and resistance in the British West Indian colonies reinforces Mathurin's perspective. She concludes that slave women 'retained the greatest independence and cultural autonomy' and 'were in the vanguard of the cultural resistance to slavery which helped individuals survive the slave experience' (Bush 1985: 34). In the 'private' lives of the slaves, women reconstituted the family system and built viable communities (Bush 1985: 34; cf. Heuman 1985: 6), which in turn laid the basis for other subtle forms of resistance on the slave plantations. Bush (1985: 34) writes:

It was this cultural strength ... which helped women resist the system in their more 'public' lives as workers. In the fields cultural defiance was expressed through language and song. Language in particular was an important element in black identity and cultural unity, a major form of defence against dehumanization. ... Women field hands were experts in the use of the rich Creole language which, with its *double-entendres* and satire, was frequently employed as subtle abuse of whites. ... Through such channels women helped to generate and sustain the general spirit of resistance.

Bush (1985: 39) notes that women also greatly contributed to the informal proto-peasant slave economy through their cultivation, marketing and higglering roles (cf. Mintz 1974: 180-213; Olwig 1985: 41). Slave women were also involved in slave rebellions and 'were crucial in transmitting the spirit and tradition of resistance to their children through song and oral tradition' (Bush 1985: 47).

Especially pertinent to the thesis of this essay is Bush's analysis of female domestic slaves (Bush 1985: 46-7), which challenges both the negative stereotypes of passive slave women advanced by historians and Wilson's view of the origins of Afro-Caribbean women's so-called Eurocentric respectability:

> In discussing modern Caribbean culture ... Peter Wilson has claimed that, because they were treated differently from black men, black women were 'more readily and firmly attached' to the alien society of the whites from the earliest days of slavery. Unlike men, they were able to improve their social standing through concubinage but in so doing were forced to adopt white values and accommodate to, rather than resist, slavery. ... Though undoubtedly a small minority of women followed this pattern, the indications are that it was far from typical. Women were in the vanguard of cultural resistance to slavery and, despite their alleged advantages, it seems that the majority of women rejected rather than encouraged the sexual advances of white men, regardless of the penalties this might incur.

Bush (1985: 37) also highlights the paradoxical situation of female domestic slaves who were not only under most pressure to conform to European culture, but whose resistance to this was as a result also the most creative: 'Of all slaves, domestics exhibited the greatest duality of behaviour and were in the most contradictory position. Though outwardly they were obliged to conform more than field slaves to European culture and values, they employed covert and subtle means to retain their cultural integrity and to protest their enforced enslavement.' This suggests that many slave women, rather than being willing mistresses to white men, were masters of the subtle form of slave resistance typified by the 'Quashee' personality identified by Patterson (1973: 174-81).

More recent work by Beckles (1988; 1989) on Barbados further substantiates the tradition of Afro-Caribbean female slave resistance (cf. Bush 1990; Morrissey 1989).

## Conclusion

In this chapter I have argued that, while Wilson's theory of reputation and respectability has many strengths, including the elucidation of the social life of Afro-Caribbean men, it has major weaknesses which obscure our understanding of Afro-Caribbean women. In particular, I challenge Wilson's thesis that Afro-Caribbean women are passive imitators of Eurocentric cultural values of respectability; that the counter-culture of reputation is male-oriented; and that cultural resistance to colonial culture is therefore confined to Afro-Caribbean males.

By contrast, in this chapter I contend, through both the case of Martha Brae at the very heart of Anglophone Afro-Caribbean society and comparative evidence in the regional literature, that Afro-Caribbean peasant women do not subscribe to Eurocentric respectability and that they participate in the main dimensions of reputation identified by Wilson. Women are therefore central to the Afro-Caribbean peasant cultures of resistance, rooted in the tradition of slave resistance, which emerged in response to colonialism and the plantation system (cf. Mintz 1974: 131-250).

Moreover, I show that in his analysis of Afro-Caribbean women Wilson falls into the very trap that he identifies for other social anthropologists of the Caribbean region, namely a preoccupation with the family and household. For, as Powell (1984: 117), in her recent overview of the multiple roles of Caribbean women, notes: 'The dynamics of women's lives are not clearly understood, mainly because of assumptions which apply for men but not necessarily for women. There has been a one-sided emphasis on women's role in the family and limited recognition or systematic assessment of their non-familial activities.' In addition, Wilson adopts a Eurocentric interpretation of the Afro-Caribbean family and household.

Powell (1984: 118) calls for '"new" approaches' to the study of Caribbean women and highlights the significance of the Women in the Caribbean Project undertaken during the Decade for Women (1975-85) at the University of the West Indies, where research on Caribbean women is being conducted by Caribbean women. The present chapter is offered both as a contribution to developing this indigenous perspective and as part of a wider growing concern with understanding the lives of Caribbean women among scholars beyond the region.[19]

In so doing I also respond to the challenge in Wilson's analysis of reputation and respectability as a model for Anglophone Afro-Caribbean societies that 'the onus is on others to prove otherwise or to offer alternatives' (Wilson 1973: 215). The perspective I offer here puts aside the functionalist-pluralist debate (and its synthesis in Wilson's theory of reputation and respectability) and relocates the analysis of Anglophone Afro-Caribbean peasant communities within the context of a critique of Eurocentric interpretations of dependency and hegemony.[20] For it reveals that these communities and their cultures, rooted in a long tradition of slave resistance to colonialism and the plantations, are a dynamic outcome of class conflict in the capitalist world system (cf. Besson 1979; 1984; 1984a; 1987; 1987a; 1992; Mintz 1974: 131-250).

This interpretation rejects the orthodox Marxian view that the masses are passive recipients of the culture of the ruling classes, and Wilson's implicit application of this view to Afro-Caribbean women; showing instead that the subcultures of subordinate classes, including women, may be active modes of resistant response to the dominant culture (cf. Besson 1984a: 19; 1986; 1992). This perspective therefore corrects the over-emphasis in dependency theory on metropolitan-satellite relations, highlights the internal class dynamic, and demonstrates that independent thought and action by the powerless (both men and women) is only constrained, rather than destroyed, by dependency and hegemony (cf. Ambursley and Cohen 1983; Austin 1984; Smith 1978). This is especially so in the case of the post-slavery peasantries who forged free communities with Afro-Caribbean cultures rooted in slave resistance, which have completely transformed the Eurocentric values of imposed colonial culture and the plantation system (cf. Besson 1989c).[21]

## Notes

1   Earlier drafts of this chapter were presented at the Sociology Department Seminar of the University of Aberdeen in May 1987, at the Twelfth Annual Conference of the Society for Caribbean Studies in Hoddesdon (Hertfordshire) in July 1988 and at the Centre for Gender Studies in Hull in June 1989. My thanks to all those who commented on these presentations. Fieldwork in the Jamaican peasant community of Martha Brae and other Trelawny villages was conducted over the period 1968-90 and funded in part by The Carnegie Trust for the Universities of Scotland, the Social Science Research Council and the University of Aberdeen Fund for Travelling Allowances. I am grateful to these bodies for their financial assistance. I also thank the people of Martha Brae, both men and women, who allowed me to participate so fully in their lives and peasant community. I use the concept of 'peasant' as defined by Dalton (1967: 265-7; 1971) to denote a broad middle category between the two extremes of 'tribal' and 'post-peasant modern farmer', with socio-economic organization typified by subsistence production combined with production for sale, incomplete land and labour markets, the virtual absence of machine technology, and the retention of traditional social organization and culture to a significant degree. Dalton's definition encompasses various sub-types, including the 'hybrid/composite peasantries' of contemporary Latin America and the Caribbean and, within this sub-type, the 'reconstituted peasantries' of the Caribbean may be further distinguished (Mintz 1974: 132). Martha Brae is such a reconstituted peasant community (Besson 1984a; 1987: 13; 1987a; 1988).

2 The concept of 'crab antics' is based on an analogy with a barrel of crabs all trying to climb out, but pulling each other down so that 'only a particularly strong crab ever climbs out' (Wilson 1973: 58). The associated proverb identified by Wilson for Providencia is also found in Martha Brae.

3 The peasant village of Martha Brae was founded on the ruins of the former planter town of Martha Brae, as a variant on the Baptist Church-founded village theme (see for example, Besson 1984a, 1987a). Martha Brae therefore has two histories, as planter town and peasant village. Yet only the former Euro-Caribbean history is recorded, while the latter Afro-Caribbean history remains a hidden history (cf. Mintz 1971). A monograph, 'Martha Brae's Two Histories: Culture Building in a Caribbean Society', is in preparation.

4 The plantation system in Trelawny, as elsewhere in Jamaica and the Caribbean region, reflects both continuity and change (cf. Beckford 1972; 1975). Two large corporate plantation 'centrals', consolidated from many of the formerly individually-owned estates, engross most of the parish's fertile land. One is an expatriate family corporation; the other, previously controlled by multinationals, is now state owned. Other former slave plantations remain as 'properties' or large farms among the local planter class (Besson 1988: 40-1).

5 Most village land is held by 'Born Ya', those born within the village, while immigrants or 'strangers' tend to be landless tenants. Among the Born Ya the core of village land is held as family land by the 'old families', cognatic family lines who have inherited such land from ex-slave ancestors who purchased land in Martha Brae. Other Born Ya hold family land of more recent origin. Most immigrants to the village have no freehold land in Martha Brae, though some hold rights to family land in other Trelawny villages. A few strangers and some younger members of old families have managed to purchase land within the village, which in some cases is being transformed to family land. On Martha Brae's two histories see note 3 above.

6 This process of transformation entails a reversal of imposed colonial culture, namely the inversion of the features of European legal freehold. Legal freeholds in the wider Jamaican society tend to comprise extensive tracts of land, are private property, alienable, marketable in the capitalist economy, validated by legal documents, and acquired through purchase, deed of gift or testate inheritance. Intestacy was traditionally defined on the basis of legitimacy, male precedence, primogeniture and legal marriage. Houses on legal freeholds are considered part of the real estate, and land use is governed by the capitalist values of maximizing profits and production. The customary institution of family land in Martha Brae contrasts in all respects. Generally only a few 'square chains' in size, family land is regarded as the inalienable corporate estate of the family line. Rights to family land are essentially validated through oral tradition and, while initially acquired through purchase, are customarily transmitted through intestacy. The definition of intestate heirs is based on unrestricted cognatic descent, which includes all children and their descendants regardless of sex, birth order, residence or legitimacy, while marriage is not regarded as a basis for inheritance. Houses are distinguished from family land and considered moveable property, and the use of family land is governed by a complex of values forged within the peasant community. Family land is the spatial dimension of the family line, reflecting its continuity and identity, and provides inalienable freehold rights, house sites, a spot for a kitchen garden, a place for absentees to return and, traditionally, before the advent of the village cemetery, a family burial ground (Besson 1984: 58-60; 1987a: 103-4).

7 A square chain is one-tenth of an acre.

8 One of the differences between the two variants of the revival cult, revival Zion and pocomania, is the differential emphasis on obeah and healing. While Zionists are regarded 'as more experienced in matters of healing', pocomania is seen as having 'better practitioners of obeah, ... considered evil by the Zion cult' (Seaga 1982: 13). While participation in both variants is predominantly female and women can be leaders in either cult, leadership in Zion and pocomania is generally female and male respectively (ibid: 5, 8).

9 In revival, the term 'bands' is used to denote one or more groups within the cult (Seaga 1982: 6).

10 This suggests a shift from revival Zion to pocomania, an interpretation consistent with the predominance of male leaders in pocomania in contrast with mainly female Zion leadership (see note 8 above).

11 The reputed incident involved elements of both pocomania and Rastafari. The prophecy therefore highlights the dynamics of competition between the predominantly female Zion cult and the more male-oriented pocomania and Rastafarian cults (cf. Besson 1989b; Seaga 1982: 5, 8).

12 Again, this suggests a shift from Zion to pocomania (see notes 8, 10 and 11 above).

13 In Martha Brae the female/male dichotomy of yard and ground is modified by a flexible division of labour, which allows women without resident spouses to cultivate provision grounds (cf. Olwig 1985: 117-19).

14 My forthcoming monograph on Martha Brae includes a history of this market (Besson in preparation).

15 Falmouth's weekly Ben' Down market, a clothes and dry goods market, is held on Wednesdays in contrast to the food markets on Fridays and Saturdays. As many of the higglers in the Wednesday market spread their wares on the ground outside the market-place, both customers and higglers have to bend down to select goods for purchase and sale; hence the market's name.

16 'Icing bodies' refers to preserving corpses with ice prior to burial, for example for wakes. There is a morgue in the Falmouth hospital which serves Trelawny parish, but villagers say it has only five drawers one of which is reserved for 'dem what squash out a road', i.e. road accident victims. If the morgue is full, the corpse is 'iced' in the village. The nickname Sam Isaacs derives from Jamaica's leading morticians.

17 Female pet names appear to be adopted from childhood to express individuality in contrast to the given name at baptism. The comparison and contrast with male nicknames requires further research.

18 Although the Sistren Theatre Collective is based in urban Kingston, many of the women are migrants from rural communities (Ford-Smith 1986a: xvii-xviii).

19 This chapter is written from both perspectives in that I am a Jamaican affiliated to a university outside the Caribbean region.

20 While Wilson's theory and the present chapter are focused on Anglophone Caribbean rural communities, there is sufficient evidence to suggest that the reinterpretation offered here has wider relevance to the non-Hispanic Afro-Caribbean variant. Such evidence includes family land and the cognatic descent system (Besson 1979; 1984; 1987); bilateral kinship networks (Olwig 1981; 1981a; 1985); conjugal patterns (Horowitz 1967); and peasant marketing systems (Mintz 1960).

21 In this chapter I also go some way towards providing 'the necessary research' urged by Wilson (1973: 233) on relations between Afro-Caribbean indigenous cults and the community. In addition, my analysis of Martha Brae develops Wilson's argument regarding the need for a new Caribbean history to replace the region's Eurocentric history, and the role of land in this new history (Besson 1979; 1984; 1984a; 1987; 1987a; 1988; 1989c; 1992; in preparation; Wilson 1973: 225; cf. note 3 above). The theme of Afro-Caribbean cultural transformation of Eurocentric values is explored more fully in my forthcoming monograph on Martha Brae's two histories (Besson in preparation; cf. note 6 above).

# References

Ambursley, Fitzroy and Robin Cohen (1983) 'Crisis in the Caribbean: Internal Transformations and External Constraints'. In Fitzroy Ambursley and Robin Cohen (eds). *Crisis in the Caribbean*. London: Heinemann, 1-26

Austin, Diane J. (1984) *Urban Life in Kingston, Jamaica: The Culture and Class Ideology of Two Neighbourhoods*. New York: Gordon & Breach

Barrett, Leonard E. (1977) *The Rastafarians: The Dreadlocks of Jamaica*. London: Heinemann

Barrow, Christine (1976) 'Reputation and Ranking in a Barbadian Locality'. *Social and Economic Studies*, 25 (2) 106-21

Beckford, George L. (1972) *Persistent Poverty: Underdevelopment in Plantation Economies of the Third World*. London: Oxford University Press

—— (1975) 'Caribbean Rural Economy'. In George L. Beckford (ed.) *Caribbean Economy: Dependence and Backwardness*. Kingston, Jamaica: Institute of Social and Economic Studies, University of the West Indies, 77-91

Beckles, Hilary McD. (1988) *Afro-Caribbean Women and Resistance to Slavery in Barbados*. London: Karnak House

—— (1989) *Natural Rebels: A Social History of Enslaved Black Women in Barbados*. London: Zed Books

Berleant-Schiller, Riva (1977), 'Production and Division of Labor in a West Indian Peasant Community'. *American Ethnologist*, 4 (2) 253-72

Besson, Jean (1974) 'Land Tenure and Kinship in a Jamaican Village'. 2 vols, Ph.D. dissertation, University of Edinburgh

—— (1979) 'Symbolic Aspects of Land in the Caribbean: The Tenure and Transmission of Land Rights among Caribbean Peasantries'. In Malcolm Cross and Arnaud Marks (eds) *Peasants, Plantations and Rural Communities in the Caribbean*. Guildford: University of Surrey/Leiden: Royal Institute of Linguistics and Anthropology, 86-116

—— (1984) 'Family Land and Caribbean Society: Toward an Ethnography of Afro-Caribbean Peasantries'. In Elizabeth M. Thomas-Hope (ed.) *Perspectives on Caribbean Regional Identity*. Liverpool: Centre for Latin American Studies, University of Liverpool, Monograph Series No. 11, 57-83

—— (1984a) 'Land Tenure in the Free Villages of Trelawny, Jamaica: A Case Study in the Caribbean Peasant Response to Emancipation'. *Slavery and Abolition*, 5 (1) 3-23

—— (1986) Review of Diane J. Austin (1984) *Urban Life in Kingston, Jamaica: The Culture and Class Ideology of Two Neighbourhoods*. New York: Gordon & Breach. In *Man* (NS) 21 (2) 353-4

—— (1987) 'A Paradox in Caribbean Attitudes to Land'. In Jean Besson and Janet Momsen (eds) *Land and Development in the Caribbean*. London: Macmillan, 13-45

—— (1987a) 'Family Land as a Model for Martha Brae's New History: Culture Building in an Afro-Caribbean Village'. In Charles V. Carnegie (ed.) *Afro-Caribbean Villages in Historical Perspective*. ACIJ Research Review No. 2, Kingston, Jamaica: African-Caribbean Institute of Jamaica, 100-32

——— (1988) 'Agrarian Relations and Perceptions of Land in a Jamaican Peasant Village'. In John S. Brierley and Hymie Rubenstein (eds) *Small Farming and Peasant Resources in the Caribbean*. Winnipeg: University of Manitoba, 39-61

——— (1989) Review of Karen Fog Olwig (1985) *Cultural Adaptation and Resistance on St John: Three Centuries of Afro-Caribbean Life*. Gainesville: University Presses of Florida. In *Plantation Society in the Americas*, 2 (3) 345-8

——— (1989a) 'Introduction'. In Jean Besson (ed.) *Caribbean Reflections: The Life and Times of a Trinidad Scholar (1901-1986). An Oral History Narrated by William W. Besson*. London: Karia Press, 13-30

——— (1989b) 'Religion as Resistance in Jamaican Peasant Life: The Baptist Church, Revival Cult and Rastafari Movement'. Paper presented to the Workshop on The Rastafari Movement: Symbols, Continuity and Change in the Caribbean, Institute of Social Studies, The Hague, September

——— (1989c) 'Martha Brae's Two Histories: Towards an Afro-American Cultural History — A Caribbean Case Study'. Paper presented to The Program in Atlantic History, Culture and Society, The Johns Hopkins University, Baltimore, November

——— (1992) 'Freedom and Community: The British West Indies'. In Frank McGlynn and Seymour Drescher (eds) *The Meaning of Freedom: Economics, Politics and Culture after Slavery*. Pittsburgh: University of Pittsburgh Press, 183-219

——— (in preparation) 'Martha Brae's Two Histories: Culture Building in a Caribbean Society'

Braithwaite, L. (1975) *Social Stratification in Trinidad*. Kingston, Jamaica: Institute of Social and Economic Studies, University of the West Indies. First published 1953

Brana-Shute, Gary (1976) 'Drinking Shops and Social Structure: Some Ideas on Lower-Class West Indian Male Behavior'. *Urban Anthropology*, (5) 53-68

——— (1979) *On the Corner: Male Social Life in a Paramaribo Creole Neighbourhood*. Assen: Van Gorcum

Brierley, John S. (1988) 'Kitchen Gardens in the Caribbean, Past and Present: Their Role in Small-farm Development'. Paper presented to Twelfth Annual Conference of the Society for Caribbean Studies, July

Brodber, Erna (1983) 'Oral Sources and the Creation of a Social History of the Caribbean. *Jamaica Journal*, 16 (4) 2-11

Bush, Barbara (1985) 'Towards Emancipation: Slave Women and Resistance to Coercive Labour Regimes in the British West Indian Colonies, 1790-1838'. In David Richardson (ed.) *Abolition and its Aftermath: The Historical Context, 1790-1916*, London: Frank Cass, 27-54

——— (1990) *Slave Women in Caribbean Society 1650-1838*. London: James Currey

Campbell, Horace (1980) 'Rastafari: Culture and Resistance'. *Race and Class*, 22 (1) 1-22

——— (1985) *Rasta and Resistance: From Marcus Garvey to Walter Rodney*. London: Hansib

Clarke, Edith (1953) 'Land Tenure and the Family in Four Communities in Jamaica'. *Social and Economic Studies*, 1 (4) 81-118

——— (1957) *My Mother who Fathered Me: A Study of the Family in Three Selected Communities in Jamaica*. London: Allen & Unwin

Cross, Malcolm (1979) *Urbanization and Urban Growth in the Caribbean: An Essay on Social Change in Dependent Societies*. Cambridge: Cambridge University Press

Dalton, George (1967) 'Primitive Money'. In George Dalton (ed.) *Tribal and Peasant Economies: Readings in Economic Anthropology*. Garden City, New York: Natural History Press, 254-81

—— (1971) 'Peasantries in Anthropology and History'. In George Dalton (ed.) *Economic Anthropology and Development*. New York: Basic Books, 217-66

Dirks, Robert (1972) 'Networks, Groups and Adaptation in an Afro-Caribbean Community'. *Man (N.S.)*, 7 (4) 565-85

Durant-Gonzalez, Victoria (1983) 'The Occupation of Higglering'. *Jamaica Journal*, 16 (3) 2-12

Ford-Smith, Honor (1981) 'Women, the Arts and Jamaican Society: The Work of the Sistren Collective in Perspective'. Paper presented to the Fifth Annual Conference of the Society for Caribbean Studies, Hoddesdon, Hertfordshire, May

—— (1986) 'Sistren: Exploring Women's Problems through Drama'. *Jamaica Journal*, 19 (1) 2-12

—— (1986a) 'Introduction'. In Honor Ford-Smith (ed.) *Lionheart Gal: Life Stories of Jamaican Women*. London: The Women's Press, xiii-xxxi

Genovese, Eugene D. (1975) *Roll, Jordan, Roll: The World the Slaves Made*. London: André Deutsch. First published 1974

Henriques, Fernando (1968) *Family and Colour in Jamaica*. London: MacGibbon & Kee. First published 1953

Henry, Frances and Pamela Wilson (1975) 'The Status of Women in Caribbean Societies: An Overview of their Social, Economic and Sexual Roles. *Social and Economic Studies*, 24 (2) 165-98

Heuman, Gad (1985) 'Introduction'. In Gad Heuman (ed.) 'Out of the House of Bondage: Runaways, Resistance and Marronage in Africa and the New World'. Special issue of *Slavery and Abolition*, 6 (3) 1-8

Horowitz, Michael M. (1967) 'A Decision Model of Conjugal Patterns in Martinique'. *Man (N.S.)*, 2 (3) 445-53

Jayawardena, Chandra (1968) 'Ideology and Conflict in Lower Class Communities'. *Comparative Studies in Society and History* (10) 413-46

Katzin, Margaret (1959) 'The Jamaican Country Higgler'. *Social and Economic Studies*, (8) 421-40

—— (1960) 'The Business of Higglering in Jamaica'. *Social and Economic Studies*, (9) 297-331

Keesing, Roger M. (1981) *Cultural Anthropology: A Contemporary Perspective*. New York: Holt, Rinehart & Winston

Kuper, Adam (1976) *Changing Jamaica*. London: Routledge & Kegan Paul

Lowenthal, David (1972) *West Indian Societies*. London: Oxford University Press

MacCormack, Carol P. and Alison Draper (1987) 'Social and Cognitive Aspects of Female Sexuality in Jamaica'. In Pat Caplan (ed.) *The Cultural Construction of Sexuality*, London: Tavistock, 143-65

Mathurin, Lucille (1975) *The Rebel Woman in the British West Indies during Slavery*. Kingston: African-Caribbean Publications

Mintz, Sidney W. (1960) 'Peasant Markets'. *Scientific American*, 203 (2) 112-22

—— (1961) 'Pratik: Haitian Personal Economic Relationships'. In Viola Garfield (ed.) *Symposium: Patterns of Land Utilization and other Papers*. Proceedings of the 1961 Annual Spring Meeting of the American Ethnological Society. Seattle: University of Washington Press, 54-63

—— (1971) 'Towards an Afro-American History'. *Cahiers d'Histoire Mondiale*, (13) 317-31

—— (1974) *Caribbean Transformations*. Chicago: Aldine Publishing Company

—— (1975) 'History and Anthropology: A Brief Reprise'. In Stanley L. Engerman and Eugene D. Genovese (eds) *Race and Slavery in the Western Hemisphere: Quantitative Studies*. Princeton: Princeton University Press, 477-94

Mintz, Sidney W. and Richard Price (1976) *An Anthropological Approach to the Afro-American Past: A Caribbean Perspective*. Philadelphia: Institute for the Study of Human Issues

Morrissey, Marietta (1989) *Slave Women in the New World: Gender Stratification in the Caribbean*. Lawrence: University Press of Kansas

Ogilvie, Dan L. (1954) *History of the Parish of Trelawny*. Kingston, Jamaica: United Printers

Olwig, Karen Fog (1981) 'Women, "Matrifocality" and Systems of Exchange: An Ethnohistorical Study of the Afro-American Family on St John, Danish West Indies'. *Ethnohistory*, 28 (1) 59-78

—— (1981a) 'Finding a Place for the Slave Family: Historical Anthropological Perspectives'. *Folk*, (23) 345-58

—— (1985) *Cultural Adaptation and Resistance on St John: Three Centuries of Afro-Caribbean Life*. Gainesville: University of Florida Press

Paget, Hugh (1964) 'The Free Village System in Jamaica'. *Caribbean Quarterly*, 10 (1) 38-51

Patterson, Orlando (1973) *The Sociology of Slavery: An Analysis of the Origins, Development and Structure of Negro Slave Society in Jamaica*. London: Granada. First published 1967

Peristiany, J.G. (ed.) (1966) *Honour and Shame: The Values of Mediterranean Society*. Chicago: Chicago University Press

Powell, Dorian (1984) 'The Role of Women in the Caribbean'. *Social and Economic Studies*, 33 (2) 97-122

Robotham, Don (1988) 'The Development of a Black Ethnicity in Jamaica'. In Rupert Lewis and Patrick Bryan (eds) *Garvey: His Work and Impact*. Mona, Jamaica: Institute of Social and Economic Research and Extra-Mural Department, University of the West Indies, 23-38

Rodman, Hyman (1971) *Lower-Class Families: The Culture of Poverty in Negro Trinidad*. London: Oxford University Press

Rowe, Maureen (1980) 'The Woman in Rastafari'. *Caribbean Quarterly*, 26 (4) 13-21

Schuler, Monica (1980) *'Alas, Alas, Kongo': A Social History of Indentured African Immigration into Jamaica, 1841-1865*. Baltimore: The Johns Hopkins University Press

Seaga, Edward (1982) 'Revival Cults in Jamaica: Notes towards a Sociology of Religion'. In *Jamaica Journal Reprint*, Kingston: The Institute of Jamaica. First published 1969

Smith, M.G. (1965) *The Plural Society in the British West Indies*. Berkeley: University of California Press

—— (1965a) *Stratification in Grenada*. Berkeley: University of California Press

—— (1984) *Culture, Race and Class in the Commonwealth Caribbean*. Kingston, Jamaica: Department of Extra-Mural Studies, University of the West Indies

Smith, Raymond T. (1956) *The Negro Family in British Guiana: Family Structure and Social Status in the Villages*. London: Routledge & Kegan Paul

—— (1978) 'The Family and the Modern World System: Some Observations from the Caribbean'. *Journal of Family History*, 3 (4) 337-60

Stone, Carl (1973) *Class, Race and Political Behaviour in Urban Jamaica*. Mona, Jamaica: Institute of Social and Economic Research

Tanna, Laura (1984) *Jamaican Folk Tales and Oral Histories*. Kingston: Institute of Jamaica Publications

Wagley, Charles (1960) 'Plantation America: A Culture Sphere'. In Vera Rubin (ed.) *Caribbean Studies: A Symposium*, Seattle: University of Washington Press, 3-13. First published 1957

Wilson, Peter J. (1969) 'Reputation and Respectability: A Suggestion for Caribbean Ethnology'. *Man (N.S.)*, 4 (1) 70-84

—— (1973) *Crab Antics: The Social Anthropology of English-Speaking Negro Societies of the Caribbean*. New Haven: Yale University Press

Wright, Christopher (1984) 'Cultural Continuity and the Growth of West Indian Religion in Britain'. *Religion* (14) 337-56

Wright, Philip (1973) *Knibb 'the Notorious': Slaves' Missionary 1803-1845*. London: Sidgwick & Jackson

# III Marriage & Concubinage among the Sephardic Merchant Elite of Curaçao

EVA ABRAHAM-VAN DER MARK*

The Sephardic[1] Jewish community of Curaçao, Netherlands Antilles, was founded in 1653 and has the longest continuous history of all the Jewish communities in the Americas. With their vast extended networks covering Europe and the New World, the early settlers soon succeeded in building up large-scale international trade and shipping. Through the centuries they have engaged in importing, exporting and transhipping wholesale and retail goods, in shipping agencies and in smuggling. International trade existed in an open economy vulnerable to climatic, economic and political occurrences of all kinds in many parts of the world, events over which the merchants had no control and from which they both profited and suffered.

High risks ensured a continuously challenging situation which required great flexibility. With no economic alternatives present on the island,[2] fluctuations in business affected population trends. Lucrative trade led to immigration and early marriages, while recession resulted in emigration and the postponement of marriage. In the twentieth century, as a result of a low birth rate, assimilation and emigration, the group's size has declined dramatically. Its present 300 members, however, still have access to high positions and play a role in economic life quite disproportionate to their number. This chapter focuses on the pivotal role played by women in the group's survival.

## Marriage & Kinship

The Sephardic Jews of Curaçao have preserved their ethnic identity and position as a powerful and affluent élite considerably longer than other Sephardic commercial communities in the Caribbean and Middle America. This must be attributed primarily to the fact that the other merchants lived in societies with a plantation economy. Curaçao, on the other hand, depended on trade until the 1920s, with economic conditions and family life closely linked.

To defend the group's trade monopoly, a strong coalition of kinship units (*famiyas*)[3] functioning as corporate organizations and controlling resources such as business networks and information, as well as real estate and capital, was maintained. With separate families operating as corporations, the division of property upon inheritance could splinter the economic unit into fragments which were individually not economically viable (Wolf 1966). This led to a strong preference for marriages in which the dowry, to be transferred to the groom's family, remained within the bride's *famiya*.

Religious law and the caste-like stratification system of Curaçao (Hoetink 1958)[4] meant that Sephardic Jews had to marry within their own group. Moreover, from the beginning of their settlement, they recognized the importance of endogamy for the group's survival as a religious and ethnic unit. Marriage and the founding of a family have always been regarded as a religious obligation among Jews and the significance of this duty was strongly emphasized on Curaçao. Parents had a cultural obligation to see their children married. The ancient Sephardic custom of marrying a daughter at the bedside of her dying mother was continued until around 1900. According to Emmanuel (1970: 250-1) 'a mother could die at peace if she knew that her daughter was settled'.

The great value placed on private property encouraged high esteem for the family (Aries 1973), which was reinforced by the family's role as a focus of religious observance. Religion served as the main locus of cultural unity and identity, but as the group also had well defined economic interests, that is a monopoly of international trade and shipping, the materialistic aspects of the marriage contract acquired increasing importance. Clement (1975: 35) observes that 'kinship acts as a mechanism of class continuity whereby families are able to pass on their accumulated advantages intergenerationally'; and Banton (1978: 53) points out that 'It is much easier for a group to preserve its identity if it enjoys a monopoly and can reward successive generations for making endogamous marriages, thereby resisting assimilation in the most critical respect.'

Marriage was not considered as a union between two individuals but rather as an alliance between two families. The partners in marriage were delegates who formed a pact in which love and companionship were not required. Emotional needs were fulfilled within the extended family and the well-established personal relationships which each partner had before marriage were kept up and continued as before. With so many partners within families, most spouses had known each other since childhood (Hoetink 1958: 54). The heads of families, who carried primary responsibility for marriage arrangements, tried deliberately to serve the interests of their family by seeking to form an optimal combination, that is one in which through an alliance of bride and groom, the largest possible amounts of property, money and social status would be united. Parents determined the actual spouse as well as the age of marriage. Early marriages, which obviously increased a parent's control over a daughter's virginity, were preferred. By narrowing down their ideal of the 'right' marriage to one between cousins or other close relatives, most parents limited the range of acceptable partners. As Karner (1969: 12) explains:

> With the range of acceptable partners being well structured and very limited, two patterns developed: the first one is cross as well as parallel cousin marriage within one's own *famiya*; the second is marriage between members of extended families. The former consolidated the family position and at the same time safeguarded its material possessions from dispersal. The latter solidified the entire group.

In certain families this pattern was repeated through the centuries. However, although first cousin marriages were typical for the group as a whole, the wealthiest families were the most demanding in their selection of marriage partners for their children. It was in the rich families that first cousin marriage flourished most. There were also marriages between men and their sister's daughters and, although the case of a man marrying his father's sister was considered problematic (Emmanuel 1970: 272), it was not prohibited. Endogamous marriage resulted in a social cohesion which promoted a strong group identity. Yet the group was highly stratified according to wealth, power and status. With each family trying to maximize combinations of capital, business information and instrumental networks through marriage relationships, family ties became a most valuable resource in themselves.

## Demography & the State of Business

Two serious obstacles to marriage were the indispensable dowry and the very low ratio of men to women. The Emmanuels refer repeatedly to the problems women faced in finding a spouse: 'Marriageability of a girl depended on her dowry'. They speak of 'the untold sacrifices and privations endured by parents in raising dowries for their daughters' and discuss how 'finding suitors for the girls has always posed a serious problem' (Emmanuel 1970: 234, 182 and 268). As men travelled and many of them emigrated and married abroad, there was always a considerable surplus of women.[5]

The oligarchical commercial organization[6] put limits on the group's size through migration and exerted careful control over the age of marriage and the marriage rate. Family relationships, associated with the family-owned firm which spanned generations, predominated over all other relationships. Within the community, rich families formed the ruling élite, dominating religious as well as non-religious affairs.

Notwithstanding the fact that the most affluent families consistently married among themselves, because of the scarcity of males, men had some chance of marrying upwards (hypogamy). The marriage prospects of poor girls, on the other hand, were bleak. Besides the families whose men have been described as 'merchant princes' and 'the Rothschilds of the Caribbean' there was always a number of people who depended on the financial support of the community for their survival. The young girls among them might apply for a dowry from the religious congregation, which held special funds for this purpose.[7] During times of recession, however, not all requests would be granted. Moreover, the *Parnassim* (Board of the Synagogue) had the authority to set certain conditions, as is illustrated by the following example (Emmanuel 1970: 177):

> In 1737, Rachel, the orphan [sic] daughter of Abraham Aboab, wanted to marry Isaac Salas. Her widowed mother applied for the amount customarily bestowed upon an orphan as her marriage portion. The *Parnassim* forbade the wedding because they did not approve of a young man who had no means to earn a living. Salas left for Suriname and Rachel never married.

The importance of dowries is indicated by the numerous passionately fought conflicts and lawsuits they caused within this small community. The squandering of a woman's dowry by her husband was considered a valid reason for her relatives to demand divorce as, besides the financial loss, the family's honour and reputation were at stake. One example is that of the daughter of *Haham* (rabbi) Jessurun who married David Arias in 1739. The *Haham*, who as religious leader of the community enjoyed high status, gave his daughter a generous dowry and, moreover, guaranteed payment for any purchases made by his son-in-law. The latter used the dowry to buy a ship and go into business. But seven months after the wedding he was deeply in debt and fled to Jamaica, leaving his father-in-law the task of satisfying his creditors. The Board of the Synagogue threatened to discharge its rabbi because of the embarrassment of having him involved in various lawsuits. The marriage was dissolved (Emmanuel 1970: 117).

As dowries depended on the state of business, marriage rates and the economy were closely intertwined. The effects of economic ups and downs on the group's numbers and on the marriage rate are clearly indicated by the Emmanuels' studies. An economic depression resulted in a decline in the number of Jews in Curaçao from 1500 in 1750 to 1200 in 1775. With the onset of the American Revolution, however, Curaçao became a supplier of arms and ammunition to the American armies. 'The island became a small paradise of terrestrial abundance ...

[and] family life flourished' (Emmanuel 1970: 262). The marriage age fell and the number of children per family increased to an average of nine or ten; it was not unusual for a woman to become a grandmother by the age of 35. But lean years followed after 1781. Men emigrated and the existing surplus of women increased. In 1810 there were 386 adult women to only 263 adult men in the community.

And so the cycle continued. The prosperity of the merchants depended to a large degree on the political and economic climates of the nearby Spanish colonies of what are now Venezuela and Colombia. After Bolívar's victories in the early nineteenth century, Curaçao suffered a severe down-turn in business activity and again a number of Jews left the island. Emigration continued until 1850 and between August 1847 and January 1849 not one marriage was registered in the community (Emmanuel 1970: 347).

But from 1850 onward the community enjoyed another period of affluence. The Emmanuels comment that a study of the documents of the years 1850 to 1880 'leave one amazed at the quantity of money disposed of by the Jews in their trans-actions' (Emmanuel 1970: 347) and particularly note the very lavish dowries of those years. However, relations with the frequently changing government of Venezuela deteriorated. In 1882 Venezuela put an additional duty of 30 per cent on goods from the Antilles and closed the ports of both Maracaibo and Coro, which were vital to Curaçao's trade. Business on the island dropped alarmingly and another wave of emigration started.

Most of those who left the community settled in various parts of Venezuela, Colombia, the Caribbean, Central America and in New York.[8] Karner (1969) points out that the various waves of emigration led to the formation of satellite communities and to the strengthening of relations with the Jewish groups into which the migrants were absorbed. Emigration did not mean an end to one's group membership. Expatriates stayed in touch with the mother community of Curaçao and their descendants would sometimes return and intermarry into the local Jewish group.

Social control was strong. Those who did not conform to the rules might no longer be considered part of the family. Marriage to a person not approved of by the family led either to loss of status or to forced migration. If the migrant couple did well, the original affront might be forgotten and their line readmitted to the family. If not, they entered into oblivion as far as Curaçao was concerned. Many of the Jewish families on the island had instances of such black sheep (Karner 1969: 15-16).

## The Value of Women

In his study of the ethnic allegiance of the Chinese in Jamaica and Guyana, Patterson (1975: 338-9) observes that: 'Over the years ... those Chinese who were most successful economically have been the very ones who had been most endog-amous. Women have become the means whereby wealth is exchanged, shared, consolidated and kept within the group, all this while performing the equally valuable task of perpetuating the group. As such, they have become highly valued and jealously guarded.' This also applies to the Sephardic women of Curaçao. They were expected to preserve the purity of blood lines and the values of the patriarchal society. However, the continuously low sex ratio weakened women's position, especially in the case of the daughters of the less affluent.[9]

The female sex ratio must have strengthened the already strong preference for male babies. Sons had great value, not only because they might bring wealth in the form of dowries into the family, but also because of their role in religious practices, in continuing the family name, and as successors in the family business. The birth of a son was an occasion for great rejoicing. The father received various honours in the synagogue and the customary festivities lasted for two weeks. Daughters were seen differently: 'If a woman unluckily gave birth to a daughter, the tropical climate of Curaçao would drop to freezing, first in the home of the unfortunate mother and then in the home of her in-laws' (Emmanuel 1970: 126). This attitude has been quite persistent. A woman, who today is in her fifties, told me that upon the news of her birth, her father, who already had two sons, wept bitterly. In 1731 the society *Misphat Habamot* (Justice to Daughters) was founded 'to boost the morale of families depressed over the birth of a daughter'(Emmanuel 1970: 126).

The double standard of sexual morality and the asymmetry of the roles of men and women in Curaçao's Sephardic Jewish community were typical of the Latin American upper and middle classes. Hoetink used the term *complejo de virginidad* (virginity complex) to characterize the cluster of values around the role of women. Their virginity before and chastity after marriage were of utmost concern. Separation of the sexes, constant chaperoning and social control were supposed to take care of a woman's reputation.

In fact, rebellion against the strict rules did take place. The Emmanuels devote a whole chapter to 'complicated marriages' and the problems and conflicts arising from rumours of children born to unmarried Jewish women, girls of 'questionable behaviour' and premarital sex. They state: 'when a young man who had fallen in love and promised marriage, in a moment of weakness "succumbed to the over-powering hold of the tropics" and the couple ultimately married, they would be denied all synagogue honours and the blame would remain with them for a long time. Moreover, if the girl's father was an employee of the community, he would be dismissed and if he was receiving community aid his monthly allowance would be cut off, unless it could be proved that the girl had been forced.' The very fact that this regulation was enacted in 1752, reaffirmed in 1756 and made more rigid in 1786, indicates that there were always some women who chose to go against the rules, even if the risks taken were great because of the punishment that might be heaped upon them and their families.

All work in the house was performed by slaves and, after emancipation, by servants. The daily care and discipline of children was left to the *jaja*, the black nanny. Yet one should not conclude that women lived lives of enforced leisure. They were the managers of domestic affairs and social life with its many celebrations, elaborate dinners and social gatherings.

The gallantry and courtesy shown to women by men underlines the social distance between the sexes (Van den Berghe 1970) and through law and custom women's role in the family was carefully circumscribed. The religious community was male-dominated, but it did provide a cultural milieu in which a varied range of human associations was carefully identified and regulated. Sexual and matrimonial patterns were spelt out in detail. Great deference was paid to motherhood. Some status giving criteria cut across gender lines: older women, like men, shared in the reverence due to age that was inspired by the customary emphasis laid on the authority of parents.

A woman's place in the household was secure and her kinship connections remained a crucial determinant of her condition. The weakening of the marital bond was the price paid for membership in a wider group, which had its rewards, for dispersal of affection and loyalty involved numerous persons who accepted responsibility for a woman's welfare. Moreover, while pre-mortem transmission of wealth in the shape of a dowry was tied to marriage, a woman would also inherit in her own right upon her parent's death, which gave her greater freedom (Goody 1983: 61).

## Concubinage

Men lived quite differently from women. Through their trade they travelled widely and were constantly in touch with people of different cultures. They found it impossible to observe all their religious prescriptions to the letter and displayed a striking liberalism in religious affairs. In the nineteenth century this group was among the first to introduce various innovations in the synagogue and one faction within the Sephardic community opened a Reform Temple, eight years before German Jews opened one in New York.[10] They had a busy social life, outside the home, centred around the synagogue and various secular clubs. They also had sexual encounters with black women.

Arranged marriages promoted concubinage and children born from this relationship. These were also encouraged by colonial conditions. Writing about the eighteenth century, the Emmanuels mention that there were fewer than six white families in Curaçao without any Afro-Caribbean relatives. A wide range of relationships existed, from a single fleeting, exclusively physical contact to more enduring forms of concubinage (Hoetink 1958). It was customary for mature men to install one or more women in their own separate houses. This practice, which was institutionalized and called *kerida*, was more prevalent among the Sephardim than among the Dutch white Protestants.

The rigid endogamy of the Jews, their greater affluence and their willingness to accept the practice of maintaining mistresses and 'outside' children, with which they had been familiar in Spain and Portugal, may have contributed to the popularity of *kerida*. Wives were socialized into pretending complete ignorance of the Afro-Caribbean children who frequented the large kitchens and servants' quarters. An old lady said, 'We never, never talked about it. But we did whisper about it.' Another woman wondered what her grandfather had meant by his often repeated statement: 'A lady should never enter the kitchen'. A wife who, in the 1930s, followed her husband to the house of his mistress and confronted him was blamed by the community for her 'outrageous behaviour'.

Male interviewees gave the most enthusiastic descriptions of the beauty, vigour, firm breasts and white teeth of black women. Some accounts of physical characteristics suggested a description of pedigree animals. For a black woman, having a relationship with a white man was one of the very few ways to acquire upward social mobility in Curaçao's caste-like society. But only a minority of those who had such a relationship ever reached the status of *kerida* and for most of these life was not easy. Nevertheless, they were envied by their sisters because of their light-coloured children. The fact that these sometimes were given a better education and achieved higher positions in society must have been their reward.

A few extracts from case-studies gathered during the 1970s may give some understanding of what life was like for these women and their children. Señora S's daughter tells her story:

My mother was the mistress of L. They met around the turn of the century, when she was 17 and after about a year 'el a sake di'e kas' (he took her away from her parent's home) [an expression which means that the relationship has become stable and the man installs the woman in her own house]. Their relationship lasted 15 years and they had four children together. He travelled a lot but always wrote the most beautiful letters [the letters, which have been treasured, indicate a sincere love affair. E.A.]. Although L was married and had children he was totally devoted to my mother. As business was slow he decided to move to Caracas and my mother and her children moved too, accompanied by a maid. We lived in a nice house and my mother was always elegantly dressed. The house was in the same neighbourhood where L lived with his family. When we went for a walk we often met his children and their nurse. The maids of the two families were friends and our maid often took us to L's house where we played in the kitchen. There was an air of secrecy about these visits, as we were not supposed to be seen by Mrs L. In that period and in that milieu a lady would not enter the kitchen, but one day a door was left open and I saw what struck me as an immensely fat lady. Our maid was startled, and later, on the way home, she told me, 'You have seen Mrs L.' The incident made a deep impression on me.

After a few years both families returned to Curaçao. But the economic situation had declined even more and after a relatively short time L decided to settle in New York. While my mother was preparing to move my brother fell ill and our departure had to be postponed. He had an operation which was not really successful and he remained in poor health. My mother used this as a reason to delay the trip. There may have been other reasons too. Caracas was near Curaçao and she was soon fluent in Spanish but New York may have frightened her. Letters and remittances kept coming regularly. Then, after three years, we no longer heard anything. There was a horrible period of insecurity, not knowing if he had died or what had happened. My mother was desperate. She felt humiliated and could never believe that L had deliberately rejected her. Then finally, she realized that she was on her own and had to take care of her children. She worked very hard as a cook and lived a rather isolated life. Her main purpose in life was to see her daughters legally married.

## Señora M's story told by her daughter:

Both my parents are children of Sephardic fathers. My mother was born in 1915. She is the daughter of A [a son of the most prominent Sephardic family of the twentieth century]. He never got married but had several women and children. Seven of these children, from four different women, have been acknowledged but not given his name. My mother was an only child but she considers the six others as her closest relatives, as near as brothers and sisters, and they have always remained very close. The three Curaçao women were also close, but the fourth was Colombian. She could not stand the idea of sharing a man with several other women and she left for Bogotá. A sent someone after her begging her to come back but she refused. [The term *combles* refers to the relationship between two or more women of the same man, who visit each other and have a good relationship with each other. One male interviewee commented 'and why not? they eat from the same hay-rack'.] My mother dislikes talking about her youth. She has very bitter feelings about her father. But she is ambivalent. It does mean something to be a descendant of such an illustrious family, with such a rich history and so much wealth and influence. My grandfather lived alternately in New York, Havana and Curaçao. When he was on the island he sometimes called for his children, mostly the sons. They had to use the back door and were permitted only in the kitchen and sometimes on the porch but never in other parts of the house.

One of the sons was unusually bright and his teacher wrote to New York and requested that my grandfather send him to secondary school. He replied politely that the matter would be discussed as soon as he could come to Curaçao. That year he did not come and the matter was never mentioned again. When A died his fortune went to his unmarried nieces. There was nothing for his children. His brother, however, arranged to give each acknowledged child $25,000. My mother and her half-sisters and brothers still insist that this uncle was much more human than A. He sometimes invited one of the boys for a conversation on the porch. Considering the period, that was very liberal. His unmarried sisters always sent for the children to run errands and do odd jobs around the house. They hated this but could not possibly refuse. My mother feels very proud of her father's name (although he did not give it to her) but is very resentful of the way she and the others were treated. After the relationship with A broke off, my grandmother made her own living, sewing clothes and making cakes to sell. She never had another man because they would all be of a lower status than A and by living with a black man she would have embarrassed A's family.

Señora E's story told by her daughter:

My mother E had a relationship with D. She knew that marriage was out of the question but she wanted very much to have a child, and when after some time she did not become pregnant, she consulted a physician. Shortly afterwards, I was conceived. I was born in 1937. Sometimes D gave my mother a little money for me but never anything for herself. When I was three years old, D married in New York and my mother learnt about it from the newspapers. She was furious because he had never told her anything about his marriage plans. Directly after the honeymoon he tried to get in touch with her but she refused to see him. He tried to win her back and sent a letter suggesting that they should meet once a week. My mother returned his letter. D had an office in the centre of town which I passed every day on my way to school. On the way back home I used to drop in and would get some candy or a small present. But I had to check first to see if Mrs D was present as in that case I was not allowed to visit. My mother supported the two of us by selling home-made cakes and pastries. There was never enough money but everything was proper and clean. When children asked me where my father was I told them that he lived in New York. His mother was curious, she wanted to see me and sent maids with all kinds of stories in order to get me to her house. But my mother would not allow me to go there. When I was 15, an aunt whom I had often met at the office was going to emigrate to Venezuela and she begged E to let me visit her to say farewell. She made it rather dramatic by saying that she might never see me again. So I was allowed to visit her and at the same time meet my grandmother, who was very pleased. Later, after his divorce, D again tried to revive the affair with E but she did not want it. She had a number of affairs with other men and also had a marriage proposal but she decided to stay single. At the age of 38 she decided to stop having anything to do with men and dedicated herself totally to me. I did well in school and later got a job as an announcer at the broadcasting station. All D's relatives have been extremely kind to me and I am his only child. We meet on Sundays for lunch and we have travelled together. He can be very generous but also extremely stingy.

The father's relatives are proud of this talented woman who plays an active role in the island's cultural life. Señora E is still a beautiful and dignified woman. She says, laughing:

I was smart not to get married, otherwise I might have to nurse an old sick man today. Now I am free to do whatever I want. When I had to bring up my daughter and also had to take care of my mother, I never had any money, never enough to make ends meet, but still we had fun. I have had a good life.

The contrast between the first and the last case study, Señora S and Señora E, is striking. Apart from the different personalities and the considerable differences in the status and wealth of the two Jewish men involved, the main variation must be explained by the changes in the relations between the social groups on the island that took place in the twentieth century, and the changes in behaviour and feelings that went with it.

The case studies indicate the importance of status and upward mobility. In general it can be said that the mistresses of wealthy Sephardim were raised above the social stratum to which they had belonged before the relationship began. Even after the relationship was over, many of these women made considerable sacrifices to keep up a life style that was in accordance with middle-class values of respectability in order to secure the social mobility of their children.

Generally, children of Sephardic fathers were better treated than those of Dutch Protestants. Hoetink (1958: 83) points out that bright young sons were most useful as reliable employees in the family business. Some of them got their father's name, which even the most superficial inspection of the current telephone book of Curaçao will prove. Just how the Afro-Caribbean child of a Jewish father was treated depended on a variety of factors. The most important were the child's somatic characteristics, which were so crucial in a society in which racial distinctions have long dominated all other divisions. Other factors were the relationship between the parents, whether or not the father was married, the benevolence and affluence of the father's relatives and the child's social training, 'good manners', intelligence and personality. After a man's death his relatives sometimes withdrew all the privileges and support that the 'outside' child had been receiving from the father. On the other hand, as the case study of Señora M shows, the relatives could be more generous than the father.

According to the closeness of the relationship to a Sephardic man, the black population referred to the 'outside child' as *yu di Judio* (child of a Jew) or *nieto di Judio* (grandchild of a Jew). Of someone who is related to the Sephardic group but not as a child or grandchild, it is said that *e tin sanger di Judio* (he or she has Jewish blood), an expression which can also be used for someone who is conspicuously successful in business or has a gift for languages. From among the numerous Afro-Caribbean offspring of Sephardic fathers, a group came into being, the *Yu di Judio*, which generally socialized together and intermarried. They lived in a particular part of town (Pietermaai) and even as early as the beginning of the eighteenth century a number of them achieved prosperity (Hoetink 1958: 83).

The Jewish fathers of 'outside' children were pragmatists who employed a strategy of co-option of their coloured offspring. Concubinage gave them the benefits of a category of children which, if necessary, provided labour but could not make any legal demands and were excluded from inheritance. Due to the rule that only children of Jewish women can belong to the religious community, and the explicit rule (until the 1960s) that excluded black and brown people from membership of the synagogue, the *yu di Judio* never represented a threat to the distinction and group identity of the Sephardim.

The *yu di Judio* belonged to the faith of their black or brown mothers and were Roman Catholic. Having a higher status within the Afro-Caribbean population (which is over 90 per cent Roman Catholic), they have always been in demand as godparents. Some of them had over 100 godchildren. Thus, through the institution of *compadrazgo* (godparenthood) they built up large networks of personal relations with black families. This has served some of them well in their political careers.

Although some women and men in this category are in business, the group is disproportionately represented in high positions in politics and the bureaucracy. It has also made important contributions to the island's cultural life. As the stratification system of the island has undergone considerable change and people's ascribed and achieved statuses have been given a different significance and meaning, the *yu di Judio* have been re-evaluated and co-opted by the Sephardim who lacked sufficient children to occupy the positions to which they had access.

## Epilogue

Sephardic family and social life was preserved for 250 years without significant changes. However, during the last decades of the nineteenth century change set in. As Curaçao became connected with Europe and the United States through the services of several steamship lines (which were almost exclusively represented by Sephardic family firms) women started to accompany their husbands on long trips to Europe and North America. Their stay abroad was still to a large extent 'programmed' by the group, yet, these trips represented a break from the omnipresent social control of the island community.

After a period of political instability and economic decline beginning in the 1880s, the group's isolation gradually ended and a process of individualization set in. Industrialization, which started with the building of the Shell oil refinery in

1917, caused radical changes in all sectors of society. But already the birth-rate of the Sephardic group had decreased drastically (Karner 1969) as couples started to practice birth control. This should not only be interpreted as women's resistance to large families. It may also have been the policy of the male heads of families who felt the pressures of the large *famiyas*, which always had some sons or cousins who were neither gifted nor enthusiastic about commerce, yet nevertheless had to be found a place in the family business. At approximately the same time many families expressed the opinion that cousin marriages might be dangerous for the health of children born from such unions. It seems plausible that this sudden disapproval of the long preferred close marriages was a rationalization behind which rebellion against the stifling custom of endogamy was hidden.

In the first decades of this century many women remained unmarried because of a lack of suitable partners, but individuals began to rebel. Some wives insisted on divorce, one even to marry her lover, and some men made it clear that they were not interested in the opposite sex. A few Sephardic sons started living with women of the Latin American 'cabarets', which caused so much commotion on the island. Although their families would not permit a marriage, they stayed with these women until their deaths. One man requested that his family should let him marry the black mother of his children. Unprecedented as this was, the couple were finally allowed to marry in the 1960s after having lived together for 40 years. As more men emigrated and married abroad, several Sephardic women married foreigners. This was true in the 1930s and especially in the 1940s, during and after the Second World War. These foreigners were mostly Dutch, non-Jewish professionals and naval officers.

If one evaluates all twentieth-century marriages in the Sephardic community, it becomes obvious that the vast majority of them are typical cases of hypogamy. Moreover, a scarcity of sons resulting from the low birth-rate led to women inheriting the fortunes of several families. Generally speaking, hypogamy increases the power and authority of the wife because it is she who, through her father, brings status and wealth. The offspring of these unions bear non-Jewish names but, nevertheless, belong to the Sephardic group and the Jewish community through descent in the female line. They have access to what is left of the Sephardim's power resources and will largely determine the group's fate in the coming decades.

With increased authority, Sephardic women no longer had to tolerate such practices as concubinage, which were obviously not in their interest. Since 1824, when the Sephardim gave up their large degree of legal autonomy and came under Napoleonic law, as it was introduced into the colony by the Dutch, the Sephardic Jews never married according to community property agreements. This implies that Sephardic women do not remain married because of economic circumstances and it is the men who are in a vulnerable position because divorce may threaten their status and high standard of living. Besides, European husbands who had come into the family were not familiar with the *kerida*. In the 1930s, *kerida*, as an institutionalized form of concubinage among the Sephardic élite, was on its way out. Of the *yu di Judio* born in this century, the youngest and last generation consists of people who today are in their late forties. Another reason behind the disappearance of this form of concubinage of white men and black women and the hypergenation (the raising of a woman's status through concubinage) that was associated with it, appears to have been the period of full employment for black men which followed upon industrialization in the 1920s and lasted until the 1960s. This economic change meant that it was no longer better *per se* to be the concubine or 'outside' child of a white man than the wife or legitimate child of a black man.

## Notes

\*   This chapter was written in the early 1980s.
1   Its members are Sephardim whose ancestors lived in Portugal and Spain before the expulsion of Jews from the Iberian peninsula. The majority of early Jewish colonists in Curaçao came from Amsterdam. Others emigrated from Brazil when the Dutch had to give up their colony in Pernambuco in 1654. Small numbers came directly from Portugal and Spain, others via Suriname, Guadeloupe and Italy.
2   The early efforts of some Sephardic Jews to develop plantations were a failure. Because of poor soil and irregular rainfall, Curaçao never had a plantation economy. Hoetink (1958) points out that the plantations that did exist were often a status symbol rather than a source of income.
3   The group's kinship system was the bilateral, extended family, consisting of all recognized relatives on one's mother's and on one's father's side, along with the kinsmen of one's spouse.
4   Until the 1920s Curaçao's population consisted of three groups, the Dutch Protestants, the Sephardic Jews and the coloured population, which were differentiated according to rank and status. Relationships between these groups have been characterized as caste-like by Hoetink (1958).
5   In the permanent surplus of women in the Sephardic group, one encounters the opposite of the situation found in some Caribbean societies which, because of absenteeism, always had a shortage of white women. Writing on Jamaica in the eighteenth century, Mathurin (1974) calls white women 'a small, troubled minority' and points out that 'they came to embody the phenomenon of absenteeism in its most extreme form: by the 1770s the greatest scarcity of white women was to be found among the families of the largest estate owners. As women and mothers, the rigours of the climate, and their children's education could give constant cause for frequent and prolonged trips home.' Parry and Sherlock (1971) mention Jamaican parishes in the late eighteenth century, with one white woman to seven men. Absenteeism in the Caribbean has been described by various authors (Van Lier 1949; Parry and Sherlock 1960; Douglas Hall 1954; Patterson 1967; Mathurin 1974) as typical white élitist phenomenon. In Curaçao, however, although there always were some Dutch public officials and military men whose stay in Curaçao was temporary, the Dutch Protestants on the island did not tend to absenteeism either. This certainly holds true for the Huguenots among them, but may be primarily explained by the fact that the Curaçao plantations were not very profitable and therefore few of the planters and their families could afford to travel extensively.
6   Describing economic life at the end of the nineteenth century, Gomez Casseres (1976) points out that, in international trade, capital was highly concentrated in the hands of a small number of family firms. 'The type of commerce upon which the island depended promoted an oligarchical organization ... international commerce was carried out by relatively large, multifaceted firms, with significant capital endowments and exclusive international ties.' This also holds true for the eighteenth century and for the latter decades of the seventeenth century and is evidenced in tax lists, real estate holdings, lists of shipowners and lists of dowries. Although many Sephardim owned real estate, they were not tied to the land. Compared to landowning élites they were flexible and mobile.
7   Families without means might apply for a dowry from the community fund, while some orphans got dowries from a charitable fund in Amsterdam to which Sephardim contributed during prosperous times.
8   See the Emmanuels (1970: 822-40) for a list of places where Sephardim from Curaçao have settled over the centuries.
9   The sex ratio as used here is the number of males per 100 females.
10  The reason for the schism that resulted in the foundation of Temple Emmanuel in Curaçao was not disagreement about religious matters but rather economic rivalry between two of the most prominent families.

## References

Aries, Philippe (1973) *Centuries of Childhood*. New York: Random House

Banton, Michael (1978) 'Ethnic Groups and the Theory of Rational Choice'. In *Sociological Theories and Race*. Paris: Unesco

Clement, Wallace (1975) *The Canadian Corporate Elite: An Analysis of Economic Power*. Toronto: McClelland & Stewart

Emmanuel, Isaac and Suzanne (1970) *History of the Jews of the Netherlands Antilles*. Cincinnati: American Jewish Archives

Gomez Casseres, Benjamin (1976) 'Economic Development, Social Class and Politics in the Caribbean: A Historical Comparison of Curaçao and Barbados'. Senior thesis, Brandeis University

Goody, Jack (1983) *The Development of the Family and Marriage in Europe*. London: Cambridge University Press

Hoetink, Harmannus (1958) *Het patroon van de oude Curaçaose Samenleving*. Aruba: De Wit

Karner, Frances (1969) *The Sephardics of Curaçao: A Study of Sociocultural Patterns in Flux*. Assen: Van Gorcum

Mathurin, Lucille (1974) 'A Historical Study of Women in Jamaica from 1665 to 1844'. Unpublished Ph.D. thesis, University of the West Indies, Mona, Jamaica

Parry, J.H. and P.M. Sherlock (1971) *A Short History of the West Indies*. London: Macmillan & Company Ltd. First published 1956

Patterson, Orlando (1975) 'Content and Choice in Ethnic Allegiance: A Theoretical Framework and Caribbean Case Study. In Nathan Glazer and Daniel Moynihan (eds) *Ethnicity: Theory and Experiences*. Cambridge, Mass: Harvard University Press, 305-49

Van den Berghe, Pierre (1970) *Race and Ethnicity*. New York: Basic Books

Wolf, Eric (1966) 'Kinship, Friendship and Patron-Client Relations in Complex Societies'. In Michael Banton (ed.) *The Social Anthropology of Complex Societies*. London: Tavistock, 1-20

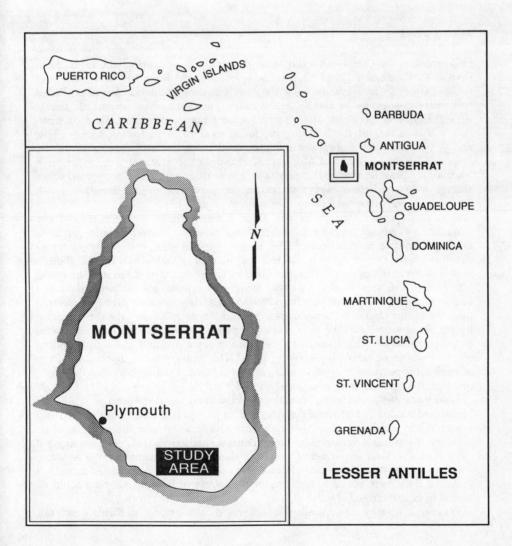

# IV Changing Roles in the Life Cycles of Women in Traditional West Indian Houseyards

LYDIA MIHELIC

PULSIPHER

Yvette's House
Dada's House

## Background

Still extant in the Caribbean today, though rapidly disappearing due to modernization, is a residential unit often called a houseyard.[1] Found in both rural and urban settings,[2] houseyards were the first place of residence for many West Indians who are now in middle age or older. They embody a way of life that is several hundred years old. In a very real sense houseyards are an historical institution that is one of the building blocks of modern West Indian society. This study, based on ethnographies and measured maps of ten houseyards on the Eastern Caribbean island of Montserrat, examines the place of women in these traditional domestic spaces. It shows how female roles and use of houseyard space change over a lifetime as maturation, mating, reproduction, education, work experiences and aging take place. (See map on page 49.)

Houseyards usually range in size from a sixteenth to a half acre and are commonly occupied by two or more small wooden chattel houses (or their modern concrete incarnations).[3] The houses vary in size, but a typical house measures 6 by 12 feet or 10 by 20 feet and usually contains two rooms, though additions have often been built or two houses joined to create more interior space. The houses are surrounded by other structures: sheds, animal pens, detached kitchens, ovens, work benches, laundry facilities, showers and privies. Scattered over the entire yard is an array of plants: food plants cultivated for consumption by people or animals in the yard and other plants tended because they are useful as ornamentals or medicinals or for performing some practical chore like fending off mosquitoes or scrubbing cooking pots.[4] The entire yard is marked off from adjoining property by a fence, a hedge of useful plants like bamboo, aloe or agave, or some other perceivable boundary (Mintz 1974: 245).

Usually one of the residents, often the oldest woman, owns the land on which the houseyard sits, or has informal rights to it. This person is in charge of the yard and others live in it either because they pay rent or have permission to live there, often by right of kinship. Occasionally the residents actually own their own houses and only rent the land on which the house stands. This arrangement was more common in the days when most houses were of wood and constructed in such a way that they were portable, because then the array of houses in a yard could be added to or rearranged at will.

Whereas a houseyard typically has several dwellings and multiple residents, what really defines this domestic unit is the spatial patterning of life within and without the house. In fact the house is often viewed primarily as formal space. For example, on Montserrat, where the bulk of this research was conducted, the standard two rooms are referred to as the 'hall' and the 'chamber' regardless of actual use and they typically contain a rather regularized set of possessions, which may be infrequently used but which symbolize the resident's status. The house is also a place for secure storage, for sleeping and for shelter from the rain. The yard, on the other hand, is where most of life is lived. It is less formal, has fluid spatial allocations and is where people prepare food and eat, tend their domestic animals and plants, wash clothes, repair possessions, sew, tend babies, train toddlers, do countless chores and converse — in short, it is the place where most social transactions are conducted.

Most houseyards have several residents — some have as many as 20 or 30. Residence in a yard may be attained through a variety of circumstances ranging from close kinship with the head of the yard to a purely business transaction wherein a yard resident pays rent and is only peripherally involved in yard activities. The relationships of those who occupy a particular house in a yard are varied and include the following possibilities: a mother and her young children (occasionally visited for the night by one of their fathers), an older woman and several of her adult children (sometimes male, but more often female) and their children, adult (uterine)[5] siblings and their children, a single adult with 'borrowed' children,[6] a lone single adult, a sexually cohabiting couple with only their common children, or with their common as well as 'outside'[7] children, or a couple living alone (usually elderly) who have no common children.[8]

It is possible for a houseyard to have only one occupied house with only one resident. Although this situation is recognized by the practitioners of houseyard culture as abnormal, in fact it occurs more and more frequently as modernization and migration draw multi-generation households apart, often leaving one elderly person, most commonly a woman, alone in a yard that once rollicked with life. Such an individual will often be heard to lament the condition of solitude.

## The Literature

Houseyards, as described and discussed here, while rarely called precisely that, have long been recognized as an elemental feature of West Indian life, being found in rural as well as urban settings. *Caribbean Transformations* by Sidney Mintz (1974), in which the houses and yards of rural Puerto Rico, Jamaica and Haiti are examined, is perhaps the best known of the studies. R.T. Smith's most recent study, *Kinship and Class in the West Indies* (1988) makes repeated reference to houses and yards as primary sites of residence, especially for the urban lower class. Brodber's *A Study of Yards in the City of Kingston* (1975) explicitly recognizes that houseyards are often multi-dwelling. Clarissa Kimber's (1966; 1973) studies of Caribbean gardens also document the spatial relationships of rural houses and yards. In a study of family land, Edith Clarke's book, *My Mother who Fathered Me* (1957: 55ff.) gives a detailed description of multi-dwelling houseyards in a rural Jamaican village.

The historical literature contains a number of references to the domestic spaces of slaves and freedmen, describing them as clusters of houses and outbuildings around central activity areas, interspersed with economic plants and animals and inhabited by people linked through kinship and friendship (Wentworth 1834; Olwig 1985; Craton 1978; Handler and Lange 1978). Writing in Jamaica in 1818, one author (Anon. cited in Higman 1974) describes a slave habitation: 'In some instances whole families reside within one enclosure: They have separate houses, but only one gate. In the centre of this family village the house of the principal among them is generally placed, and is in general very superior to the others.'

Another writer in Jamaica in 1825 describes a multi-dwelling houseyard very similar to that of Miss Joy's yard described later in this chapter; the yard with five houses included the 18-member extended family of an African-born matriarch and yard head, Bessie Gardner (Higman 1974).

Archaeological findings in Jamaican and Montserrat slave villages confirm the general pattern of a cluster of dwellings interspersed with activity areas; but as yet archaeological evidence of domestic plants and animals is not firm (Higman 1974; Howson 1987).

Architects have shown increasing interest in the role of the built environment in both embodying and reflecting the deep structure of a culture and in reproducing social relationships peculiar to it; but their relative unfamiliarity with conducting or interpreting ethnographic research to complement their understanding of building techniques and of spatial design has often prevented cogent phenomenological analysis of a particular material culture. An exception is Amos Rapaport (1969) who offers numerous observations pertinent to this study.

Jon Goss (1988) states that geographers have also failed to analyse adequately the form and meaning of the spatial patterning of the built environment. I found useful his suggestion that an analysis of the spatial arrangement of 'floorscape', adapted in this case to 'yardscape', might reveal inherent ideas about gender roles by delineating zones of interaction.

This study of West Indian traditional houseyards was originally designed to help interpret archaeological data from Caribbean plantation slave villages.[9] In recent years archaeologists have sought ethnographic data that will help them to interpret artifact assemblages and distribution patterns and to discern the behaviour that resulted in a particular signature of human activity on the landscape. Typically these ethno-archaeological studies have collected data from modern informants who are as similar as possible to the culture group being studied archaeologically. In this case historical research on the physical characteristics and domestic activities of slave villages revealed a strong similarity in form and function to modern houseyards. In order to learn more, a systematic examination of the material culture and spatial and temporal patterning of present day houseyard life was designed. The results, reported elsewhere (Pulsipher 1986; 1986a) show that houseyards are, indeed, useful analogues for interpreting archaeological data from slave villages, for they not only provide information about the signatures that West Indian traditional lifeways leave on the landscape, but also reveal the cognitive processes and behaviour that produced those signatures.

The comprehensive nature of the study and the attention given to the behaviour that produced particular patterns in the landscape make it possible to use the houseyard data for purposes beyond the original. In this case I am using the information to better understand the spatial patterning of the life cycles of traditional West Indian women. Because the sample is small, only minimal statistical analysis is attempted.

I chose to survey and map ten yards in which I had known the residents from between five and sixteen years. Most of the data were collected in 1985, when I was aided by 16 Earthwatch volunteers who were assigned in teams of two or four to a particular yard.[10] The terrain and all structures and items of material culture were mapped, as were all economic plants (i.e. those cultivated, tended or toler-

## Figure 4.1: Miss Joy's Yard

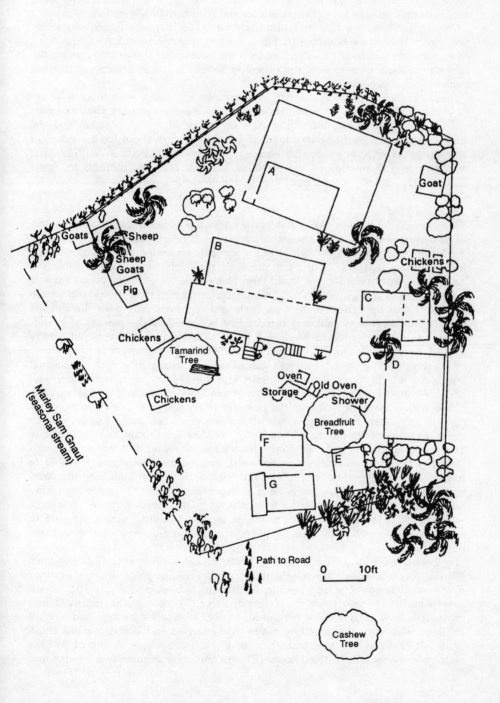

ated for their potential use). All yard residents and their kinship relationships were recorded. For at least two weeks the research teams spent several hours a day observing life in the yards, mapping all activities, noting who performed which tasks and what material culture and resources were used. Oral histories were collected from the recognized head of the yard or other willing yard residents and photographs of the residents and their activities were taken. ·

Among the questions that needed answering for archaeological purposes were: who spent time in the houseyards? How was their time occupied? And what kind of a signature did their activities leave on the landscape? It was in pursuing the answers to these questions that information about the spatial features of the life-cycles of women began to emerge.

The oral histories revealed how the yards came into being, how those who are now heads of the yards reached that position and how the present yard residents gained the right to live there. The data on household[11] composition and the mapping of houseyard activities made it possible to learn about the life-cycles of women as reflected in the spatial economy of domestic activities. The following narrative is a distillation of the pertinent material gleaned from the ten yard studies. Occasionally specific cases are cited to illustrate a point.

*Creating a Yard*
The origin of the custom of living in yards undoubtedly lies in the plantation past, as discussed above. Further research may very well reveal that specific yards and the kin-groups that occupy them actually antedate emancipation, but most yards today are not that old. Of the ten yards in this study, seven were established around the time of the Second World War. This period is significant because it was a time of rapid change: agricultural reorganization which rearranged land tenure patterns, new opportunities to earn cash and increased access to the outside world. The houseyard land was usually first occupied by the parents or grand-parents of the current yard head; and though the land usually was not legally owned, the right to occupy it was passed on to succeeding generations.

For example, 80-year-old Joy Ryner gained the right to a quarter acre of marginal land along Marley Sam Ghaut in Kinsale, Montserrat from her grandmother who had cultivated a ground in the vicinity. When Miss Joy moved an old wooden house with a thatched roof onto the property in the 1940s no one challenged her right to live there. In the mid-1940s, after years of no children, Miss Joy's sister gave her nine-month-old daughter, Molly, to Miss Joy to raise. Later, Miss Joy 'borrowed' another young boy to raise from a friend. As head of this small family Miss Joy began to add houses to her yard, renting them whenever possible to friends and relatives. She was able to finance this expansion by selling her culti-vated crops and through various other entrepreneurial activities, such as making guava jelly and guava cheese for sale, raising goats, sheep, pigs and chickens, working as a laundress for a prominent family, breaking stones for sale to construction projects and running an informal day-care centre for the neigh-bourhood babies.

By 1984 Miss Joy's yard consisted of seven houses with a total of 24 residents (Figure 4.1). She lived, together with an adult grand-nephew and yet another unrelated 'borrowed' young boy, in a concrete two-roomed house (A), which overlooked the whole yard. Her original house (B), now much improved and expanded, was occupied by her niece, Molly, who, after having had several children with several succeeding mates, had married and borne her last child. With Molly lived her husband, their seven-year-old son and one of Molly's teenage 'outside' sons. A third house (C) was rented by an unrelated woman and her four children. The fourth (D) was occupied by another of Molly's sons, his common-law wife and their three children. The fifth (E) was rented by the adult son of the mother in house three; the sixth (F) by an unrelated woman and her four children and the seventh (G) was lived in occasionally by Miss Joy's elderly brother who spent most of his time with women friends in other yards. In 1986, under a programme to rationalize landholdings, the government surveyed Miss Joy's yard and gave her title to the land.

Although Miss Joy's yard was the largest in the study, the histories of the other nine yards run roughly parallel to it with the number of people living in the other yards varying from 1 to 14. Six of the yards were also founded by women on land acquired through the female line. The remaining three were founded by men on land acquired through ancient family connections that could not be clearly recalled; but one of these three male-founded yards has been headed for the past 50 years by the daughter of the original male founder. Of the ten yards, three were headed by males in 1985. Table 4.1 is a summary of information about the ten yards showing the number of households according to the taxonomy given above, the gender and age make-up of each household, the estimated decade in which the yard was founded, the gender of the founder, and the gender and age of the present head of the houseyard.

From the information in Table 4.1 we learn that women are most often the heads of houseyards (seven out of ten) and also the most common heads of households (14 out of 23, or 65 per cent). Perhaps more significantly, household types 1 and 2, both of which are headed by women, when taken with the three single-female households, account for 73 per cent of the total population of the ten yards, whereas households headed by men accounted for just 25 per cent of residents. And so this evidence corroborates once again the matrifocal, matrilocal character of the West Indian family discussed by many writers (see Smith 1988; Clarke 1957). It should also be noted that the classic nuclear family (woman, man and their common children), so often used as a standard by North American or European analysts of modern and historical West Indian mating patterns (Frazier 1939; Fogel and Engerman 1974; Higman 1975; Gutman 1976; Jagdeo 1984; Smith 1962; Pleck 1972) was entirely lacking in the ten yards. Only five of the 23 households were occupied by cohabiting couples and they accounted for just 15 (21 per cent) of the yards' residents. All the households of more than two people were made up of the common and 'outside' children of one or both partners.[12]

*Yards as Female Space*
The observation by geographers Zelinsky, Monk and Hanson (1982: 330) that cross-culturally domestic or private space is the purview of women while public space is where men are active, and geographer Bonnie Loyd's (1975; 1976) idea that domestic interiors are female landscapes, are particularly appropriate to this analysis of West Indian houseyards, which are not only places of female activity but were also often founded and designed by women. Though the statistical analysis of the ten houseyards reveals that women played a strong role in their creation and residential composition, it was through observations of daily life in the yards that gender/space relationships and age-graded gender/role assignments were clarified.

In addition to being the heads of most yards and of most households, during the day women are overwhelmingly the primary occupiers of the yards. It is they who organize and oversee the various activities that support the social and economic reproduction of the yard, providing continuity from one generation to the next. R.T. Smith (1988: 138) makes the point that in the Caribbean, whereas women

## Table 4.1: Summary of Information on the Ten Houseyards

| Family Name of Houseyard Head | House | Mother and young children | Older mother, adult children and grandchildren* | Adult siblings, children of one or both* | Single adult, children or borrowed children | Single adult, male or female | Co-habiting couple, in-common children | Co-habiting couple, in-common & outside children** | Co-habiting couple, no common children | Males 15 and over | Males under 15 | Females 15 and over | Females under 15 | Total residents in household | Yard founded by female or male, date of founding (approx.) | Gender and age of present yard head (house A) and of household head (houses B - G) |
|---|---|---|---|---|---|---|---|---|---|---|---|---|---|---|---|---|
| Cabey | A | | X | | | | | | | | 3 | 4 | | 7 | F 1940 | F 46 |
| | B | | | | | m | | | | 1 | | | | 1 | | M 25 |
| Dyett | A | | | | | f | | | | | | 1 | | 1 | M 1930 | F 79 |
| Fenton | A | | | | | | | | X | 1 | | 1 | | 2 | F 1890 | M 82 |
| | B | | | | | f | | | | | | 1 | | 1 | | F 80 |
| Hogan | A | | | | | | | X | | 1 | | 1 | | 2 | M 1940 | M 70 |
| Jeffers | A | | | | | | | | X | 1 | | 1 | | 2 | M 1970 | M 68 |
| Roach | A | | | | | f | | | | | | 1 | | 1 | F 1950 | F 86 |
| Ryner | A | | | | X | | | | | 1 | 1 | 1 | | 3 | F 1940 | F 76 |
| | B | | | | | | | X | | 2 | 1 | 1 | | 4 | | F 46 |
| | C | X | | | | | | | | 1 | 1 | 1 | 2 | 5 | | F 32 |
| | D | | | | | | | X | | 1 | 1 | 1 | 2 | 5 | | M 30 |
| | E | | | | | m | | | | 1 | | | | 1 | | M 20 |
| | F | X | | | | | | | | | 1 | 1 | 3 | 5 | | F 25 |
| | G | | | | | m | | | | 1 | | | | 1 | | M 80 |
| Silcott | A | | X | | | | | | | 2 | | 2 | 1 | 5 | F 1940 | F 49 |
| Tuitt | A | | X | | | | | | | | 1 | 2 | | 3 | F 1940 | F 86 |
| | B | | | X | | | | | | 1 | | 1 | 2 | 4 | | F 25 |
| | C | | X | | | | | | | 1 | | 2 | 1 | 4 | | F 55 |
| | D | | | X | | | | | | 3 | | | | 3 | | M 25 |
| Taylor | A | X | | | | | | | | | 1 | 2 | 4 | 7 | F 1940 | F 32 |
| | B | | | | | m | | | | 1 | | | | 1 | | M 35 |
| | C | X | | | | | | | | | 1 | | 1 | 2 | | F 14 |
| Total Households | | 4 | 4 | 2 | 1 | 7 | 0 | 3 | 2 | | | | | | | |
| # persons/hsehld | | 19 | 19 | 7 | 3 | 7 | 0 | 11 | 4 | 19 | 11 | 24 | 16 | 70 | < - # persons/category | |

Notes: * Adult siblings sharing a house are almost always siblings through the mother when they are half siblings.
** Co-habiting couples with no common children are most often over forty and have married each other after having children with others.

interact in houseyards, there is no space where closely related men routinely, frequently and informally interact while performing life's tasks. Space for interaction among men tends to be linked with public, leisure or non-productive activities in bars and on street corners.

### Male Behaviour

An individual's first experience with gender/space customs comes from the child care system of the yards in which males and females are treated differently. This treatment shapes the child's later relationships to the yard. As male children pass the toddler stage they are encouraged to be adventurous and boisterous and to take on responsibilities that will take them out of the yard. Even a seven-year-old boy may have goats to take to pasture or other small animals to tend, or he may be asked to fetch water from the spring or neighbourhood stand-pipe, or to run errands. Young boys are often expected to walk up into the hills to tend their mother's or grandmother's mountain gardens. As eight to ten year-olds, males remain frequent occupants of the yard, interacting with their adult female relatives, helping to prepare and eat the main meal of the day, doing homework under supervision, performing yard maintenance tasks, such as sweeping and helping with the care of younger children, but increasingly boys spend hours on the periphery of the yard and then roaming in small groups further afield. As males reach their teens they become more loosely attached to the yard, roaming yet further, staying away longer, eventually reaching the stage where they live in the yard only part of the time, occasionally spending weeks or months away, often at the home of a girlfriend or male pal. Yet, it should be noted that males in their late teens and beyond still help their female relatives in the yard and, in fact, are in many cases the primary male role models for the children of their sisters and female cousins, fixing formula, changing nappies, bathing and dressing babies and playing with toddlers.

This close interaction between young men and their sisters' and female cousins' children was found on all five of the study sites that contained young adult males. Eric Greenaway, one of Miss Joy's grand-nephews is a member of the Rastafarians.[13] He keeps busy as a skilled carpenter; but in his spare time, while doing maintenance jobs around Miss Joy's yard, he constantly interacts with the children in what outsiders might term a 'fatherly' way but which should more appropriately be called an 'avuncular' way, though only some of the children actually are his nieces and nephews. He has been observed to set down his tools to comfort a sobbing child or help feed a baby. He is so focused on what the children are doing that in the midst of repairing a door he discerns when a toddler is about to fill his pants and whisks him off to the bushes so as to reinforce toilet training and save a nappy from the laundry pile. No one takes much note of this. It is the behaviour expected of a young male.

Boka is another Rastafarian who spends four days a week up in the mountains cultivating his various cash crops. On Thursdays he rides his donkey down to the yard he shares with his brother, sister, mother and baby niece. There he repairs the outbuildings, sweeps the yard and spends hours playing with his niece, bathing her and dressing her in a pretty dress for a walk around the village. The father of the child visits the yard but appears to have a much more reserved, almost ceremonial, relationship with the baby. Steadroy, a young police cadet, spends Sunday afternoons playing with his sister's children, changing the baby and fixing its formula.

While most males eventually establish themselves in a houseyard, this may not happen until quite late in life when they set up a permanent residential union with a female. Very frequently, men continue well into middle age to maintain a house or part of a house in the yard of their consanguineal female relatives. This dwelling will be considered his primary residence, though he may spend weeks away at the home of a girlfriend who, in turn, most commonly lives in the yard of her mother, grandmother or aunt. An adult male is expected to contribute money and services to any yard in which he spends time, the proportional amount being determined by his relationship to the women there, as well as the time spent, and whether or not he has fathered children in the yard.

Vonella Taylor's 35-year-old brother, Charles, maintains a house in the yard they shared with their mother until her recent death. Vonella is now the head of the yard; but Charles comes and goes several times a week and can be counted on for financial assistance during lean times, such as the summer of 1987 when the fathers of two of Vonella's children died.

### Female Behaviour

Females are more likely than males to spend most of their lives living in one yard. The changes wrought by maturation, mating, motherhood, the birth and death of kin, work, migration, eventual marriage and finally ageing, create consonant changes in their roles within the yard.

When female toddlers become ready to make contributions to yard life, they are steered in the direction of particular domestic activities. Like male children, their first helpful role will be as a child care assistant; but as they mature, laundry, house cleaning (interior), and food preparation, as well as child care, are empha-sized — skills that girls proudly demonstrate to visitors. Vonella Taylor's pre-teen daughters claim to love washing the endless piles of laundry that collect on two old iron bedsteads in their yard. In Miss Joy's yard Gracelyn, a teenage mother of three, is happily engaged nearly every morning in scrubbing clothes by the corner of her house where the water can run into her garden. Harking back to the era before water was piped into yards, she cheerily calls to visitors, 'See, I'm down by the riverside washing again.'

Except when in school, girls aged between 5 and 12 are expected to stay in their yards and are rarely allowed to roam with children of their own age, as the boys regularly do. Trips to the store are allowed but a prompt return is expected and 'liming' on street corners will bring a physical reprimand. At the age of 90, Edith Tuitt remembered that when she was a child confinement of young girls to their yards was much more strictly enforced than it is today; in fact even grown women were punished for straying. 'All we couldn't leave we parent's house and go to the street. We have to stay by we mother. Even I was a married woman with two kids, when me mother see me liming on the street she get on me and beat me and me have to stand for it.'[14]

As girls reach their teens special care is taken to guard against unsupervised contact with males of any age over puberty; but it would be wrong to assume that the goal is to prevent all sexual contact. Rather, the idea is to delay it until a suitable mate has presented himself, suitability being determined by the girl's preference and evidence that the male intends to take a long term interest in her and in any children that may result (Clarke 1957: 105; Jagdeo 1984: 60-4). There is no expectation, however, on the part of the male, the girl or her family, that the relationship will be for life; and in most cases the girl will continue to reside in the yard of her mother, with the male only visiting and eating some of his meals there.

Historical evidence indicates that it has long been common for a teenage girl to begin her biological reproductive role in the yard of her youth (Olwig 1985: 119-22). This study confirms that such is still the case with the young mother only slowly assuming an adult role in the yard. In times past she might have cultivated her own or her mother's subsistence plot and, occasionally, engaged in waged agricultural labour or domestic service, leaving her children in the care of her older female relatives. Today, young mothers are increasingly returning to school, taking training courses, or finding jobs in town, while their female kin or women in neighbouring yards care for their children.

Joycelyn Cabey had her first child at the age of 17 and, by 1987, had had another and then a set of twins. The three different fathers, one student and two seamen, make only occasional contributions to the children's support. At no time were her mother or her childless sisters, one working in a factory and one a junior teacher in the secondary school, heard to comment with anything but pride on Joycelyn's reproductive success. The children were cared for in shifts by Joycelyn, her mother and sisters, all of whom held jobs in town, but spent most of their spare time in the yard. The two sisters each built additions onto the family home in part to accommodate Joycelyn's children and in part to allow themselves space for privacy. For the time being Joycelyn is content to work as a waitress; but she is a stylish woman with plans to emigrate soon, long before her four toddlers are grown. An uncle plans to take one child, the other three will stay in her mother's houseyard looked after, as they have always been, by her female kin.

Anisa Taylor's situation is also illustrative. She was 14 in 1985, living in her Aunt Vonella's houseyard with a newborn baby whose 17-year-old father visited often. By 1987 Anisa was back at school, the baby in the daily care of her aunt and the father working in Antigua.

As a woman matures, she may migrate and leave the system entirely for many years, sending home remittances to support her kin; or she may begin to assume more autonomy and responsibility within the yard and by middle age have taken on major responsibilities as a financial contributor to the yard and as an organizer and supervisor of the many domestic activities. Often the middle-aged woman will move into the house of the yard head, physically taking over the central space. Yet she will usually continue to defer to the wishes of the more senior woman in the yard — an aunt, mother or grandmother. Meanwhile the older woman will continue to prize her autonomy, taking care of her own business, looking after her own needs.

As Miss Joy Ryner ages, her niece Molly, who moved into Miss Joy's original house when she married, has taken over much of the yard management, unobtrusively supervising the day's activities from one of the two front stoops. Daily Miss Joy continues to make her rounds, checking the condition of the animals and the laundry and being sure the children have done their chores. Encouraged to maintain her physical strength and autonomy for as long as possible, at 83 she continues to cultivate her ground, to tend plants around the yard, to cook for herself, to organize the children in cash-producing activities (such as breaking stones or making guava jelly) and to manage the cash earned. When in need of rest she occupies her accustomed place on the front stoop chipping coconut for fowl food or holding one of the many babies being cared for in the yard. Miss Joy's authority is still very evident, a position she maintains with a quiet presence, while Molly ensures that everything goes smoothly.

Edith Tuitt rules her yard with a colourful personality, a quixotic temper and commanding physical authority; and between her two middle-aged daughters, who share her fiery personality, the line of succession to yard headship is under contention. When she neared 90, her eldest daughter, Margaret, moved into Edith's tiny house. Even though Margaret had recently married an old friend, in the event of Edith's death, she wanted to secure her position over her sister

Alberta as successor to yard headship. Now Edith and Margaret often occupy the front stoop of Edith's house, surveying the entire yard and keeping track of all that goes on, especially the comings and goings of Alberta. Like Miss Joy, Edith Tuitt remains productive and in charge — continuing to tend her animals, cultivate her ground, and cook a pepperpot which she shares with her great-grandsons or whoever is hungry and currently in favour. She verbally lashes misbehaving children, prepares cassava meal and bakes wheat bread on Sundays. All the while Margaret and other family members assist, deferring to her judgement.

When there is no middle-aged woman to take over in a yard, the problem often preoccupies the ageing yard head. Nora Dyett and Mary Roach each live alone in their yards. Though both raised 'borrowed' children when they could not have their own, these children have emigrated to England. The women lament that there is no family to share their days; but worse, there is no-one to whom to hand over the yard. Mrs Roach is thinking of marrying again, though she is 90, just so that she can pass the yard on to the much younger gentleman who has helped her in small ways for some time. Mistress Dyett at 83 is trying to talk her 'borrowed' daughter into returning to Montserrat from London. Mr Jeffers now 72, who married for the first time about ten years ago and whose children by previous mates have all migrated to England, solved the problem of a lonely old-age in a yard bereft of extended family by giving his son in London a portion of the yard and contracting with a local builder to build his son a modern concrete retirement home with a big front porch overlooking his own house and yard and the Caribbean Sea in the distance. He hopes this will entice his son and family to return.

## Analysis & Conclusions

Geographer Jon Goss (1988) sees the built environment as the physical expression of a way of life, reflecting its culture and providing the physical milieu for the reproduction of social meaning and ideology. Though other geographers share this view (for example, Tuan 1974), it appears as a strong theme in many of the more recent works of architectural theorists (Bertelot and Gaume 1982; Hillier and Hanson 1984) and is also fundamental to archaeological interpretation (Hodder 1978). What then is the cultural meaning of the West Indian houseyard? What does the use of houseyard space over the course of lifetimes tell us about West Indian ideas of proper gender roles, of the meaning of family and of family daily life? If the slave-yard and even the African compound are its historical precursors, what has been the carry-over of meaning into the new world? And how is the houseyard reflecting and responding to the modernization that is swamping other aspects of West Indian culture, including much of the built environment?

First the historical question: moving from the present to the past, it seems likely that the houseyard way of life has its roots in slave domestic space. Preliminary analysis of the archaeological research for which this study was originally conducted strongly indicates that the houseyard organization of space also existed in slave villages. The houses were of similar size and construction, the artifact distributions indicate strong continuity in the content and spatial organization of domestic space. And archaeological evidence from the surrounding landscape indicates continuity in modes of resource exploitation. Whether or not the similarities in spatial organization of buildings and material culture also indicate similarities in cultural meaning is more difficult to discern. For example, we have not as yet found a way of testing archaeologically for the existence of matrifocality and

matrilocality, or for the roles of adult males in slave village life; but despite the
continuing debate over the meaning behind slave domestic relationships,[15] there
is no strong reason to suspect very different past perceptions of either family and
family life or of how resources should be used (Edwards 1793; Stewart 1823;
Wentworth 1834; Young 1801).

The possibility that slave domestic life was, in turn, organized along African
models is also strong, though much more research is needed to draw the lines of
connection carefully. A brief perusal of the literature turns up numerous similarities, all of which deserve further examination. The houseyards set up in Jamaica
by female slaves straight from Africa confirm not only the domestic model, but
matrilocality. The ramifications for gender/space organization of matrilineal
descent rules are suggested in V.W. Turner's study of village life in the Belgian
Congo. He explains that due to maternal descent rules there, the role of men as
brothers of women and uncles of their children is more enduring and more crucial
to attaining power and status in the village than their roles as husbands and
fathers. And, in fact, a headman's children are naturally rivalrous with his nieces
and nephews, whom he may regard as closer kin than his own children (Turner
1957). While no connection can as yet be shown between these customs and those
of the Caribbean, it is important to keep such possible explanations in mind when
noting the domestic spatial behaviour of males and females in the Caribbean,
especially the child care roles of brothers and uncles as noted above.

This study of the gender-specific use of houseyard space and the more sociological works of writers such as Edith Clarke and R.T. Smith together suggest a
number of ideas about how West Indians view family or domestic relationships.
First of all the nuclear family is not very important at all; rather, the term family
means kin connected to you through the female line. Long-term relationships are
reserved for maternal consanguineal kin; and males, rather than being disfunc-
tional in the family or marginalized, as some (Smith 1962; Greenfield 1966; Patterson 1967) have suggested, play out their roles most often in their mother/son and
sister/brother and uncle relationships. That is, as participants in family life they
are less important as fathers than they are as sons, brothers and uncles.

Perhaps the most interesting stages in the female life cycle in houseyards at the
present juncture in history are represented by the teenage mother and the elderly
yard head. Today, in recognition of economic changes that make it desirable for a
woman to be able to earn a regular cash income, at least some post-primary or
even post-secondary education and a job outside the yard are considered appropriate. Interestingly, the demands of modernization, which in many situations
around the world present a conflict between the woman's social and biological
reproductive roles in the domestic sphere and the need for her to be productive in
the cash economy, have not necessarily been met by very distinctive changes in
Montserrat yard organization or in mating patterns. As in the case of Joycelyn
Cabey and Anisa Taylor, the information from this houseyard study as well as
more comprehensive statistical data indicate that many young women are still
having their first children as young teenagers with young men who are also
thinking about further education, training for a skilled position, or migration, as
future options. It is the houseyard institution, which so successfully meets their
needs and those of their children, that allows these young women to see
themselves without much conflict as both mothers and students or workers and,
in the future, as possible short or long-term migrants, absentee mothers and career
women. Marriage, though occasionally discussed as an option, does not rank high
as an early goal. Marriage is more likely to come, as it did for Molly in Miss Joy's
yard and Margaret and Alberta in Mrs Tuitt's, and for Mmes Hogan, Jeffers and

Fenton, long after their children have grown up. My observations lead me to conclude that in houseyards the children of teenage mothers are considered more as progeny of the kin-group than of the biological mother, an assessment confirmed, if only obliquely, by Jagdeo (1984: 76ff.) and Clarke (1957: 100). The widespread pattern of behaviour as well as interviews with the consanguineal kin of young mothers indicate that there is acceptance of the idea that having babies is the explicit social reproductive role of a young girl. Other yard residents support this by taking over most of her mothering duties, leaving her free to pursue an education, training, migration or local employment. Indeed, the life stories of many successful West Indian professional women reveal that they had their first children while young girls living in their mother's houseyard.

Finally, it must be noted that within the overarching umbrella of communal support within yards, everyday practice is to instil in all yard residents the value of personal autonomy including a measure of economic independence; and this value persists in treatment of the elderly. What is noteworthy is that the times at which residents are encouraged to enjoy autonomy varies by gender and age. For males it comes early with first goat-tending, then errands and then the freedom to roam at will as young adults so long as chores and yard obligations are taken care of. For teenage girls it comes with the freedom to take a lover, have a child and yet not be tied down to the drudgery of endless child care. For adult women it comes in the form of the opportunity to take a job or emigrate with the knowledge that children and parents will be attended to by kinsfolk. Or for those who stay in the yard maturity brings increasing authority that does not diminish with old age. In fact, the houseyard provides a hospitable milieu for productivity well into advanced age, as exemplified by the numerous cash-producing activities engaged in by the elderly yard heads, and ensures that the autonomy and authority that go along with productivity are fully enjoyed. Though modernization is introducing some adjustments, the ability of the houseyard system to meet the needs of women over a lifetime persists.

## Notes

1   The term houseyard is used here for the sake of clarity, but in common parlance the term is more often shortened to 'yard', as in 'that woman lives in my yard', meaning she lives in a different house but in a cluster of houses in a defined space in which the speaker lives. In the chronicle of her life as a slave in the Eastern Caribbean, Mary Prince refers to 'yards' in such a way as to give the impression that they constituted a residential spatial pattern similar to the one I discuss here.
2   Several studies have focused on urban houseyards in Jamaica. In addition to Brodber (1975), see especially Diane J. Austin (1984).
3   Houses built of concrete blocks on a concrete slab are increasingly popular in the Eastern Caribbean, ostensibly because they offer better protection against hurricanes, rain and insect damage. Such houses are called 'wall houses' and have become a status symbol. For some time these houses were built in the same dimensions as the traditional wood houses and were arranged like them, several to a yard. Many of the yards in this study contain a mixture of wood and concrete houses. Increasingly, new houses are being built according to a standardized western model, containing a living-room, several bedrooms and an interior kitchen and bathroom. This aspect of modernization and the ways in which such an architectural model modifies yard life are not discussed in this chapter.
4   Green breadfruit leaves are slowly burned in an open tobacco can to chase away mosquitoes. A member of the *compositae* family, the 'pot-scrubber bush' or 'cattle-tongue' has a profusion of scratchy-surfaced leaves that are quite effective in cleaning dirty dishes and pots. A patch of the plant will often be found close to where people in a yard commonly wash dishes.
5   West Indians tend to figure kinship through the female line and live in matrilocal patterns, hence half-siblings through the maternal line (uterine) tend to live together and be much closer than half-siblings through the male line.
6   The custom of 'borrowing' children is old in the Caribbean. Several writers in the eighteenth and nineteenth centuries mention that slaves frequently raised children they had not borne, sometimes to take care of the needs of an orphan, but more often the mother would freely give up her child to a childless sister or close friend so that the adoptive parent could have the companionship and loyalty of a child as it grew to adulthood. This custom is still very common today.
7   Outside children are those born either before marriage or present liaison, or those parented by a mate other than one's spouse or present mate. Women rarely bear outside children while married or even

while cohabiting with a man; but men commonly father outside children while married. Edith Tuitt reports that her husband, whom she married at age 15, at one time had three women pregnant at the same time that she was expecting his child. For a discussion of the more subtle connotations of the concept of outside and inside, see R.T. Smith (1988: 117ff).

8 Elderly married couples living without children usually have had children with other mates before they married.

9 This study was done to complement part of the interdisciplinary study of Galways plantation on the island of Montserrat. A delay in completing archaeological excavations in the Galways slave village has delayed the publishing of a complete report on the use of this study in the interpretation of that site.

10 The Center for Field Research, Watertown, MA funded the houseyard study in 1985. Included with the grant were the services of 16 volunteers recruited by Earthwatch (a sister organization to the Center for Field Research) who did much of the field research under my supervision.

11 There is much discussion about the use of the term household to describe West Indian traditional residential patterns. First the matter was clouded by the preoccupation of researchers with charting the nuclear family and their refusal to recognize that nuclear families were not a useful norm in this situation. Once this was recognized they became preoccupied with showing economic units, but households (and certainly houseyards) are often not discrete economic units. Since households clearly exist and the problem is primarily one of definition for first world researchers, I try to think of households as sub-units of family and houseyard life only, with, as yet, no firm notions of the economic roles they may play.

12 In household D in Miss Joy's yard, the outside children visited but did not continuously live in the house. In the Hogan house, Mrs Hogan's outside daughter, born prior to her marriage, and her daughter with Mr Hogan, were raised together; but by 1985 they had long since grown and migrated.

13 The Rastafarian movement, which started in Jamaica, has spread to the Eastern Caribbean and been reinterpreted to suit the circumstances of the various islands. On Montserrat many lower-class males have been attracted to the loosely defined philosophy of self sufficiency (usually based on subsistence agriculture), environmental consciousness, down-playing of materialism, musical creativity, and ganja (marijuana) smoking. Though held in low esteem by the middle class, many 'Rastas' appear to be particularly hard working and conscientious citizens.

14 Taped interview with Edith Tuitt, summer 1986.

15 For a brief discussion of the discontinuity between historians' and anthropologists' interpretations of the Afro-Caribbean family, see Karen Fog Olwig (1985: 190-2).

# References

Austin, Diane J. (1984) *Urban Life in Kingston, Jamaica: The Culture and Class Ideology of Two Neighbourhoods*. New York: Gordon & Breach

Bertelot, Jacque and Martine Gaume (1982) *Kaz Antiye*. Pointe-à-Pitre: Éditions Perspectives Créoles

Brodber, Erna (1975) *A Study of Yards in the City of Kingston*. Mona, Jamaica: Institute of Social and Economic Research, Working Papers, No 9

Clarke, Edith (1957) *My Mother who Fathered Me: A Study of the Family in Three Selected Communities in Jamaica*. London: George Allen & Unwin Ltd

Craton, Michael (1978) *Searching for the Invisible Man: Slaves and Plantation Life in Jamaica*. Cambridge: Harvard University Press

Edwards, Bryan (1793) *The History, Civil and Commercial, of the British West Indies*. 2 vols. London: John Stockdale

Fogel, Robert W. and Stanley L. Engerman (1974) *Time on the Cross*. Boston/Toronto: Little Brown & Company

Frazier, E. Franklin (1939) *The Negro Family in the United States*. Chicago: University of Chicago Press

Goss, Jon (1988) 'The Built Environment and Social Theory: Towards an Architectural Geography'. *Professional Geographer*, (40) 392-403

Greenfield, Sidney M. (1966) *English Rustics in Black Skins*. New Haven: College & University Publishers

Gutman, Herbert G. (1976) *The Black Family in Slavery and Freedom, 1750-1925*. New York: Pantheon Books

Handler, Jerome S and Frederick W. Lange (1978) *Plantation Slavery in Barbados: An Archaeological and Historical Investigation*. Cambridge: Harvard University Press

Higman, Barry (1974) 'A Report on the Excavations at Montpelier and Roehampton'. *Jamaica Journal*, (8)

——— (1975) 'The Slave Family and Household in the British West Indies, 1800-1834.' *Journal of Interdisciplinary History*, (6) 261-87

Hillier, H. and J. Hanson (1984) *The Social Logic of Space*. Cambridge: Cambridge University Press

Hodder, Ian (ed.) (1978) *The Spatial Organization of Culture*. London: Gerald Duckworth & Company Ltd

Howson, Jean M. (1987) 'Report of the Summer 1987 Archaeological Research at Galways Village'. Unpublished

Jagdeo, Tirbani P. (1984) *Teenage Pregnancy in the Caribbean*. New York: International Planned Parenthood Federation

Kimber, Clarissa (1966) 'Dooryard Gardens of Martinique'. *Yearbook of Pacific Geographers*, (28) 97-118

——— (1973) 'Spatial Patterning in the Dooryard Gardens of Puerto Rico'. *The Geographical Review*, (63) 6-26

Loyd, Bonnie (1975) 'The Home as a Social Environment and Women's Landscape'. Annual meeting of Association of American Geographers, Milwaukee. Cited in Zelinsky et al., *q.v.*

——— (1976) 'Women's Place: The Landscape of Interiors'. In Pat Burnett, *Women in Society* (mimeo). Cited in Zelinsky et al., *q.v.*

Mintz, Sidney W. (1974) *Caribbean Transformations*. Chicago: Aldine Publishing Company

Olwig, Karen Fog (1985) *Cultural Adaptation and Resistance on St John: Three Centuries of Afro-Caribbean Life*. Gainesville: University of Florida Press

Patterson, Orlando (1967) *The Sociology of Slavery*. London: MacGibbon & Kee and Rutherford: Fairleigh Dickenson University Press

Pleck, Elizabeth H. (1972) 'The Two-parent Household: Black Family Structure in Late Nineteenth-Century Boston.' *Journal of Social History*, (6) 3-31

Pulsipher, Lydia (1986) 'Ethnoarchaeology for the Study of Caribbean Slave Villages'. Symposium and Workshop on Ethnohistory and Historical Archaeology, Johns Hopkins University

——— (1986a) *Models to Guide the Archaeology of West Indian Slave Villages*. Charleston: American Society for Ethnohistory

Rapaport, Amos (1969) *House Form and Culture*. Englewood Cliffs: Prentice-Hall Inc.

Smith, M.G. (1962) *West Indian Family Structure*. Seattle: University of Washington Press

Smith, R.T. (1988) *Kinship and Class in the West Indies*. Cambridge: Cambridge University Press

Stewart, John M. (1823) *A View of the Past and Present State of the Island of Jamaica*. Edinburgh: Oliver & Boyd

Tuan, Yi-Fu (1974) *Topophilia: A Study of Environmental Perception, Attitudes and Values*. Englewood Cliffs: Prentice-Hall

Turner, V.W. (1957) *Schism and Continuity in an African Society: A Study of Ndembu Village Life*. Manchester: Manchester University Press

Wentworth, Trelawny (1834) *West India Sketch Book*. 2 vols. London: Whittaker & Company

Young, William (1801) *A Tour through the Several Islands of Barbados, St Vincent, Antigua and Grenada*. London

Zelinsky, Wilbur, Janice Monk and Susan Hanson (1982) 'Women and Geography: A Review and Prospectus'. *Progress in Human Geography*, (6), 317-66

# V  Women's Place is Every Place: Merging Domains & Women's Roles in Barbuda & Dominica

RIVA BERLEANT-SCHILLER & WILLIAM M. MAURER

In the United States some women wear a button that reads 'Women's place is every place'. This slogan is meant to counter the belief that women's place is in the home. Yet both clichés express the western assumption that social life is divided into two spheres, the public, usually dominated by men, and the domestic, usually dominated by women. This division is not just an ethnocentric assumption; it is also a construct that until recently has succeeded in illuminating gender cross-culturally.

In her introduction to *Woman, Culture and Society* (1974) Michelle Rosaldo argued that gender inequality begins with the conceptual and psychological linking of women with birth and child-rearing. This association 'leads to a differentiation of domestic and public spheres of activity' and underlies those aspects of social organization and human psychology that relate specifically to gender (Rosaldo 1974: 23). Sex roles and the relationships between men and women can be analysed in terms of two spheres of activity, the public and the domestic. Public activities 'link, rank, organize or subsume particular mother-child groups', whereas domestic activities 'are organized immediately around one or more mothers and their children' (Rosaldo 1974: 23). Sherry Ortner (1974) widened the dichotomy, proposing that male things become associated with extra-domestic 'culture' and female things with domestic 'nature'. She later developed this distinction into a concept of prestige structures from which gender ideologies are extrapolated (Ortner and Whitehead 1981).

In the Caribbean, the public/domestic distinction holds up best when we think about men's role (for example, Anderson 1986; Berleant-Schiller 1977; Moses 1976). The more we think about public and domestic spheres in relation to women's activities, the less distinct the two domains become (Barrow 1986; Durant-Gonzalez 1977; Gussler 1980; Sutton and Makiesky-Barrow 1977).

In this chapter we explore the ways in which the public and domestic domains merge in women's roles in two islands of the Lesser Antilles, Dominica and Barbuda. We are concerned not only with differences and similarities between the two islands, but equally important, with a critical evaluation of the public/domestic dichotomy. We examine women's roles in the intra-island economy and informal social organization and analyse these roles in relation to recent generalizations in anthropology about gender domains. We show how women's roles become integral to a range of social and economic processes that are not confined within the household. We are not concerned with the status of women or the evaluation of their roles, either by folk or observers' criteria. We argue that the study of gender in the Caribbean can contribute to a comparative regional understanding of social networks, economic exchange and informal social control. Our work is based on field research, which we carried out separately,

Maurer in Dominica in 1987 and Berleant-Schiller in Barbuda at various times from 1971 to 1987.

## Gender Research in the Caribbean

Many scholars have applied the public/domestic dichotomy to the study of women's roles in the Caribbean. Patricia Anderson, for example, analysed four fundamental features of gender in the Caribbean, all of which relate to the household. Women, she states, support their own households with household and extra-household work and achieve influence through their domestic and maternal roles. Status, on the other hand, they achieve through affiliation to men. They defer to men's decisions in the public realm, and exercise power only within the household (Anderson 1986: 291-324).

Although Anderson's analysis is typical, it is not universal. Judith Gussler, for example, does not question the dichotomy, but she demonstrates the flexibility of the domestic sphere as it relates to social and economic realities on St Kitts. Where resources are scarce cooperation becomes essential 'and the social system itself depend[s] on the ability of the female to be mobile, flexible and resourceful, rather than tied to a specific structure or role' (Gussler 1980: 208).

Christine Barrow, going further, argues that the conventional assignment of public roles to men and domestic roles to women is a stereotype that does not fit the Caribbean, 'where women are perhaps outstanding in their continuous contribution to economic and community life' (Barrow 1986: 131-76). The work of Constance Sutton and Susan Makiesky-Barrow also challenges the separation of domains. Barbadian women, they show, are neither confined to domestic units that are linked to the outside through men, nor are they 'submerged within kin groups' (Sutton and Makiesky-Barrow 1977: 313). Rather, the overlapping of domestic and community spheres renders such a dichotomy useless for understanding sex roles and gender ideologies.

The Caribbean evidence clearly necessitates a rethinking of the original dichotomy. We show that the personal and familial relationships and activities that are located within the walls of the household do not necessarily imply and do not fully constitute a social role. Women's work includes tasks that maintain the household, but the social importance of these tasks defines a social role that extends well beyond the domestic and into the public, and in fact blurs the distinction between the two.

Women's household work fosters a set of social roles and activities that link the private and public: networking, marketing and religious activities are a few general types. Distinguishing between work and roles allows us to see the public nature and public importance of women's social roles founded on, but not bounded by, house-based work. This work immediately influences the public sphere. The significance of women's work in the Caribbean is different from that described elsewhere. In Andalusia, for example, 'Women can regularly leave the home for shopping ... [but] their domestic role is reinforced: marketing is necessary for the upkeep of the household' (Brandes 1981: 217). In Dominica and Barbuda, the work of women keeps up the household, but their roles become public when this work also contributes to economic and community life. Indeed, many women's tasks are carried on in public, which is no less public because the milieu is female. We must avoid the circular thinking that defines activities carried on in public as private because the activities themselves maintain the household and only women are present.

## Barbuda & Dominica

Barbuda and Dominica are two very different islands of the Lesser Antilles. Together they form a microcosm of the range of Caribbean physical environments and their disparate physical features are associated with differences in economy, history and land use. Neither is at all typical, though such a statement begs the question of whether any Lesser Antillean island can be called typical. Indeed one of the great challenges in Caribbean research is reconciling the unmistakable pan-Caribbean commonalities. These two islands, therefore, can be used as a laboratory from which to derive hypotheses for regional research.

Barbuda, one of the outer Leewards, is a dry, flat, limestone island of about 160 square kilometres. Its high point is only about 40 metres above sea level. There are no streams on the island; Barbudans depend on dug wells, modified sinkholes and rain cisterns for their water. No hills break the continuous sweep of the northeast Trades. The effects of desiccating winds on vegetation have been intensified by human land uses of the last three centuries. Since the first settlement in the seventeenth century grazing livestock, woodcutters, shifting cultivators and charcoal burners have altered the landscape and changed the once-dominant evergreen scrub forest into a variety of drought resistant plant communities that range from a scattered, goat-bitten thorn scrub through cactus and zerophytic scrub forest to remnants of the old vegetation in areas protected from grazing (Harris 1965).

Recurrent drought thwarted the development of plantations in Barbuda and, from its earliest English settlement, the island was given over to the raising of livestock and provisions. Attempts at commercial plantation crops repeatedly failed (Berleant-Schiller 1978). On the fringes of the colonial plantation economy, Barbuda was also outside the ordinary mode of English colonial government in the Caribbean. For 200 years, until 1870, the Codrington family held the island as its private fief on lease from the British crown. Barbuda eventually became a dependency of the colony of Antigua and Barbuda.

In this history and setting an unusual community developed. After emancipation the freed people of Barbuda became a community of subsistence and small cash producers, all living in a single village, Codrington, and holding in common all the unparcelled lands outside the village walls. Barbudans still hold the vast flat bushlands in common, although house sites are now deeded and have begun to nibble into commonlands. The island is beginning to yield to tourism and to pressures on the land from the Antiguan central government and foreign development interests (Berleant-Schiller 1987). Nevertheless, many of the 1400 inhabitants still carry on their old productive pursuits — fishing, lobster-diving, shifting cultivation, making charcoal and keeping cattle, goats and sheep on open range. Since emancipation, emigration and remittances have been necessary adaptations to the island's meagre resource base.

Dominica, located midway between the French islands of Guadeloupe and Martinique, is of volcanic origin. Steep valleys separate the high peaks, some as high as 1380 metres. The island occupies about 790 square kilometres, much of which supports a dense tropical forest crossed by hundreds of streams. Abundant rainfall (200 centimetres a year) coupled with difficult terrain hindered the development of large-scale plantation agriculture on the island, though there has been more commercial agriculture on Dominica than on Barbuda. Now the banana industry dominates the economy. Many Dominicans also engage in some form of food production for the household and for local sale in markets in the two largest towns, Roseau and Portsmouth. Roseau, the capital, has about 20,000 residents; Portsmouth about 8000. Small villages are scattered along the coast.

French settlers entered Dominica at the end of the seventeenth century, but it was ceded to Britain in 1763. In 1979 Dominica became an independent state in the Commonwealth Caribbean. There are some 83,000 largely Afro-Caribbean English and French patois-speaking inhabitants and about 700 Caribs who remain in a small reserve on the windward coast.

Dominica and Barbuda are prototypical 'high' and 'low' islands, with all the differences in moisture, plant communities and human ecology that this basic distinction implies (Burrows 1956). Nevertheless, both are characteristically Caribbean products of the large-scale physical, cultural and economic processes that shaped the region. Both islands have meagre resources and a narrow economic base with the consequent poverty relieved more by the possibilities of emigration and of subsistence production than by the tourism to which so many Caribbean national hopes are attached.


## Merging Domains in Dominica

An understanding of the ways in which Dominica's rugged terrain and inhos- pitable coastline have hindered development and communication is crucial to an understanding of Dominican gender roles. Travel is so difficult that, as one infor- mant put it, 'transportation *is* communication'. Going to Roseau to sell vegetables, for example, means taking every village shopping list, every message to a friend and every bit of business that needs the facilities of the capital. Informants tell of the days before transinsular roads, when women gathered up children, vegetables, bags and business and set out on the Chemin Letang, a rough footpath through the interior to get to market on Saturday morning.[1] Many people walk this path even now. The village of Grand Bay, in the south of the island, has long had closer economic, political and familial ties to Martinique, which was easier to reach by boat than was Roseau by foot. It is still a community set apart (Caribbean Agro- Economic Society 1977).

Nevertheless, Dominican society remains closely-knit and this integration is achieved through women's work and women's roles. Social networks have an important communication function, facilitated by women. Dominicans say, as do people everywhere in the Caribbean, 'This island one big family you know!' This conceptualization of community as family alerts us immediately to the problems of applying a domestic/public opposition in the region. During six months of fieldwork in Dominica I rarely met anyone anywhere whom I could not trace to my landlady's family and the families tied to hers. These families are spread over the whole island and often include people not linked by birth.

Two case accounts will illustrate the role of women and men in two linked networks. They will show how familial communication becomes public communi- cation and how domains begin to merge as women go about their tasks.[2]


## Case 1: Frances Louis

Frances Louis is a retired woman of 63 (IV 7 in Figure 5.1).[3] She is comparatively well-off and is known island-wide as a no-nonsense woman who respects others and commands respect, partly as a consequence of her long public career as a

teacher, nurse, administrator, secretary, political activist and member of the Red
Cross and several agricultural, marketing and credit organizations. Her involve-
ment in social and political organizations is not atypical of women in Dominica.
At the time of writing, four women, all friends of Frances, occupied the four
highest political positions in Dominica (Prime Minister, Speaker of the House of
Assembly, Magistrate and Mayor of the Capital).

**Figure 5.1: Frances Louis's Family Network**

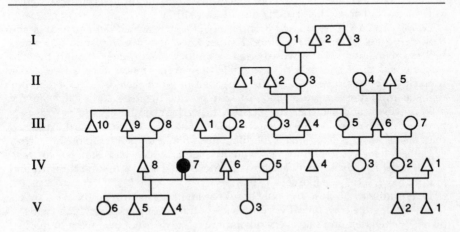

At present Frances lives alone. Her three children (V 4, V 5, and V 6 in Figure 5.1)
are abroad. Savings, pensions, boarders, occasional part-time government projects
and her own cottage industry, producing and selling cocoa, jellies, juices and
chickens, all make up her income. She has never been married and although her
children all bear the surname of their father, she speaks nothing of this man except
his name: Robert Robinson (IV 8). He belonged to a prominent Dominican family,
which was founded by two brothers who first came to Dominica from the UK (III
9 and III 10). One settled in the northeast and one in Roseau. 'You see how many
Robinsons there are in Dominica?' an informant said. 'Well, then you know them
boys they wasn't just with one woman! They came and populated the island.'

After Robinson left, Frances 'shacked up' for a year or two with a man named
Munro (IV 6). When Munro later had a daughter, Adele (V 3), by another woman,
Frances considered her a step-daughter and maintained a close relationship with
her. The Munros are also an enormous family, mainly owing to another relative of

Frances's, David Munro (not in Figure 5.1), a legendary figure in Dominica. He and Frances feel warm toward each other but rarely meet. By his own account and that of many others, David Munro is father of innumerable children around the island. Thus Frances is linked, through the Robinsons and Munros, to two huge families which are themselves linked to other families.

In spite of these connections, Frances holds greater affective ties to her kin reckoned through the women in her network. These ties are channels for the exchange of moral and economic support, as the following story illustrates. Bernard and Harold (V 1, V 2), both in their twenties, are the sons of the daughter of Frances's father and his second wife (III 6 and III 7).

Several years ago Bernard and Frances met at a store where Bernard works and took an instant liking to each other. Neither knew they were related, as Frances had never maintained ties with Bernard's mother, Alexis, even though the two women had the same father. Meanwhile, however, Frances took a dress to a friend's shop to be mended. Alexis happened to work there and 'remembering' that she and Frances were related, asked to borrow the dress for a fête.[4] She fell sick, however, and sent her son Bernard instead. When he arrived at Frances's house with the dress, each was amazed to see the other. When Bernard explained that his mother, Alexis, had sent him, they realized their relationship. They explained their compatibility as common 'blood', which had 'spoken' to them through the friendship they had formed. Alexis died soon after and Bernard and Harold have since been like sons to Frances.

These examples disclose the extent and nature of kin networks; the next shows how they operate economically. Frances keeps a flock of chickens, which yields 24 birds for slaughter and sale every other month. She does not take them to market, but sells them mainly to relatives reckoned through her mother and mother's sisters, III 2 and III 3 in Figure 5.1. Three of her customers, for example, are related distantly through a mother's sister who married a Syrian immigrant (III 3). By this connection Frances is linked to the five large and influential Syrian and Lebanese commercial families in Dominica (see Myers 1981: 103). This link connects Frances into the families of the majority of the inhabitants of the Roseau area. Through these families Frances can buy any non-food item she could want.

Frances's female relatives link her to families all over the island. Frances's mother's other sister (III 2) married a man from a small village in the north. Although Frances has not much kept up her ties in the north, she is friendly with those members of the Jones family who live in Roseau. Frances's mother's mother (II 3), the daughter of a French immigrant who founded another large family in the south of the island, is her link to the south. Through her mother (III 5), also the daughter of a Frenchman, Frances has ties on the east coast. In Roseau, some distant relations of her mother's run a small shop where Frances can obtain her food without depending on the unreliable Saturday market.

Thus Frances is connected to all the major families of Dominica. With extension and a little effort she can find a blood connection to anyone she chooses. The following case study (a family that is itself a small branch of Frances's network) demonstrates how these connections are activated in practice.

## Case 2: The Joneses

Albert Jones (age 35) and Cynthia Jones (age 34) live in Roseau (V 8 and V 9 in Figure 5.2). Cynthia's family, the Stephens, came from a small village in the north, but most of them have moved to Portsmouth. Her mother (IV 12) heads a household there, which includes the wife of one of Cynthia's brothers and her four children (V 11 and V 13-6) and Cynthia's two daughters (VI 1 and VI 2). Cynthia's brother (V 10) is in the United States.

**Figure 5.2: The Jones's Family Network**

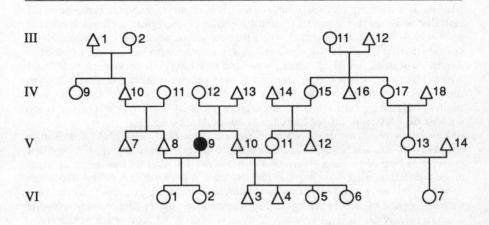

Several years ago a distant relative of Cynthia's brother's wife died, leaving a granddaughter, June (VI 7), with no one to care for her. Cynthia's mother's house was full, so Cynthia agreed to take in June. Note that Cynthia's kinship tie to June is entirely through women except for the initial brother-sister link, which is of course a tie through the mother.

When I asked Cynthia what would happen if one of Albert's relatives were in a similar situation, she replied that the child would be the responsibility of Albert's 'people'. It is standard practice in Dominica for the kin of women of a single household to share that household in times of need, even if the husband objects. This objection, however, is only a symbolic claim of male authority in the household.

These cases demonstrate the scope and effectiveness of women's networks in providing support. Now we will see how women use these networks to surmount the island's enormous barriers to communication. Indeed, these networks are integral parts of a Dominican communication system, which telephone and radio contacts complement rather than supplant and in which women's participation is critical. Men can and do spread news around the island, but most Dominicans agree that men get their news from women in the first place. In this section I show first how news spreads and second how the communication functions of women's tasks and networks become an integral part of the politico-jural domain. I discuss food gardening, marketing, washing and hair-plaiting.

Of all women's activities in Dominica, there are only two that can be considered non-economic, although they are allied to economic activities. These are hair-plaiting and washing clothes (which in the Dominican countryside is a household task that is not done for pay). Dominican women spend hours each week plaiting each other's hair in complicated styles that are a source of pride to them. News spreads during these plaiting sessions, as any woman who has just returned from Roseau will bring word of deaths, wars and anything else newsworthy. While I was in Dominica, Fiji, a fellow member of the Commonwealth, underwent a coup d'état. We first heard of this from a woman who got the news from her hair plaiter, who had heard it on the local radio news at one o'clock. The US news stations on television did not carry the story until that evening.

More important is washing, where news and debates of immediate significance to daily life are exchanged. The majority of Dominican women still do their laundry at one of the 365 rivers and streams on the island. Here news spreads among different communities who use the same stretch of water. The issues are serious, such as coming elections, government corruption, grassroots unrest and the emergence of a new and possibly threatening cult in the country. As one woman said while doing her wash, 'Any news you need, you get it at the river. The ones close to two rivers spread the news that way. All news, personal, family, marriage, religion, even politics, it starts at the river'.

Still more important and more complex than these, however, are women's food-producing and marketing activities. As in many parts of the third world, the growing of vegetables and root crops is the work of women, whereas the produc-tion of export crops, in this case bananas and some citrus, is the work of men. Dominican women share in the work of export agriculture, but also maintain their own small food gardens and raise small stock. Cooperative labour exchange is a feature of both kinds of agriculture, although it is declining among men.

Koudmen or journée, as cooperative labour exchange is called, mainly occurs among men during house construction and land clearing.[5] Informants say that it is declining in men's agricultural work as a consequence of land fragmentation and increasing competition. Yet, whether working their own food plots or the export plots of their male connections, women continue to participate in and enlist cooperative groups for weeding and harvesting. Although women's food produc-tion is essential and is carried on without male help, it is not perceived as distinct from men's agriculture. It is regarded by women and men alike as 'helping' and is devalued. Nevertheless, even as a household activity of women it engages the network and furthers, through koudmen, social integration and news dissemina-tion.

Many writers have noticed the social roles of marketing in the Caribbean, though its communication role has been comparatively neglected (for example, Durant-Gonzalez 1977; Legerman 1962; Mintz 1959, 1961; Norvell and Thompson 1968). Men exchange news from different parts of the island while they wait with their crop at the banana boat. Significantly, this is often news they heard from wives and women friends who picked it up at the river or elsewhere. Meanwhile, at Roseau market the largest forum for information and debate occurs among women of all classes and from all parts of the island.

Roseau market is held on Mondays, Wednesday, Fridays and Saturdays. Monday is the day for hucksters to buy produce that they take in their small boats to other islands of the Eastern Caribbean and exchange for manufactured goods. Huckstering also brings new ideas and products onto the island. The trade has long been important in the economic and political development of the island and the hucksters themselves command a great deal of influence (Honychurch 1984: 63; Homiak 1986).

Yet it is not only the hucksters who spread news and ideas into, out of and within Dominica. The Saturday market is the greatest means for intra-island communication. Women and a lesser number of men from all over the island begin their cash and social transactions as early as 4.00 a.m. and as late as noon. Although the former are the stated reason for market day, the latter are often more important. I observed a friend for an hour and a half making seven cash transactions and 22 social ones. I went to market not only for food, but to see friends from parts of the country I could not reach. One Saturday I was with my landlady as she discussed political committee business with a fellow committee member. Another member, a man, came up and jokingly said, 'So you come here to discuss the grant meeting!' My landlady replied 'We come here to discuss EVERYTHING'.

Both purchasers and vendors have their regular, understood spots at the market, even though vending spaces are supposed to be available on a first come, first served basis. Furthermore, vendors from each locality tend to congregate, making it easy for anyone who wants to send a message to a particular village. Many women engage in the social transactions of the market almost unconsciously, whereas others are fully aware of its social functions. Many men, however, are unaware of the communication networking. One man who became my close adviser expressed disbelief when I told him what I had learned from a woman at the market. After seeing it for himself he said, 'Well, that's Dominica for you' and dismissed the activity as a silly women's thing. Communication networking is thus devalued even though many Dominicans rely on it to get news, spread ideas and influence others.

There is a decided political tint to these activities and many a social movement in Dominica is said to have begun with an incident at the market. Although networking at the market is founded on a household maintenance activity, it not only influences the political and jural domains, but constitutes them. In one instance I found out about the nomination of a city council candidate at the same time and from the same source as a newsman from the Dominica Broadcasting System — a woman who heard it from a friend who heard it at the river from someone who heard it at the market. The radio station carried the story soon after.

Thus intra-island communication takes place in Dominica primarily through the work of women. Although men contribute to the spread of news, they usually receive it from women in the first place. This communication is not only on a personal level. Rather, it has political, integrative and economic functions that warrant a rethinking of the public/domestic dichotomy.


## Merging Domains in Barbuda

We have made a domestic or home-based distinction between social roles and work and have pointed out that the carrying out of domestic tasks does not necessarily imply a wholly domestic role. We have seen in Dominica how women's roles function in (and partly constitute) the public sphere. Now we look at Barbuda, different in many ways but also historically marginal in the regional plantation economy.

There are no problems of communication in Barbuda (as there are in Dominica) and there is no market. Both these contrasts are related to physical and demographic differences. Barbuda's 1400 people all live within walking distance of each other, the village terrain is perfectly flat and the vegetation is open. Barbudans also say they are one family and the saying is true: anyone can trace a connection to anyone else. Everyone has convenient access to provision grounds and grazing on the commonlands, though Barbudan plots, always at risk of drought, lack the richness and variety of food gardens in well-watered islands such as Dominica (Berleant-Schiller and Pulsipher 1986). Nor is much cash cropping possible in Barbuda: only in years of adequate rainfall might a few cultivators grow a little cotton and a surplus of pigeon peas and ground nuts for export. There is, nevertheless, local buying and selling of meat, fish, fruit and vegetables and of course there are a few small shops for a limited range of imported foods and goods.

These contrasts (absence of market, more meagre and proportionately fewer subsistence gardens, negligible cash cropping and ease of communication) immediately suggest questions about gender contrasts between the two islands. Are there other opportunities in Barbuda for autonomous feminine roles which might help constitute a public domain? If not, should we advance the hypothesis that gender roles in Dominica are a function of the requirements of communication, economic production and distribution, of the wider structural and economic complex, or of the absorption of men into cash cropping? If they are, should we understand gender itself as an independent variable in the nature and working of Caribbean society, or should we seek some other commonality between the two islands which might account for women's roles?

In Barbuda the domestic role of women is very apparent, they are noticeably responsible for supporting and maintaining households. The various ways in which Barbudan patterns of land tenure, inheritance, child-rearing, house ownership and household composition bolster the domestic aspect of women's roles are discussed in an earlier paper (Berleant-Schiller 1977), so need not be reiterated here. At the same time, men's work and men's roles have a very definite integrating social effect and men's clusters and networks are important economically and socially (Berleant-Schiller 1977). Yet this is not to say that the entire role of women coincides with their domestic tasks, or that there is necessarily a sharp division between public and domestic domains. Those are still the very questions we explore. Let us approach them as we did for Dominica, in relation to women's networks, women's tasks and the locus of women's tasks.

We saw how moral and material support flows through women's networks in Dominica and how encompassing these networks are. The same is true of Barbuda, where we find multiple links between people and where people are quick, in the most ordinary contexts, to identify each other as kin. Children provide an important link with other households and the role of mother and household manager is important (perhaps paradoxically) in merging the domestic and public spheres. As the following example illustrates, even when activities are centred around the physical house, in their managerial functions women use and extend the network ties they have acquired through producing, consuming and distributing their resources.

Lilliane, aged 24, lives with her four brothers, all in their twenties and her three children. The house itself was bequeathed jointly to Lilliane and her brothers by their mother. Even without further details we can see that such a situation implies a number of things about women's roles: in the household there is only one adult woman; there is no husband-wife pair and no father-child relationship; the house itself was owned and bequeathed by a woman. Additional details will clarify what implications Lilliane's domestic activities have in the extra-household sphere.

The men who contribute materially to the household are Lilliane's four brothers and the two fathers of her three children. These six men work the typical range of Barbudan jobs for men: lobster-diving, fishing, charcoal-making, cultivation and intermittent wage labour. They provide money and kind; Lilliane uses these as she sees fit. Thus her role as household head makes her a centre for the redistribution of basic economic goods, over which she has decision-making power. In these functions the support of herself and her children is her first concern and she must be able to juggle her resources if any of the men should cut or withdraw their contributions. Her own contributions of labour, garden provisions and money from her own charcoal kiln will always provide minimal support.

What, if any, public functions do her roles as manager, redistributor and provider of resources have? Most of Lilliane's managerial activities, aimed at supporting herself and her own children, do indeed link and organize households centred on mothers and their children and in some instances subsume them. Her resources are inseparable from a network of complex and shifting social relationships among persons and households. Her brothers have children in other households; her children link her to two complete and separate sets of kin and their households; the fathers of her children are also members of and contributors to the households in which they live. Here we should note that in the Caribbean the question of where some men and children 'live' is not always either clear-cut or settled and in fact is symptomatic of the merging domains we have mentioned. These social and economic connections pass through nodal women such as Lilliane, who are household heads and redistributive agents. Goods, services and even children flow from household to household.

Let us look more closely at Lilliane's three children. Through their fathers they create links between households. The fathers give to Lilliane, but the link is more complex than that. The ties of affinal kinship between Lilliane and her children's paternal grandmothers and aunts (ranged in several households) open up channels for the exchange of goods and services. These households can and do provide a temporary home for a child when the child, or Lilliane, or the aunts and grandmothers find it suits their needs. Thus Lilliane's role as mother is a public asset in its potential for linking and organizing private mother-child groups. Her brother's children have identical and reciprocal economic and kinship functions for Lilliane and open up her household to the needs of their mothers. This situation is similar to the one we described for the Joneses and Stephens in Dominica, though the matrilateral bias is less pronounced. In any case, women's support networks are broadened and enhanced through their children, i.e. through their roles as mothers, even though most of the tasks of motherhood take place within the home.

The place of men in the linking we have just described also argues the case for merging domains. Men have their own male networks of workmates, kin and neighbours, but their roles as sons and brothers and fathers tie them into inter-household networks as providers of some of the resources that women manage and distribute.

Like Dominican women, Barbudan women keep their own provision grounds, though they may also work plots jointly with their husbands. Men, too, keep their own provision grounds. However, cooperative labour exchange in agriculture no longer exists in Barbuda, though informants remember it from the 1920s and earlier. Food gardening, therefore, does not draw Barbudan women into any public sphere. Men, however, exchange labour in house construction, as they do on Dominica. If we consider building a house to be a household task, then here is another example of merging domains in men's work that applies to both islands.

Barbudan women also launder and make charcoal. Since there are no rivers or streams in Barbuda, the women gather at two or three of the public wells to do their washing. Laundering is a time for socializing and gossip, but since news travels so easily in Barbuda anyway it does not have the vital communication function that washing does in Dominica. Its gossip function should be noted, however, since gossip is an important means of informal social control. Charcoal-making, carried out in the bush, is the work of couples, or single women, or single men, or a pair of cooperating kin, either male or female and may be done either for export sale or home use. In any case, it has little or no public or integrating function although it is very important economically for those who undertake it.

There are other kinds of women's work that do make use of domestic roles and that do draw on networks and thus merge with the public domain. Among these are small-scale entrepreneurial activities that attract women who in other Caribbean places might become higglers. They include, for example, retailing in small amounts what the women have purchased in large amounts — kerosene, cooking oil, matches, school supplies and sweet drinks. Women use their connections to obtain these goods from Antigua and sell to their loyal customers. Some women bake cakes and pastries for sale. Usually such goods are sold from the back door. Women also hawk in public, on the walkways and streets: fish brought in by mates and boyfriends, fruit from their own trees, garden surplus, ice cubes, flavoured ices ('frozen joy'), or desirable produce brought from Antigua, such as tomatoes, garlic or carrots. At dances and fêtes they sell cooked foods. All these bring together the public and domestic domains and, to some extent, draw on network ties in the form of loyal buyer-seller relationships.

In the absence of a market these pursuits and their social concomitants are less obvious and less elaborated than in Dominica, but just as clearly they demonstrate the association between networks and economic pursuits. The area in which social and economic activities coincide is also where the domestic and public spheres merge, for it is here that women widen the social roles founded on domestic tasks. But how does the communication function of women's networks in Dominica fit into this association? If we think of the economic sphere as where the distribution of valued goods is dealt with in a society, we immediately see that, given the difficulties of communication in Dominica, news may be regarded as a valued good, flowing through the same network of relationships sustained by and used for moral and economic support.

It is not only through kin and neighbourhood networks, however, that Barbudan women act in public roles, nor are all their public roles founded on domestic tasks. They also assume a role in informal social control by means of gossip (which is unceasing) and through public tirades ('cussing out') against those whose violation of ideal codes has injured them directly and personally. One cussing out I witnessed was staged against a woman and her daughter-in-law, although the latter was not present. The daughter-in-law had fled to New York after her husband had slashed her, leaving six children in the care of their grandmother, her husband's mother. The graphic tirade publicly exposed the women's neglect of the six children, the 'worthless vagabond' of a son and the grandmother's alleged prostitution. It was performed at the gate of the grandmother's house by a woman whose husband was trapped inside for the duration; it was as effective as a sermon and certainly more entertaining.

Over the course of their life cycles women's roles also change. Once past high school young women rarely appear on the street in groups, except when they are walking to church. They do their socializing at the wells or in the yards, whereas groups of young men are highly visible in public. But when women and men alike pass into middle age their social worlds begin to merge; the men spend more time at home and the women become more publicly gregarious and engage in more activities conventionally defined as public. Once past their forties, persons of both sexes share favourite late-afternoon congregating places in the shade; older men and women renew the friendly kinship-influenced relationships across the sexes, which they had dropped after childhood. Although there are very few formal public roles and opportunities available to anyone in Barbuda, women do become more visible. One woman, for example, ran for a seat on the local governing body, the Barbuda Council, after having brought up 11 children. Another woman in her forties, who had taken in sewing at home and worked as a laundress while her children were growing up, opened a tavern and also became active in local party politics. Of seven tiny shops in Barbuda, three are run by older women. There are, however, no formal public roles to compare with those of Dominica.

## Conclusion

Despite their differences, both Dominica and Barbuda demonstrate that the public/domestic dichotomy, useful as it has been for initiating an understanding of gender, cannot be applied universally. We have seen that women's networks in these islands and, in all likelihood, throughout the Caribbean, link women and their households and create channels for the distribution of resources that are essential to everyone. The public functions of women's networks include communicating news, reinforcing social norms, reviving and maintaining social ties and providing moral support. These social and cultural goods are as much essential resources as are economic goods and services. We have also seen that public and domestic domains are hardest to distinguish in zones where social networks and economic pursuits coincide, as they do, for example, in marketing and *koudmen*.

In Dominica, women's activities foster social roles that not only bring women into the public domain, but constitute the public domain. Public life in Dominica could not function without the integrative role of women effected through their marketing, washing, plaiting and networking activities. In Barbuda, where everything is on a smaller scale, private relations have public significance, as the case of Lilliane demonstrates. Personal relationships, inter-household kinship ties and small-scale commercial relationships are socially integrating, even though there is no market and no communications problem. Because of their differences in productive economy, topography, land use, social structure and demography, Dominica and Barbuda exhibit differences in some of the public roles of women and in the degree to which women's roles constitute the public domain. Yet in each, the social importance of women's 'domestic' tasks places women in 'public' roles. In each, the two domains merge, both economically and ideologically.

This merging shows that a public-domestic dichotomy is not universally useful in explaining status differences. Our data suggest that the study of gender may productively focus on kinship, economic associations and the ideology of the household, without necessary reference either to relative statuses or to organizational dichotomies, as perceived by actors or described by observers. This is not to say that status differences and inequalities between men and women as groups do not exist, but that they are separate questions that might better be explored as phenomena of class, productive economy, male economic dominance, economic development and scarce resources, perceived or real.

We have mainly focused on women's pursuits related to economic production and reproduction. One reason for this was our concern to show that tasks and roles are not always coterminous; we also wished to supply an example of public social roles founded on household work. But women do other things that may demonstrate the merging of the public and domestic spheres which should also be investigated. These include women's activities in religious organizations and mutual support societies (which are discussed in Chapter 8). The cases of Dominica and Barbuda also raise questions about the relationship of resource abundance and paid employment to women's mobilization. Further, considering children as resources available to adults poses questions about the role of children as participants in the production and consumption of community resources.

Our work on Dominica and Barbuda also raises questions that are specific to the Caribbean. Why, for example, have Caribbean societies been the most resistant to applications of the public/domestic dichotomy? Can further work on merging domains be integrated with the abundance of work on gender inequalities, class and economic change in the Caribbean, even while the two endeavours remain conceptually distinct?

The Caribbean is an extraordinarily varied region, yet pan-Caribbean cultural phenomena are obvious. It is therefore an ideal region in which to focus widely on manageably bounded problems, such as those we have presented, with the possibility of achieving conclusive results. We have been able to combine our interest in gender relations as a live anthropological issue with our dedication to the Caribbean as a research area. We hope that in doing so we have demonstrated the significance of the region for current discourse in anthropology.

## Notes

1  Meaning 'lake path' because it runs past the freshwater lake (Letang) deep in the island's interior.
2  All personal names in this chapter have been changed. Where knowledge of a person's European ancestry is significant, pseudonyms reflect this ancestry. Place names that might reveal identity have been omitted.
3  Numbering is consistent in Figures 5.1 and 5.2. Many persons are left unrepresented so that the major connections explained in the text will be clear.
4  'Remembering' relationships when convenient is a feature of Dominican family politics. Large family networks often drop members who take spouses of lower status and who dissolve marriages. Those involved in common-law relationships are more likely to be dropped.
5  Langrish (1973) refers to this practice as *jeuner*, although in Dominica the preferred spelling is *journée*. The more common term is *koudmen*

## References

Anderson, Patricia (1986) 'Conclusions: Women in the Caribbean'. *Social and Economic Studies* (35) 291-324

Barrow, Christine (1986) 'Finding the Support: Strategies for Survival'. *Social and Economic Studies*, (35) 131-76

Berleant-Schiller, Riva (1977) 'Production and Division of Labour in a West Indian Peasant Community'. *American Ethnologist*, (4) 253-72

—— (1978) 'The Failure of Agricultural Development in Post-Emancipation Barbuda: A Study of Social and Economic Continuity in a West Indian Community'. *Boletin de Estudios Latinoamericanos y del Caribe*, (25) 21-35

—— (1987) 'Ecology and Politics in Barbudan Land Tenure'. In J. Besson and J. Momsen (eds) *Land and Development in the Caribbean*, London: Macmillan, 116-31

Berleant-Schiller, Riva and Lydia M. Pulsipher (1986) 'Subsistence Cultivation in the Caribbean'. *New West Indian Guide*, (60) 1-40

Brandes, Stanley (1981) 'Like Wounded Stags: Male Sexual Ideology in an Andalusian Town'. In Sherry Ortner and Harriet Whitehead (eds) *q.v.*, 216-39

Burrows, E.G. (1956) 'Topography and Culture on Two Polynesian Islands'. *Geographical Review*, (28) 214-33

Caribbean Agro-Economic Society (1977) 'Proposals for Development of the Grand Bay Area, Dominica'. In John Cropper (ed.) *Proceedings of the 11th West Indies Agricultural Economics Conference*, Trinidad: University of the West Indies, 123-37

Durant-Gonzalez, Victoria (1977) 'Role and Status of Rural Jamaican Women: Higglering and Mothering'. Ph.D. dissertation, Department of Anthropology, University of California at Berkeley

Gussler, Judith D. (1980) 'Adaptive Strategies and Social Networks of Women in St Kitts'. In E. Bourguignon (ed.) *A World of Women: Anthropological Studies of Women in the Societies of the World*. New York: Praeger

Harris, David R. (1965) *Plants, Animals and Man in the Outer Leeward Islands, West Indies*. University of California Publications in Geography, vol. 18, Berkeley: University of California Press

Homiak, John (1986) 'The Hucksters of Dominica'. *Grassroots Development*, (10) 30-7

Honychurch, Lennox (1984) *The Dominican Story*. Roseau, Dominica: The Dominica Institute

Langrish, Paul (1973) 'Dominica Land Management Authority: Project Proposals for the Procurement and Development of 10,000 Acres over Five Years'. Unpublished manuscript, Botanic Gardens, Roseau, Dominica

Legerman, Caroline J. (1962) 'Kin Groups in a Haitian Market'. *Man* (62) 145-9

Mintz, Sidney W. (1959) 'Internal Market Systems as Mechanisms of Social Articulation'. In *Proceedings of the American Ethnological Society*. Seattle: University of Washington Press, 20-30

—— (1961) 'Pratik: Haitian Personal Economic Relationships'. In *Proceedings of the American Ethnological Society*. Seattle: University of Washington Press

Moses, Yolanda Theresa (1976) 'Female Status and Male Dominance in Montserrat, West Indies'. Ph.D. dissertation, Department of Anthropology, University of California at Riverside

Myers, Robert (1981) 'Post-Emancipation Migrations and Population Change in Dominica: 1834-1950'. *Revista/Review Interamericana*, (11) 87-109

Norvell, Douglas and Marian Thompson (1968) 'Higglering in Jamaica and the Mystique of Perfect Competition'. *Social and Economic Studies*, (17) 407-16

Ortner, Sherry (1974) 'Is Female to Male as Nature is to Culture?' In Michelle Rosaldo and Louise Lamphere, *q.v.*, 67-87

Ortner, Sherry and Harriet Whitehead (eds) (1981) *Sexual Meanings: The Cultural Construction of Gender and Sexuality*. New York: Cambridge University Press

Rosaldo, Michelle (1974) 'Woman, Culture and Society: A Theoretical Overview'. In Michelle Rosaldo and Louise Lamphere, *q.v.*, 17-42

Rosaldo, Michelle and Louise Lamphere (eds) (1974) *Woman, Culture and Society*. Palo Alto: Stanford University Press

Sutton, Constance and Susan Makiesky-Barrow (1977) 'Social Inequality and Sexual Status in Barbados'. In A. Schlegel (ed.) *Sexual Stratification*, New York: Columbia University Press

# PART 2

# The Intersection of Reproduction & Production

Caribbean women have some of the highest levels of economic activity and lowest fertility rates in the developing world (Table 1.1). During slavery this was also true but after emancipation birth rates rose and female participation in the labour force gradually fell only to be reversed again in the last three decades.

Both reproduction and production have been influenced by migration. During periods of high male out-migration, as in the early years of this century, women were forced to move back into the labour force. Today, many women are migrating overseas independently as well as with their families and some Caribbean countries have more female than male emigrants. Women migrants to North America and Europe enter into professional, though poorly paid, jobs such as nursing, while migrant West Indian men tend to be concentrated in unskilled or semi-skilled work. Women migrants also retain their ties with their families in the Caribbean more than men and are more likely to send remittances, especially if they have left children to be raised by relatives in their natal country.

Women who do not migrate are increasingly becoming involved in grassroots organizations. Many that were originally set up for charitable and social purposes have been used by national political parties, though without giving women themselves power. As women take control of their own bodies and increase their economic autonomy they will be able to play a greater role outside the home and local community.

# VI  Women in Guadeloupe:
# The Paradoxes of Reality

HUGUETTE DAGENAIS*

In the North American imagination, Caribbean islands are associated with sunny holidays, sensuality (the three 'S'es — sea, sex and sun — in whatever order one places them) and a certain *douceur de vivre* unknown in temperate regions. It takes catastrophes like the Gilbert and Hugo hurricanes, a film such as *Sucre Noir*[1] about the living conditions of Haitian cane workers in the Dominican Republic, or assassinations of people like Maurice Bishop in Grenada or those that have taken place in Haiti since February 1986, to attract the general population's attention to the darker sides of Caribbean reality. At another level, a similar dichotomy exists with regard to intellectual analyses of the region. Still, too often, the Caribbean region, which I deliberately limit here to the islands, is either simply assimilated into Latin America, with isolated chapters in books on the latter devoted to one island (usually a large one), or is considered as a cultural area in itself but with the local specificities often hidden in a more or less homogenized portrait. In fact the Caribbean defies all broad generalizations (Dagenais 1988a). Though there are striking similarities between the islands stemming from their shared geographical situation, colonial past, dependent economies inherited from and still dominated by the plantation system logic and their Creole cultures, one cannot disregard the immense cultural, demographic, economic and political variations existing between them. Because of this, the Caribbean region — 'this dust of islands' (*cette poussière d'îles*) as some French authors have described it — deserves closer examination. Guadeloupe[2] in particular needs further study, being, in my judgement, one of the lesser known countries of the region.

Through this lack of precise analysis, ambivalent images of Caribbean women have emerged. Popular representations of the region portray them as sexual objects and publicity props; the tourist industry presents them as sensual mulattoes with endless free time to enjoy the beaches and, of course, the (male) visitors. This is one side of the mother/whore dichotomy which characterizes the dominant thinking on women's roles in Caribbean society. The other side is found mainly in anthropological and sociological literature on the Caribbean family. Until the recent development of feminist studies, with the exception of Haitian *madan sara* and Jamaican higglers, women were largely invisible as social actresses in the regional social science literature. Only their role as mothers was recognized and this was mainly in works dedicated to the so-called concept of 'matrifocality' (Dagenais 1984). However, such recognition has to be examined with a critical eye.

* Writing this chapter in English was made possible for me by the constant collaboration of my partner, Lee Cooper. The research projects on which it draws have been made possible by grants from the Social Science Research Council of Canada and the Fonds FCAR pour la Formation de Chercheurs et l'Aide à la Recherche of Quebec.

While women are portrayed as mythical black matriarchs and super-women whose courage and abnegation seem without limits (Mathurin 1977; Wallace 1979), they are also described as possessive and castrating mothers whose power over their sons is highly harmful to them and to men in general (Dagenais and Poirier 1985; Gautier 1985).

Fortunately, feminist research has begun to demystify Caribbean women and to make them more visible as full active participants in the economic life of their countries. But this area of study itself has some glaring omissions. Although there is a fair amount of feminist research in the Anglophone and Spanish-speaking territories (though, as everywhere, somewhat marginal in its impact), there is very little in the French areas. Moreover, links between feminist researchers in the region are restricted by language barriers; while there is collaboration between researchers from the different English-speaking territories,[3] communication is still embryonic between English and French-speaking territories.[4] In the latter, even though there was no feminist research before the 1980s, Guadeloupean intellectuals, like their counterparts in France, have succeeded in portraying feminism as an outdated fashion.[5] In addition, the nature of the communication channels (which are partly inherited from the colonial past and partly determined by the politico-economic factors affecting each country) are such that the results of feminist research on the Caribbean are disseminated faster in metropolitan France, Britain, The Netherlands and North America than within the region itself.

In this chapter I survey the position of Guadeloupean women from a materialist feminist point of view, focusing on the productive and reproductive dimensions of their daily lives. After presenting general contextual data on Guadeloupean economics and women's circumstances in relation to education and health, I look at women's work and maternal activities and at certain aspects of male-female relations, comparing, when appropriate, Guadeloupean women with their counterparts in metropolitan France. I deliberately use the term 'work' in preference to the term 'production', for I believe it more appropriately describes the multiplicity of women's activities and has fewer economic connotations. Similarly, while I am in general agreement with Edholm, Harris and Young (1977) about the triple content of the concept of reproduction (reproduction of manpower, biological reproduction and broader social reproduction), I place more emphasis than they do on the time and energy women expend on the daily caring activities resulting from biological reproduction; these are empirical facts which even feminists do not pay enough attention to in the various theoretical debates. In considering women's work and motherhood I begin with 'where women are', but keep in mind their daily lives 'as problematic' (Smith 1987) and try never to lose sight of the dialectical relations that tie them closely together in gender relations and of the overall social organization.

To do this I analyse a range of official statistics which, for French territories like Guadeloupe, are considerable, regular and of high quality. I question and examine them from the standpoint of women and through the qualitative insights and data gained from my field research in this island since 1983.[6] I believe that despite a male bias (especially concerning the labour market) and their incapacity to give a complete picture of women's economic contribution (which should include women's production in the domestic sphere and informal sectors), these supposedly neutral numbers and percentages, often automatically broken down by sex, when interpreted with critical feminist insight can still give useful information on social inequalities and on women's inferior position in society. Thus, using common statistical development indicators, I highlight what seem to be the best indicators of women's well being (Townsend and Momsen 1987) and I interpret as indicators of women's working conditions the statistics on lodging and household equipment.[7] This approach situates my analysis at the heart of the power relationships involving Guadeloupean women and all women in patriarchal and capitalist societies, power being basically defined here in terms of the control and autonomy individuals and groups can exercise over their own destiny and over their social environment — people, institutions, ideologies and practices.

## Statistical Overview

Located in the 'arc' of the Lesser Antilles, some 7000 kilometres from metropolitan France, the archipelago of Guadeloupe is divided into 'mainland Guadeloupe', itself an archipelago including Grande-Terre island to the east and Basse-Terre island to the west separated by the narrow Rivière Salée, and the 'dependencies' (the islands of Marie-Galante, Désirade, St Martin, St Barthelemy and the archipelago of Les Saintes). In January 1986 its total population was estimated at 333,378, a 1.9 per cent increase over the 1982 general census (G. Gautier 1986). With a land area of 1780 square kilometres, Guadeloupe is the second largest territory of the Lesser Antilles. It has a moderate population density (198 persons per square kilometre in 1988 with an annual increase of 0.2 per cent), which is much higher in reality because rugged mountains, including the Soufrière volcano (altitude 1476 metres), occupy the whole central section of Basse-Terre island.[8]

After three centuries of colonial rule, two of which were dominated by slave labour production, the law of 19 March 1946 made Guadeloupe one of the five French overseas *départements* or DOMs (*département français d'outre-mer*) and its population was then granted full French citizenship. This particular political status, so very different from that of any of the other newly independent territories in the region, was granted after years of demands for equality and social justice by left-wing politicians, foremost amongst whom was the well known Martinican poet and politician, Aimé Césaire. Today this political status is lived out with many ambiguities, including aspirations to independence,[9] by the local population of whom more than 80-85 per cent are of African ancestry.[10]

There is no doubt that the progressive extension of French metropolitan social welfare programmes, family allowances, and educational and health policies brought about by DOM status has improved living and working conditions in this former colony. Usual macro-social indicators such as gross national product (GNP) and life expectancy at birth are quite high in Guadeloupe compared to most other Caribbean islands.[11] In 1987, the per capita GNP in US dollars was $3190 (compared to $4230 in Martinique, $5330 in Barbados, $5520 in Puerto Rico, $960 in Jamaica, $360 in Haiti and $1440 in neighbouring Dominica) and life expectancy was 73 years compared to 55 in Haiti. However, the picture is somewhat different when comparisons are drawn with metropolitan France, where the GNP is almost four times higher (US$12,860 in 1987), life expectancy slightly higher (75 years) and unemployment rates are three to four times lower, even in the poorest *départements* (Conseil Economique et Social 1987: 45, 60). In fact, as I briefly show, expressions like 'false growth' (Albertini 1974), 'apparent prosperity' (Conseil Economique et Social 1987) or 'mal développement' (Armet 1983) used by local analysts would all be more appropriate to describe the 'distortions' (Buffon 1982) and the total 'dependence' of the Guadeloupean economy on metropolitan France.

Though still considered to have an agricultural vocation, over the last 20 years Guadeloupe has seen the importance of its primary sector shrink by more than half; the tertiary sector has continued to grow and the secondary one, consisting of young light manufacturing industries, remains economically in a middle position. The continuation of this process has resulted in an ever increasing polarization of the labour force towards the unproductive tertiary sector where, as Table 6.1 shows, 65 per cent of employment is concentrated (Gautier 1988: 4). Thus, instead of the constant surpluses found in its trade balances before the Second World War and the 81 per cent coverage of imports by exports in 1950, by 1985 the value of Guadeloupe's exports, consisting almost entirely of sugar and bananas shipped to the metropole, amounted to only 12 per cent of that of imports, which are largely made up of metropolitan consumer goods (48 per cent) including food products.

Table 6.1: Percentage of Labour Force by Broad Economic Sectors in Guadeloupe 1967, 1974, 1982

| Economic Sectors | 1967%* | 1974%* | 1982%** |
|---|---|---|---|
| Primary | 32.4 | 22.2 | 15.0 |
| Secondary | 26.2 | 22.8 | 20.1 |
| Tertiary | 41.4 | 55.0 | 64.9 |

Sources: *Buffon 1982:25; **Conseil Economique et Social 1987:48

This commercial deficit has meant that only through the transfer of public funds (via social security and family allowance programmes, military and civil service expenses, public loans, etc.) from the metropole, which collectively represent more than a third of the island's GNP, can the average Guadeloupean standard of living be artificially maintained at a relatively high level. However, this fact alone tends to gloss over large remaining differences between Guadeloupe and metropolitan France. For example, the amount of money paid through various social programmes to people in Guadeloupe represents only 33-45 per cent of the level distributed in the metropole (1982), while the minimum salary remains some 17 per cent lower and the gross available income per household is more than 50 per cent lower (FF 16,563 as opposed to FF 37,934 in 1985) (CES 1987: 53).

There are also profound 'inequities in individual situations' (Buffon 1982: 22). A case in point, local civil servants, like their metropolitan counterparts living in Guadeloupe, receive a 40 per cent income supplement to compensate for the island's higher cost of living. Yet, every Guadeloupean citizen suffers from the very real 17.3 per cent higher price level (excluding housing); food alone is almost one and a half times more expensive than in the metropole for similar metropolitan type products which have to be imported.[12] Guadeloupean people spend some 30 per cent of their budget on food as against 23 per cent by the metropolitan French (Diman-Antenor 1988: 13). Even taking into account the fact that those who grow their own food or eat primarily local produce spend less on this item, it is easy to understand how this high cost of living affects low income people, among whom are found the majority of female heads of households.

Associated with the economic situation has been an important current of emigration towards metropolitan France involving 3-4 per cent of the population each year, mainly young people between the ages of 20 and 29. However, the movement is slowing down and, since 1975, there has been a consistent trend towards return migration. Even so, taking into account the rapid decline in birth and fertility rates in the 1960s and 1970s, which will be discussed later, the population of Guadeloupe remains young: the average age is 27 (compared with

36 in metropolitan France in 1982); the proportion of persons less than 15 years of age is presently 31.2 per cent (21.1 per cent in the metropole). Yet, compared to 1974, when more than half (52 per cent) of the people were under 20, the population is getting older and some experts predict problems in about 50 years when people born during the 'demographic explosion' will reach retirement age (Guengant 1987). Paradoxically, it is immigrants from other islands in the Antilles, accounting for a mere 3 per cent of the Guadeloupean population, who contribute most to the maintenance of the fertility rate above the threshold of population renewal. In 1985, for example, 6.4 per cent of the births registered in Guadeloupe were to mothers born in Dominica and 5.4 per cent of births were to Haitian mothers, two territories where fertility rates are high (Gautier 1987: 14).

The proportion of urban population is not very high in Guadeloupe (45.7 per cent in 1985) compared to many other territories in the region (Cuba 71.8 per cent; Puerto Rico 70.7 per cent; Martinique 71.1 per cent and Trinidad 63.9 per cent) (*Etat du Monde* 1988: 326-7, 332-3). However, given the hypertrophy of the tertiary sector and the sexual division of labour, women of working age are more numerous than men in the two main cities.[13] Especially notable is the massive presence of women heads of households who constitute 46 per cent of the female population in Pointe-à-Pitre (the biggest city and commercial capital) and 43 per cent in Basse-Terre, the administrative capital, while female-headed households represent 34 per cent of all households for the *département* as a whole (Diman-Antenor 1986: 51-2). This preference among female heads of households for cities and the services they provide has been well documented elsewhere and one can presume that the causes are similar in Guadeloupe.[14] Yet the good road system, at least as far as major roads are concerned, makes it quite simple to commute daily in and out of the cities and cheaper housing in the countryside enables 70 per cent of the people working in Pointe-à-Pitre to live elsewhere. Guadeloupe has a large number of fairly new motor cars on the road. In 1986 alone 5600 private new cars were registered (about 6000 at the beginning of the 1980s). That same year the total motor car fleet contained about 75,000 vehicles, including nearly 2000 trucks (Roudil 1987). Thus, in the *département* as a whole, there is about one motor vehicle for every five persons. Most of the car owners, however, are men while women constitute the vast majority of the bus passengers (along with school children at certain times of the day). This difference is noteworthy because, despite recent improvements in the number and comfort of commuter buses, public transport is still very time and (human) energy consuming compared to speedy private car transport, not forgetting the strain caused by the noise, the crowds and some drivers' quite personal driving styles.[15]

These global statistics on cars and roads seem to confirm the impression visitors get of relative prosperity as they drive along Guadeloupe's principal roads, noting the many large houses located on the cool mountain sides or hills, where access is difficult and electrical and water connections expensive. However, behind the façade of this apparent luxury is the fact that about a third of the homes, particularly in the rural areas, have no running water and two-fifths are overcrowded. Even so, the main city, Pointe-à-Pitre, with its public housing developments of concrete apartment blocks and towers, often with graffiti-covered walls and garbage-littered surroundings, is a far cry from most third world cities and their shanty-towns. In Pointe-à-Pitre's *Assainissement* quarter (literally 'cleaning-up district') the shacks have been torn down or carted away to be replaced by modern stores, banks, offices and apartment buildings, needed because of the increase in urban growth over the past 15 or so years.

A corollary of this construction boom is that the most impoverished urban Guadeloupeans and recent Dominican and Haitian immigrants continue to be grouped at the edges of the city, in Boissard and Carenage, two neighbourhoods isolated from the rest of the population more by the epithet 'ghetto' and the disproportionate attention of the island's media than by their geographical location. In Boissard, which has an entrance just opposite Pointe-à-Pitre's large modern hospital centre, the most important in the *département*, the rate of babies dying before or during the first week of life was estimated at 77 per 1000 in 1983 compared with a *département* average of around 26 per 1000 (Bangou et al. 1988).

Even so, the poverty is not immediately visible to a visitor to Guadeloupe. There are no children with distended stomachs, suffering from rickets and begging tourists for money, as one sees in Haiti and elsewhere in the Third World. Children attend schools culturally and administratively similar to those of metropolitan France. But the island's system has serious problems. For example, even taking into account the fact that emigration to the metropole is mainly of young people with more formal education than those remaining behind, it is worrying that 70.23 per cent of the population were without any diploma in 1982 (CES 1987: 42). Problems begin in the first year of school (*cours préparatoire*), which 20 per cent of the children have to repeat. This pattern continues throughout primary school, with only one child in three arriving at the secondary level without repeating. In addition, only about a quarter of children will reach the *baccalauréat* level, where the success rate is 52.1 per cent overall compared to 63.7 per cent in France (Cazenave 1986; Cazenave and Briand 1986). These figures indicate progress, but not enough to keep critics from seeing the Guadeloupean school system as a failure in socio-economic, cultural and linguistic terms. One has to remember that although French is the national language, it is a second language on the island. For most children Creole is their first and only language before formal schooling and, in general, it remains the language spoken at home and outside school (see Bebel-Gisler 1976 and 1985).

The position of women in the educational sector deserves particular attention. Overall, it is much the same as in most Western countries: girls succeed better than boys, more often obtain their secondary level diploma and are concentrated in the humanities rather than the sciences. Even though they have more diplomas, they are more often unemployed (40 per cent of women aged between 20 and 24 compared with 34.9 per cent of men). However, because of the particular economic situation, the Guadeloupean female labour market, as we shall see, is much narrower and more rapidly saturated than the female one elsewhere. As a result, the proportion of young women among migrants to metropolitan France (55 per cent) is higher than that of men, and 58 per cent of migrating students are women. In the metropole, Guadeloupean young women stand a much better chance of finding jobs related to their levels of training (Cazenave 1986).

Finally, in this general survey of Guadeloupe from the standpoint of women, one cannot ignore health statistics. The *département*'s average yearly medical expenditure per capita is high (FF 2214 in 1980; FF 3312 in 1983, the latter corresponding to about US$550) (Thery 1986: 93); it has been estimated that about 13 per cent of household expenditure went on medical costs in the early 1980s (Diman-Antenor 1982: 56-9). In 1984 there were 12 hospital beds per 1000 people and one doctor for each 1045 people, but nearly two thirds of these 309 medical doctors were concentrated in the Pointe-à-Pitre and Basse-Terre urban areas (Thery and Lefait-Robin 1986). In its medical care system, Guadeloupe is definitely closer to the Western developed countries than to many other neighbouring territories, a position reflected in the rapid drop in infant mortality to 15.3 per 1000, a rate that is now among the lowest in the Caribbean. But again these global statistics obscure profound inequalities. Though low in comparison with developing countries, Guadeloupe's infant mortality rate is still nearly double that of metropolitan France (8 per 1000) (*ICAR* 1988: 2-3). The perinatal death rate is still more than one and a half times the French one (18.8 per 1000 compared to 11.5) and, in 1983, the proportion of deaths from perinatal infections in Guadeloupe (2.5 per cent of all infant deaths) was eight times that of France (0.3 per cent). Even though the percentages are low, the proportion of Guadeloupean women dying from pregnancy complications and genito-urinary pathologies is higher than that of metropolitan women (respectively 2.0 per cent and 0.3 per cent of all deaths in Guadeloupe as opposed to 1.6 per cent and 0.0 per cent in the metropole). The DOM's modern health care system has failed to eliminate the infection by pathogenic parasites of 44 per cent of the population — 2 per cent of all deaths in Guadeloupe are from infectious and parasitical diseases compared to 0.5 per cent in France (INSEE 1983: 27-30). As Auguste Armet (1983: 47) explains, this system puts a priority on treatment, not on prevention, whereas the Antillean pathology in fact largely remains a transmittable one, in other words, a pathology of under-developed countries.

From this perspective, the 'tropical paradise' portrayed in the publicity brochures, which each year attract thousands of North American and European tourists, is a distortion of the life led by many Guadeloupeans. As this brief portrait of the *département* shows, numerous contradictions and paradoxes characterize Guadeloupean society today. With this social and economic profile as a background, I now turn to the work and reproductive activities of Guadeloupean women.

## Women at Work

In this analysis, women's work in Guadeloupe is divided into two broad categories. The first covers their activities in the labour market. Socially recognized and taken into account in the economic and demographic statistics, these paid activities are the most 'visible' kind. The second category includes all other kinds of work accomplished by women:[16] paid and usually quite visible under-the-table jobs (called *travail noir* in French); work as 'helpers' in domestic, farm or small commercial enterprises; small-scale and more or less regular domestic market production and services; specific forms of female mutual help (*coups de main*); and the very real 'invisible' free domestic work which is by far the most regular, but 'which no one (neither economists nor husbands) considers as work' (Michel 1983: 66). This diversity of activities makes this second category look like a large residual one, but it also provides a good illustration of the difficulty of artificially separating activities that are intertwined parts of women's daily lives.

### The Labour Market

According to Guadeloupe's most recent general census (1982) 51.8 per cent of the population between the ages of 15 and 64 are women. Of every 100 women iN this category, 13 are students, 34 have jobs, 13 are unemployed, 23 remain at home and 12 are retired. Counting as 'economically active' those who have a job or are unemployed, nearly half (47.8 per cent) Guadeloupe's women are in the labour market, an important increase from the 40.7 per cent reported in the 1974 census. Women make up 43.2 per cent of Guadeloupe's total labour force and 40.9 per cent of the employed, but half (50.2 per cent) of the unemployed. For every 100 women in employment, 87 are in the tertiary sector (probably one of the highest concentrations in the world), eight are in agriculture and five are factory workers. Despite women being seen as the main beneficiaries of the 'tertiarization' process (which incidentally increases female job ghettoization because of the limited number of existing professions in Guadeloupe), they actually hold only 55.3 per cent of the jobs in the tertiary sector as against 22 per cent in the primary sector and 10.6 per cent in the secondary one. Between 1974 and 1982 the number of men employed in the tertiary sector increased by 28 per cent, while the number of women grew by 33 per cent. However, when one considers that in this sector, as in the others, the top jobs are invariably held by men, one has to conclude that women have not been the only ones to have benefited from the tertiarization process.

**Table 6.2: Proportion of Women in the Socio-Professional Categories and Sub-Categories 1982**

| Categories | | | % |
|---|---|---|---|
| | Sub-categories | % | |
| Agricultural producers | | | 26 |
| Agricultural salaried workers | | | 21 |
| Industry and commerce | | | 26 |
| | Industry owners | 23 | |
| | Craftsmen | 9 | |
| | Fishermen | 1 | |
| | Large commercial businessmen | 23 | |
| | Small shop owners | 60 | |
| Liberal professions, upper managers | | | 32 |
| Middle managers | | | 56 |
| Employees | | | 58 |
| Workers | | | 21 |
| | Overseers | 5 | |
| | Tenured public sector workers | 13 | |
| | Other workers | 9 | |
| | Seamen and fishermen | 1 | |
| | Skilled worker apprentices | 7 | |
| | Unskilled labourers | 51 | |
| Service personnel | | | 79 |
| | Cleaning women | 97 | |
| Other categories | | | 8 |
| People without paid employment | | | 60 |
| | Unemployed | 50 | |
| | Persons at home | 95 | |
| | Students | 53 | |
| | Military personnel | 00 | |
| | Retired | 53 | |
| | Other inactive | 47 | |
| Total population 16 years old and over | | | 51.8 |

*Source:* General Population Census of Guadeloupe 1982. Percentages calculated by author

When one looks at the statistics from other viewpoints the subordinate position of Guadeloupean women in the labour market is even more starkly revealed. Table 6.2 illustrates the important gap between high and low prestige jobs, with

women heavily represented in the lower categories of unemployed and service
personnel (60 and 79 per cent respectively). Included in the category 'service
personnel' is the only linguistically feminine sub-category — cleaning lady (*femme
de ménage*) — which is 97 per cent female. In the higher prestige categories the
situation is more ambiguous; if women represent almost a quarter (23 per cent) of
the global category of 'managers/owners in industry and commerce', it is because
they account for 60 per cent of 'small shopkeepers'. The proportions of women
increase as we go down the socio-professional categories and sub-categories; they
constitute 32 per cent of workers in the liberal professions and executive managerial category, 56 per cent in 'middle management' and 51 per cent of unskilled
workers. Even in the public sector, where women account for 55 per cent of the
employees and about half of the tenured positions, they are more numerous than
men among non-tenured employees (about 60 per cent). In 1986 only 4.7 per cent
of employed women, as compared to 15.1 per cent of employed men, were in the
category of 'independent workers and employers' (Basso and Tranap 1980: 10). As
a result there is a wide gap between women's and men's average salaries; a
Ministry of Labour inquiry revealed that in 1985 salaries for men were 19 per cent
higher than women's among workers and 21 per cent higher among employees
and intermediary professions.

**Table 6.3: Proportion of Women in Ten Professions
with Highest Proportion of Women**

| Professions | % women | % women in labour force |
|---|---|---|
| Services | 90.0 | 27.1 |
| Office work | 66.7 | 17.4 |
| Teaching | 60.9 | 10.8 |
| Agriculture & connected activities | 23.9 | 8.6 |
| Commercial salaried work | 58.9 | 7.1 |
| Commerce | 56.1 | 7.0 |
| Health | 68.2 | 6.8 |
| Social Services | 77.7 | 1.7 |
| Food Services | 59.0 | 1.5 |
| Sewing, hat & basket-making | 66.1 | 1.4 |
| TOTAL | | 89.4 |

*Source*: General Population Census of Guadeloupe 1982 (percentages calculated by this author)

   Though the ghettoization of women's employment is not specific to Guadeloupe,
its rhythm and scope are. Guadeloupe's 'ghettos' of women's work are narrower
than those in France. Thus, when one adds up the number of female workers in
the ten 'regrouped professional categories' (*professions regroupées*, according to the
census) in which women are most strongly represented, the total accounts for 90
per cent of all employed women (see Table 6.3). To get the same percentage for
Guadeloupean men, one must add three times as many professions, whereas in
metropolitan France a similar operation results in a much smaller concentration of
women in twice as many categories, i.e. 45 per cent of the female work force in the
20 most 'feminized' professions (*Femmes en Chiffres* 1986: 46). A similar picture
appears when one looks at figures over time, as in Table 6.4: in a little less than 30
years, the number and proportion of employed women in teaching, office work,
service jobs, business, health and social services has risen considerably, with

increases ranging from 113 per cent to 962 per cent. At the same time women have become less dominant in the traditionally feminine craft sectors (sewing, hat making, basketry), in agriculture and in shopkeeping. In the case of sewing, the decrease is partly due to shifts in production towards the informal economy. My observations suggest that many women are paid to sew for private individuals (acquaintances, neighbours or others) and that there are also seamstresses (many of them Haitian immigrants) working at home for the new, tourist-oriented clothing shops. In agriculture, the decrease is explained in part by the overall decline of this sector (Poirier and Dagenais 1986), while that of small shopkeepers is due to the control of an important part of retail food distribution by large supermarkets located on the outskirts of the cities, and to men taking control over the means of transport.[17]

**Table 6.4: Evolution in the Proportion of Women in the Labour Force in Certain Professions between 1954 and 1982**

| Professions | % 1954 | % 1982 | % variation |
|---|---|---|---|
| Agriculture & connected activities | 39.6 | 8.6 | - 76 |
| Sewing, fashion, basket-making, etc. | 18.3 | 1.4 | - 92 |
| Office work | 4.2 | 17.4 | +314 |
| Commercial employees | 3.5 | 7.1 | +102 |
| Industrial & commercial owners | 10.6 | 7.0 | - 33 |
| Services | 12.5 | 27.1 | +117 |
| Health and social services | 0.8 | 8.5 | +962 |
| Teaching | 2.2 | 10.6 | +381 |
| TOTAL | 91.7 | 87.7 | |

Source: General Population Census of Guadeloupe 1954, 1982 (percentages calculated by this author)

*Unemployment and Underemployment*
Even so, statistics on employment are incomplete without those on unemployment. Between 1980 and 1986, when the last two labour force censuses were taken, the Guadeloupean labour force increased by 26 per cent, but among the 29,200 new persons concerned, 18,600 had not found employment; at present two persons out of three seeking formal work do not find any, especially among young people. Even if the creation of 11,000 new jobs 'has been of benefit only to women' (Gautier 1988: 5; Cazenave 1988: 17), as demographers like to stress, it does not erase the fact that, for all age groups, with the exception of the oldest, women's rates of unemployment are always higher than men's (see Table 6.5) and sometimes double.

Another characteristic of unemployment in Guadeloupe is its longevity; it lasts 'practically 20 months on an average' and 'always four to six months longer for women than men' (Domenach and Guengant 1981: 9). Notwithstanding these differences, it is evident that young workers of both sexes find it difficult to accept such enforced inactivity. Some 60 per cent of unemployed men and women say they would be prepared to accept any kind of work, though both groups would clearly prefer it to be full time. Here another assumption seems to be unfounded, for 80 per cent of the women concerned (and 95 per cent of the men) expressed a preference for full-time work (Domenach and Guengant 1981: 9-10). This readiness to find any kind of employment is confirmed by the 'Jobs Wanted' columns in the local daily newspaper. Even though this is not generally the most usual or efficient means of finding a job in Guadeloupe, it is a visible one; twice as many women as men (and mainly young ones) place such advertisements in the newspaper.[18] Reading them regularly, as I have over the years, one gets a clear sense, not only of the strong desire driving these women to find a job at any price, but also of the particular perception these women have of female employment. Thus, young women job seekers frequently mention, for example, that they are qualified and looking for a typist's job but would 'consider any reasonable offer', or would be willing to do selling, baby sitting or house cleaning as well; such readiness to lower one's job expectations is less obvious in men's advertisements.

**Table 6.5: Unemployment Percentage by Sex & by Age-Groups 1986**

| Age-groups | M% | F% |
|---|---|---|
| 15-24 years | 56 | 68 |
| 25-29 years | 24 | 45 |
| 30-39 years | 10 | 22 |
| 40 years & over | 9 | 8 |
| TOTAL | 22 | 33 |

*Source:* Cazenave 1988: 16

The problems of the labour market in Guadeloupe, however, are not simply confined to unemployment. Perhaps as important is underemployment, which is a marginal phenomenon in metropolitan France (where it is confined to young people looking for a first job), but which in Guadeloupe 'represents a real sub-population ... it does not represent transitory situations but a structural group, squeezed between very high unemployment and an employment market whose resources are limited' (Basso and Tranap 1988: 12).

According to the 1986 employment census, 'one woman out of three compared to 20 per cent of males' is underemployed — underemployment being mainly manifested by part-time work where women predominate (G. Gautier 1986: 33). This means that the situation prevailing in 1980, when only 51.8 per cent of employed women compared to 68.3 per cent of men were in 'normal activity', i.e. working 40 hours a week and gaining at least the minimum wage, has not positively changed. As a consequence, many people continue to hold more than one job, a phenomenon called multiple employment or *polyvalence* in Guadeloupe. It is considered a tradition, especially for rural men who often shift from agriculture to fishing or other day labour jobs with the seasons. According to Gérard Gautier (1986: 34), a statistician from INSEE, 'in Guadeloupe 36 per cent of the men in underemployment have a secondary activity or many simultaneously, four times out of five in agriculture or fishery, compared to only 16 per cent of the women'.

### 'Inactive' Women, Invisible Work

Gautier's comment shows how far the particular kind of work undertaken by women outside the regular labour market remains invisible. He fails to acknowledge that, under the unequal sexual division of labour dominant in Guadeloupean society, most women have continual (though socially 'inferior') jobs in the domestic sphere, jobs they fulfil every day to maintain their homes, children and spouses and which are added to any other job they might hold outside their homes. When all the time spent at the work place, on the journey to work, taking and picking up children, doing last minute shopping and performing multiple household chores is added up, it is surprising that as many as 16 per cent of women still find time to seek a second formal job, even if driven by economic necessity. Though many women claim to teach their sons as well as their daughters to help out with household chores and take care of their own clothes, systematic observations and precise questioning on the subject show that, by and large, in Guadeloupe domestic work remains women's work (*c'est l'affaire des femmes!*).

Participation by Guadeloupean men is usually limited in time (Sunday morning breakfast) and scope (precise chores like putting out the rubbish, or expressions of parental authority like meeting their children's teachers). How individuals internalize cultural norms about the sexual division of labour becomes particularly obvious when daughters or females other than the mother are living in a household, or when, both spouses being on the labour market, a maid is hired. In these cases, the mother or wife's tasks can be considerably lightened. But it is the men, not the women, who are the real winners; with the moral pressure taken off them, they feel free to enjoy fully the privileges of spare time and rest.

On the other hand, the multiple small 'informal' jobs which many women do in addition to their main (formal or informal) occupation and which they perform inside or close to their home, are simply not taken into account, neither in economic statistics nor in people's minds; they are 'naturally' associated with household chores. This implicit assumption, added to the knowledge of how little money each small job provides, certainly explains in part the apparent indifference of the government to the phenomenon of the black economy (*travail noir*). It is also plausible that the government values this state of affairs more highly as a political security valve than as an eventual source of additional tax revenue. Thus today in Guadeloupe, and in the countryside in particular, there is a quite large female informal sector of work which is unaccounted for and which differs in scope, but not in nature, from the general situation in the Third World. If statistics on female jobs were based on empirical reality rather than on formal criteria, the profile of Guadeloupe's female workforce would be quite different, especially in the agriculture and service sectors.

Taken together, several factors (low wages in the informal sector, high underemployment and unemployment rates, a large pool of 'inactive' women willing to work, and a potential clientele made up mainly of civil servants or other employees who receive a 40 per cent income supplement) create a situation in Guadeloupe in which there is an important market for various female skills such as dressmaking, child care and certain types of housework (for example, washing, ironing and cleaning). Women willing to do these tasks do not hesitate to contact prospective customers personally.[19] It is not uncommon for middle-aged, uneducated rural women to accumulate five or six different small paid jobs in the same week, interspersing them with their own usual domestic activities. Such a work week might include doing someone else's cleaning, washing and ironing for one or two days a week, tending one's own garden for another day and then selling one's own and perhaps a neighbour's surplus vegetables on market days, performing the long process of making *boudin Creole* (blood sausage) and afterwards selling it at home or at the market place during the weekend (Dagenais 1988). Yet all these activities, which can easily total more than the regulation 40 work hours a week, might bring in barely enough money to assure daily subsistence for a family.

In the rural areas very few women are registered as *agricultrices* or *ouvrières agricoles*, and some of those who are conscious of the inequity of such a situation find it hard not to be able to write 'agricultural producer' (*agricultrice*) on the various government forms they must fill out when they have worked all their lives as such. In addition to the inadequacies of formal statistics for small scale and family agriculture and the general decline of this economic sector, the gradual disappearance of female jobs through the mechanization of agriculture and women's lack of access to land are equally important explanatory factors (Poirier and Dagenais 1986). Yet when a researcher expresses, as I have, the desire to know more about women's work in agriculture, she has no problem obtaining bona fide informants; many people recognize that their aunt or their mother 'has done farming all her life'. Subsistence agriculture remains largely a women's affair, but it also remains an important economic asset for many households, particularly in the countryside, but also for other family members now living in the city. Statisticians studying household consumption in Guadeloupe have no difficulty acknowledging their incapacity to find and include this 'home production and consumption' (*autoconsommation*) into their accounts. It remains for them to acknowledge also that it is mainly women who accomplish this 'production originating from agriculture, animal husbandry, fishing or hunting' (Diman-Antenor 1988: 14).[20]

## All for the Sake of Love

Guadeloupean women themselves sometimes have difficulty identifying their unpaid domestic activities as real work. They may easily regard sewing for their family during their evening and weekend 'free time' as leisure, yet this is what many women are employed to do; the same point holds for the baby sitting many so-called 'inactive' women perform to help a daughter, neighbour or sister in the labour market, or for the work women often do to help a child's or spouse's small business.

In fact, in Guadeloupe, mainly women tend the small family bars, businesses, or tiny grocery and snack shops known as *lolos*; as saleswomen, barmaids, secretaries and accountants, these women often single-handedly ensure their smooth running and profitability. Some women own their own *lolos*, but most are owned by men who entrust their daily management to their wives or concubines. However, unless the male 'provider' gives his spouse a salary as a family assistant, the economic contribution of these small business women remains invisible and they, like all 'housewives', remain most vulnerable economically if the couple separates.

One way of assessing the specificity of women's domestic work is to use statistics on household equipment and lodgings as indicators of their working conditions; in the most literal sense, it is also a way of beginning where women are in their daily lives. In doing so, one realizes that if the conditions of domestic work in Guadeloupe are undeniably better than in many other Caribbean territories, they are not as favourable as they look from general statistics and, in the *département* itself, they differ according to social class and location. For example, while practically all housing in Pointe-à-Pitre has running water, toilets and a bath or shower, the situation is different in the rest of the *département*. At the time of the 1982 census, 51 per cent of all main residences in Guadeloupe possessed all three conveniences cited above. But the percentages were much lower (38.8, 28.4 and 26.2 per cent respectively) among unemployed persons, agricultural producers and agricultural workers. Similarly, no matter what domestic appliances are considered, it is always in the households of small farmers and hired hands and in the socio-professional categories where women are the most numerous that the conditions of comfort and of household equipment are the worst. The 1984/5 budget inquiry[21] shows that less than a third of these households owned a washing machine and only two out of five, compared to half the general population, had a telephone (Diman-Antenor 1988a: 39-40).

For the women concerned these percentages are no abstraction; a house without running water and toilet means the drudgery of supplying water several times a day from the nearest public fountain and the unpleasant chore of emptying the chamber pot every morning; it means that one must ensure the hygiene of the whole family by using the disposable water as rationally as possible. No running water or electricity also means washing by hand several times a week, especially if there are young children, and ironing with heavy flat irons. It also means the absence of television to keep children occupied on their return from school and to replace going to the cinema, an outing which in any event many cannot afford. The case of domestic workers is particularly striking. The women who spend their working days cleaning other people's homes are themselves badly housed: in 1982 over 40 per cent of them lived in one or two rooms, 44 per cent lived in housing without running water and approximately one third were without electricity; they have few household appliances to help accomplish their own domestic chores and if they themselves are household heads the situation is even worse. Present-day Guadeloupe is organized in such a way that domestic work is relegated to a particular group of women — the most economically and socially disadvantaged. For this reason the question of men's participation in household work cannot be looked at in the same manner as elsewhere. It is a cruel irony that women in Guadeloupe continue to be called 'queens of the home' (*les reines du foyer*).

We have seen that, despite the work they accomplish, Guadeloupean women have very little social power. In fact a large part of their economic contribution is not even recognized. Keeping in mind our same minimal definition of power and starting out as before from the daily experiences of women, I would like now to consider their contribution in the field of reproduction, examining women from the viewpoint of motherhood and the male/female relationships which undergird it. But first I would like to outline the statistical context within which to place these social relationships.

## Reproduction & Men/Women Relationships

*From 'Natural Fertility' to 'Birth Control'*
Having been the objects of Malthusian angst during the 'demographic explosion' from the 1930s to the mid-1960s, when the annual number of births per year more than doubled, in the 1980s Guadeloupean women began to arouse contrary concerns.[22] From 35 per 1000 (1960-4) the crude birth-rate dropped to less than 20 per 1000,[23] and the annual increase in population growth dropped from 3 per cent (1954-60), a rate which would have doubled the population in 23 years, to 0.2 per cent (1974-82), a phenomenon which occurred despite a parallel sharp reduction in the child mortality rate (from 46.8 per 1000 in 1970 to 19.5 per 1000 in 1981) (Guengant 1983; Gautier 1986a). In this 20 year period the average number of children born per woman between the ages of 15 and 49 dropped from nearly six (5.8) in 1960-4 to close to five (4.6) ten years later to below three (2.6) in 1980-3 (Gautier 1986a: 30). However, a more realistic portrait of women's fertility can be obtained from the Guadeloupean Fertility Study of 1975 done with a representative sampling of the population. This study reveals that the average number of children born per woman (15 to 49 years of age) was 4.8, but it also shows that 30 per cent of the women at the end of their fertility cycle (40 to 49 years old) had had

nine or more children, 64 per cent of them had had five or more, 20 per cent had three or four, and less than 10 per cent were childless.

To complete this paradoxical demographic picture, what is perhaps more important to make clear from a feminist point of view is the fact that the sharp reduction in the fertility and birth-rates happened during a period when, due to the slowing down of the exodus of young Guadeloupeans to the metropole and the important, though numerically smaller, flow of return migrants,[24] the percentage of women of reproductive age living in the *département* increased significantly from 36 per cent in 1970 to 51 per cent in 1985 (Gautier 1987a: 3).[25]

As can be seen, birth and fertility rates do not always follow demographers predictions; motherhood is a cultural and psycho-social phenomenon determined by the dynamics of the relationships between women and men (somewhat more complex than what the demographers call 'the dynamics of unions') and by the economic and socio-cultural factors affecting the life trajectories of women. In Guadeloupe, as we have seen, the labour market presents serious difficulties for women. On the one hand, high levels of unemployment and underemployment practically constitute an invitation for young people to emigrate, while on the other hand the economic insecurity generated by such a situation is hardly an incentive for women to have large families. Moreover, like their counterparts elsewhere in the world, Guadeloupean women in employment are becoming less and less willing to renounce working for pay and the economic autonomy it brings (limited though it may be) to bear large numbers of children. Hence, despite extensive social programmes, the proportion of women heads of households in the labour market in 1982 (50.3 per cent) is higher than that of the women who are spouses of heads of households (45.8 per cent).

Moreover, in my view, the rapid change in the fertility of Guadeloupean women is an illustration of how women behave when effective birth control methods are put at their disposal. Results from the Guadeloupe Fertility Survey show that two-fifths of women aged 45 years and over would have preferred to have had fewer children (Charbit and Leridon 1980: 172). This clearly demonstrates that in the past many births were unwanted. Paola Tabet reminds us that reproduction is the cornerstone of gender relations. There is no 'natural fertility' and the notion of women's fertility control[26] should include, not only pressures to limit fertility, but also pressures (collective and individual) to reproduce (Tabet 1985). Given the sexual division of labour in society and among couples, and given also in Guadeloupe the high proportion of women-headed households, the time cost of children is very 'real for the wife; hence when she takes charge of the fertility decision, family size is likely to fall' (Robinson 1987: 323). Otherwise why would Guadeloupean women, usually considered as the 'traditional element' in society and often blamed for their supposed 'submissiveness' to tradition, have so spontaneously adopted new methods of birth control such as the pill and the IUD?

*Contraceptive Practices*

The pill and IUD, however, are the means rather than the causes of the movement toward a lowered birth-rate. As Cases, Guengant and Lauret (1980: 46) note, this general tendency had already started in Guadeloupe when the first family planning centres opened in 1964. One can therefore conclude that the already existing wish of women to control their pregnancies favoured the introduction of these centres. Women themselves played an important role in creating the Guadeloupe Family Planning Association (*Maternité Consciente*) and in assuring the spread of birth-control information throughout the population. The first 'volunteers' to go from door-to-door contacting women at home, meeting them as often as possible in the absence of men, were often mothers who had decided, with or without the agreement of their spouses, to have no more children. At the time, these women needed considerable courage and determination to withstand the wrath of the Roman Catholic Church, the threats from some of their clients' spouses and all the gibes directed against them by public opinion.

Nevertheless, the use of modern contraception should not be overly emphasized, for, at the time of the 1975 Fertility Survey, only 30 per cent of women between the ages of 15 and 49 were using contraceptive methods and, among them, only 40 per cent were using either the pill, the IUD or the condom. This means that to avoid unwanted births, many Guadeloupean women continue to rely on rather uncertain methods like Ogino, showers, jellies, coitus interruptus, or local recipes to make a child 'pass by'. The condom and coitus interruptus, depending on men's willingness and control, have decreased in popularity in favour of the pill and IUD, which can be used without the partner's knowledge. On the other hand, local abortion recipes are often dangerous to the health of women, as shown in several of the testimonies collected by France Alibar and Pierrette Lembeye-Boy (1981: 162-3). It is not surprising, then, that legal abortions are numerous. From a study of a sample of doctors, Jean-Pierre Guengant (1982: 38-43) estimates that about 2400 voluntary terminations took place in Guadeloupe in 1979 alone, a figure six times greater than the number, similarly estimated, for the period 1965-9 and corresponding to a rate of 40 abortions for every 100 live births. In addition, in 1980 three out of five women aged 40 years and over (58 per cent) had already been sterilized, which is an indication of how far Guadeloupean women have been willing to go to avoid unwanted pregnancies.

It is evident that all these changes are not only individual but also cultural. Yves Charbit, a French demographer who has been studying the region for over 15 years, sees them as 'the sign of a break with deeply held values', for 'everybody knows that in the Antillean context, children are considered as gifts of God' (Charbit 1987: 174). Without disputing this interpretation, I think it is more likely that Caribbean women often accepted unwanted children because they thought it was God's will, or their destiny, and there was not much they could do about it anyway. One must also not forget that many of these 'gifts from heaven' are not raised by their biological mothers. Guadeloupean authors Albert Flagie (1982) and Dany Ducosson (1983) stress how adolescent single mothers, in particular, entrust the rearing of their children to their families, even though they might resume the responsibility a few years later. Although this widespread custom does not necessarily mean that a child is deprived of care and affection, it is still a more or less disguised form of abandonment, which calls into question the women's apparent acceptance of an unwanted child.

In addition, in the Caribbean context, it is a euphemism to say that children are entrusted for their upbringing to their mother's or father's family, for it is primarily the grandmothers and eventually the other women of the household (older sister, aunt) who undertake this responsibility. There has never been an in-depth study of these generous grandmothers and we do not know how they really cope with their resumptions of motherhood. Praise of 'Guadeloupean mothers' and the 'magnificent stereotype into which they have been confined' (Alibar and Lembeye-Boy 1981, I: 28), associated with the overall insistence of authors of all allegiances on matrifocality (if not matriarchy), should not make us forget the real flesh and blood women who, as we have seen, often had to accept more childbirths than they would have wished and who also often had to rear them alone.

*Single Mothers and Women Heads of Households*

A third of Guadeloupean households (compared to a fifth in France) are headed by women, many of whom live alone, but to get a clearer picture of the burden of motherhood, one has to look at the 65,000 or so households with children. Among these households, 20 per cent are mono-parental, of which 90 per cent are headed by women; among the 80 per cent bi-parental households one out of ten is built around a concubine couple. However, there are more women 'exposed to the risk of pregnancy', as demographers would say, than shown by such civil status data. There are in fact two times more unmarried women in unions with a 'friend' without cohabitation than there are in concubinage, both types accounting for about 40 per cent of the women in all unions (married, concubinage or 'friend'), a phenomenon which largely explains the 50 per cent or so 'illegitimate' birth-rate. Among the mothers, 'isolated parents', i.e. those who rear their children alone, have on average as many dependants (3 or 4) as couples and close to a third of them even have five or more. According to the 1975 Fertility Survey, half the women of reproductive age were under 20 at the time of their first union, and 30 per cent were under 18. Among 15 to 19 year-old Guadeloupean girls, 78 per cent had never been in a sexual union, but about 5 per cent were married or in concubinage and 15.8 per cent were involved in a relationship with a so-called 'friend'. Of all these young women 6.2 per cent had children and, among them, about one-fifth had two or more (Charbit and Leridon 1980: 42-74). In fact, while the fertility of women over 20 has decreased markedly, teenage pregnancies remain about the same, translating into a birth-rate of about 60 per 1000 for this age group (Guengant 1983).

However, these statistics only partially reflect the situation of teenagers; many more girls get pregnant but they seek abortions.[27] More frequent childbirths and abortions are the main differences between the sexual behaviour of Guadeloupean teenagers and their counterparts in France and other Western countries, where first sexual relations occur at about the same age, i.e. between 16 and 16.5 years of age. The situation in Guadeloupe needs further analysis. Far from being positively viewed, Guadeloupean teenage mothers are often portrayed as compulsive and immature by local psychologists, psychiatrists, medical doctors, social workers, sociologists and statisticians, whose discourses manifest profound Freudian and Lacanian influences. In Guadeloupe, psychoanalytic explanations of family life, child behaviour and male/female relationships are common and, surprisingly, even among the most severe critics of ethnocentric foreign theories. Also widespread are explanations based on a supposedly collective Guadeloupean mentality of passivity and economic dependency. Without denying the unconscious and psychological dimensions of sexual behaviour, it seems as appropriate (if not more so) to explain the behaviour of teenagers and mothers from the vantage point of their material life conditions.

It is not by coincidence that the highest levels of fertility and the highest proportions of women raising their children alone in the Caribbean are always found among women who are the least educated and the most economically deprived (see Charbit 1987; Charbit and Leridon 1980). These are the persons whose job options are the most restricted and for whom the possibilities of financial autonomy are least certain. As Carol Susan Vance (1979: 254) reminds us at the end of her study of female employment and fertility in Barbados, 'the introduction of birth control does not necessarily alter reproductive decisions, although it has the potential to do so. ... Although contraception provides the technology for women to avoid children from new partners, it has not altered their economic options or established a new power base which would permit or encourage them to make this choice.'

Consequently, given the amount of prestige associated with being a mother in Caribbean societies, for many women motherhood might present itself as a socially acceptable way (and the one with least potential loss) of securing a marriage or, more simply, of maintaining an alliance with a man. Such a strategy is especially inviting to teenagers, for whom motherhood also constitutes the passage to adulthood. Strategically then, Vance argues (1979: 253), for economically deprived women, motherhood may function:

> as a choice amid very limited and constrained options, akin to a lottery. Some will win, and each woman takes a chance that this strategy will succeed for her, despite abundant evidence that it fails for many. Women's evaluations of strategies at hand probably emphasize short-term consequences and thus compare the strategy of supporting oneself vs receiving supplementary income from a ... partner.

In the case of teenagers, however, the absence of adequate sexual and contraceptive information is clearly an important factor. There is no systematic sex education programme in Guadeloupean schools and many mothers find it difficult to talk about the subject with their daughters. As a result, piecemeal information is gathered from friends and classmates at school, or from magazines and romantic novels. Teenage responses to anonymous questionnaires answered at the beginning of some sex information classes, which the CGIEF[28] was asked to organize in several Guadeloupean schools, confirmed that many young people of both sexes were ignorant about the female reproductive cycle and were full of fears and prejudices about menstruation and male impotence. The bravado of some of the youth in Guadeloupe, as elsewhere, who speak freely about sex, the pill and other related subjects, may well conceal real ignorance about conception and contraception.

## Men/Women Relationships

However important they are, economic factors and adolescence cannot in themselves account for the fact that in the two highest socio-professional categories 44.1 and 38.5 per cent of working mothers are raising their children alone (Charbit 1987: 87). These apparently contradictory data have to be situated within the context of men/women relationships in Guadeloupe, which are largely antagonistic. Such antagonism is of course present in any patriarchal society, but in Guadeloupe, as in the rest of the Caribbean, it is well imbedded in the cultural representations of gender relations and, as such, is a highly complex subject to study.

It is a subject that does not lend itself to objective quantitative inquiries or clear general declarations; directed qualitative research is no easier to realize, for people's sensitivities on this subject have to be respected. Moreover men, in particular, generally resent political analyses of gender relations, even though many of them speak quite freely about polygamy, sexuality, violence, or jealousy. What happened to *Le Couteau seul ... La Condition féminine en Guadeloupe*, a book co-authored by France Alibar, a Guadeloupean, and Pierrette Lembeye-Boy, a metropolitan who had been settled in Guadeloupe for many years at the time, is a good illustration of how sanctions are imposed on 'transgressors'. Intellectuals accused the authors of being unscientific because they used sociological data derived from in-depth interviews with volunteer women and because they did not assume that poverty was the key causal factor. The leftists, who are mainly responsible for such family problems in Guadeloupe (helped by the French state and women on social security) and not Guadeloupean men, called them traitors to the cause of independence. Many others in the general public accused them of having exaggerated the 'dramatic' side of men/women relations by presenting a 'biased' picture stemming from the deliberate selection of women informants who all had problems. Feminist researchers and Guadeloupean women considered the two volume book a useful document and an example of successful non-academic research,[29] but, as noted previously, the feminist opinion remains very marginal in Guadeloupe today.

Even so, testimonies collected in 1984 through in-depth interviews with over 150 lower and middle-class women and from over 30 men show that the private oppression of women has not disappeared. Double standards still obtain in education, sexuality and the freedom of movement. 'Lock up your hens, the roosters are out' is how women as well as men often refer to just such a double standard. Mothers and fathers readily admit that they control their daughters closely but that 'with boys it is different'. For girls the restriction of movement and of encounters with boys takes the place of sex education, while for boys it is assumed that as soon as they become sexually active they know what there is to know. Most men interviewed in 1988 freely admitted that they never used a condom with any woman. Either they considered that it was their partner's responsibility to use contraceptives, or, as some said, they undertook their responsibility by paying for an abortion when a partner told them she was pregnant. Interestingly, preliminary indications from 1988 interviews seem to suggest that the threat of AIDS is prompting some mothers to encourage their teenage children to use condoms.

If women are not simply the passive victims of male polygamous behaviour and relations between the sexes constitute a dynamic involving actions and interactions, why should Guadeloupean men continue to boast about their virility by having multiple and simultaneous sexual unions? Though there are also women who have multiple unions and become involved with several men, there is a major difference between the two practices: for women these are successive unions; rarely are they involved with more than one partner at a time, whereas men frequently have one or more women 'outside' at the same time as a wife or concubine 'inside' at home. Such male behaviour is considered normal, natural and justified as such, especially by men,[30] on the basis of a so-called uncontrollable male sexual instinct and/or of a psychological heritage from slavery (Dagenais 1988). In fact many women seem more or less to expect such behaviour from men and often describe it with a certain fatality — 'what can a woman do about it?'

This does not mean, however, that women do not suffer from this double standard. While men can be quite open about their 'sexual adventures', especially with their male friends, women are expected to act as if they were indifferent to the whole situation, in private as well as in public. Consequently, 'to keep their dignity' they 'close their eyes'. As one 50 year-old rural woman explained: 'in the beginning I used to revolt, to shout; then I became very depressed'. Today she no longer reacts, but feels 'sad and hopeless'. Men usually expect their wives to act 'as if they did not know'; they particularly resent any manifestation of 'jealousy' and when women do show it, the men do not hesitate to threaten to leave or resort to physical 'punishment'.[31] In fact, questions from a wife or concubine about their behaviour after they had spent a night out or come in late frequently serve as a catalyst for wife beating. Interviews with women suggest that male threats to leave the house are effective, particularly with women who have young children and are economically dependent on their man ('Where could I go? I have no place to go, no money'). One does not need to be a psychologist to understand how destructive such situations can be to a woman's self esteem.[32] The situation is made worse because the double standard of sexual behaviour makes it impossible for women to retaliate in similar vein (i.e. to go out with other men or take a lover). Neither the husband, extended family nor general public would ever tolerate such behaviour from women.

### An Unintentional Attack on the Power of Men by the State

Only in 1975 were the metropolitan 'orphan' and 'single parent' allowances extended to unemployed women raising children on their own in overseas French *départements*. Before then, it was easy for a man, even if he were not rich, to use his economic contribution, modest and sporadic as it may have been, to obtain the sexual and domestic services of a woman. Today, orphan and family allowances place women in a better position to 'negotiate' with men; moreover, these benefits can modify considerably the rules of the game when a couple breaks up. For example, if a man ceases to provide for the needs of his children, economic security for the woman no longer consists of desperately holding onto him or of immediately beginning to search for another provider, which always involves the risk of a new pregnancy. It is not the presence but rather the absence of a man which confers eligibility on a woman for 'orphan' and 'single parent' allowances. It is not difficult to imagine the contribution this social policy is making to the individuals concerned, not only in their male/female relationships, but also in the way in which male and female roles in the family unit are collectively represented.

The introduction of the single parent allowance, which Alibar and Lembeye-Boy regard as a sophism, has outraged certain strands of public opinion in Guadeloupe, which generally supports one or other of two derogatory views about it and the women who receive it. On the one hand, are those who hold that a very large number of women benefit from these allowances. In fact, only about 15 per cent of the family units receive family allowances (see A. Gautier 1986).[33] Women are being accused of symbolically and in fact throwing out their men in order to become eligible for the allowance, of preventing men from legally recognizing their children and, even, of conceiving babies for the sole purpose of benefiting from the allowance. On the other hand, it is sometimes alleged that these women receive the benefits not for their children, but to support their 'friend' so that he can do nothing. They are accused of using their family allowances to buy cars or other luxurious gifts for their men. In fact critics of the allowance can provide no end of examples of how the system is being abused.

Either way, it is the women who are blamed and it is their sexuality that the critics feel should be brought under control. No attempt is made to understand why some women might need to take the desperate measure of conceiving babies and living off the state in order to survive economically. Nor is it taken into account that for most of these beneficiaries the allowances provide only a temporary solution, but none the less one that could well enable at least some of them to escape the harassments of a violent or drunken partner. Even if the state's action in this matter is coloured by political opportunism, given the difficult situation in the labour market for women, there is no legitimate reason why women should be denigrated when they are acting in a way designed to give their children better chances in life. No derogatory references are ever made to men and their sexual responsibilities. Nothing prevents a man who might feel sexually exploited from leaving the woman in question or from simply using a condom. Nothing obliges men, either, to accept the gifts they label as immoral. In fact, Guadeloupean men did not wait until 1975 and the 'single woman' allowance to marginalize themselves from women and the family unit.

In the Caribbean literature, matrifocality, the instability of couples and the large numbers of 'illegitimate' children are often thought to result from the depressed economic situation, with its high levels of unemployment and underemployment and the consequent impossibility of many of the less privileged males to provide for the needs of their families. In addition to being paternalistic, this thesis is ethnocentric and moralistic, two biases readily recognized today by the very scholars — the anthropologists — who did a great deal to disseminate the theory in the first place. But such reasoning is also sexist, which is far less readily admitted. Not only does it implicitly presume that the economic responsibility of a family should be mainly or solely the duty of a man, but in putting emphasis on the poverty of men when women are even poorer, it practically amounts to excusing men collectively for their lack of individual responsibility.

## Conclusion

The Guadeloupean women who have emerged from this brief examination of their situation are a far cry from the mythical 'super woman' ideal and Guadeloupe is far from being a 'matriarchal society'. Guadeloupean women do not participate in the social power structure and do not have the wherewithal to control or even influence decisions that directly affect them (such as abortion and contraception). Their specific economic contributions are mainly accomplished in and associated with the domestic sphere and, as such, they remain as invisible in popular gender representations as they do in the national accounting balance sheet. Given the actual levels of unemployment and underemployment and given the subordinate position of those sectors of the economy employing large numbers of females, one cannot foresee the future being any different from the present for young women. Since the power of women is not increasing significantly, it is probable that the most impoverished of them will continue for some time to be dependent on the state in order to escape being dependent on men. Additionally, the prestige now associated with motherhood might be seriously attenuated by the prejudices currently surrounding the special family allowances for single parent women. No matter what happens, any attempt to analyse social and economic changes and the position of women must always take sexual politics into account. That being so, this chapter will have been worth writing if it leaves the reader with a more balanced and less glamourous view of Guadeloupe's reality and the daily existence of Guadeloupean women.

## Notes

1  *Sucre noir* was produced in 1987 by Michel Regnier of the National Film Board of Canada. It provoked interesting reactions in Quebec, such as spontaneous movements to boycott the Dominican Republic as a main winter tourist destination.
2  Guadeloupe's sister island, Martinique, has a similar socio-economic profile, but with slightly higher wealth and educational indices and lower birth and fertility rates. However, since Guadeloupe is less well known and since there are sufficient differences in the composition between the two populations, I will treat the two *départements* separately. Moreover, Martinicans and Guadeloupeans prefer to affirm their separate identities.
3  Concrete examples of collaboration in feminist research are the policy oriented Women in the Caribbean Project (WICP) (1979-1982) developed by the Institute of Social and Economic Research (ISER) of the University of the West Indies under the coordination of Joycelin Massiah (see *Social and Economic Studies*, 35 (2 and 3) 1986) and the different ongoing projects (on agriculture, free zones, history, poetry) of the Caribbean Association for Feminist Research and Action (CAFRA). For information on CAFRA's projects and activities, see *CAFRA News*, its quarterly newsletter published in Tunapuna, Trinidad.

4   My own language limitations keep me from being categorical about intellectual communication between the French and Spanish islands, though it appears to me to be the same as between the French and English territories. However, feminists from Spanish and English-speaking islands seem to have closer contacts, but the extent of the movement is not yet obvious to a foreign observer.

5   In my view, this denigration, together with the implicit accusations of treason being levelled against 'foreign' feminist ideas by leftist male intellectuals, very effectively squashed any interest in women's studies in Guadeloupe and maintained a taboo among Guadeloupean women against the use of the word feminism. Better inter-island and inter-linguistic communications during the Decade for Women might have fostered more feminist research and action in the French territories. Though the absence of a social science faculty at the Université des Antilles et de la Guyane is an inhibiting factor and though the number of potential feminist researchers is necessarily limited by demography, there is no doubt in my mind that a courageous book like France Alibar and Pierrette Lembeye-Boy's *Le couteau seul* (1981) could have served as a departure point for more in-depth scientific research from a woman's point of view.

6   This comprises two successive research projects entitled *Condition féminine en Guadeloupe* and *Travail et fecondité dans la Caraïbe: Guadeloupe, Haiti et Trinidad.* They are interdisciplinary studies with myself as coordinator and the demographers Joel Gregory and Victor Piche from Montreal University acting as co-researchers; demographers Jean Poirier, Ghislaine Neil and anthropologist Danielle Leveille were our research assistants; anthropology and sociology student auxiliaries were recruited in Quebec, Guadeloupe and Trinidad. For obvious reasons fieldwork in Haiti has had to be delayed. More data on Guadeloupe from these two projects can be found in Dagenais and Poirier 1985; Dagenais 1984, 1988, 1988a, 1988c; Poirier and Dagenais 1986; Poirier, Dagenais and Gregory 1986.

7   I am not referring here to the totally artificial indexes such as GNP and GDP over which there is a general agreement, but to the sectoral statistics usually broken down by sex. Looking at statistics to answer questions pertaining to women also permits the researcher to identify areas where information is lacking (Dagenais 1988a and 1988b).

8   For a detailed physical and social geographical presentation of Guadeloupe, see the in-depth study in two volumes (and over 1100 pages) by geographer Guy Lasserre (1981) and his beautiful atlas, *La Guadeloupe* (1982).

9   Local left-wing political parties and independence movements have shown little concern for women's problems and their discussions about what social programmes might best benefit the poorest women are consequently rather muddled. There are, however, some well known socialist and communist militant women involved in what could be called reformist feminist groups, with the Communist Party's Union des Femmes Guadeloupéennes being particularly active and outspoken.

10  One can only estimate the proportions of the different ethnic groups in the Guadeloupean population, for (unlike the Trinidad & Tobago census) none of the official documents or statistics contain any reference to ethnicity. Judging from the generally darker complexions of the overall population it seems that there are fewer 'mulattoes' in Guadeloupe than in Martinique; the percentage of the 'dominant' Creole white minority has been estimated at 1-2 per cent and it is believed that about 25,000 people are of Indian descent. But, considering the patronyms appearing on electoral lists and his personal knowledge, a local Indian politician estimates their numbers between 40,000 and 50,000, i.e. between 12 and 15 per cent of the population (Moutoussamy 1987: 16). There are also two other minorities, namely the well-integrated Syrian-Lebanese community which specializes in commerce and the highly mobile white metropolitans, consisting mostly of public servants, teachers, military personnel and private sector managers and executives who come to Guadeloupe to work for short or long periods.

11  It has almost become a cliché among statisticians and economists to describe Guadeloupe (and Martinique) as a small island of prosperity in a region of great poverty.

12  This shows that Guadeloupeans have over the years developed culinary tastes very similar to those of people in the metropole. Today, one can find in Guadeloupe's supermarkets almost anything available in Parisian stores; the main impediments to a European lifestyle are the prices.

13  In 1982, the time of the last general census, the proportion of women in the population of Pointe-à-Pitre did not exceed 56 per cent and at Basse-Terre, the capital, it was just below 54 per cent, both percentages having dropped 1 per cent between the last two censuses (1974 and 1982).

14  For analyses of the situations in Quebec, Montreal and Paris, see the articles by Andrée Fortin, Anne-Marie Seguin and Paul Villeneuve, Damaris Rose, Jeanne Fagnani and Chantal Balley in 'Espaces et Femmes', special number of *Cahiers de géographie du Quebec*, 31 (83) September 1987.

15  Death and injury statistics from car accidents are quite high in Guadeloupe; the powerful new cars and very good highway system provide strong temptations to drive fast. But the topography also has to be taken into account, especially along the western coast and in the centre of mountainous Basse-Terre island, where sharp curves, steep hills and narrow roads often make bus travel a risky adventure in the relatively old vehicles working this region. For example, on the Côte-sous-le-Vent Caribbean Sea coast, there are many inland mountain roads and lanes, off the tourist track and too narrow for two cars to pass but where, surprisingly, local buses make regular runs several times a day.

16  Dagenais and Poirier (1985) base the categorization on social recognition (visibility) and the relations of production, i.e. whether the woman is subject or not to exploitation.

17  Since irrigation was started on the Côte-sous-le-Vent there has been a significant increase in vegetable production; Basse-Terre's market is livelier, its stands are more colourful and attractive and its vegetables more abundant. In the summer of 1984, for the first time I saw two men behind stalls. One explained that he was simply accompanying his mother who had come with her produce in his pick-up; the other was so busy improving the appearance of his stand, already the largest and most attractive, that I simply observed his behaviour. Obviously, such men are still few in number but one cannot help but wonder if this small commercial activity could attract more men in the future, now that there are more and better quality products to sell.

18  Some women upon their return from the metropole also use these advertisements; it is obvious by the way they are written that they consider their metropolitan work experience as an asset. Their reasoning is correct, for many employers in Guadeloupe believe that they get better quality work from employees who have previously worked in France.

19 I myself have often been offered such services by local women who assumed that I was a metropolitan; elsewhere, I have analysed the ambiguities in situations of this kind (Dagenais 1985).

20 Hunting is necessarily a marginal activity in Guadeloupe, for there are no big game and very few small wild animals to hunt. Fishing is marginal too, but more frequent, especially among men living in coastal communities. However, most fishermen cannot invest in a boat big and solid enough to go far enough from the coast for the operation to be economically profitable in the long run.

21 The first results of the 1984/5 budget inquiry for Guadeloupe, Martinique and French Guiana came out in September 1988; so far the available statistics have only been broken down into broad categories and still need to be analysed sociologically.

22 Ironically, the same demographers now seem worried about over-population, as witnessed by the title of an article by Gérard Gautier (1987), 'Guadeloupe, An 2000: Surpopulation?' The author bases his question on a set of hypotheses which take into account the fact that while the number of deaths will not increase significantly, the cohort of women born during the 1965-75 demographic explosion will soon reach childbearing age. He compares a projection of 365,000 inhabitants in Guadeloupe for the year 2000 with the 332,200 enumerated in 1985. Fortunately he also has the prudence to declare that 'a statistician is not a futurologist' and cannot forecast future social changes.

23 It took 50 years for European countries to reach this birth-rate level at the beginning of the twentieth century (Guengant 1983; Gautier 1986a).

24 The migration of 100,000 youth of both sexes to the metropole between 1960 and 1980 has certainly been an important factor in lowering the birth-rate in Guadeloupe. Guengant estimates that 41,000 births were avoided in Guadeloupe by this population transfer. However, he is careful to note that this estimate is greater than the actual number of registered births (32,500) by Guadeloupean women living in the metropole during the same period (Guengant 1983: 38). The discrepancy seems to be accounted for by the fact that, on the one hand, a considerable number of the women migrants who left to work in the metropole were single and better educated than average and, on the other hand, a variety of changes in the life styles of the migrating couples may have inhibited or modified their desire to have children. For a start, for parents who did not want to send their children back to a grandmother in Guadeloupe, as a certain number did, baby-sitting costs were higher and more complicated to organize in the metropole.

25 It is difficult to understand why such a paradox has not also struck the numerous demographers and analysts working on Guadeloupe, but I have yet to see such a link made in their publications.

26 The continuing use of the apparently neutral terms 'fertility' and 'birth control' helps to obscure the fact that it is women's fertility and not that of males that is at stake and that it is still women who bear almost all the responsibility for contraception. Very few demographic and sociological/anthropological studies have ever been made on male fertility and male attitudes towards these topics. In the Caribbean region, one can cite studies by Abdullah 1973; Allman et al. n.d.; Dann 1987 and Dagenais 1988.

27 It is relatively easy for adolescent girls to get an abortion without the knowledge of their parents and at an affordable price; there seems to be in circulation a list of doctors who are quite willing to earn a little 'extra' money on the side.

28 Centre guadeloupéen d'information et d'education familiale. In addition to information and education, the CGIEF is authorized to give psychosocial pre-abortion counselling to women, as required by French law.

29 The two authors are not professional researchers, but high-school teachers. The book originated from a desire expressed in a women's discussion group to get women from different milieux to speak of their daily lives. Though the title refers to a broader reality than that actually covered and though at some point the authors claim that the testimonies presented in the book are generally representative of male/female relationships in Guadeloupe, the 60 detailed life histories none the less provide good social insights into the antagonistic relationships in which many Guadeloupean women are involved. As French ethnologist Jeanne Favret-Saada (1986: 103) notes, it is not that Alibar and Lembeye-Boy selected women for whom male/female relations presented problems, but that the male/female relations were a problem for all the women who were interviewed; the nuance is important.

30 So normal that, at a meeting held in December 1978 at the Psychiatric Hospital in St Claude, entitled 'Sexuality: Auto-experiences and Conclusion: To be 16 Years Old in Guadeloupe' (cited in Alibar and Lembeye-Boy 1981, II: 9), a well known populist local politician declared, 'Be faithful — to all your loves'; 'A man's heart is like a cathedral: there is the main altar and lateral chapels. Place your wife in the main altar and frequently replace the female saints of the lateral chapels by other female saints.'

31 The men in our exploratory research who admit to having been physically violent with a woman or women in their past usually put the blame on the woman for having pushed them to it by her jealousy; they had to punish her (Dagenais 1988).

32 This type of sexual behaviour might also provoke animosity and antagonism between men. After all, how can a man have full confidence in a friend when he knows he has seduced the wife of another one? (Dagenais 1988).

33 This percentage comes from the Caisse des Allocations Familiales de la Guadeloupe's 1982 report and is cited by Arlette Gautier in an unpublished working paper.


## References

Abdullah, Norma (1973) *Fertility and Family Planning among Men in Trinidad and Tobago*. St Augustine, Trinidad: University of the West Indies, Institute of Social and Economic Research

Albertini, Jean-Marie (1974) *La fausse croissance*. Montreal: Centre for Caribbean Research

Alibar, France and Pierrette Lembeye-Boy (1981) *Le couteau seul: La condition féminine aux Antilles*. 2 vols, Paris: Éditions caribéennes and Agence de coopération culturelle et technique

Allman, James, Ginette Desse and Antonio Rival (n.d.) 'Condom Use in Haiti'. Unpublished document

Armet, Auguste (1983) 'Mal développement et dépendance sanitaire et sociale.' *Carbet*, (1) 35-61

Bangou, Jacques, Marie-Line Lambourdière et al. (1988) 'Intervention en péri-natalité dans un quartier défavorisé: l'experience de Boissard'. Paper presented at the Annual meeting of the Caribbean Studies Association, Pointe-à-Pitre, May

Basso, C. and A. Tranap (1988) 'Le monde du travail: Le tertiaire plus avant'. *Antiane eco*, 7 (July) 10-13

Bebel-Gisler, Dany (1976) *La langue créole, force jugulée*. Paris: L'Harmattan and Montreal: Nouvelle Optique

——— (1985) *Les enfants de la Guadeloupe*. Paris: L'Harmattan

Buffon, Alain (1982) 'Transferts et déséquilibres de croissance: Le cas de la Guadeloupe.' *CARE*, 9 (April) 13-31

Cases, C., J-P Guengant and E. Lauret (1980) *L'évolution démographique et la situation en 1979*. Paris: INSEE-SIRAG

Cazenave, Jacques (1986) 'Avoir 20 ans dans les années 80.' *Antiane eco*, 1 (November) 16-19

——— (1988) 'Le chiffrage du chomage.' *Antiane eco*, 7 (July) 16-19

Cazenave, Jacques and Jean-Paul Briand (1986) 'Aspects du monde éducatif.' *Données sociales, INSEE*, (11) 96-116

Charbit, Yves (1987) *Famille et nuptialité dans la Caraïbe*. Paris: Presses universitaires de France (Cahiers de l'INED no 114)

Charbit, Yves and Henri Leridon (1980) *Transition démographique et modernisation en Guadeloupe et en Martinique*. Paris: Presses universitaires de France (Cahiers de l'INED no 89)

Conseil Economique et Social (CES) (1987) *La situation économique et les conditions du développement des départements d'outre-mer*. Official journal of the French Republic, 9-10 November

Dagenais, Huguette (1984) 'L'Apport méconnu des femmes à la vie économique et sociale aux Antilles: Le cas de la Guadeloupe'. *Anthropologie et sociétés*, 8 (2) 170-87

——— (1985) 'Une éxperience humaine complète: La recherche sur le terrain en Guadeloupe'. In Serge Genest (ed.) *La passion de l'échange: Terrains d'anthropologues du Quebec*, Chicoutimi: Gaetan Morin, 135-7

——— (1988) 'Du point de vue des dominants: Reflexions théoriques et méthodologiques à partir d'une recherche en Guadeloupe'. In *Les rapports sociaux de sexe: Problématiques, méthodologies, champs d'analyses*, Proceedings of the International Round Table held in Paris 24-26 November 1987, I. Paris: CNRS Atelier/Production/Reproduction, 106-13

——— (1988a) 'Introduction: Pour les femmes, un autre développement'. *Recherches féministes*, 1 (2) 'Femmes et développement: Mythes, réalités, changements.' 1-17

——— (1988b) 'Quand la réalité fait éclater les concepts: La situation des femmes et du développement en Guadeloupe, en Haiti et à Trinidad'. Paper presented at the annual meeting of the Canadian Institute for the Advancement of Women (CRIAW), Quebec City, November

—— (1988c) 'Entre la nature et l'amour: Le travail invisible des femmes antillaises'. In *Femmes: Livre d'or de la femme créole*, IV, Pointe-à-Pitre: Raphy Diffusion, 145-53

Dagenais, Huguette and Jean Poirier (1985) 'L'envers du mythe: La situation des femmes en Guadeloupe'. *Nouvelles questions féministes*, 9-10 (Spring) 53-83

Dann, Graham (1987) *The Barbadian Male: Sexual Attitudes and Practice*. London: Macmillan Caribbean

Diman-Antenor, D. (1982) 'Economie et santé en Guadeloupe'. *CARE*, 9 (April) 54-67

—— (1986) 'Groupes sociaux, modes de vie, cadre de vie'. *Données sociales, INSEE*, (11) 48-74

—— (1988) 'Que fait-on de son budget?' *Antiane eco*, 5 (January) 13-15

—— (1988a) *Les budgets des ménages 1984-1985*. Pointe-a-Pitre: INSEE

Domenach, Hervé and Jean-Pierre Guengant (1981) 'Chômage et sous-emploi dans les DOM'. *Economie et statistiques*, 137 (October) 3-23

Ducosson, Dany (1983) 'Adolescents des "ghettos" de Pointe-à-Pitre'. *Les temps modernes*, (December) 1080-100

Edholm, Felicity, Olivia Harris and Kate Young (1977) 'Conceptualizing Women'. *Critique of Anthropology*, 3 (9-10) 101-30

*Etat du monde 1988-1989* (1988) Paris: Editions la Découverte/Montreal: Boréal

Favret-Saada, Jeanne (1986) 'Antillaises Revisited'. *Nouvelles questions féministes*, 13 (Spring) 101-4

*Femmes en chiffres* (1986) Paris: Centre national de documentation sur les droits des femmes (CNID), Institut national de la statistique et des études économiques (INSEE)

Flagie, Albert (1982) 'Baroches, quartiers de la ceinture urbaine de Pointe-à-Pitre'. Doctoral thesis, 2 vols

Gautier, Arlette (1985) 'Sous l'esclavage, le patriarcat'. *Nouvelles questions féministes*, 9-10 (Spring) 9-33

—— (1986) 'Politique familiale et familles monoparentales en metropole et dans les DOM depuis 1946'. *Nouvelles questions féministes*, 13 (Spring) 89-100

Gautier, Gérard (1986) 'La population'. *Données sociales, INSEE*, (11) 3-12, 33-6

—— (1986a) 'Regard démographique. Guadeloupe et Martinique: vers la stabilité'. *Antiane eco*, 1 (November) 29-31

—— (1987) 'Naissances et reconnaissances'. *Antiane eco*, 2 (February) 14-15

—— (1987a) 'Guadeloupe, an 2000: Surpopulation?' *Antiane eco*, 3 (May) 3-5

—— (1988) 'Guadeloupe: sous pression'. *Antiane eco*, 7 (July) 1-5

Guengant, Jean-Pierre (1982) 'Demographic Trends in Guadeloupe'. Occasional Papers, Caribbean Family Planning Federation, 1 (August)

—— (1987) 'Fécondité et démographie dans la caraïbe'. *Guadeloupe maternité*, 11 (December) 111-18

*ICAR* (Information Caraïbe) (1988) (717), 20 November

INSEE (Institut national de la statistique et des études économiques) (1983) *Données sociales, INSEE* (Les dossiers Antilles Guyane), (5)

Lasserre, Guy (1981) *La Guadeloupe*. I, *La nature et les hommes*; II, *Les îles et leurs problèmes*. Bordeaux: CNRS

—— (under the direction of) (1982) *Atlas des départements français d'outre-mer III: La Guadeloupe*. Paris: Editions du Centre national de la recherche scientifique and University of Bordeaux, Talence, Centre d'études de géographie tropicale (CNRS)

Mathurin, Lucille (1977) 'Reluctant Matriarchs'. *Savacou*, (13) 1-6

Michel, Andrée (1983) 'Inégalités de classe et de sexe et système agro-alimentaire en milieu rural en Amérique latine, *Nouvelles questions féministes*, 5 (Spring) 59-76

Moutoussamy, Ernest (1987) *La Guadeloupe et son indianité*. Paris: Editions caríbéennes

Poirier, Jean and Huguette Dagenais (1986) 'En marge, la situation des femmes dans l'agriculture en Guadeloupe: Situation actuelle, questions méthodologiques'. *Environnement caraïbe*, (2) 151-86

Poirier, Jean, Huguette Dagenais and Joel Gregory (1986) 'Démographie et approche féministe: Reflexion méthodologique à partir d'une recherche en cours'. *Cahiers québécois de démographie*, 14 (2 October) 277-83

Robinson, Warren C. (1987) 'The Time Cost of Children and other Household Production'. *Population Studies*, (41) 313-23

Roudil, J.C. (1987) 'Automobiles: Les petites ont la cote'. *Antiane eco*, 3 (May) 22-3

Smith, Dorothy (1987) *The Everyday World as Problematic*. Boston: Northeastern University Press

Tabet, Paola (1985) 'Fertilité naturelle, reproduction forcée'. In Nicole-Claude Mathieu (ed.) *L'arraisonnement des femmes: Essais en anthropologie des sexes*. Paris: Editions de l'école des hautes études en sciences sociales, 61-146

Thery, D. (1986) 'La consommation médicale'. *Données sociales, INSEE*, (11) 93-4

Thery, D. and R. Lefait-Robin (1986) 'L'offre de soins'. *Données sociales, INSEE*, (11) 82-92

Townsend, Janet and Janet Henshall Momsen (1987) 'Towards a Geography of Gender in Developing Market Economies'. In Janet Henshall Momsen and Janet Townsend (eds) *Geography of Gender in the Third World*. Albany: State University of New York Press, 27-81

Vance, Carol Susan (1979) 'Female Employment and Fertility in Barbados'. Ph.D. thesis, Columbia University, New York

Wallace, Michèle (1979) *Black Macho and the Myth of the Super-Woman*. New York: The Dial Press

# VII The Development & Role of Women's Political Organizations in Guyana

LINDA PEAKE

Guyanese people have a long history of organized struggle and, though sketchily documented, women's involvement has always been present. This chapter, which presents a historical overview of Guyanese women's political participation in the colonial and post-colonial development of their country,[1] aims to document the experiences of Guyanese women, to analyse the interrelationship between the nature of women's organizations and the form they have taken and to examine the extent to which women have benefited from national liberation.[2] The emphasis on women's ability to exert control over their lives should not obscure the broader societal constraints that have subordinated Guyanese women over time. The historical context is that of a former British colony with an avowedly socialist regime within which a racially divided political system has been constructed.

Any attempt to analyse the political involvement of women in Guyana has to be viewed within the framework of the country's history. To understand how official policies and material conditions have affected women, both under colonial rule and subsequently, three critical factors have to be taken into account: the impact of slavery and indentured labour; the inheritance of a dependent economy; and the strategies employed for national development by the post-independence government. With independence in 1966 and a government committed to cooperative socialism it might have been expected that changes would occur that would benefit women. Under socialism, women's status should improve for a number of reasons: private property is restricted; strategies for full employment should open up possibilities of economic independence for women; the official ideology is committed to egalitarianism and, hence, women's emancipation; and the revolutionary nature of socialism should transform the social formations and cultural practices that had worked against women's equality (Randall 1987).

It is within this framework that the nature and form of women's political involvement in Guyana's development are traced. Three aspects are considered: first, the range of women's activities in the so-called private sphere of the home and community and the degree to which these have been recognized as political activities; second, the extent of the representation of women in the public sphere of formal politics, within both political parties and the state apparatus; and third, the 'existence, influence and degree of independence of specific women's political organizations and the concern of the latter with identifiably feminist, as distinct from generic, political, objectives' (Molyneux 1981: 26).

The chapter is divided into four sections. The first specifies the historical roots of the present structure of women's political participation, charting the emergence of a large and varied network of primarily social-welfare women's organizations, designed to promote an increased participation by women as citizens. The second section portrays the transformation of these precursors of women's political organizations to their present-day configuration in Guyanese politics as wings, or associated organizations, of political parties. The third section examines transformations in the productive and reproductive spheres of women's lives. The chapter concludes with an assessment of the extent to which women's political (party and non-party) organizations in post-independence Guyana have been an important dynamic for socio-economic and political change leading towards the emancipation of women.

## From Benevolence to Taking Control

African slaves were first taken to the area now known as Guyana as early as the 1620s to work on sugar plantations. Over the following two centuries the area was governed by the Dutch, French and British, until 1814 when it was finally ceded to Britain. It appears that a class divide between white women and slave women was established as early as the first half of the seventeenth century. This divide was to remain uncontested for over 200 years. By the early nineteenth century, miscegenation between Europeans and African slaves (henceforth referred to as Afro-Guyanese) had produced a category of coloured women who grew up between these two classes, freed women, born of a slave mother and a slave-owning father. By 1831, 29 per cent of the whites, 46 per cent of the slaves and 60 per cent of all freed persons were female (creating a ratio of white : slave : freed women of approximately 1 : 41 : 5). Both white and free women followed European dress and social customs and the private domain of the home was seen as the natural place for these women to be. The public sphere of business, politics, government and slave control was the domain of men.[3] This strict demarcation of the public and private sphere of society limited social interaction between slave women and white women to the domestic slaves in the household.

With the abolition of slavery in 1838 and the subsequent introduction of indentured workers from India and elsewhere, the social structure of the population underwent a dramatic shift. Many Afro-Guyanese women left the sugar plantations and entered domestic service in the urban areas of Georgetown and New Amsterdam. The Indo-Guyanese indentured workers were granted agricultural land after completing their period of indenture and they established their own villages in the rural areas. Yet working women of both racial groups played a part in the labour struggles at the turn of the century (see also Chapter 16). As Rodney (1981: 157) explains: 'From time to time, estate disturbances started in the weeding gang, which was essentially the women's sphere. During the major disturbance at Plantation Fields (Berbice) in 1903, a key role was played by the veteran indentured woman named Salamea.' Rodney (1981: 205) goes on to show how, in the 1905 urban riots in the capital, Georgetown, women took a prominent role:

Of the 105 persons convicted in the Georgetown Magistrates Courts as a consequence of the riots, 41 were female. Another 95 persons were charged but had the charges withdrawn or dismissed; and of these 19 were female. The implication could well be that at least one in every three rioters was a woman, a credible ratio given the large proportion of women in the city of Georgetown at the time.

Meanwhile, the social activities of church-connected white and freed women extended from Sunday-school teaching to fund raising for religious purposes. These activities also attracted white women from the plantocracy and administration so that by the end of the century the tradition of engagement in socially uplifting activities among upper-class women was well established. It was involvement in this unpaid charity work that allowed these women to make forays into the public world and to see themselves as the moral guardians of colonial society. In the 1930s, one British Guianese woman (cited by Dingwall 1931: 6) still saw her role in enhancing social progress in precisely these terms:

Let all us women participate in this social uplift. Prove yourself day by day in everything you say and do, a good Christian and worthy citizen. ... Organize societies and clubs that will help to stem the tide of temptation. Remember that there is no sphere into which your activities cannot climb; no mass of sordidity [sic] which your influence cannot permeate; no depth, but your sympathy can reach to cleanse and purify.

By the early twentieth century both white women and coloured women of the colonial élite had established a number of friendly societies and social welfare organizations. Many of the church organizations were divided along ethnic lines, such as the (Portuguese) Ladies of Charity, the (Chinese) Chrysanthemum Workers and the (British) Young Women's Christian Association and the British Guiana Dorcas Society (Table 7.1). The activities of these organizations focused on providing financial aid for widows and 'respectable' women and children who were in financial difficulties. Numerous friendly societies and branch lodges of the Free Gardeners and Druids of Great Britain also aided the growing numbers of working-class women by providing precursors of present-day health and life insurance policies. Undoubtedly, the most popular organizations for white women to be involved in were the social welfare ones, where women's roles were viewed as natural extensions of their caring role in the family. The Girl Guide Movement, set up in 1924 in Guyana by Lady Thomson, provides an example and aimed at developing a 'fuller and better knowledge of practical housekeeping, mother-craft and citizenship' (Bayley 1931: 25).

A number of social welfare organizations established in the late nineteenth century centred around providing aid to those 'less fortunate', though some also attempted to improve the appalling environmental conditions of the urban-based working class. First, in 1890, came the Children's Protection Society, which was concerned with the prevention of cruelty to children and with raising funds to provide 'nourishing' meals for needy children. One of its members, Lady Chalmers, wife of a chief justice, went further, raising funds to build 'model homes' for the working class. Legal complications brought the closure of the society and its members joined the Child Welfare Movement, later the Infant Welfare and Maternity League, established in the early years of the twentieth century by Lady Egerton, wife of the governor. Funds provided by the government and the municipal council of Georgetown enabled the league to employ (mostly Afro-Guyanese) women as nurses and health visitors to provide both ante- and post-natal care. A further development, also at the instigation of Lady Egerton, was the opening in 1913 of the British Guiana United Home Industries and Self-Help Association, whose purpose was to assist women of meagre financial means to earn a livelihood by making craft items at home for sale.[4] Targeted at the same group of women was a charitable organization, the Gentlewomen's Relief Association, which provided a retirement home for elderly women living on their own. During the inter-war period these organizations, and others, continued to flourish and in 1931 yet another organization, the Working Women's Guild, aimed at promoting cottage industries, was established by Lady Denham, the wife of a colonial official.

These women's organizations of the late nineteenth and early twentieth century shared a number of characteristics. The vast majority were headed by wives of colonial officials. Whilst this allowed these benevolent organizations to act as channels through which the colonial powers could establish a 'European' way of life, it almost certainly also gave them a high degree of influence and status in Guyanese society. The first associations to emerge united women from élite white groups to perform unpaid community services. But by the beginning of the twentieth century, the Guyanese élite was becoming fractured by racial and class differences and white women alone could no longer presume to be the moral guardians of the era.

**Table 7.1: Chronology of the Formation of Women's Organizations in Ghana**

|        | Social & Welfare | Religious |
|--------|------------------|-----------|
| 1890s  | Children Protection Society (1890) | Ladies of Charity<br>Chrysanthemum Workers |
| 1900s  | Infant Welfare & Maternity League | YWCA |
| 1910s  | Self Help Depot (1913)<br>Child Welfare Movement (1914)<br>Gentlewomen's Relief Association | British Guiana Dorca Society |

|        | Social & Welfare | |
|--------|------------------|--|
| 1920s  | Girl Guide Movement (1924) | |
| 1930s  | Working Women's Guild (1931)<br>Sunshine Workers (1931) | |

|        | Social & Welfare | Political |
|--------|------------------|-----------|
| 1940s  | Women's League of Social Services (1940)<br>Federation of Women's Institutes | WPEO (1946) |

|        | Political |
|--------|-----------|
| 1950s  | WPO (1953)<br>Women's Auxiliary of the PNC (1957) |
| 1960s  | Women's Auxiliary of the United Force (1965)<br>WRSM (1967)<br>WAC of the TUC (1967) |
| 1970s  | CASWIG (1973) |
| 1980s  | WAB (1980)<br>Women's Section WPA (1982)<br>Red Thread (1986) |

Consequently, a new type of association appeared, aimed not only at aiding unfortunate individuals, but also at improving environmental conditions and establishing quasi-state welfare institutions. In addition, a new mode of organizing was exhibited, that of mutuality. Organization members were still of a high social status but, most importantly, they were often of different racial groups. The hegemony of European culture was such, however, that, although a number of these organizations were not composed of members of the (white) classes that owned and managed the production process, their aims emulated those of white women's groups. Their activities were largely domestic. They did not work to change the status quo, nor even to question the role and place of women within it.

These organizations were extremely important, however, in providing a new social space in which women could manoeuvre for power within the community. Their political leverage came from this network of like-minded individuals connected by informal social ties. This very structure allowed them to flourish. Occupying the interstices between the public and private spheres, they did not pose a threat to male-based formal institutions engaged in the exercise of official authority. Moreover, once mobilized, these everyday contact networks of neighbours and kin so familiar to women, effectively removed the barricades that had confined women to the domestic sphere. The influence of these organizations was evident, not only in that they set new social standards of education, health and welfare, but also in that they allowed women to introduce such issues into public debate. They thus extended both the basis and the scope of women's activities. For example, by pressing for the extension of state services such as housing and health care provision, they helped to provide and consolidate social services. Welfare provision became increasingly a social and political issue.

Undoubtedly, one of the greatest contributions women of the colonial élite made to the future participation of Guyanese women in the political development of their country was their Victorian zeal for the benefits of education to be brought to those 'less fortunate' than themselves. Hence, by 1900 various secondary school scholarships for working-class children had been created. Girls were still largely trained for domestic work or primary school teaching, but by the 1920s a privileged few had started to enter commerce and public sector work. This trend became so marked that the governor declared that women should instead direct their attention to nursing and the male nurses who then dominated the profession were replaced by women. Within a few decades a number of educated Guyanese women were potentially ready to emerge on the political scene.

It was not until the Second World War, however, when the leverage of these organizations was extended beyond the household, outside the women's networks and across social, economic and racial divides, that the extent of their influence became evident. Nowhere was this more apparent than in the setting up of the Women's League of Social Services. As a result of the exigencies of wartime conditions, in 1940 a number of women's charitable organizations banded together to form the Women's League of Social Services. Not only did this allow them to coordinate their efforts, but it also led to new activities such as the 'meals-on-wheels' service and the establishment of Women's Institutes in rural areas.

During the war the League moved in an important new direction — into civic affairs. As Kilkenny (1984: 7) explains:

Lectures on local government, law and justice, and social welfare were sponsored; a Women's League member served on the Government's Cost of Living Survey Committee; suggestions were submitted to the Advisory Welfare Committee; and a memorandum was submitted to the British Guiana Congress of General Workers on the working conditions of domestic servants. A Women's League Sub-Committee made successful representation to Government protesting a proposed amendment that would have adversely affected fund raising activities by charities.

One member of the League, Frances Stafford, attributed the members' desire to do more than mere charity work to the 1945 expansion of the franchise to include the majority of women and to allow them for the first time to sit on the Legislative Council. However, another member, Winnifred Gaskin, saw 'meaningful change' resulting less from the wider franchise than from the combined efforts of League women and working-class women working through the Legislative Council.[5] She went even further to suggest that in order for women to initiate change they needed to establish a women's political party. Although Winnifred Gaskin had been calling for women to unite for over 18 months, this was the first indication that the Women's Political and Economic Organization (WPEO) was to be formed.

## From Taking Control to Sharing Power

The development of these women's organizations and their move towards militancy was paralleled by the rise of trade unions and proto-political parties. After the Second World War, increased anti-colonial fervour resulted in the emergence of the Political Affairs Committee (PAC) in November 1946 and its subsequent evolvement in 1950 into the (Marxist) People's Progressive Party (PPP). This party won a resounding victory in the 1953 general election. However, political tensions developed within the PPP and, in 1955, these led to a split between one faction led by Indo-Guyanese Cheddi Jagan and another led by Afro-Guyanese Forbes Burnham. In 1957, having won the support of the Afro-Guyanese in the PPP, Forbes Burnham renamed his faction the People's National Congress (PNC). With this development the nationalist movement split irrevocably along racial lines. Both the PPP and the PNC contested the 1957 general election, which the former won. The PPP had been in power for less than five months, however, when the British government suspended the constitution. During what was to be a six-year period from 1957 to 1964, although in office, the PPP was not in power. The next election (in 1964) was again won by the PPP, but the PNC came to power a few months later through forming a coalition with the small Portuguese-led United Force, effectively giving it majority rule. There is widespread agreement that the PNC gained power only through the backing of the British and United States governments. Thus, it was the PNC that was to lead the country to independence in 1966, with the PPP as its major opposition. The emergence of the women's wings of these parties is examined in this section.

*Women's Political and Economic Organization (WPEO)*
The WPEO was launched on 12 July 1946, a few months before the formation of PAC. It was jointly created by Afro-Guyanese Winnifred Gaskin and Janet Jagan, the Canadian wife of Cheddi Jagan. Both overtly political women, and women from the traditional pre-war organizations were active in setting it up. Its aim was 'to ensure the political organization and education of the women of British Guiana in order to promote their economic welfare and their political and social emancipation and betterment' (WPEO records, quoted in Kilkenny 1984: 8). It set about encouraging women to register as voters for the forthcoming 1947 election. Indeed it urged women in the charitable organizations to exert pressure on local government to bring about improvements in social welfare in general and in housing conditions in particular (Earle 1977). Within the first three months it attracted approximately 160 members, both working and middle-class women.

One of its first tasks was to expose the cramped and unhygienic living conditions of the urban-based working class. It set up a housing committee to investigate housing conditions in Georgetown. The committee launched a media campaign, which gained international support (including that of the British Labour Party), and as a result a number of improvements were made to dwellings. However, various attempts between 1946 and 1948 to organize campaigns to press for higher wages and shorter hours for domestic servants met with little success. This failure may be attributed either to the attitude of some WPEO members who had come from traditional women's organizations and viewed domestic service as a preparation for family life, to victimization by employers of domestic servants who engaged in the campaign, or to the nature and hours of the work, which isolated the women from one another and led to a high turnover of domestic servants (WPO 1983).

But the WPEO's main activity was as a pressure group organizing for the extension of the franchise. Three WPEO members ran unsuccessfully for the 1947 Legislative elections. The Executive Council of the WPEO was itself divided on the issue of running candidates in national elections. These political differences led to organizational tensions within the WPEO and the eventual resignation of a number of executive members. Kilkenny (1984: 17) saw its demise as inevitable — 'its keen interest in politics and its ability to attract a broad cross-section of women were at one and the same time its strong point and its Achilles heel.'

Though the WPEO had a short life,[6] it was part of a deep-rooted continuity of long-term habitual cooperation, which had broken from the semi-invisibility of community life to enter public politics during a period of severe social upheaval and political unrest. It was women's entry into formal politics that gave them a platform from which to fight for women's equality. Whilst they may not have achieved their specific goals of winning seats on the Legislative Council and of universal suffrage, the work of the WPEO led a number of women to reassess their roles within society and to demand the equality that was rightfully theirs. And their pressure group activities undoubtedly influenced the colonial administration, which waived the property and literacy qualifications for voters and introduced universal suffrage shortly afterwards, in 1953. Thus the WPEO was successful in its broad aims of educating women about their political and economic rights as members of the community, and in training leaders for future elections at municipal and national levels.

*Women's Progressive Organization (WPO)*
In May 1953 another women's political organization arose to replace the WPEO. A month after the PPP had won the elections, the WPO was formed with three of its five founding members (Janet Jagan, Jessie Burnham and Jane Philips-Gay) being the first women to enter parliament as MPs in the PPP Assembly. In June the provisional secretary of the WPO, Jessica Huntley, spelt out their platform (WPO 1983: 11): 'It [the WPO] stands for a better educated woman who can bring up her children in surroundings of security; it stands for the raising of our living standards and it stands for peace and friendship among the peoples of the world and for the ultimate liberation of our women from colonialism and poverty.'

But when the PPP split along racial lines in 1955, Jessie Burnham and Jane Philips-Gay joined the PNC, causing the WPO to lose most of the Afro-Guyanese section of its leadership. The WPO was revitalized, however, after the PPP's successful election result in 1957 and, over the following few years, it was vociferous in its demands for political and economic equality and equal opportunities. Unlike the PPP, the WPO was not banned under the state of emergency, but restrictions were placed on its activities. Still, it managed to provide party members and the populace at large with news and information, which was passed on by women party members (largely ignored by the colonial establishment) who, acting as couriers, carried and distributed party pamphlets from their market baskets. Moreover, it gradually branched out into the rural sugar growing areas, where support for the PPP was greatest, to win the votes of peasant women, female sugar workers and housewives. Its activities, in keeping with its political philosophy, largely focused on women in waged work.

To this day the political philosophy of the WPO, like that of the PPP, remains Marxist-Leninist. As such it advocates an end to all forms of exploitation, oppres-

sion and racism and supports the struggle for world peace, democracy and socialism. Its views on the emancipation of women are firmly rooted in the belief that
this will be achieved by the large-scale entry of women into the workforce and the
socialization of housework. In keeping with its commitment to Marxism, the WPO
places the subordination of women in an international framework. Indeed, as
early as June 1953 it established links with the Women's International Democratic
Federation (WIDF) and now has connections with approximately 200 women's
organizations world-wide.[7]

One of the WPO's earliest activities was to organize domestic workers (the most
exploited sector of working women) and to claim better conditions for women in
the Indo-Guyanese dominated sugar workforce. In the long term, the efforts on
behalf of the former were largely unsuccessful, though a Domestic Workers Union
was registered and functioned for approximately five years (Mohammed 1986).
But through exerting pressure on various unions and the Sugar Producers' Association the WPO was able to argue for maternity benefits, shorter working days, an
increase in pay and a change in the pension age for female sugar workers (WPO
1983). More generally, the WPO claimed to be fighting for the interests of all
working women, including housewives. This struggle was not only organized
through specific campaigns for particular groups of workers but also through
campaigns for improved social conditions. During the 1960s, for example, primary
education was made compulsory, children were given milk and pre-natal classes
were set up to teach women about childbirth, nutrition and child care (WPO 1983).

The WPO also campaigned for more women to join the organization and, after
the PPP won the 1961 general election, claimed to have evolved into a militant
mass democratic women's organization. Since the 1964 election, however, the PPP
has been out of government and the WPO has, consequently, had little or no influence over government policy. But it has remained active, both internationally and
locally. It has organized sessions for men on cadre development to counteract
'cultural backwardness' and has arranged for female PPP members to be sent
overseas to attend universities in socialist countries. In addition the WPO holds
'bottom-house' meetings for women in rural areas on Marxist philosophy, WPO
history and sex education, in which it questions the view that sexual activity is
primarily for the pleasure of men, provides information on birth control and
campaigns against the use of De-po Provera. It has recently strengthened its
connections with the women's arms of trade unions not under PNC control and,
likewise, with women's religious organizations (Hindu, Muslim and Christian) in
an effort to raise the social and political consciousness of its members.

*Women's Revolutionary Socialist Movement (WRSM)*
In 1957, in the same year as the formation of the PNC, the idea of a women's arm
was mooted. According to one report by President Forbes Burnham (Burnham
1980) it was at the annual Congress of the PNC that a number of Afro-Guyanese
women (who had left the PPP to join the PNC) suggested the idea to him and he
gave his agreement. The Women's Auxiliary was to form the backbone of the
party: it became especially active at election times, helping to mobilize women
voters. In between elections it 'organized rallies, lectures, numerous kinds of fund
raising activities and campaigned from house to house' (Baber and Jeffrey 1986:
75). In addition, it served as a domestic unit, catering (literally) for the needs of the
male PNC members. Essentially, however, between 1964, when the PNC came to
power, and 1976, the Women's Auxiliary played only a minimal role outside
election times. But in 1976 it abandoned its back seat role and saw itself instead as
the Vanguard of the Vanguard (Party). This transformation was signified by a

name change and the Women's Auxiliary became the Women's Revolutionary Socialist Movement mandated to advance the full integration of women into the political life of the party (WRSM 1980). This change in emphasis was an integral part of the PNC's transformation from a party focused essentially on nationalism to one with a Marxist-Leninist ideological orientation. As a result there was a reshuffling of WRSM members and, 'by the time its designation changed in January 1976, the organization consisted of a few old stalwarts, many of whom held one of its offices, and a small group of younger people [women] attracted by the new socialist orientation' (Baber and Jeffrey 1986: 75).

There is, to the best of my knowledge, no written material on the political philosophy of the WRSM, but, in 1985, its major objectives (WRSM n.d.) were as follows:

(1) To promote the full participation of women in all phases of community and national life with special emphasis on the discovery and development of talent and leadership among women of our country.
(2) To increase labour efficiency and development in women and an awareness of the significant role they need to play in the challenging but rewarding task of nation building.
(3) To improve the economic status of women. They are encouraged to establish cooperatives, livestock rearing, cottage industries and handicrafts.

Further information from interviews with the WRSM's National Executive Committee (WRSM 1985) confirmed that it still saw itself as a vanguard organization focusing on making women aware of the role they had to play in the development of a socialist state. It does not see itself as a mass participation organization, though in 1985 it claimed to have issued 18,021 membership cards to women. Membership tends to fluctuate and estimates vary. Baber and Jeffrey (1986), for instance, state that in 1983 the WRSM had only 825 members.

WRSM women are present, however, in all ten administrative regions of Guyana, but only in five have mandatory conferences taken place to establish regional committees. WRSM regional committees plan programmes for the sub-regions, districts and neighbourhoods and report back on these to the leadership each month. Thus, no decisions below regional level are taken by WRSM members. At the national level the WRSM has links with the highest level of decision-making through the PNC. The Chairman (sic) of the WRSM is a member of the Central Executive of the PNC, as are two other members but in different capacities. Links with the ruling party have also benefited the WRSM in relation to its income-generating projects for women. As the chairman of the WRSM is the widow of the former president, the WRSM has been able to gather project funds which otherwise might have remained inaccessible. The absence of a national Women's Bureau before 1981 also led to the channelling of funds to the WRSM. Funding for its projects comes both from local sources, such as the Guyana Cooperative Agricultural and Industrial Development Bank, and from international development agencies, such as the US Voluntary Fund (now UNIFEM) and UNICEF.

The WRSM claims to have commenced its project-based activities in 1972. These were initially oriented towards reducing food distribution problems by providing such services as work-place canteens and shops. Since then the WRSM has progressed to small semi-industrial projects, reflecting the move from cottage-based industries to small business enterprises. It now has three categories of project (distributive, semi-industrial/industrial, and agricultural) for which it has established its own commercial outlet — Vanpro Enterprises.

*Women's Section of Working People's Alliance and Red Thread*

The two party scenario of the PNC and PPP, with their respective women's arms, remained unaltered until 1979, when the multiracial Working People's Alliance (WPA) was set up. Prior to its formation as a political party, the WPA consisted of a small group of people who met once a fortnight to discuss their multiracial socialist alternative to the Marxist-Leninist PPP and the (by now) cooperative socialism of the PNC. Few women were active in the group and, despite support from some male members, there were not enough of them to establish a women's section. Furthermore, not until mid-1981, a year after WPA leader Walter Rodney had been assassinated, did the wave of harassments and arrests to which party members had been subjected begin to abate. As a consequence, it was only in 1983, following the ban on the import of certain basic food items, that the WPA started to canvass its grass roots support and decide to set up a Women's Section.

In 1983 the Women's Section of the WPA held its first national conference of women at which it resolved to 'build the multiracial unity of Guyanese women of different strata in defence of the most oppressed ... and ... pay special attention to joining in the defence of the rights and interests of the Amerindian women and children of Guyana' (WPA Women's Section 1983). Over 100 women were present at the conference, including Afro-Guyanese, Indo-Guyanese and Amerindian ones. They established 17 women's groups, but then encountered problems in meeting. Not only was there insufficient guidance from the WPA Women's Section because of conflicting pressures of WPA work on their time, but women were afraid of being identified as WPA supporters in case their husbands or children were victimized by PNC 'thugs'. Consequently, despite a promising start, the section remained dormant until 1985 when a women's officer (who was also the international secretary of the WPA) was appointed and a six-page document on women was included in the WPA's political programme.

With the services of an international secretary it became possible to renew contacts with various women's and political organizations throughout the Caribbean and beyond. These, in turn, led to discussions among Women's Section members about whether organizing women as political party members was the most effective way of mobilizing women into taking control of their own lives. The decision was taken to discard the WPA Women's Section and establish the first non-party political women's organization in Guyana, Red Thread. Thus, while most of the organizers are WPA members, the 120 women employed on its projects are not. Originating in the Women's Development Project in October 1986, its focus is on consciousness raising and income-generating projects for women and schoolgirls. With the aim of working with women towards 'collective self-development and self-organization', it has set up projects in four communities (WDP 1987). These projects not only utilize women's existing skills, such as sewing, but also encourage non-traditional skills such as making school exercise books and selling copies of school textbooks. The latter are currently available only on the black market at a price of G$400 but the women reproduce the books and sell their copies for G$60 (approximately £1 or US$2) (Kwayana 1990). Red Thread also carries out consciousness raising through educational activities such as training sessions with Sistren, the Jamaican women's theatre group, and research into the working lives of Guyanese women. This programme is designed to enable the women to engage in analysis of the material conditions that mould their life chances.

## Impact of Women's Political Organizations on Women's Lives

A number of factors have limited the impact of women's political organizations in Guyana on women's liberation. First, the issue is closely associated with national liberation and this has been hampered by unemployment, national debt and high levels of out-migration, all of which have acted as material and ideological constraints on the emancipation of women. But even more detrimental has been the nature of the regime itself (Peake 1987). It has become increasingly clear over the years since independence that the PNC state lacks mass support, largely as a result of its mismanagement of the economy and its declining commitment to socialism. This helps explain the third factor mitigating against the emancipation of women, namely the belief that socialism itself is sufficient for the purpose. Consequently, until recently there has been a tendency to deny that there is a need for autonomous women's organizations to campaign for feminist objectives. Given this background, what impact, if any, have these women's political organizations had on the lives of Guyanese women? I turn first to the arena of politics itself to see how far these organizations have become part of a democratizing process in which the participation of women in political life is promoted.

*Political Changes*
There is sufficient evidence from a wide variety of sources to show that there is no doubt that political democracy is non-existent and that the electoral process has been subverted. Energies within the PNC are devoted to keeping itself in office and this has occurred not with the approval of the Guyanese people but at their expense. The inequalities inherent in PNC policies also manifest themselves in those adopted by the PNC associated women's organizations. Apart from the WRSM these include the Women's Advisory Council of the Trades Union Congress (WAC of the TUC), the NGO Conference on the Affairs and Status of Women (CASWIG) and the Women's Affairs Bureau (WAB).

Although there are women in these organizations who are genuinely concerned about the emancipation of women, they are constantly constrained by the framework within which they operate. Moreover, many of their members are accessories to PNC attempts to rig the electoral process, thus denying women the ability to participate fully in political activity. Hence, the PNC women's organizations have kept decision-making firmly within the control of a small group of PNC women, most of whom are married to PNC male members. Cross-linkages between the WRSM associated organizations are so numerous that their activities can only be viewed as part of the PNC's state machinery.[8]

Female representation on the PNC's Executive Committee, however, is minimal. Of the 15 Cabinet members, none are women and in the Central Executive Committee there are only three women out of 25 members. Obviously women's representation at higher levels of economic decision-making remains low. The picture is only slightly less depressing with respect to other government posts; women form only one-quarter of the members of the National Assembly. The tendency, as in the vast majority of both socialist and capitalist countries, is for women to be concentrated at the lower levels of the political hierarchy. Although the PNC vice-president is a woman, women's representation in political bodies rarely exceeds one third. There are 23 women MPs out of a total of 65. A third of the representatives on the National Congress of Local Democratic Organs and a quarter of those on the Regional Democratic Councils (RDC), for instance, are women, but there are only three female RDC chairpersons. This picture is repeated in connected spheres. In the legal system, for example, there are only two female judges and five female magistrates and there are no women on the Board of Directors of State Corporations (WPO 1983). The overwhelming majority of women in positions of power are members or supporters of the PNC and hence of the WRSM, as all female PNC members automatically become WRSM members.

The WRSM and its associated women's organizations appear subordinate to the party and to its socio-economic priorities. As such, the political mechanism for questioning the effect of State policies on women is the responsibility of the WPO and (until 1985) the WPA's Women's Section. Having said this, it remains to be seen whether the WRSM and its associated organizations have had an autonomous sphere of influence over policy determination in areas directly affecting women. Given the Guyanese government's (official) socialist political philosophy, there already exist guidelines that can be used to evaluate the efficacy of these women's political organizations in promoting the interests of women (Molyneux 1981):

(1) In socialist states there is an official ideology that recognizes the need to liberate women from their oppression and, concomitantly, to redefine female and male roles. The extent to which this ideology is addressed can be measured through constitutional and legal changes;
(2) Central to this liberation is the notion of economic independence, which is measured in attempts for women to enter into waged work;
(3) In order to accelerate transformations in the economic sphere, social change is also encouraged with the state usually accepting a certain degree of responsibility for the reproduction of labour power and social welfare provision such as health care, housing and education.

Each of these three areas will be investigated in turn.

*Constitutional and Legal Change*
Apart from the granting of universal suffrage in 1953, it was not until 1975 that any significant legislative changes for women took place.[9] A year after the start of the United Nations Decade for Women (in 1975), a State Paper on Equality for Women was tabled in parliament. It set out policy guidelines relating to the full integration of women into the country's development, outlawing sex discrimination in the fields of employment, recruiting, education and the provision of housing, goods and services. In 1980 the PNC government reiterated its commitment to the full participation of women in national development and made another statement on the prohibition of sex discrimination. This was Article 29 of the People's New Constitution (Government of Guyana 1980: 25):

Article 29 — Equality for Women

(1) Women and men have equal rights and the same legal status in all spheres of political, economic and social life. All discrimination against women on the basis of their sex is illegal.
(2) The exercise of women's rights is ensured by according women equal access with men to academic, vocational and professional training, equal opportunities in employment, remuneration and promotion and in political economic and social activity, by special labour and health protection measures for women, by providing conditions enabling mothers to work and by legal protection and material and moral support for mothers and children, including paid leave and other benefits for mothers and expectant mothers.

## Table 7.2: Legal Changes Affecting Women

*Legal Changes that Redefine Relations between the Sexes*

A. *Equal rights within marriage*
— minimum age of marriage of 16 for both sexes;
— a recognition that the services of a wife in the home should be taken into account when determining rights to property acquired during the period of marriage;
— a recognition that when a husband's earning capacity is impaired, women should maintain their husband;
— national insurance and income tax anomalies to be ironed out;
— common law unions to be recognized.

B. *Ending of rights previously enjoyed only by men*
— a child's acquisition of citizenship through either parent;
— unilateral divorce grounds;
— both women and men to have legal custody of children and both be required to maintain them;
— illegitimate children to be allowed to succeed to the property of their fathers;
— equality of treatment by employers of female and male employees as regards terms and conditions of service

*Legal Changes that Affect Women as Childbearers and Rearers*
— revocation of the Bastardy Act under which the mother of an illegitimate child may be punished 'as a rogue and a vagabond' for neglecting or deserting her child;
— changes to protect women from indecent assault, incest, abduction and prostitution.

## Table 7.3: Women's Formal Sector Occupations in British Guiana, 1851-1970

| Year | Domestic Servants | | Agricultural Labourers | | Other | | Women in the Workforce | |
|---|---|---|---|---|---|---|---|---|
|  | Total no. | % | Total no. | % | Total no. | % | Total no. | % |
| 1851 | *5,547 | 6.0 |  |  |  |  |  |  |
| 1861 | 9,100 | 18.0 | 28,674 | 69.3 | 3,583 | 12.7 | 41,357 | 46.2 |
| 1871 | 8,484 | 12.6 | 37,606 | 69.1 | 8,320 | 18.3 | 54,410 | 39.7 |
| 1881 | 14,563 | 16.5 | 40,833 | 59.9 | 12,793 | 23.6 | 68,189 | 40.7 |
| 1891 | 19,934 | 22.0 | 41,162 | 54.4 | 14,516 | 23.6 | 75,612 | 41.2 |
| 1911 | 29,867 | 31.8 | 40,923 | 48.5 | 13,527 | 19.7 | 84,330 | 44.1 |
| 1921 | 30,007 | 36.6 | 31,126 | 40.5 | 15,679 | 23.0 | 76,812 | 43.1 |
| 1931 | 16,314 | 31.1 | 18,754 | 38.1 | 14,122 | 30.8 | 49,190 | 33.5 |
| 1946 | 13,314 | 26.8 | 13,613 | 33.5 | 13,653 | 39.7 | 40,580 | 27.8 |
| 1960 | 13,944 | 38.0 | 9,307 | 25.4 | 13,405 | 36.6 | 36,661 | 22.7 |
| 1970 |  |  | 3,900 | 10.8 |  |  | 36,055 | 19.0 |

*Sources*: 'Occupations of Gainfully Occupied Population 1871-1921 with approximate extensions for 1931 and 1946, *British Guiana Census*, 1946; Anon (1980) 'Review of Employment of Women in Guyana, 1975-1980', mimeo; 'Table of major Occupational Groups' *British Guiana Census*, 1960.
*Note*: * Figures include both men and women.

In order to put these constitutional provisions into effect a committee was appointed to make appropriate amendments to Guyanese law. The committee made 35 recommendations and, by 1984, eight of these had been implemented. These were concerned with affiliation and maintenance, equating women's and men's pension rights, outlawing bastardy, equating rights relating to the acquisition and division of property, and women's employment. For example, the Factories Act, which prevented the employment of women in factories at night, has been repealed and certain categories of workers, such as clerks, hotel workers and sugar workers, have won the right to minimum pay levels. In the public sector women have won equal pay and benefits with regard to paid leave and retirement. A further step towards attaining equal rights for women was taken in July 1980 when Guyana signed the United Nations Convention on the Elimination of all Forms of Discrimination against Women.

Whilst these legally binding documents recognize that all Guyanese women have been discriminated against on grounds of their sex, legal changes have largely benefited middle-class women, such as those in the civil service and medical professions, with sufficient finances and knowledge to secure access to courts of law to ensure their entitlement to equal rights. It appears that too much emphasis should not be put upon this official commitment to end sexual discrimination. But, at the same time, neither should an attempt to formalize legal equality between the sexes be seen as totally irrelevant. The official commitment to liberate women has already brought about changes in government policy, especially in relation to education and housing and, as such, may well have a multiplier effect, creating expectations in other areas of government policy (Peake 1986, 1987a). Most revealingly, however, there have been no real attempts to bring to an end the most extreme forms of exploitation. Protective legislation for a minimum wage and improved conditions of work for domestic servants and other low-paid workers such as laundresses and waitresses have not been instigated. Many Indo-Guyanese women still work in rice and sugar fields as unpaid family labour. And it is generally accepted that there has been an increase in the number of women turning to prostitution in order to make ends meet.

In what sense can we measure the impact of legal changes on women's daily lives? Molyneux (1981) recognizes two areas on which legislation in socialist countries has concentrated: measures to redefine relations between the sexes, and protective legislation affecting women in their reproductive roles as childbearers and rearers. Guyanese legislative changes fit neatly into these two categories, as Table 7.2 shows. They were determined by the PNC policy on the family, which is underlain by a conservative ideology that fails to problematize both the family as the basic unit of society, and female and male relations within society. These legal changes affect women not as individuals *qua* women, but as wives and mothers. As Randall (1987: 203) explains, the Western model of the family is effectively preserved and enshrined, both as the norm to be aspired to and as the stabilizing block of society so essential to the reproduction of labour power.

> The family has an important socializing function, transmitting if not attitudes of positive support for the existing regime, at least a tendency to accept authority and to adhere conservatively to the way things are as normal ... the family household system which, in so far as it assists in the ideological as well as the physical reproduction of economic relations, is clearly a force for political stability. Although this family system is no longer strictly patriarchal, it is still premised upon women's main responsibility for child care and the home.

It appears that legislative change aimed at the emancipation of women is not a principle to which the PNC state is committed as part of the supposed goal of achieving a more egalitarian society. As in a number of socialist countries, it is merely an integral part of its wider development goals.

*Changes in the Sphere of Production*
Though women have obtained some degree of constitutional and legislative equality, there are major obstacles in the economic and social spheres, which hamper them in their struggle for equality. A dual sector economy, high levels of unemployment and lack of training opportunities encourage the persistence of a sexual division of labour, sex-segregated occupations and the view that women's jobs should be less well paid and valued. There is, however, growing socio-economic diversity amongst women (as Table 7.3 illustrates). In the second half of the nineteenth century, apart from work in agriculture, a large number of women were also employed as domestic servants and general labourers. Formal labour force participation of women peaked in the first decade of the twentieth century (a similar pattern is found in the Eastern Caribbean, see Chapters 15 and 16), but during the 1920s many women left the formal sector. Although in the 1930s the majority of women were still employed in the rural areas as agricultural labourers and in the urban areas as domestic servants, changes in the employment pattern of women were taking place. As Standing (1979: 53) comments: 'Dualism has particularly affected female workers who have been eased out of the labour force. The causes are not known, but mechanization and high unemployment are likely to have been the main factors. What is particularly striking is the extent to which women have been pushed out of the agricultural labour force in recent years.' By 1960, 38 per cent of female formal sector workers were in domestic service, for the first time surpassing the number of women working in agriculture. The following statement from the WPO (1985) illustrates that the diversification of women's jobs is a trend that has continued into the 1980s:

According to our estimates, the percentage of women in unskilled jobs such as domestics, sugar workers, cleaners, vendors, (home) laundresses, waitresses, etc., amount to more than 70 per cent of the working women, semi-skilled workers another 20 per cent, including shop clerks, typists, cashiers, (home) seamstresses, garment and factory workers, and skilled workers in the nursing and teaching, the legal and medical professions etc., only 10 per cent.

The number of women entering university and certain professions, such as nursing and teaching, has declined with the enforcement of the prerequisite of a year's compulsory national service for the attainment of university degrees and promotion. Women are more commonly engaged in various commercial activities in the informal sector, such as dressmaking, food preparation, presentation and selling, and prostitution. However, in Guyana the process of women's removal from the formal sector has manifested itself most markedly in the growth of trading. This activity originated during the period of slavery when slaves were given small plots of land on which to grow vegetables and women began to sell their surplus produce in the local markets. Many Afro-Guyanese women are as mobile as men and they have been able to develop an extensive, unofficial import-export business in street market goods. Street trading is a common activity for both Afro- and Indo-Guyanese women. Until the economic crisis of the mid-1970s, and especially the high levels of retrenchment from the state sector in 1978/9, their operations were on a local level, collecting agricultural produce from farms to sell in market places. Now, however, the women traders travel overseas, taking out plantains, pineapples and sometimes gold and bringing back items that are scarce or unavailable in Guyana.[11]

Not only do more women than men occupy the lowest paid jobs, but unemployment is also higher among women than men because fewer women than men are unionized and, in the rural areas, they have few employment opportunities. The WPO (1983a) estimates that fewer than 1 in 20 women have acquired their occupations through WRSM training programmes and those who have are in occupations that reveal the gender stereotypic nature of their training. Although figures are unavailable, it is unlikely that WRSM projects have led to employment for more than a few hundred women and not all of these jobs have been permanent. This low figure could be justified if the WRSM had been focusing its attention on other activities concerning women. This does not appear to be the case as the following section shows.

*Changes in the Sphere of Reproduction*
The third criterion to be discussed is the extent to which the state has accepted responsibility for the various activities and resources associated with the reproduction of labour power, namely housing, health care, education, child care, welfare benefits and so on. It is perhaps in this sphere that the breakdown of Guyanese society is so visibly obvious. And it is women, especially those who head households, who have been particularly affected by government policy. The following quotation from a State Paper on Equality for Women (1976: 1) expresses the official view in relation to these issues:

Many of the causative attitudes have changed over the past decades as a result of alterations in the pattern of the family, as well as in the structure of the economy and of society generally. The portion of the life-span of the average woman which is taken up with child-bearing has markedly contracted. This, together with the lengthening of her life expectancy due to better medical facilities, has left her with more free time which continues to increase as more labour-saving devices tend to become available to her. Improvements in health and education have enabled her to tackle many jobs which in earlier times would have been thought capable of being undertaken only by men. Changes in the general social climate inspired by events abroad and by the political evolution at home as well as the development and expansion of the economy now in progress, have combined to add many vocations to the narrow category of domestic service, nursing, teaching, typewriting and telephone operating to which women were in earlier days confined.

The above extract reveals that Western middle-class images of women have been projected onto Guyanese women, with the government adopting a 'Beveridge' type view of women surrounded by modern kitchen equipment and severely underestimating the amount of work women actually do. Time spent in biological reproduction may have declined with increasing access to birth control, but the average number of children was more than four per family in the 1970s, with the fertility rate falling to 2.8 a decade later (see Table 1.1). While life expectancy for women has increased by five years over the last decade to 72.3 and is five years longer than that of men, the infant mortality rate at 30 per 1000 live births is still the worst in the English-speaking Caribbean (IBRD 1978; Kwayana 1990). Moreover, in 1984, 71 per cent of children below the age of five were suffering from malnutrition (Baber and Jeffrey 1986). Approximately a third of households are headed by women and 70 per cent of these have no formal source of income (Buvinic et al. 1978). With a devaluation of the currency in 1989 as a result of IMF austerity measures, the minimum wage in March 1990 of G$36 a day did not even purchase a gallon of rice (G$45). Shortages and high prices are endemic for most goods, including food items produced locally. As a result women spend many hours in queues trying to buy food or incur extra work growing food to compensate for shortages in the shops and markets. Facilities provided by the state are grossly under-funded and the health care and education systems barely function.

In addition, there has been no concerted attempt to socialize the domestic sphere or to equalize the burden of housework. The effect of these omissions on women's control over their fertility and on their responsibility for children and the home are now examined.

In the same way as the PNC government actively promoted a family form alien to the historical and contemporary experiences of the majority of Guyanese women, so too has it been reluctant to concede to women the opportunity to control their own fertility. There have, however, been some changes in women's lives as a result of contraception. Condoms, for instance, are available for men, but contraception is still seen as a woman's responsibility. Available contraceptive devices, for which women have to pay, include the IUD, De-po Provera (though the WRSM deny its existence) and the pill (but supplies are unreliable and have a high oestrogen level). According to some sources, though illegal, a number of women also use abortion as a method of contraception. Although openly practised, these abortions are costly and unreliable and obviously undesirable.[12] But they do enable women to have more control over their fertility, resulting in fewer women having to spend their adult lives constantly engaged in childbirth and child care. But given that Guyanese society regards women primarily as reproducers, birth control is still frowned upon in some rural areas because of ignorance, superstition and religious influences. Moreover, as Randall (1987: 179) asserts, 'measures to promote fertility control only really increase women's life options if they provide greater, more informed choice.' The use of De-po Provera and illegal abortions carried out in unsanitary conditions can hardly be said to contribute to this process. They are, indeed, abuses of a woman's control over her own fertility.

In relation to family planning a policy of spaced births is endorsed. Its implementation and monitoring, however, depend on a rudimentary system of maternal health clinics, far from comprehensive in geographical coverage. Although free, shortages of qualified staff, equipment and drugs have led to a low standard of ante- and post-natal care. However, given the low population density and high level of out-migration, political backing for family planning is non-existent.

Issues of sexuality and sexual relations have only recently been addressed. The WRSM's 1980 Third Biennial Convention considered a Family Code and established a study group to discuss paternity, prostitution, abortion, rape and other related topics (WRSM 1980). But by 1985 it had still not adopted an official position on abortion, for it feared this would cause divisions between its members. But, given the unsatisfactory nature of certain issues relating to sexuality (for example, male partners still had to give their written consent before a woman could have a hysterectomy), they were considering further discussion.

Child care is obviously the most important concern to women responsible for children and the home, yet since 1976 the WRSM has set up only two day-care centres — one in the Rupununi and one in Corriverton (Georgetown). Women working in the government sector, while not receiving help with child care, do have paid maternity leave at a rate of 60 per cent of the mother's wage for 13 weeks, but this is less generally available in the private sector (WPO 1983a). However, since the majority of women are employed in the informal sector, they are not eligible for this benefit.

It is probably in the area of housework that least has been achieved. There have been no serious attempts to free women from their dual roles through the socialization of domestic work. Other than to say that men should be encouraged to develop a responsibility for domestic work, the WRSM has done nothing to help this become a reality. Like the benevolent women's societies of the early twentieth century, the WRSM has assumed that women are responsible for the home and children, yet has failed to make any policy arrangements to provide practical assistance to them. Its resemblance to these earlier women's organizations is further revealed in the following section.

## Evaluation

Why have women in Guyana benefited so little from the process of national liberation, given their active involvement in it? Despite an apparently progressive constitution espousing legal equality between women and men, and despite women's concerted action over the last 40 years in both the political and economic spheres, women are still inadequately represented on political decision-making bodies. Throughout the economic recession they have been increasingly pushed out of the formal sector and 'relegated' to the private sphere of the family and the informal sector. And there appears to have been no substantial change in gender consciousness over the years. Women's increased involvement in income-generating activities in the informal sector has not served to alter the boundaries of the public and private spheres of Guyanese life. The division between public 'productive' labour and private 'unproductive/reproductive' labour has been maintained, with the result that women's subsistence and commodity production has remained socially invisible. Political activities are still considered to be what takes place in relation to the state (not the home or community) and issues of biological reproduction, domestic work and sexuality are still seen as personal and private.

The maintenance of patriarchal social relations and their institutionalization in the Western model of the nuclear family has been a crucial component of the building of the modern Guyanese state. It is a state characterized by a centralization of power within a male élite group, which not only forms the government but also maintains control over the economy, the military, the legislature, the media and all forms of communication in the country. Any surplus value has been distributed among the (mainly male) members of the PNC, allowing it to create its own state-class by which it can monopolize politics and maintain political stability.

Women are largely excluded from this state-class, a situation illustrated by the low level of their representation on state decision-making bodies. The fact that a nominally socialist political party has achieved control of state power — indeed has put itself above it — and that certain sectors of the economy have been nationalized, has clearly not brought exploitation to an end. Not only do the economic interests of the dominant PNC élite benefit from this state of affairs; their interests, as men, are also served. Male dominance is secured both by presenting the sexual division of labour as natural, i.e. women's place is in the home, and by ensuring there has been no threat to their 'institutionalized male supremacy' (Randall 1987).

This combined preservation of male interests and of PNC state objectives has adversely affected women, specifically in relation to employment, and generally in the reinforcement, through coercion and persuasion, of a view of the family household system as the cornerstone of social and political stability.

Within this framework what have the WRSM and its associated organizations been able to achieve? Given that they have access to PNC policy-making channels, it is they who have had the greatest potential for making changes to women's daily lives.

The WRSM does appear to have achieved some positive objectives. It has tried to deal with women's increasing aspirations both by formulating women's programmes and projects and by articulating official state support for them. As a result some educational and legal inequalities have been abolished. Outside Guyana the WRSM has maintained international links with women's organizations such as WIDF, and the CARICOM Women's Desk (based in Georgetown). All these links are helping to break down isolation and to promote a Caribbean women's movement. Women in the WRSM and its associated women's organizations have been raising funds to assist 'needy' women, training women in crafts and domestic skills, encouraging better nutrition and child rearing practices, and producing goods and services for sale. But these are precisely the same activities as middle-class and professional women were engaged in at the turn of the century. It is in this vein that their activities have to be viewed. Despite its official status as the wing of a political party, the WRSM is following in the footsteps of the pre-independence social welfare organizations.

Any significant advances the WRSM and its associated organizations might have made are far outweighed by their failings. Politically, the WRSM concentrates on fund raising, election campaigning and mobilizing women in PNC membership drives. In fact it only seems to act as a political unit to mobilize women into PNC forms of political and economic organization[13] and, as such, is unrepresentative of the interests of the majority of women. It does not have mass support among women and has not attempted to use campaigning skills to involve the mass of women in political activities or even to secure more female representatives within the PNC. Not only does the WRSM seem to have nothing to say about its political philosophy in relation to women, it also vehemently denies being a feminist organization. Socialism and feminism are seen as mutually exclusive, with the latter viewed only in crude terms as an adjunct of colonialism (WRSM 1985). Women's problems are seen as an integral part of the wider problems of society, which have to be addressed by both men and women. Hence, there is at least one male PNC member on the WRSM executive.

While the WRSM's members see one of its major objectives as 'the full participation of women in all aspects of national life', it has not attempted to secure the large-scale entry of women into formal sector employment — it claims that 'development has to come first' (WRSM 1985). It in fact only encourages women to participate in the development process when this happens to suit the government; women's needs are invariably secondary.

The WRSM's current position on the activities of women traders crystallizes its general viewpoint. Trading represents the only growing area of women's employment in the country and is a valuable source of foreign exchange. But in the eyes of the WRSM it constitutes the bringing in of non-essential items, the undermining of the state's system of distribution and the non-payment of overheads. Essentially, female traders are thought to undermine the government's development efforts and, consequently, the WRSM seems determined. to ban them.

It is through such strategies that the WRSM helps promulgate gender inequality, not only by failing to tackle prevailing discriminatory structures, but also by adding to them through promoting gender-stereotyped training programmes. Neither have its employment schemes for women, whether in cooperative development enterprises or in small-scale businesses, been integrated into the formal sector economy. As a consequence of its focus on certain welfare type activities and income-generating projects, women have come to be classified as a dependent welfare group — as consumers rather than participants. Placing women's concerns within the welfare sector, which is the first to be cut in periods of retrenchment, merely institutionalizes women's subordinate status in Guyanese society.

After 1964, when the PNC came to office, the WPO and (for a few years in the 1980s) the WPA Women's Section drew attention to the attack that had taken place on human rights. They focused on the rights of women to participate in free and fair elections, to have employment, to be able to live in hygienic conditions without fear of malnutrition, to live free from fear of political and racial discrimination and male violence and to promote world peace and disarmament. It was in their attempts to organize, unite and mobilize women against PNC policy and practices that these women's political organizations had a progressive role to play. As arms of socialist political parties they are not politically autonomous, but rather act as pressure groups operating within socialist ideals. Indeed the only common characteristic shared by the WRSM, the WPA Women's Section and the WPO is that they act as supportive organizations for their parent parties. But, unlike the WRSM, the WPO engages in consciousness raising and political education, as does the successor to the WPA Women's Section, Red Thread. The latter is in fact a feminist organization, which supports women regardless of their political affiliation or racial group, not only at election times but also on a daily basis.

## Conclusion

As throughout the Caribbean, by the early twentieth century women's networks in Guyana included church groups, mother's unions, professional organizations and service associations. These religious and social groups played a significant role in establishing the welfare state in Guyana. Their flexible, non-bureaucratic mode of organizing gave women an opportunity to participate in improving their social situation and allowed them to develop valuable organizational and leadership skills. Although important potential channels for social change, the location of these groups in the private sphere led to their marginalization, with their members isolated from any formal development initiatives. It was not until the formation of the WPEO, with its focus on the social and economic constraints facing women, that a breakthrough to the public sector occurred. More recently, these women's organizations have been brought under the umbrella of CASWIG and, while ostensibly NGOs, they have aligned themselves with the PNC government. As such, although they press for more support and resources for women, they have not challenged the PNC system.

The women's political organizations in Guyana formed since the Second World War can be split into two camps — for and against the PNC. The position of women in the PNC government's women's associations seems largely symbolic: the majority have been content to play traditional supportive roles for the party. They have not promoted the needs, nor defended the interests or the political advancement of the mass of women. Although, during the 1975-85 United Nations Decade for Women, they urged the government to affect legal changes that would redefine relations between the sexes, there has been little sign of improvement in women's access to basic needs, such as employment, health care and housing. They lack the ability (and interest) to develop a women's movement because they were not established on the democratic principle of listening to women and channelling their voices to the government. Reforms that have taken place have not been with the participation of women, but have rather been handed down to them and have been of limited usefulness.

Only with the development of a politics of empowerment, which would allow women to organize with more independence, to speak out free from fear or victimization, to gain access to information and services, in fact to win the power to act to meet their needs, will the conditions of the masses of women fundamentally change. With its dual emphasis on income generation and consciousness-raising around issues of class, gender, race and political transformation, this empowerment approach is currently being advocated by Red Thread. The type of political involvement it espouses is a primary mechanism for social change, for it has the potential to create alliances of women whose interests crosscut those of the male political party élite. Although some WRSM women are more committed to the interests of women than to their male colleagues, empowerment has never been promoted by women's organizations within the sphere of PNC influence. Guyanese women, it appears, will have to turn to organizations outside the PNC'S orbit to win their right to true political involvement in their country's future.[14]

## Notes

1 I would not have been able to write this chapter, nor indeed would have wished to, were it not for the friendship and support of a number of Guyanese people. For pointing to or providing me with relevant information I am particularly indebted to Andaiye, Indira Chandrapal, Roberta Kilkenny, Patrice Lafleur, Karen de Souza, Gail Teixera, Faustina Ward-Osborne and the WRSM National Executive Committee. However, I claim full responsibility for interpreting the information. I also wish to thank Sally Marston, Ruth Pearson and Jan Penrose for their comments on an earlier draft. In addition, I wish to explain why this chapter has been written by a non-Guyanese. As a white Western feminist, my attempt to analyse the interrelation between women's exploitation and oppression and the national liberation of Guyana could well be interpreted as yet another expression of Eurocentric cultural imperialism. But this point of view denies the reality of the world system within which women are linked to each other through the international division of labour. The question of whether women in countries that have achieved national liberation now have more access to economic and political power is still unclear. This chapter is a contribution to that debate and, as such, I hope it will be accepted on these terms by both Guyanese and non-Guyanese women. The background research was undertaken in 1985, when I spent three months as a visiting lecturer in the Department of Geography at the University of Guyana, and during a return visit in December 1988. Interviews were conducted with officials in the WPO, WRSM, CASWIG, WAC of the TUC, WPA Women's Section, Red Thread and with a number of Guyanese women who were not represented in any of these organizations.

2 I am not suggesting that Guyanese women form a homogeneous group. They are divided by race, colour, class, social and economic status and place of residence and their experiences differ accordingly. However, by virtue of their gender they are all, regardless of other attributes, subject to male subordination. Accordingly it is their unifying feature as a gender-defined social group that is of prime importance in this analysis.

3 There were a few exceptions to this rule when women inherited property. One example was Mrs Margaret Burns, who in the mid-1880s was 'the leading Creole lady in Berbice, with a fine store on the Strand and several other properties, including a cattle ranch' (Rodney 1981: 107).

4 Their work included 'needlework of every description, fancy work, baskets, articles in wood, both plain and inlaid, raffia and felt work, novelties for Christmas, guava jelly, hot sauce, tamarind syrup, sweets, guava cheese, cakes, Indian curios, stuffed alligators, hammocks and balata ornaments' (Anon. 1931: 59).

5 Guyanese women had first attained a limited franchise in 1928 when eligibility to vote included property and income qualifications and the ability to read and write. These criteria effectively excluded the vast majority of women who were functionally illiterate. In 1945 the franchise was extended and by the 1947 election the financial qualification was further reduced. The literacy requirement was retained, however, effectively disfranchising the 22 per cent of women who could not read or write (Kilkenny 1984). Not until 1953 were all women entitled to vote.

6 The WPEO made no official statement about its demise, but its Executive Committee functioned until June 1948 and the Congress until April 1949 (Kilkenny 1984).

7 The WIDF is the largest international body of women's organizations. Formed in 1945, it has consultative status in UNESCO and on the UN Social and Economic Council.

8 For example, the president and vice-president of the WAC of the TUC are first and second vice-presidents of CASWIG. Along with the chair of CASWIG, they are all members of the WRSM, as is the director of WAB, who is also assistant general secretary of the PNC. Funds also pass between the organizations, with WAC, for example, being shareholders in the WRSM projects.

9 A number of constitutional changes relating to women's equality have taken place in Guyana since 1904, when separate property rights were conferred on women. The only women with property at this stage, however, were from the white élite and emergent middle class. As measures indicative of the emancipation of women they were isolated gestures.

10 This article, however, is part of the Directive Principles of the Constitution and is not enforceable by law.

11 To the best of my knowledge, only two studies of Guyanese traders have been conducted. A 1985 survey by Dann (1985) of 90 traders, 25 of whom were women, and a 1988 survey of 123 female traders by Holder (1988). They reveal that the vast majority of women traders are between the ages of 20 and 35 and are likely to be single household heads supporting children and other dependent relatives. Approximately 70 per cent of the women had completed secondary education and, apart from trading, which was a full-time occupation for half to three-quarters of them, they were also employed as government workers, teachers, nurses, typists and provision farmers. They engaged in trading through sheer economic necessity usually brought about by unemployment, desertion by male partners and having to supplement other sources of income. They travelled as far as Suriname, Brazil, Trinidad, Barbados, Venezuela, Miami and New York and the majority had experienced problems with airline customs and immigration officials, which usually resulted in them giving bribes in order to continue their trading activities. While some traders always bought specific items, especially clothing, shoes and foodstuffs, others simply purchased any 'cheap' goods. While some secured orders from regular customers, others sold their goods on the street, often with the help of their children. Finance to set up their trading activities was usually loaned by families or friends who acquired foreign currency on the black market.
12 Evacuation and couterage operations, performed by both doctors and nurses, are available in the public hospitals and these are used to bring on spontaneous abortions.
13 The WRSM links directly to the policy-making structures within the PNC. Its position is made clear in the 1988 telephone directory where it is listed under the heading 'Other Government Departments'.
14 Since the time of writing this chapter in 1989, there have been significant developments in the Guyanese political system, in particular the deposing of the PNC government and the election on 5 October 1992 of a PPP-dominated government led by Cheddi Jagan. His cabinet has only one female member, Gail Teixeira, the new Minister of Health.

## References

Anon. (1931) 'The British Guiana United Home Industries and Self-Help Association'. *British Guiana Women's Centenary Effort, 1831-1931*, Georgetown, Guyana, 59-60

—— (1980) 'Review of Employment of Women in Guyana, 1975-1980'. Georgetown, Guyana, mimeo.

Baber, C. and H.B. Jeffrey (1986) *Guyana, Politics, Economics and Society*. London: Frances Pinter

Bayley, M. (1931) 'The Girl Guide Movement'. *British Guiana Women's Centenary Effort, 1831-1931*, Georgetown, Guyana, 25-7

Burnham, L.F.S. (1980) 'Address to the 3rd Biennial Convention of the WRSM'. *Report of the 3rd Biennial Convention of the WRSM*, Georgetown, Guyana

Buvinic, M., N. Youssef and B. von Elm (1978) *Women Headed Households: The Ignored Factor in Development Planning*. Washington DC: International Center for Research on Women

Dann, G. (1985) *The Role of Women in the Underground Economy in Guyana*. Ann Arbor, Michigan: University of Michigan, mimeograph

Dingwall, M. (1931) 'Women and Social Progress'. *British Guiana Women's Centenary Effort, 1831-1931*, Georgetown, Guyana, 3-6

Earle, C. (1977) 'Women in Guyana's Politics'. *Caribbean Contact*, (December) 19

Government of British Guyana (1946) *1946 Population Census*. Georgetown, Guyana: Government Printer

—— (1960) *1960 Population Census*. Georgetown, Guyana: Government Printer

Government of Guyana (1980) *Constitution of the Cooperative Republic of Guyana*. Georgetown, Guyana: Government Printer

Holder, Y. (1988) *Women Traders in Guyana. Consultancy Report*. Santiago: Economic Commission for Latin America & the Caribbean/Caribbean Development & Cooperation Committee

IBRD (International Bank for Reconstruction and Development) (1978) *Social Indicators Data Sheet*. Washington DC: IBRD

Kilkenny, R. (1984) 'Women in Social and Political Struggle: British Guiana 1946-1953'. Paper presented at the 16th Annual Conference of Caribbean Historians, Barbados, April

Kwayana, E. (1990) *Public Talk, 3rd March 1990*. Toronto: Ontario Institute for Studies in Education

Mohammed, P. (1986) 'Domestic Workers'. In P. Ellis (ed.) *Women of the Caribbean*, London: Zed Books, 41-6

Molyneux, M. (1981) 'Socialist Societies Old and New: Progress towards Women's Emancipation'. *Feminist Review*, (8) 1-34

Peake, L. (1986) *Low Income Women's Participation in the Housing Process: A Case Study from Guyana*. London: University College, Development Planning Unit, Gender and Planning Working Paper No. 10

—— (1987) 'Guyana: A Country in Crisis'. *Geography*, (72) 41-4

—— (1987a) 'Government Housing Policy and its Implications for Women in Guyana'. In C. Moser and L. Peake (eds) *Women, Human Settlements and Housing*, London: Tavistock

Randall, V. (1987) *Women and Politics*. 2nd ed. London: Macmillan

Rodney, W. (1981) *A History of the Guyanese Working People, 1881-1905*. London: Heinemann Educational Books

Standing, G. (1979) 'Socialism and Basic Needs in Guyana'. In G. Standing and R. Szal (eds) *Poverty and Basic Needs*, Geneva: International Labour Office

State Paper on Equality for Women (1976) *Sessional Paper No. 1/1976, 15.1.76*. Georgetown, Guyana: Government Printer

WDP (1987) *Needlepoint*. Georgetown, Guyana: Women's Development Project, mimeograph

WPA Women's Section (1983) 'Resolution Passed by Conference, Women in Struggle for Bread and Justice', 4 July

WPO (1983) *Forward with Women's Struggle*. Georgetown, Guyana: WPO

—— (1983a) Questionnaire by WIDF to the 1985 World Conference to review the results of the UN Decade for Women

—— (1985) *WPO Answers Justice Bernard*. Georgetown, Guyana: WPO, mimeograph

WRSM (n.d.) *Brief History of the WRSM, 1957-1984*. Georgetown, Guyana: WRSM, mimeograph

—— (1980) 'Report of the 3rd Biennial Convention of the WRSM'. Georgetown, Guyana: WRSM

—— (1985) 'Personal interview with the WRSM National Executive Committee'. Georgetown, Guyana: WRSM

# VIII Neighbourhood Networks & National Politics among Working-class Afro-Surinamese Women

ROSEMARY BRANA-SHUTE

Working-class, urban Afro-Surinamese women have participated in informal clubs and voluntary associations for generations. Many of these societies or sodalities are religious in orientation and are affiliated with established churches. Many others, however, are perceived by their members to have strictly social aims: companionship and entertainment. Known variously as *straati vereningen* or *sport vereningen* or *dansi vereningen* (street, entertainment or dance clubs), they are all overwhelmingly female in membership. In the late 1950s, with increasing politicization of the population and an increase in the number of political parties, many of these club members began to participate actively in national political campaigns and in the discussion of political issues. Because of the close cooperation between club members, based on previously existing ties of residence, kinship, shared sexual division of labour and common adaptations to economic marginality, those national political parties successful in recruiting club members as party workers found that these women could deliver the votes of a neighbourhood. This reliance on working-class women to muster the vote in their neighbourhoods continued after political independence from The Netherlands in 1975, ceasing only after a military coup in February 1980 prohibited political parties from operating. Elections in 1987 briefly revived political parties and their support groups. The result was a return to a semblance of civilian rule without the enthusiastic political contests and hope in the future that was characteristic of the pre-1980s.

In this chapter, after briefly describing some important characteristics of Suriname, I examine the working-class, urban, Afro-Surinamese clubs (which have been so important to political mobilization at the urban neighbourhood level) and explain why their membership is almost exclusively female. Attention is directed both to the socio-cultural context of these clubs and to the political activities of these women, with a view to explaining how and why they worked to deliver electoral victories. Given that the males rather than the females in the political parties benefit most from this effort, I ask why women work so hard to secure positions of power for men. The remainder of the chapter probes changing demographic and political patterns that seem likely to alter permanently and radically the influence, if not the very existence, of these female organizations.[1]

## National Context

Until it became an independent republic on 25 November 1975, Suriname was a Dutch plantation colony tucked between French Guiana and Guyana on the northeast coast of South America. It has one of the most heterogeneous populations in the Western hemisphere, with no one ethnic group holding a clear majority among its 382,000 inhabitants.[2] The largest group, making up 37 per cent of the population, is the Hindustani, who are descendants of East Indian contract labourers imported between 1873 and 1917 to work on the plantations after the abolition of slavery. Creoles (Afro-Surinamers), descended from European settlers and Africans sold as slaves to plantations between the seventeenth and early nineteenth centuries, constitute about 31 per cent of the population. The Javanese, who account for about 15 per cent, were also introduced as contract labourers for faltering plantations between 1891 and 1939. Maroons (known as Bush Negroes in Suriname), whose ancestors were African slaves who escaped from the plantations into the rugged interior, make up 10 per cent. Chinese, Amerindians, Guyanese, Lebanese, Europeans and Jews, the latter present as a distinct group in the country since the seventeenth century (see Chapter 3), add to the array of ethnic styles, religions, languages, cuisines and values.[3]

Virtually all students of contemporary Suriname have remarked on its deeply-ingrained social and cultural pluralism, whereby groups are separated one from another through such boundary-maintaining mechanisms as residence and settlement patterns, source of livelihood, language, religion and the residual influence of divisive colonial policies and practices transferred in part to large political parties based on ethnic membership and solidarity (Dew 1978). Even the national language, Dutch, is largely relegated to the capital city of Paramaribo, to bureaucrats, élites, the well-educated and the upwardly mobile (Eersel 1971). Almost all ethnic groups maintain a 'mother tongue', even as the young enter schools to face instruction in Dutch, a second or third language for many. Sranan Tongo, a local Creole language and traditional 'mother tongue' of the Creoles, has been in use in Suriname since the seventeenth century (Voorhoeve and Lichtveld 1975: 273-84). It is *de facto* the national language; it is the one most Surinamers know and thus serves for cross-ethnic communication among the masses, despite the increasing incursion of Dutch, especially among the better educated.

Economically, in this century the national Surinamese treasury has been dependent on bauxite extraction and smelting, with rice, wood and tropical products augmenting exports. All these commodities rely on world market prices, which are largely outside Surinamese control (Hawkins 1976). Locally, under-employment and unemployment levels are chronically high, especially for the young and for females. A world recession in the 1970s, high and rapid price increases (especially difficult for a country dependent on foreign imports for everything from food to glass) and chronic maldistribution of wealth, services and opportunities have only intensified competition between ethnic groups for whatever political and economic spoils are available. A military coup in the 1980s increased competition for resources, for the military co-opted both power and the national treasury, redirecting resources and patronage for its own aggrandizement. A massacre of civilian opponents in 1982 resulted in a drastic loss of foreign aid to punish the military, a loss that exacerbated the country's rapid slide from a standard of living among the highest in the Caribbean in 1975 to one of the lowest and still declining in 1990.

Since the Second World War and especially since the 1960s, all ethnic groups have been migrating in increasing numbers from rural, formerly plantation, districts, into Paramaribo; nearly 70 per cent of the population now resides in and around the city, making Paramaribo the most primate of all new world cities (Cross 1979: 77). Historically, the city has always been primate, in that it was the centre of trade, commerce, government and, for the élite, culture. Increasing urbanization, particularly by Hindustani, Javanese, Chinese and Maroons, has brought changes into a city which traditionally had served as a European and Creole professional and cultural stronghold. The growing presence of recent migrants in the city, the increasing political and national self-consciousness of the population, universal suffrage in 1948, home rule in the 1950s and an increase in the utilization of educational opportunities by all groups led to political events which reflected and occasionally exacerbated inter-ethnic rivalry. Political affiliation was not strictly ethnically determined, but the association was so close as to remain, even in 1990, part of public wisdom: party and ethnicity support each other (Brana-Shute 1979).

It would, however, be a mistake to perceive Surinamese problems as purely ethnic rivalries, though Surinamers themselves often explain their political history and conundrums in this way and politicians may play this for whatever mileage they can get. Colour, class, religious and gender divisions exist within ethnic groups as well. The focus in this chapter is on one segment of one ethnic group: working-class Creole women in Paramaribo. The configuration described is distinctive in several ways. Being working-class distinguishes them economically, socially and culturally from upper and middle-class Creoles. Being Creole distinguishes them from their female and class counterparts in other ethnic groups. Certainly being female simultaneously constrains them and allows them opportunities that are different from those of male citizens (Coleridge 1958).

## Pre-Coup Social Clubs

Following the end of slavery in 1863, many voluntary associations emerged and thrived in working-class Creole neighbourhoods in Paramaribo (Pierce 1971: 65-76). We know very little about their origins and activities before the 1950s, but since then almost all have been social or religious in nature and all are overwhelmingly female in membership. The social clubs were begun by women for their own enjoyment (Coleridge 1958: 92-3). They have evolved into both mutual support networks and broker institutions tying domestic and neighbourhood networks to the national political parties favoured by Creoles.

The basic reason for the essentially female membership is that working-class Creole women are more cohesive as a group than working-class men. A number of shared social characteristics that strengthen the ties between these women contribute to this cohesion (Brana-Shute 1976: 158-64). Creole kinship has a strong female bias. The maternal side of the family is generally favoured and localized, most prominently among the lower and working classes for whom legal marriage is less common than among more advantaged Creoles of the middle and upper classes. Mother-child bonds are generally stronger than affinal ties, as even most married men will acknowledge. Men, when present, often play relatively weak domestic roles (Pierce 1971; Buschkens 1974; Brana-Shute 1979).

Female-headed households remain a more frequent occurrence among the less well-off. Women who head their households have increased responsibility and decision-making authority and wider experience in the domestic and economic spheres. Many middle-aged and elderly working-class Creole women own their own homes, no matter how humble, and have resided in their neighbourhood for some length of time. Some have inherited from their parents or mother, so that they and their families are associated with their neighbourhood and its development and lore. Others have worked long to buy their own house and yard (Coleridge 1958: 91). When mates separate, the male is almost always the one who moves on. As in other areas of Surinamese life, women are less mobile than men;

while preferring secure and permanent residence, they are simultaneously constrained by limited marketable skills and resources. However, permanency does have its advantages: one is known in the neighbourhood; one has a 'place' in its social life; and the cost of housing, especially for those who own their own homes, is often minimal. To move elsewhere would necessitate making new friends and neighbours with whom favours, goods and services may be exchanged, a situation which demands time for friendship and mutual trust to develop. A move would also necessitate money; these women have little to spare.

Creole women, like Creole men, accept a division of labour based on gender. Although traditionally the women are closely tied to the domestic realm, this does not mean that they do not participate in the labour force. The public or formal sphere is not a male preserve and historically it never has been in Suriname. However, women who are working-class and Creole share the disadvantages of their class as well as their gender: less income, less steady employment, less education and fewer marketable skills than other Creoles, male or female. Even when a woman works for wages, the management of the home and the rearing of the children remain her responsibility. Especially for working-class Creole women, wage labour is often a necessity for the family's economic survival rather than a question of choice. Householding is often perceived as an occupation, for it takes time, money and managerial expertise. Own-account businesses ·run by women (such as making and selling small handicraft items and home processed foods, marketing fruit and taking in laundry and sewing) frequently keep them close to home, in or near the neighbourhood and often in close contact with other women. In the city, working-class women work in the company of other women much more than in the company of men.

There is also a sexual division of leisure; much of the lower and working-class Creole woman's leisure time is spent, as with work, in the company of other women.[4] They chat together, go to parties together and even make politics together. In sum, and not discounting the importance of financial contributions by men, working-class Creole women learn to live with and to depend more on other women and children than on their male peers.

By contrast, men generally work outside these domestic units and neighbour-hoods and establish individual ties with other men (and women) dispersed throughout the city, among whom they divide their time and their money. Relaxation is generally taken in the company of other men, drinking and conversing in rum shops. It is precisely because women have developed vested interests in their local neighbourhoods, based on kinship, friendship, stable residence and the shared patterns and responsibilities associated with their class and gender, that they can organize themselves effectively and without the suspicion with which outsiders are scrutinized.[5]

Because household responsibilities devolve almost exclusively on females and consume much time, energy and money, these women 'make do' by utilizing other female contacts to increase their access to markets, jobs, bargains and services. Assisting and depending on other females obligates them to other women, but also opens up networks to be exploited. Wise women maintain this reciprocity and broaden their contacts with and through other women, even outside their neigh-bourhoods. The frequent absence of men, rather than acting as a constraint on women, often allows them greater independence in decision-making, in use of time and money and in establishing their own social relationships.

This degree of independence does not guarantee that a working-class woman will join a social club. Probably only a minority of women would be 'socially eligible' for membership. She is more likely to join a club if she is at least in her early forties. By that age there are no infants at home for whom she is directly responsible. Her older children will be able to care for younger ones, or she may be a grandmother with the care of grandchildren resting mostly on their mothers. She will have more time available and be more mobile, whether or not she holds a job. She should own her own home, or have somehow stabilized her financial situation. The young or really poor cannot afford the time and money spent in club activities. By the time she is in her forties she will have developed a core of close friends and a network of good neighbours with whom she has learned to cooperate. Finally, she must be 'respectable' (*lespeki* in Sranan Tongo), which is an important aspect of her reputation. This will mean that she is recognized as courteous, cooperative, trustworthy and as leading a scandal-free life. The latter is not correlated with being legally married; so long as she is not regarded as promiscuous, the civil status of her intimate relationship(s) is not an issue. Good humour and an ability to wield traditional Creole proverbs and Sranan Tongo is a plus. If she is thought to be greedy or stingy, to have a malicious tongue, or to appear to move in on other women's spouses or mates, she is unlikely to be appraised either as respecting herself, or being worthy of respect.[6]

A social club is formed or joined when a number of these women and their close friends formally organize to create new opportunities for cooperation and fun outside the home and immediate neighbourhood. A number of neighbourhoods are linked through social clubs. Memberships range from about 30 to 100 or more women, though most appear to number under 100. The club constitutes a change in social relationships in that it is a large group effort not determined exclusively by kinship and residence. Some members may be related, but that is an unimportant aspect unless the women are also close and cooperating friends. More important than residence is distance, as the travel time to meetings and parties can be an effective and expensive barrier to full and frequent participation in activities and contact with other members. Membership in a social club allows a woman to move beyond what could be called strictly household-maintaining activities. It offers emotional support, some redistribution of wealth, informal managerial training and something important and usually difficult to achieve for working-class women: entertainment. At meetings members call each other 'sister' or 'mother,' which is symbolic of the close cooperative roles they anticipate.

A club has a slate of officers and regular meetings. It will also have a colour, a name and often an insignia by which it is known. Decisions, including elections of officers, are arrived at by consensus, for a conscious effort is made to minimize conflict. Members unable to attend a function will always be kept informed by their 'sisters', who will visit or pass by their houses in the normal pattern of a week, on the way to and from the markets, or in the afternoons or evenings after much of the work of the day is done. Dances and commemorative celebrations are frequent and often open to outsiders, who pay entry fees and, in effect, help subsidize the club and minimize the costs incurred by the members. Sometimes one club will invite another club to participate in its activities, thereby increasing acquaintances and, in the case of a lavish well-organized affair with fine food and drink for everyone and music for a full afternoon or evening of lively dancing, increasing the reputation and status of the host club's members. On occasions a club will organize a weekend excursion to a rural district to enable its members to meet their counterparts in rural organizations, visit old friends and relatives less frequently seen and talk to members of political clubs.

Though clubs are not perceived of as offering social services, they are in effect used as a forum in which to exchange food and labour, disseminate information about jobs, government agencies and policies, bargain prices and discuss political developments, moving the information by 'mouth newspaper' (*mofo koranti*) between members and from members back to neighbours and kin outside the club (see Chapter 5).

Members' birthdays are celebrated with dances, gifts and songs arranged by the club 'flower committee', which controls much of the money. Birthdays are very important occasions to Creole Surinamers, especially the 'big years' that mark every decade and half decade of a person's life. The clubs recognize this and reinforce their special role in a 'sister's' life by playing a prominent role in the celebrations, if not actually hosting the party. In times of illness or death the club extends money, services and emotional support. In times of food shortages or political crises, the same networks are tapped, with the same attention to detail and efficiency as in normal times.

## Pre-Coup Political Clubs

Many of the women who belonged to social clubs also belonged to a branch of the largest national political party associated with the Creole population in Suriname, the NPS (Nationale Partij Suriname).[7] These branches are called *kernen* (in Dutch *kern* means nucleus, kernel or gist). In fact, the memberships of the social clubs and the *kernen* strongly overlap in the city. According to NPS rules, a *kern* consists of at least 100 registered party members, male and female, of a particular locality who choose to meet regularly to advise party leaders and in turn to be informed of party positions on various issues and strategies. Not all *kernen* meet year in year out, the main reason being the tendency of party officials to approach constituents mostly when votes are needed and because Creole Surinamers rely more on individual personal contacts between elections. The social clubs help to fill this gap between elections, as many club members are individually well-connected to the party and can informally gain access to favours or information which may be passed back to club 'sisters' as well as kin and select neighbours.

*Kernen* most frequently meet when word comes from party headquarters that it is time to gear up for the campaign. At that time all the skills and networks developed by the club women come into play. Most of the *kern* members, especially the active ones, are older Creole women. Social club officers are often *kern* officers. The formal structure of the *kern* reflects the social club's structure, except for the addition of a secretary charged with taking notes and the so-called 'mother' whose role is undefined but symbolic of the party itself, which will nurture and protect its own 'children'. Although *kernen* have no 'flower committees', social club officers extend their duties to include high political party officials on their birthdays too, reminding them that they are 'brothers' with obligations to 'sisters'. They organize club members into groups that personally visit party leaders with flowers and songs; club members expect the recipients to remember their faces, names and organization in the future. Thus, in 1979, at a birthday party held for the then NPS prime minister of Suriname at a comfortable, but not lavish, home of a loyal party worker and friend, working-class *kern* leaders and members paraded into the feast, sang songs, pledged their party allegiance and, sitting next to and among the middle- and upper middle-class wives of the ruling (male) politicians, shared in a dinner of traditional Creole food. It was at once a 'rite of passage' for the prime minister and a 'rite of intensification' for the NPS.

Much of the efficiency of campaigns at the local level was attributable to the activities of *kernen* and these *kernen* were able to play this role because they grew out of the social clubs. Although men were also members of *kernen* and a man was almost always elected or appointed head of a *kern*, the energetic *kernen* were essentially the social clubs with political duties appended to regular club business. In the process they assumed the additional function of broker institutions between the neighbourhoods and the national party headquarters. The *kern* merely provided another opportunity for these 'sisters' to realize additional social, entertainment and potential economic gains by participating in the political process and winning.

It is worth emphasizing the importance of the political process as entertainment. Most working-class women have few opportunities for leisure and fun. Political campaigns, as well as social clubs, are usually exciting, full of stories, gossip and rumours, with emotional swings of elation from an anticipated victory to explosions of indignation at the public accusations of opponents. *Kern* meetings were generally in the evenings or at weekends and constituted opportunities to go out, to be seen and to see others as well as a chance to collect some information and perhaps to pass some along. The NPS traditionally organized excursions during campaigns in order to bring its message to the rural districts. Buses and meals were provided, as were speeches and festivities to cap the day. Many of the *kern* members from Paramaribo, especially women, participated as often as they could. Party leaders and followers would elbow each other; political gossip and rumours would be told and inspected; stories and jokes would fill the day. The entire process was re-enacted time after time, district after district and neighbourhood after neighbourhood, in back yards and in public parks at mass meetings.

Also important was the medium in which the party message of the party was broadcast: especially in Creole working-class areas in town and in the rural districts, the language used was Sranan Tongo. The images, metaphors and proverbs (*odo*) are Creole. A party platform may be for national consumption but it is sold most effectively to the Creole working class when packaged in what is perceived to be traditional Creole style (Brana-Shute 1976: 174-5).

Where clubs and *kernen* blended the women performed a wide variety of jobs, which ensured the bulk of a neighbourhood's votes for the party. Their work left party élites free to put their propaganda across quietly in social and business circles, where the working class, especially women, have no regular access. The *kernen* also recommended candidates for the party lists; they know the people who, by past experience, have proven willing to help local people, through patronage and/or through efforts to ameliorate the problems of working-class residents in general. *Kern* women have withheld contributions of money and services when *kern* advice was clearly overlooked, especially when it appeared that a snub was intended or if party officials were acting as if they were superior to their neighbourhood constituents. During a campaign the club networks operated to communicate party strategies, canvass votes, collect money, check voter registration lists, teach people how and for whom to vote,[8] ridicule disbelievers, put pressure on waverers,[9] pack mass public meetings, wear the party colours like walking advertisements, physically get voters to the polls, (including the men in the corner rum shops), help count and verify the votes and, finally, celebrate the victory.

It would be erroneous to claim that these politically-keen women also make important party decisions. They do not, but politicians are aware of the enormity of their contribution during the campaigning. They are courted, if somewhat feared and resented. More than one politician has chilled at the prospect of women being given high-level, decision-making positions, which are presently male-dominated. When questioned one claimed that these women are 'unreasonable. They want solutions and don't know how to compromise [to get them]. If they don't like what you say or how you behave, they can kill you with a *churi*,[10] a sophisticated and eloquent version of the Bronx cheer. This sentiment was repeated by others. In part because of the small-scale, personal nature of the society, 'mouth newspaper' is effective. Politicians are seen, spoken to and talked about often. Club women know personally, or via their contacts, the accomplishments and peccadillos of many of the well-placed. They rarely have any compunctions about advising politicians about problems and needs. Politicians able or willing to aid individuals or to arrange something for someone are remembered; so are the ones who cannot or will not respond.

In sum, although these women as an interest group do not decide on the mechanics or substance of how problems will be solved at the national level, they do deliver much of the vote and they did influence how much attention was given to issues such as prices, jobs for the young and for women and expanded health and educational facilities. Interviews with politicians and party workers in the 1970s confirmed the existence of real pressure exerted by these women individually and especially in groups.

Why then, if Creole women are so influential, do they not occupy more high political offices? Put another way, why do women work so hard to secure decision-making positions for the men? Although there is a precedent in Surinamese history for women in high political office (though never the highest) and even for a women's political party,[11] 'women's issues' have been insufficiently attractive to organize women as an interest group or constituency on their own behalf. Working-class Creole women largely agree that women have a 'greater understanding' of the problems families have to face daily and that women 'work harder'. After lengthy discussions in some social clubs about the demand to place more women in key national positions, it was generally agreed that, when it came to experience, women, not men, knew what problems Surinamers faced; that women would work harder than men because they were more concerned with immediate results and changes than with egos; that women would understand the need for jobs and lower food prices more than men, who spend much of their time away from the home, the market and the children. They agreed that more women need to be in positions of power. In the end, however, the party leadership argued for patience, saying that a vote for a women's party would divide the Creole vote and possibly pass the government over to another ethnic group. The women backed off. It was ethnic solidarity that was accepted as the first necessary step to Surinamese development. Issues of class and gender were played down in the face of a perceived threat to the Creole group as a whole.

There are other explanations as well. Women have less education than men; they earn less money and hold more marginal jobs. This leaves them insecure in a larger public arena. Many women persistently underrate their own abilities, even in the light of their accomplishments. Surinamers, perhaps because of the colonial experience, put high value on education and polish in their leaders and working-class women, though proud and outspoken in many ways, feel the difference between themselves and those men and women who have had a good formal education (generally in The Netherlands) and speak Dutch with ease.

Some of the very characteristics that allow women to work and cooperate together serve to fence them out of power positions. Their networks are not limited to the domestic sphere, but the only functioning networks that are sensitive to them are based in local neighbourhoods. In this sense their networks are introverted, constantly re-intensified at that level. Working-class men link up with the broader occupational hierarchy outside the neighbourhoods; this experience and their diffuse social life expands their networks farther afield. While the women tend to cooperate to reinforce what they have in small groups, the men tend to individualize to broaden their contacts and experience (Brana-Shute 1979).

In addition, it is important to recognize that many of the gender stereotypes of what is proper for women are accepted by the women themselves: public life is widely accepted as a predominantly male domain, with room only for the exceptional woman. The customary division of labour usually allows women less free time than it does men, as women carry both financial and domestic burdens. Lower-class women can exchange services and favours but they rarely have the security, surplus and experience to dispense patronage (matronage?).

One could turn this around and say that they are not financially independent, which seems to be a prerequisite for power in many parts of the Caribbean, especially for women. One needs to be able to afford to lose bids for power without being dependent on the winner for one's family's livelihood. For women who accept an ideal of respectability, political infighting and campaigning means exposure to *ad hominem*, ridiculing and sometimes vicious and libellous verbal public attacks that can challenge and diminish respectability. One needs both independent financial stability and the ability to put up with and survive personal abuse in order to be a woman on her way to the top in politics. It should surprise no one, then, that most women in high political positions in Suriname have been appointed rather than elected.

Also real are continuing colour and class divisions that separate women. In Suriname this is further complicated by ethnic differences, class divisions within ethnic groups, religious differences within and between ethnic groups and the varying degrees of economic and social independence allowed women, which depends as much on one's ethnic group and age cohort as on class affiliation. In a society in which skin shade has been closely correlated with class, the Creole working class is clearly darker complexioned, less educated and more traditionally Creole than Dutch in world view, language and religious practice. This has important implications for the development of female leadership in Suriname. The very women with enough education and wealth to enter the fray to attain decision-making positions in public life are traditionally the employers, not the comrades, or their darker skinned, lower status female counterparts.

There is also a cultural component to the historical animosities based on colour and class, an aspect that continues to stratify the Creole population. The Sranan Tongo term *malata* (mulatto) has traditionally been used to denote much more than skin shade. It is a reference to the offspring of Creoles who adopted Dutch, Christian and Western practices and values as standards of excellence; most of these people were lighter skinned and had been part of the local colonial élite in Suriname since the nineteenth century. *Malata* is a term of derision used commonly to refer to people who are haughty and arrogant, who behave as if their 'clear' skin were a warranty of natural superiority. As a counterpoint there is the Sranan Tongo term *nengre* (Negro), which refers less to black skin than to those who adhere to the traditional Creole values and practices that evolved under slavery and, in some senses, oppose the Westernized standards of the *malata*.[12] To say that someone is a real *nengre* is often a compliment and recognition of a person's worldly knowledge, personal carriage, understanding and appreciation of Creole folk culture and religion and the ability to use Sranan Tongo as an eloquent primary (though not exclusive) language. The working-class Creole women referred to in this chapter are clearly *nengre*, a self-perception based on culture as well as class. This perception of themselves as *nengre* poses a challenge to those who come from other ethnic or class groups to organize them, particularly if the would-be organizers behave as *malata*.

Gaining an insight into the meaning(s) of *nengre* helps one to understand why the club women's political activities were often extensions of faith rather than of a clearly articulated ideology. In the early days, organized political party activities were, in Suriname as in many other Caribbean countries, the prerogative of upper- and middle-class Creoles, many of whom were light complexioned and socially and economically advantaged. Until universal suffrage was extended to Suriname in 1948, only about 2 per cent of the population was eligible to vote, given the property and education requirements then in force (Van Lier 1971: 334). Broadening the franchise to include the lower classes activated discussions in Suriname (and among the Surinamese in The Netherlands) about the need for more local autonomy. This ultimately led to the emergence of a charismatic black politician, the late Johan (Jopie) Pengel, and the coalescence of most working-class Creoles into a formidable NPS constituency. In trying to answer why so few women were in positions of political power, one elderly black woman explained that *nengre* women had internalized the view that the public, more prestigious areas of life were the domains of males, but that self-respect and pride could be attained by supporting their men — *Opo na kloroe, opo den man* (Elevate the [black] colour, elevate [your] men). A pride in one's colour (and in the traditional cultural patterns associated with it) was closely tied to the political ascendancy and victory of the pre-eminent Creole party, the NPS, whose most dynamic leader appeared to champion the *nengre*. Even after Pengel's death in 1970, the NPS remained for many the party to which one maintained allegiance as a matter of loyalty and self-respect. Ignorance of the details and implications of the moderate, if not conservative, goals of the NPS does not necessarily diminish the fervour of many who continue to follow its banner. It largely remains a matter of *bribi* (belief, faith).

While one may understand the reasons for such tenacity of faith, it is important to recognize that the 1970s and 1980s were years of rapid and unforeseen political and demographic changes, which have tempered the activities, if not the beliefs, of the faithful and are altering both the context and substance of lower-class Creole life. The patterns of these changes are explored in the remainder of the chapter.

## Aftermath of the Coup

On 25 February 1980, four years and three months to the day after Suriname became a sovereign republic, a sergeants' coup toppled Suriname's increasingly moribund NPS-dominated government. For most citizens it was a stunning shock, without any historical precedent and in a country in which the military was only four years old. Though many citizens were growing frustrated with the government's ineptitude and inefficiency in dealing with economic problems, the sergeants had only specific and limited grievances against the government. They wanted it to recognize their military (trade) union (a replica of the Dutch army's union for non-commissioned officers, NCOs) and to release several of their comrades who had been gaoled and court-martialled after over a year of sporadic demonstrations and sit-down strikes by the NCOs. The sergeants' swift attack ended in the (perhaps largely unintended) collapse of the entire government. Newspaper headlines quoted one sergeant's assessment of a few hours' work: 'We only wanted a union but we got a country' (*Haagse Post* 1981: 10; Brana-Shute 1981: 26).

The new military leadership of 25-35 year-old NCOs quickly solidified its position by forming a National Military Council (NMR) composed of members from the 16 commandos involved in the early morning attack. Civilian government was abolished. Apart from that act, the new leaders appear to have possessed little in the way of a developed vision or plan for governing the country. Counselled by a variety of advisers (many self-appointed) from the smaller, progressive, 'left' political parties not tarnished by association with the fallen government, in 1981 the military and some civilians began to refer to the change of leadership as a 'revolution'. The immediate goal of this 'revolution' was to 'restructure' society by abolishing the ethnically based political parties (i.e. the predominantly Creole NPS and predominantly Hindustani VHP or Verenigde Hervormings Partij),[13] which they believed relied on patronage, graft, cronyism and the 'buddy system' (what the Dutch call *vriendjes politiek*), to the detriment of the country as a whole. All public political rallies and activities were outlawed and the national elections scheduled for March 1980 were cancelled.

On 15 March the NMR installed a civilian government, apparently recognizing that the military could not run the government by itself. The ousted government officials were kept at home under watch or in gaol for as yet undefined crimes of corruption. Through this period and into the summer of 1980, many Surinamers were willing to give 'the boys' (NCOs) the benefit of the doubt: they had kept the highly respected former president of Suriname, Dr J.H.E. Ferrier and had appointed as presidential minister a medical intern, Dr Henk Chin A. Sen, whose reputation was untainted by previous government office or affiliation with either the NPS or VHP. A number of young, Dutch-educated technocrats were tapped to head the ministries of government. The NMR continued to maintain the final veto over the civilian government, while the civilians worked to assess just what financial and bureaucratic possibilities were available for the immediate and long-range future of Suriname. The NMR members, all military, concentrated on disarming and reorganizing the police force (to foil any counter-coup attempts from that quarter). They also publicly advertised their intent to 'sanitize' Suriname of the 'old ways', by flogging looters, thieves and rapists (without trial) and by patrolling government offices to ensure that workers arrived on time and worked the full number of hours for which they were hired.

By August 1980 much of the goodwill and patience many were willing to extend to the new military and civilian government had begun to dissipate. The NCOs were clearly perceived of as less knowledgeable, sophisticated or united than people had initially thought or hoped. After what Sergeant Desi Bouterse (head of the coup and the NMR) described as a foiled counter-coup attempt by a faction of 'far left' NCOs, some members of the NMR were gaoled and the national constitution and parliament were abolished. President Ferrier, a staunch constitutionalist, was sacked when he would not quietly acquiesce. Ministers in the civilian government were frequently replaced as the NCOs still in power worked to tighten their control.

One way of 'sanitizing' Suriname and ending 'old ways' was to put the previous administration on trial. A number of ministers, including the prime minister of Suriname and head of the NPS, Henk Arron, were to be tried for crimes the new government claimed were beyond the competency of the old legal system to handle. A 'special tribunal' was appointed to hear publicly the cases against the defendants, involving embezzlement, graft, bribery and patronage, which the new government thought characterized the old. One panel of judges was replaced by another; dates for public hearings were postponed and postponed; not all the evidence seemed convincing, even to the judges appointed to hear the cases. In the end the military and civilian government convicted few on the charges and did nothing to discredit the old government in the eyes of the party faithful.

In fact, Creoles who supported the NPS before the coup interpreted the banning of the political parties, the cancellation of the March 1980 elections and the 'special tribunal' as punishment directed entirely at them: their party had been toppled, the election victory taken from them, 'their' government replaced by one they did not perceive as sensitive to their needs. Whatever qualms they may in fact have had during the former government's administration were forgotten in the light of what appeared to be clear military policies designed to put their interests last. The prohibition against political gatherings, coupled with a nightly curfew, censorship of the media and the uncertainty of the immediate future, placed a lid on *kern* meetings at the neighbourhood level. Men and women alike were frightened and unsure; tensions were increased by rumours that there were military informers and spies in their neighbourhoods and by the fear of being caught on the streets near the curfew hour. Through 1980 and into 1983, the gay sounds of birthday parties, club-sponsored dances and feasts and lively outings were rarely heard. Expenditure on hospitality was kept to a minimum as money was hoarded.

Stripped of influence and a sense of place in the order of things, by spring 1981 people in working-class neighbourhoods had begun to speak out. Women prohibited from holding *kern* gatherings assembled informally in small groups of trusted friends and neighbours. The former leader of a well-known social club and of a once-influential *kern* reported that 'the people do not support the government. We do not have our *kern*, but we walk from house to house. They cannot take away our faith [as they have our *kern*].' The old patterns were maintained quietly in house-to-house visits and discussions. Their goals had no clear design other than the catharsis of talk with the like-minded and to maintain the 'old faith' until the parties became public and legal again. This almost invisible building of barricades was a form of resistance.

The military sensed the passive resistance and fear of many segments of the population and worked both to win the support of the masses and to undermine the hold of the 'old beliefs'. Working through its administrative arm (the NMR) and under the banner of 'motivation and work', the military encouraged the formation of people's committees (*Volks Comite*) in each urban and suburban neighbourhood and in several rural villages — a model Bouterse had lifted wholesale from the Bishop revolutionary experiment in Grenada. The goal was to make contact with various 'functional groups' in each setting: church groups, youth sports clubs, the youth, and women. *Volks Comite* were intended to advise the military of local needs and wishes and to serve as conduits of aid, thus by-passing the civilian government bureaucracy. Assessed by the residents themselves, local *Volks Comite* would advise the military if a road needed to be paved, a house repaired, or electricity brought in. The military would then arrange to do its part by providing the tools, trucks, or materials necessary for the job, as well as, on occasion, a small contingent of volunteer workers.

In the working-class Creole areas of Paramaribo only one *Volks Comite* was established — in March 1981, when this model for democratic development was being most enthusiastically embraced by the military. Some young people and a smattering of adults joined. One elderly man, well known as a minor NPS party official and a neighbourhood personality, enthusiastically joined the committee, only to have his physical safety and property threatened. The threats, castigations and admonitions of disgust by neighbours, many of whom were women, forced him to move to one of the rural districts. The bulk of the urban neighbourhoods and residents remained cautious, if not passively resistant and cynical. Imposed from the outside as an extension of a government seen increasingly to be incompetent, if not downright vindictive in its opposition to the re-emergence of elective party politics, the committees in turn were exploited by people where and when they thought they could manage it. When some women who had previously been very active in *kern* activities were questioned about the apparent success of the committees, as viewed on government television news reports and from signs and banners in the streets, the response was a *churi* and a slow, careful explanation that people are not stupid. 'Sure, we will take the roads they want to pave for us, the street lights they put up and we will go dance and drink at the neighbourhood parties they throw. But never, never, will they pull the old beliefs from my heart.' When asked about the enthusiasm reported in some non-Creole areas where more committees were founded, the response was practical: 'If they have nothing, people will take what is offered them.'

In sum, the failure of the *Volks Comite* was the best-kept public secret in Paramaribo and not only for ideological reasons. In the military's attempt to de- (or re-) politicize citizens and court the support of the followers of the old parties, they by-passed the very women who lent structure and cohesion to working-class urban Creole neighbourhoods. Leadership of each *Volks Comite* was invested in young males who promoted an undefined 'revolution'. Appearing at quickly organized neighbourhood gatherings they would call for 'a new order', 'socialism', 'equality' and 'brotherhood'. A member of the NMR, also young and male, would usually appear at his side, Uzi machine gun slung casually over his shoulder. The symbols were wrong, if capturing the support of many of the women in Creole neighbourhoods was intended. First of all, the new leadership is young and male, not the older men and women of tradition. Second, the force used to take and maintain power is symbolized by the Uzi; once a sign of change and renewal for many, it soon came to be seen as a sign of oppression, even by those who initially welcomed the coup. The Uzi and the military uniforms became associated with bad manners and 'uppity' behaviour practised by impudent youngsters, according to many. Good manners, hospitality, some respect for one's elders, courtesy even to strangers: these have been the traditional elements that elicited some trust, some reciprocity, some *lespeki* among Creoles and these were elements that many working-class Creole women and men, even the young, saw missing in the 'boys trying to play men'. In their cultural context these were devastating criticisms that severely eroded the stature of those who would rule.

By the spring of 1981 the civilian government was in a bind. Its need to remain in power meant finding a delicate balance between cooperating with the military and proceeding to move ahead as if the government, in fact, were composed only of civilians. There appeared to be a real concern for reinstating a constitutional base for government and for the protection of the suspended human and civil rights, including free elections. The restitution of electoral politics, however, would probably remove the present government from office, as even government officials concede privately that the old ethnic-based politics has maintained its hold on most Surinamers. As a result there seem to be few plans, if any, to return to free elections in the near future.

In truth even followers of the ousted government admit to gains for the populace since the coup. Retired people are receiving a big increase in monthly pension payments and, for the first time, they are getting them regularly and on time, although the inflation that has accompanied a rapidly deteriorating economy has consumed the gains. The military is credited with getting the civil service to work on time and keeping it at work during the day. For women who had the responsibility for paying bills, collecting welfare cheques, arranging payment for taxes and cashing remittance cheques from relatives abroad, the disappearance of long queues is a development frequently mentioned with gratitude.

The current civilian government also appears to be more sensitive to women's needs than previous administrations. It has been appointing women to a number of relatively high positions in government, as well as supporting the creation of a Women's Desk and a Women's Institute. Although still embryonic, plans are being drawn up to implement income-generating projects for women, to increase facilities for child care and for research on women, to disseminate health information about women and children more widely and to support self-help projects for women through various ministries. With the parliament dissolved, the government proceeded unilaterally in April 1981 to remove civil disabilities in the law that adversely affected married women, an issue opposed most strongly by the Hindustani leadership before the coup (Decreet C 11 1981).

Unsure of how much time they will have to effect permanent changes in Surinamese society, government leaders appear to have decided to concentrate their energies on younger, rather than older, women. Younger women, regardless of ethnic background, are seen as more willing to work in larger community and national organizations and less determined to think in terms of ethnicity. Many of the women with whom this chapter is concerned are perceived as stubborn, traditional, ethnically loyal and eternally wedded to the 'old politics'. There is some truth in this perception. Other than as appropriate recipients of social programmes, such as old age and medical security, these older women are not readily seen as partners in 'social development'. Ironically, social development in this case may undermine the very cooperative forms that have allowed these women to secure for themselves a measure of social, economic and political status and independence.

## Demographic Changes

Suriname obtained its political independence in November 1975, as a result of pressure from the Dutch government and tense political negotiations within Surinamese society itself (Dew 1978: 175-96). Not all political parties, or ethnic groups, were enthusiastic about losing what they perceived as the stabilizing influence of the Dutch presence. The major fear was the loss of metropolitan restraint on ethnic rivalry, with the image of Guyana not far from the minds of many Hindustani Surinamers. Although Creoles and others decried this fear as unrealistic and as a ploy to pry constitutional concessions out of the then Creole-dominated government (the NPS and three other political parties in a ruling coalition as the NPK), many Surinamers of all ethnic groups migrated to The Netherlands. Fear of a change in the political climate in Suriname, fear of increasing poverty at home and of the closing of educational opportunities in The Netherlands for Surinamese children, lack of confidence in the abilities of Surinamers to run their own country and the attraction of the generous Dutch welfare system — all contributed to an unprecedented out-migration before, during and after independence. It is estimated that a third to a half of Suriname's population is in The Netherlands. A majority of that expatriate group (51.5 per cent) is female. In 1983 the Dutch government unilaterally ended free and unrestricted migration to The Netherlands, a move that slowed the stream but has not stemmed the tide.[14]

All the traditionally Creole neighbourhoods in Paramaribo have felt the direct impact of this mass migration to Holland. There is probably not one Surinamer alive who does not have a kinsman or close friend resident in The Netherlands. The departure of neighbours has meant a depletion of club members as well as separation from old friends and family members. A large number of older Creoles went to The Netherlands in part because of the social security and welfare benefits which were unavailable in Suriname; this is an age group that was disproportionately represented in many of the social clubs. There are fewer birthdays and celebrations around which to organize club activities now. With the departure of key members of clubs went some of the vitality and organizational skill needed by the group.

As owners migrated, houses and yards were rented or sold and new residents from outside the neighbourhoods moved in. Neighbourhoods in which traditionally there had been few sales of house and yard ownership to complete strangers now have opened to the market place. Concurrent with the massive emigration to The Netherlands has been an internal migration into urban neighbourhoods by rural people of Asian ancestry from the plantation districts and by Maroons from the interior, changing the ethnic character of residential areas — a change that may permanently alter the nature of local level social interaction and political participation. This seems to be a certain concomitant of migration into those areas where the new residents are not ethnic Creoles.

Particularly important in the last half of the 1970s and still continuing, is the effect of the government's attempts to increase the number and quality of houses for economically disadvantaged Surinamers. A large number of housing projects have been built on the outskirts of the capital for inner city residents. Since most urban dwellers were traditionally Creole, this process appears likely to fragment further their residential solidarity. Historically, neighbourhoods were more or less prestigious, more or less working-class, but never exclusively for either the rich or the poor. In Paramaribo proper the tenor of a neighbourhood could easily be gauged by the size and age of the large gentlemen's houses or two and three-storey wooden street-front houses, all with smaller houses hidden in the yards behind (a pattern from the days of slavery when the yard houses were for slaves). (See Chapter 4). Residential segregation by colour or class has never been a feature of Surinamese life. The new housing projects, however, do not maintain this mix: they are multi-ethnic but economically uniform. The houses are similar to one another and occupancy depends on income.

In a simultaneous development, middle and upper middle economic groups are building in areas where land prices are too high for the working class and where few houses from the past are in evidence. This was a process already underway at the time of the coup and was funded in part by the huge foreign aid package granted with independence which swamped the ability of Surinamers to control its (ab)use. Many businessmen became overnight financial success stories and the new neighbourhoods on the edge of the city boasted elaborate constructions designed to advertise that new reality.

Class segregated housing has become part of the urban landscape and it seems reasonable to assume that the contact between classes will lessen in the future as class-based residential specialization increases. The effective functioning of the social clubs, especially in political activities, is jeopardized as the frequency of contacts with party officials is lessened and perhaps increasingly relegated to planned and ritualized encounters such as public mass political meetings.

In addition to the immediate and long range implications of the internal and international migration of Surinamers, the Surinamese population is getting younger. It is now estimated that the majority of Surinamers is under the age of 16. These young people are getting more and better education in public and private schools. It is to be anticipated that the content and language (Dutch) of instruction, as well as the multi-ethnicity of the schools will create bonds between members of various ethnic groups to a degree unheard of in Suriname's history.

The links between Surinamers resident at home and abroad are also ties of communication. News travels back and forth across the Atlantic, by mail and by visiting or return migrants, about changing roles and attitudes of Surinamese women, among other issues. In Suriname itself more Creole women, especially young ones, are working full-time outside the home and out of the neighbourhood and are looking for more training and better jobs. They are joining trade unions, clubs and professional organizations with people who come together for reasons different from those of the members of the traditional clubs, which have been more tied to neighbourhood and gender. Younger women are increasingly unwilling to accept the traditional measures of prestige; instead they appear to value more and more the market-place measures of education, job, income and consumer goods. Whether this is indicative of deep changes to come, or whether it is only a manifestation of just wanting more of the same things their mothers and grandmothers sought, is not yet clear.

## Notes

1   The research on which this chapter is based is derived from fieldwork undertaken in 1972 and 1973 and updated during 1990 by correspondence and periodic visits to Suriname. A summary of my findings is contained in Brana-Shute (1976), where the domestic roles, kinship networks and friendship and neighbourhood relationships that underpin the social clubs are examined in greater detail than here. Readers interested in women's networks at the neighbourhood level may find the original paper of particular use because of its descriptive, ethnographical nature. Changes to these networks in the wake of independence in 1975 and the coup of 1980 are documented in Brana-Shute (1982). This chapter further updates the 1982 paper to 1990 in the light of a changing social and political context and a rapidly deteriorating economy. I try here to cite English sources, rather than the more abundant but less accessible Dutch ones. The most complete bibliography of sources published in English since the Second World War is in Gary Brana-Shute (1990). Nagelkerke (1980) provides the most complete bibliography of Suriname in Dutch, including many works that focus on specific ethnic groups. I am particularly indebted to Gary Brana-Shute for sharing his information on Suriname since the coup and his willingness in particular to check on club sisters whenever he visited Suriname in the 1980s.
2   Algemeen Bureau voor de Statistiek (1973) and Lamur (1973). The year 1980 was the last one in which a national census was taken and tabulated, though its accuracy has been questioned. A census is a very political instrument in Suriname because Surinamers are sensitive to the growth or decline of various ethnic groups. The migration of Surinamers to The Netherlands during the 1980s was so heavy that observers doubt that the population has increased since 1980; many suspect that the population is now smaller than in 1970. Data from the 1980 census and extrapolations and distributions are found in *Suriname Planatlas* (1988).
3   The best-known recent history of Suriname is Van Lier (1971), an update of his original work and bibliography of 1949.
4   Most studies of women in the Caribbean focus on the domestic sphere and issues of matrifocality and female-headed households, which have been the objects of scholarly, if often confused, attention for the past half century. Women's activities and relationships outside the domestic unit are unfortunately far less frequently recorded; when they are studied, their activities tend to be seen as disassociated from the domestic sphere. The result is an incomplete view, in which much of the complexity of these women's lives is missed.
5   Outsiders in this sense include new arrivals to the neighbourhood and any agents of national institutions (clergy, police, social workers, school teachers or military sergeants) who would attempt to organize the neighbourhood.
6   Pierce (1973) adopts Wilson's (1969) conceptual distinctions of reputation versus respectability to explain status competition among Surinamese Creoles. (This is also discussed in relation to Jamaica in Chapter 2.) I use the concept of respectability differently from Wilson and Pierce. Whereas they correlate respectable behaviour with an apeing of the mores, style and Christian regularity imposed during colonialism, I attempt to describe elements of behaviour that correspond to *lespeki*, which is a Surinamese cultural configuration. My own uneasiness with the reputation versus respectability model is that its sheer polarity makes it more difficult to include data that are seemingly contradictory or too complex. As a model it deals much better with men than with women, who have their own standards for measuring reputation and respectability.
7   This is not the only political party to have attracted mostly Creoles, but it is by far the largest. It is important to note that not all women in social clubs participate actively in political clubs, though most seem to. Also, not all the women in one social club will be members of the NPS; a minority will also belong to some of the smaller parties.
8   It is interesting to note that after the franchise was extended in 1948 to all Surinamers over the age of 23, a female Creole doctor wrote a stage play in Sranan Tongo (a language of very little prestige at the time) to explain the meaning and procedure of voting. The title translates as 'Miss Jane Goes to Vote' (Redmond 1972: 41-7). Apart from the doctor, who explains the procedure and may be of either sex, the characters are all female.

9  This process of campaigning, or propagandizing as it is known in Suriname, is not meant to convert
   outsiders: people of other ethnic groups are very rarely courted in the neighbourhood. Even better-
   educated Creoles who may voice support for a different party, or kind of politics, are rarely solicited
   for their vote.
10 *Churi (tjoeri)* is known elsewhere in the Caribbean as 'chups' or 'hissing the teeth'. One may use this to
   express an opinion, surprise, sympathy or disdain. It can be very disconcerting to an orator when
   someone in the audience comments on his statements with a *churi*, which will carry like a stage
   whisper.
11 The first woman elected to the national parliament (*Staten*), Mrs G.R. Schneiders-Howard, was
   supported by the *Sociaal Democratische Vrouwen Bond* (Social Democratic Women's League), an organization established by Creole market women specifically to support her candidacy in the 1938 election
   — ten years before women were even allowed to vote (Dew 1978: 53). The second female to sit in the
   *Staten* was Isabella Richards, a teacher, who took her seat in 1963; in that decade she was also the
   treasurer of the NPS (Ormskirk 1966: 211). The *Dames Comite* (Ladies Committee), led by a female
   dentist, Tine Putscher, participated in the 1949 elections but without success (Ormskirk 1966: 70). In
   1973 a new political group ran candidates under the banner of the *Verenigde Volkspartij-Surinaamse
   Vrouwen Front* (United People's Party-Surinamese Women's Front) 'representing the unlikely alliance
   of Chinese shopkeepers and militant women liberationists, men of Chinese and Chinese-Creole ancestry and women of a variety of origins'(Dew 1978: 169). Since 1980 there have been several women
   appointed at the sub-cabinet ministerial level. Suriname is unusual in that cabinet posts most likely to
   be filled by women, such as education and health, which are traditionally associated with women's
   concerns, have always gone to men. It should be added that as yet there are almost no serious studies
   on Surinamese women, especially in terms of political involvement. Parts of larger studies on family,
   health or cultural groups do deal with women (and children). Interestingly, most of what is now available is appearing in a new body of magazines published in The Netherlands for Surinamers there.
   They have been including many articles on Surinamese women, almost all short, general, based on
   older studies and/or outright polemics.
12 Hutz and Pierce (1976: 40-1) capture some of the cultural tensions among Afro-Surinamers by referring
   to Afro-Creole (*nengre*) and Euro-Creole (*malata*) Surinamers, though the terms unnaturally bifurcate
   Creoles into two opposing factions without recognizing the situational nature of both types of
   behaviours.
13 This party, formerly called the *Verenigde Hindostaanse Partij*, changed its name in 1979.
14 The *Suriname Planatlas*, section C2, 1.6, refers to the decade of 1970-80 as 'the era of mass emigration'
   during which the mean annual population growth of the country actually fell, particularly following
   independence in 1975.

## References

Algemeen Bureau voor de Statistiek (1973) *Suriname in Cijfers No. 60*. Paramaribo:
   ABS

Brana-Shute, Gary (1979) *On the Corner: Male Social Life in a Paramaribo Creole
   Neighbourhood*. Assen: Van Gorcum

——— (1981) 'Politicians in Uniform: Suriname's Bedevilled Revolution'. *Caribbean
   Review*, 10 (2) 24-7, 49-50

——— (1990) 'Old Shoes and Elephants: Electoral Resistance in Suriname'. In Gary
   Brana-Shute (ed.) *Resistance and Rebellion in Suriname: Old and New*, Williamsburg: The College of William and Mary

Brana-Shute, Rosemary (1976) 'Women, Clubs and Politics: The Case of a Lower-
   Class Neighbourhood in Paramaribo, Suriname'. *Urban Anthropology*, 5 (2) 157-
   85

——— (1982) 'Lower-Class Afro-Surinamese Women and National Politics: Tradi-
   tions and Changes in an Independent State'. In Sandra McGee (ed.) *Women and
   Politics in Twentieth Century Latin America*, Williamsburg: The College of
   William and Mary, 33-56

Buschkens, W. (1974) *The Family System of the Paramaribo Creoles*. The Hague:
   Martinus Nijhoff

Coleridge, P.E. (1958) *Vrouwenleven in Paramaribo: Suriname in Stroomlijnen*.
   Amsterdam: Wereld-Bibliotheek, 86-93

Cross, Malcolm (1979) *Urbanization and Urban Growth in the Caribbean*. Cambridge:
   Cambridge University Press

Decreet C 11 (1981) *Rechten van de Vrouw, Rechten van de Man*. Paramaribo: Minis-
   terie van Justitie, Leger en Politie en Buitenlandse Zaken

Dew, Edward (1978) *The Difficult Flowering of Suriname: Ethnicity and Politics in a Plural Society*. The Hague: Martinus Nijhoff

Eersel, Christian (1971) 'Prestige and Choice of Language and Linguistic Form'. In Dell Hymes (ed.) *Pidginization and Creolization of Languages*, New York: Cambridge University Press, 318-26

*Haagse Post* (1981) *Haagse Post Extra*. [A compendium of articles published in the *Haagse Post* magazine in Amsterdam in 1980 and 1981 on the Suriname 'revolution'.]

Hawkins, Irene (1976) *The Changing Face of the Caribbean*. Barbados: Cedar Press

Hutz, Evelyn and B. Edward Pierce (1976) 'Historical Factors Contributing to the Perception of Ethnicity among the Nengre of Suriname'. *LAAG Contributions to Afro-American Ethnohistory in Latin America and the Caribbean*. Albany, New York: LAAG/Institute for Mesoamerican Studies, State University of New York, 39-57

Lamur, Humphrey (1973) *The Demographic Evolution of Suriname*. The Hague: Martinus Nijhoff

Nagelkerke, Gerard A. (1980) *Suriname: A Bibliography, 1940-1980*. The Hague: Smits Drukkers-Uitgevers BV for the Department of Caribbean Studies, Royal Institute of Linguistics and Anthropology, Leiden

Ormskirk, Fred (1966) *Twintig Jaren NPS: 'Groei Temidden van Beroering'*. Paramaribo: n.p.

Pierce, B. Edward (1971) 'Kinship and Residence among the Urban Nengre of Suriname: A Reevaluation of Concepts and Theories of the Afro-American Family'. Unpublished doctoral dissertation. Tulane University

——— (1973) 'Status Competition and Personal Networks: Informal Social Organization among the Nengre of Paramaribo'. *Man*, 8 (4) 580-91

Redmond, Sophie (1972) *Misi Jana e Go na Stembus*. Paramaribo: YWCA, 41-7

*Suriname Planatlas* (1988) Washington, DC: Department of Regional Planning/ Organization of American States

Van Lier, R.A.J. (1971) *Frontier Society: A Social Analysis of the History of Suriname*. The Hague: Martinus Nijhoff

Voorhoeve, Jan and Ursy Lichtveld (1975) *Creole Drum: An Anthology of Creole Literature in Suriname*. New Haven: Yale University Press

Wilson, Peter J. (1969) 'Reputation and Respectability: A Suggestion for Caribbean Ethnology'. *Man*, 4 (1) 70-80

# IX The Migration Experience: Nevisian Women at Home & Abroad

KAREN FOG OLWIG

Anthropologists have long been interested in the special role of women in the West Indian family. Family studies from the 1950s and 1960s noted the absence of men in many of the domestic units and emphasized the central role of women as *de facto* household heads, rearing and providing for the children. Due to this importance of women, the family was designated matrifocal. This family system was, furthermore, often described as a variant, caused by the heritage of slavery and poverty, of a European nuclear family ideal inculcated in the Afro-Caribbean population by the colonial churches and schools (Smith 1956, 1973; Gonzalez 1970; Smith 1966). During the 1970s increasing attention was paid to the fact that although women tend to manage domestic affairs, they do this within networks of relatives and neighbours, who help with child rearing, grant economic support and provide the necessary labour. These networks have been seen to derive in part from the Afro-Caribbean heritage of the West Indians and in part from their adaptation and resistance to the constraints of oppression (Brown 1977; Gussler 1980; Olwig 1985; Sutton and Makiesky-Barrow 1977).

The focus on kin networks has drawn attention to the fact that, while women may play a central role in domestic units, men do in fact contribute to the household through support networks, though their economic assistance is often less regular than that of women. Furthermore, male support may be given to several different households, including the maternal one, the domestic units of current and prior spouses, as well as to those of their offspring. The importance of men in the extra-domestic sphere has also been emphasized in studies of men's social life (liming) in the public arena (Wilson 1971; Tobias 1975; Lieber 1976; Brana-Shute 1976; Abrahams 1983).

While women are tied to one particular domestic unit for which they assume responsibility, men have considerable freedom with respect to membership in a domestic unit and may, in fact, display allegiance to several domestic units at one time. Furthermore, women and men are delegated to different spheres: women to the private, domestic arena with its social-reproductive functions, supported by a network of kin, including men; men to the public sphere outside the home, where they engage in the money economy and associate with friends.

These two spheres reflect an ideal conceptualization of family structure, which emphasizes the importance of keeping women in the home, supported by men who act as bread winners and represent the family in the society at large. This ideal reflects British cultural values and has been introduced largely by colonial officials through the church and schools (Wilson 1969; Abrahams 1983; Olwig 1987, 1989). It does not, however, match the social and economic reality of West Indian society and West Indian women cannot be characterized as primarily dependent housewives confined to the home. Despite the fact that, 'since the formative stage of West Indian society women have been jural minors and linked *ideologically* to "domestic" activities' (Smith 1987: 167), they have played crucial roles in extra-domestic affairs, including economic ones.

West Indian women, therefore, have had to deal with the fact that they are actively involved in the greater society, even though the family ideal restricts them to the private domestic sphere. As one might imagine, this situation is less problematic within the local community, for women situate their activities within networks of domestic relations, which cushion the effect of the women's involvement in extra-domestic affairs. The women's position is more difficult (and the strategies they devise to deal with it more apparent) in the migration situation, in which they leave their home community in search of wage employment. While male migration would seem to be a natural extension of the men's position in the wider, public community, and their attempt to play the role of provider for their families, such migration on the part of women clearly constitutes a break from their domestic world of relatives and neighbours. The main problem for the women who emigrate, therefore, appears to be that of reconstituting their network in the migration destination. This process, ironically, is made difficult by the fact that, even though migrant women have left the protective sphere of the network of their natal community, they remain important in it as social and economic resources. Thus they continue to have strong obligations in their home island, which make it difficult for them to generate their own network abroad.

## Importance of Migration

Nevis has been heavily affected by migration since the abolition of slavery in 1834. It had little to offer the freed slaves other than poorly paid menial jobs as labourers on plantations that had dominated the island for centuries.[1] Emigration in search of economic opportunities abroad was an attractive alternative and, as early as 1835, 157 Nevisians left for British Guiana. By 1846, 2441 had migrated to Trinidad (Richardson 1983: 88). Emigration from the island continued throughout the nineteenth and twentieth centuries to the gold mines in Venezuela, to the large sugar plantations in Cuba and the Dominican Republic, to help construct the Panama Canal, to the domestic and industrial sectors on the east coast of the US, to the oil refineries on the Dutch West Indian islands (see Chapter 2), to the industries and public services in Great Britain, and to tourism in the Virgin Islands and the Dutch island of St Martin (see Richardson 1983). While much of the early emigration was temporary and tied to short-term economic opportunities, the more recent emigration to England and nearby West Indian islands, which has involved thousands of Nevisians, has been more permanent (Richardson 1983: 147).

In many ways Nevis presents a classic case of the effects of out-migration. During the 1960s Richard Frucht (1972: 279-81) carried out a community study on the island in which he documented the migration of thousands of Nevisians to England and the Virgin Islands. More than half the households he studied had migrant members; almost 45 per cent consisted of grandparents and grandchildren; and over 70 per cent of the household heads were above 50 years of age. A study of the island's folklore by Roger Abrahams (1983: 10-18) at about the same time showed that, as the local community disintegrated through heavy out-migration, many of the social events and cultural traditions, such as Christmas celebrations and the tea party, were on the verge of dying out.

Geographer Bonham Richardson (1983), who did research on the island during the 1970s, documents the huge impact of emigration on the island's agriculture, the mainstay of its economy. The cultivation of subsistence and cash crops on small farms, which had taken the place of plantation production by the middle of the century, declined markedly with the loss of so many economically active members of the community; in its place emerged a pattern of extensive cattle grazing which needed little labour. Furthermore, these herds of animals were 'walking banks' for the emigrants who had largely financed the increasing cattle population by investing in livestock on the island. The 1980 census (Population Census of the Commonwealth Caribbean 1980-81: 4) recorded a population of 9428, the lowest since the abolition of slavery.[2] Today it is estimated that the majority of the Nevisian-born population has settled in destinations as far away as England, the US and Canada, as well as on the nearby British, US and Dutch islands.

Though emigration has taken a heavy toll on the island society, it is incorrect to speak of a breakdown of the Nevisian community as such. Rather, the Nevisian community has redirected itself outwards to include and centre on Nevisians living and working abroad. Richardson (1983: 48) suggests that 'outside remittances account for more disposable income on the two islands than any other source, including the St Kitts' sugar industry'. The dispersed families are united primarily at burials and cultural events such as carnival celebrations, which are supported by returning migrants (Richardson 1983: 51-4, 174, 181; Sutton 1986). Nevisian geographer Carolyn Liburd (1984: 57) made a detailed study of the nature of the remittances sent to Nevis from abroad, in which she documents the increase in calls by ships transporting goods from nearby West Indian migration destinations from 61 calls in 1969 to a peak of 163 calls in 1979. A closer examination of the content of one boat arriving in November 1983 revealed not just luxury items such as antennas, mixers and liquor, but also household necessities such as beds, tables, chairs, plastic buckets, mops, brooms and foodstuffs (Liburd 1984: 59-60). Nevisians have clearly come to depend on the migrants even for the everyday essentials of life.

## Participation in Migration

Throughout the history of emigration from Nevis, men have left the island in greater numbers than women. This is reflected in population censuses of Nevis, which reveal a consistent, female bias.

Though men have been more prominent in migration, women have also been active. Statistics on post-emancipation emigration from Nevis to Trinidad show that 44 per cent of the migrants were women (Richardson 1983: 88). Female participation seems to fluctuate as employment opportunities for women vary. Thus, during the first two decades of this century, when canal work in Panama provided the major attraction for migrants, male emigration predominated and, by 1921, the proportion of males in the Nevis population had dropped to 40 per cent. During recent decades, when tourism and industry have provided ample opportunity for female as well as male employment abroad, women have emigrated in large numbers. The 1980 census of Nevis found that women constituted 55 per cent of the net migration from Nevis between 1970 and 1980 (Population Census of the Commonwealth Caribbean 1980-81: 4) and that the proportion of males in the Nevis population had correspondingly increased. Women have been involved in migration both in staying behind in the domestic unit to care and provide for a residential family and in leaving to exploit economic opportunities outside the island. Family networks have provided an important basis for women's lives both within the rural community of Nevis and in the complex societies of the migration destinations.

**Table 9.1: Sexual Composition of Nevis Population, 1844-1970**

| Year | Men | | Women | |
|------|-----|-----|-------|-----|
| 1844 | 4418 | 46% | 5153 | 54% |
| 1861 | 4734 | 48% | 5088 | 52% |
| 1871 | 5433 | 47% | 6247 | 53% |
| 1881 | 5436 | 47% | 6248 | 53% |
| 1891 | 5945 | 45% | 7142 | 55% |
| 1901 | 5605 | 44% | 7424 | 56% |
| 1911 | 5521 | 43% | 7424 | 57% |
| 1921 | 4678 | 40% | 6891 | 60% |
| 1946 | 5062 | 44% | 6326 | 56% |
| 1960 | 5653 | 44% | 7117 | 56% |
| 1970 | 5186 | 46% | 6064 | 54% |
| 1980 | 4426 | 47% | 5002 | 53% |

*Sources*: Richardson 1983: 93, 132, 146; Population Census of the Commonwealth Caribbean 1980-81: 4)

## Family Networks

The basic building block in kin networks, which provides continuity and stability in the Nevisian community, is the tie between mother and child. In general, the parent-child tie involves, on the one hand, the obligation to clothe, feed and care for the child and, on the other, the right to expect help and support from the child as soon as it is able to contribute in any way. In the West Indies the parent-child tie tends to be concentrated on the mother-child relationship, partly because it is common for young Nevisians to engage in a number of child-bearing sexual unions before settling down to one mate. This typically results in the fathers having children in several households, whereas the mothers usually have all, or at least most, of their children living with them.[3] The relative unimportance of the father-child tie in the domestic unit is reflected in a survey of Nevisian school children carried out in the mid-1980s, which showed that single mothers cared for the greatest proportion of children (38 per cent), followed by grandparents (29 per cent) and both parents (26 per cent) (Edwards n.d.: 44).

The female bias in the parent-child relationship is strengthened by the fact that children are reared in the female sphere of the household or yard, a fenced-in area inhabited by a family living in one or more houses (see Chapter 3). Though very young children can impose a heavy burden on women, they constitute an important source of labour power at quite an early age. In the rural communities, which dominate on Nevis, most households are involved, not just in domestic activities such as child care and housework, but also in some farming, including cultivating a vegetable plot and rearing livestock. Women manage these household affairs with the help of older children, who do most of the work outside the domestic unit, including fetching water at the public stand-pipe, collecting firewood or tending animals in the bush. In this way the women are able to concentrate on activities in the yard or fields, which the family either owns or leases. With the help of children women can therefore maintain an appearance of remaining within the domestic sphere, even though they are, in fact, actively involved in economic activities that extend beyond the household.

Few, if any, Nevisian households depend entirely on the limited income that can be generated from farming. Unless they have the educational qualifications to obtain a civil service job, work opportunities for women on Nevis are limited and confined to wage employment in tourism and light industry. While wage employment is regarded as attractive and suitable for women, for it takes place indoors in respectable surroundings patronized or owned by people from Western countries, it is poorly paid and often rather irregular. Remuneration is further decreased if the women must pay for child care and transport to and from work. Wage employment therefore does not grant them any sort of economic security. On the contrary, they remain dependent on the domestic units of the rural communities for basic subsistence produce and child care. For the vast majority of women, a respectable and secure life therefore depends on their ability to build networks of mutual aid and support, both on Nevis and in the various migration destinations outside Nevis.

A sexual relationship constitutes an important basis for developing networks among young women. In the short run it brings some support from the man and in the long run it produces children, who are vital future links in the mother's networks. As long as the sexual tie endures, the man usually provides some support for the woman and her eventual children; but as soon as it is cut off and the couple begin to turn toward other relationships, it is not uncommon for the man to stop providing any kind of support. This is largely because, since the father has children with other women living in different domestic units, father-child ties are subject to conflicting demands. The mother-child tie, however, is usually permanent and free of such conflicts of interest; women are therefore often the main providers for children and the main beneficiaries of support from adult children. Many young women with small children, who have only limited networks of their own, therefore prefer to remain in their mother's yard, where they can benefit from the remittances she receives.

For women without a family network, rearing children to adulthood can present great problems. For example, I.N. was 26 years old and expecting her sixth child. Her five children aged one to 12 years, all boys, were fathered by two different men and the sixth was with a third. The two fathers provided no support for the children and she would not take them to court, but her present boyfriend helped out. Without his support she would have found it difficult to manage on her part-time job as a maid. She lived by herself and her only external support came from an aunt on St Kitts, who had taken care of her when her mother died during her infancy. She placed great hope in her children and was supportive of her oldest son's desire to become a doctor. She wanted the rest to follow him in this, 'to become something big'. Her hopes were rather unrealistic, for it would be difficult for her to provide proper education for so many children on her limited resources.

This woman's expectations for her children were not unusual. The inculcation of high ambitions in children by their parents, particularly their mothers, was quite apparent in a questionnaire survey I carried out among schoolchildren on the island in 1981. It showed that most children were very career oriented, hoping to obtain white collar jobs as teachers, civil servants or professionals, even though their educational qualifications were often inadequate and their actual chances of obtaining the required training limited (Olwig 1987: 162-4). The mothers' desire to see their children do well does not merely reflect their wish for a better life for their children than they have had themselves. It also reveals that, after many years of struggle and personal sacrifice, mothers hope to see the fruits of their labour in terms of financial support from their offspring. This was emphasized by another woman, who put it more bluntly than most. 'People get children to get help, help in the home and yard, and when they become grown up they can give back what you have spent on them.'

The mother-child tie thus links women into the kin network. With help from their young children they can maintain an appearance of respectability in the domestic unit, even though their economic activities extend beyond it. As the children grow older they form links in wider networks, which provide an important economic and social context for women's lives. On an island as heavily influenced by migration as Nevis, the networks cannot be confined to Nevis, but must extend to the migration destinations within which Nevisians are involved.

## Home Community

The impermanence of sexual relationships, the difficulties in obtaining support from children's fathers and the dependence on economic assistance from one's offspring are all accentuated in the migration situation. Many of the women interviewed on Nevis had lost touch with their children's fathers through emigration, or found it difficult to put pressure on men living abroad to send them money.

One difficulty women experience in bringing up their children is that, with the influx of food, clothing and other material goods sent by migrants abroad, Nevisians have grown accustomed to a Western life style, which costs far more than the women living on Nevis can earn. The young women most satisfied with their situation were either living with mothers receiving support from abroad, or were closely connected with emigrant relatives. Some of the greatest difficulties were experienced by married women dependent on husbands living at home. One woman whose husband was a mason complained: 'If the father is not working, because he can't find any work, it is hard to find something to give the children. When there is no food in the house, the children can't understand nothing is there, and when there is no money you cannot buy the clothes that the children want. All I have is an auntie in England, who sends things sometimes, but she has children herself to look after.' This woman was looking forward to the possibility of her husband obtaining a visa to go to St Croix, so that he could work there and send money back for her and the children. She hoped that some of her children would leave the island 'to get something outside'.

It is instilled into children from an early age that if they have any 'mind' and ambition they will emigrate so that they can help the family left behind.[4] From children's answers to a questionnaire about why they wanted to emigrate, it became apparent that maternal pressure was an important factor. One young student simply replied 'because my mother told me so' (Olwig 1987: 164). Most children, who see all wealth coming from abroad, quickly perceive the importance of emigration. One woman proudly explained that her six year-old boy was already talking about whom he was going to support when he was earning good money abroad. When asked about the ideal number of children they would like to have, the women usually took it into account that some of them would be leaving the island and one warned against having too few, saying: 'If you have only one or two children, they might go away, leave you alone. But with more children, one will stay behind.'

The benefits of having reared a number of children properly and taught them to appreciate everything that their mother had done for them accrued to the older generation of women on Nevis, the parental generation of mothers. These women had seen their children leave the island during the large-scale migratory movements after the Second World War and it was quite apparent that some of them were flourishing, resting on the laurels of their good work, while others had not been quite so fortunate.

One woman who had done well was Mrs L. She had a son and daughter in England, three daughters (of whom one was a teacher) and one son in the Virgin Islands, and one daughter (a nurse) in the US. The sons seemed to be 'afraid of pen and paper' and rarely wrote, but the daughters sent letters regularly, including some money for their mother. Before writing home the daughter in England often called her brother and he would send a message and some money; the sisters in the Virgin Islands sometimes did the same with their brother. The children had paid for the building of an addition to Mrs L's house and the installation of electricity and running water. Mrs L was well satisfied with her lot and refused to move to the Virgin Islands to join her children there, as they would like her to do, preferring to stay in her own house in her home village. She explained her children's help as a mother's just reward: 'Look, I reared them, and now they keep me up, because they send me food, they send me clothes, they send me money. I reaped my reward, you understand. You sow good seed, you reap good fruit.' Her situation was in marked contrast to that of another elderly woman living down the road who received no support because she had no children. She lived in a tiny shack with no electricity or water and had to go begging for food.

For these women, migration was thus less about people leaving the island to live and work elsewhere than about extending the domestic unit to include people working abroad, in some cases thousands of miles away. The idea of the household not necessarily being a residential unit, but rather a tight network of exchanges of support, seems to be commonly accepted among the Nevisians. Many of the schoolchildren who answered the questionnaire I gave them in 1981 were unsure about whom to include in their household and a number of them listed relatives working abroad (Olwig 1987: 156-8). Ties between the domestic unit on Nevis and those who have emigrated from it are apparently so close that the emigrants are regarded as part of the household. This view is also reflected in Liburd's (1984) research on migration from Nevis since 1950, which showed 96 per cent of the households studied to have members living abroad.

In the Nevisian migration community the household is therefore less of a residential unit than a group of people engaged in the 'pooling of goods and services, placing at the disposition of its members what is indispensable to them' (Sahlins 1972: 94). Perhaps it is not so strange that West Indian households conform to those of the primitive societies analysed by Sahlins, for in many ways West Indians have become 'hunters and gatherers' in the modern world economy, on the look out for new economic opportunities.

## Leaving the Island

Great Britain and the United States have been important migration destinations for West Indians looking for unskilled work, and several thousand Nevisians have settled in these two countries over the past few decades. Today the small US Virgin Island of St John (which is dominated by tourism) and the industrial city of Leeds in northern England contain sizeable Nevisian populations. While these destinations have provided widely different social and economic conditions for these migrants, Nevisian motives for emigrating to them were similar: they wished to 'better' themselves. Men and women express this wish for betterment, however, in rather contrasting ways.

In a study of out-migration from Grenada, Tobias (1975: 135, 214) suggests that 'manliness and liming are central to Grenadian migration' and that 'freedom implies the ability to leave Grenada with the least fuss, leaving the fewest obligations behind'. For the men, who may not be tied to a particular domestic unit, with its social and economic obligations, and who are allowed to, even expected to, spend much of their time outside the home, migration in search of personal freedom and exciting adventure can be seen as a natural extension of their wide array of extra-domestic activities.

For women, however, migration presents problems. With their close association with the domestic sphere, most of them are vital members of a household (usually their mother's) when they migrate and have a moral obligation to support it, especially since many of them leave one or more of their children behind in the care of their mother. In the case of St John, over a third of the women I interviewed had left children on Nevis (usually with their maternal grandmother) and felt strongly indebted to their mothers for enabling them to emigrate. Many of the men had been able to pay much, or all, of the cost involved in emigrating, having had wage employment on Nevis and being subject to fewer domestic demands than the women. The women, on the other hand, left from their parental household and, directly or indirectly, their mothers provided the money for the passage, for the young women were in no position to earn enough on Nevis to pay for it themselves. In many cases the mother also used her extensive network of friends and relatives to make arrangements with a Nevisian abroad to receive her daughter and help her find work and a place to stay, while in the case of men, it was often male friends who helped one another in the migration situation.

By the time the young women left Nevis, they therefore knew that their mothers had already expended considerable effort and money to help them. (See also Philpott 1968: 469.) There was little doubt in the young women's minds that they were expected to remain important sources of future help and economic support to the family left behind on Nevis. This was further impressed on the children as they saw the older ones leave home and realized that their chances of migrating depended on their older siblings paying back the passage money that had been expended on them. In one case, doubts about a daughter's willingness or ability to provide support for her family on Nevis actually led a mother to refuse to give her daughter the passage money when it became her turn to emigrate:

> Three of my sisters went to England before I left for the Virgin Islands. My mother did not want me to go to England, and when one of my sisters sent passage money for me, she refused to spend it on me, but decided to repair the house instead.
>
> I had one child for a young man who had gone to England some years previously. He left with a lot of promises, but after a few months he never sent any support for my child. My mother refused to send me to England, fearing that I would get together with my old boyfriend, have more children with him and forget all about my mother and the one child I left behind. My mother told me that she had no shots to waste on hawks, and she later sent out one of my sisters who left behind five children.
>
> As it turned out, this sister married soon after going to England and had four more children. She never sent anything, and I had to help support her five children, who stayed in my mother's household, after I finally managed to emigrate to the Virgin Islands on my own and with the help of my brother on St Martin.

For women, the ability to send a money order back home after having received their first wages became an important proof of their continued loyalty. For many, however, the price of that first money order was much greater than the cash paid at the counter, for it became apparent that conditions at the new location were far more difficult than expected.

## Settlement Abroad

### (a) St John

In the 1950s, West Indians began to migrate to the US Virgin Islands in order to find wage employment in the rapidly developing tourist industry. Most of them entered the islands during the 1960s under a special labour certification programme that made it possible to hire aliens on a temporary basis, provided they were guaranteed 40 hours of work and the US minimum wage. This programme began to be phased out in 1972, but most Nevisians still lived and worked on the islands under the tenuous conditions of the certification programme.[5] For many years Nevisians therefore remained in limbo, not knowing whether their visas would be terminated and they would be forced to return to Nevis. Perhaps because of this long period of uncertainty, the Nevisians I interviewed during the late 1970s had maintained even stronger ties with their family on Nevis than they might have done had they been more secure in their migration destination.

Nevisian women found in St John a rural island that in some respects reminded them of Nevis. Until the 1950s the St Johnian population lived in scattered communities and subsisted on small-scale farming, supplemented by wage employment and remittances from migrant labourers. In the mid-1950s tourism began to develop rapidly in the Virgin Islands and St John attracted an increasing number of visitors. The island was transformed from a peaceful, rural community to a major tourist resort, attracting US investors as well as workers from nearby West Indian islands, among them Nevisians. This led to fierce competition among those attempting to take advantage of the tourism and hostility on the part of Virgin Islanders seeking to preserve their island community in the face of drastic change (Olwig 1985). While Nevisian women could enter the Virgin Islands legitimately in search of employment, they found they were resented by the local population and exploited by their employers — a situation made worse by the US immigration system.

According to the law, to qualify for a work permit the migrants had to be offered full-time employment at minimum wages. Most of the available female employment was in domestic work in private homes or hotels (guest houses), where few employers were able to offer full-time jobs or were willing to pay standard wages. Many women made informal arrangements with employers, who agreed to certify them under the conditions stipulated by US immigration law so long as they were not expected to live up to the requirements of the contract — i.e. they might pay less than the minimum wage or offer only part-time or seasonal employment. If the women reported this to the authorities they would lose their certification and be forced to leave the Virgin Islands.

Most women were willing to put up with deplorable working conditions to get the desired labour certificate. Those who failed to obtain one before their temporary tourist visas expired had to return to British territory and re-enter the US islands on a new visitor's visa. One of the women interviewed had endured one and a half years in the Virgin Islands before she finally received certified employment:

I came to my sister in St Thomas in 1967. She had planned for all of us to come, but I was the only one who made it, so I regard myself as the lucky one. I came on a visitor's visa and I had to go to the British Virgin Islands every time the visa expired. Sometimes I got two weeks' extension, sometimes as little as two days. While I was on a visitor's visa I lived with my sister and made a little money doing odd jobs, cleaning, ironing and baby-sitting for anybody who needed a little help. Of course, I was paid less than the minimum wage. ... Finally, after one and a half years, I found a certified job on St John and settled there. I did not go back to Nevis, because I had come here to help my home, and I felt that I had to stick it out. I knew there was no work on Nevis.

As soon as they started to work the women began to send regular remittances to their families on Nevis, irrespective of whether or not they could really afford it. By Nevisian standards they earned good salaries on St John (easily two to three times as much as they would have made on Nevis); however, much of this income was spent on rent and food. It was therefore quite difficult to set aside money to send to their Nevisian families, but they usually chose to eat less well or to delay paying a bill rather than disappoint their relatives. Many women also contended with poor housing, for they were unable to afford the rents demanded for better accommodation in the highly inflated tourist economy. They would resign themselves to their lot with statements such as, 'I know that I can't do better than stay where I do, because this is not my home.' This statement was typical, in fact most of them said that they did not feel at all at home on St John, but merely regarded it as a place to work and make money, not to have fun and relax. Furthermore, many stated that they did not like to 'keep company' and emphasized that they spent most of their free time at home with their children.

The only extra-domestic sphere in which they all felt free to participate was the religious one. Although the women had by and large belonged to Anglican or Methodist churches on Nevis, on St John most of them chose to join more fundamentalist denominations such as the Baptists or Seventh Day Adventists. These churches offered them a warm, often emotional environment and provided various forms of social and moral support, as well as minor economic assistance to members experiencing problems. This support was generated from the other members, however, and most of the churches actually presented a rather heavy drain on their members' economic resources, expecting them to tithe and in some cases even offer additional donations. The churches therefore constituted a parallel to the women's support networks on Nevis; also they did not encourage the women to engage in local social and economic affairs, but rather preached resignation and obedience to the word of the Bible.

In general the women found that they felt much freer on Nevis, where they had relatives and could move about as they pleased; some would try to visit Nevis every year. Several of those who were married to Nevisians had built houses on Nevis after emigrating to St John; and they regarded these houses as their real home even though they occupied them for no more than a few weeks a year. But many of the women visited Nevis far less often than would be expected given their close attachment to their family there. One reason was that, despite the short distance of only about 180 miles, the plane ticket was quite expensive. But a more important reason is that returning migrants cannot apparently come empty-handed but must live up to their Nevisian family's expectations of their great affluence abroad. As one woman explained: 'When you go back to Nevis on vacation, it is almost necessary to bring a big bag of money and six suitcases of clothes. All my relatives and godchildren come and ask me right to my face to give them something. It is really quite a rat race to go home.' Some women said they were not much better off than their family on Nevis, which was supported by all the relatives who had left the island. They did not, however, want to cause disappointment and, rather than admit that they had nothing to bring, some chose to visit less often.

One solution to the double bind of living and working on St John while maintaining expensive ties with relatives on Nevis, was to bring the relatives to the Virgin Islands. And a few early migrants did succeed in relocating their families on St John, thereby both fulfilling their family obligations on St John and drawing on their families in their everyday lives. A minority of the Nevisian women managed to resettle to the extent of forming their own families on St John and reorienting their future networks to the migration destination. These tended to be women who had their children in the Virgin Islands, either through having them sent from Nevis or having them and marrying on St John. This reorientation was most marked among those who had married St Johnians or men from other West Indian islands.

Furthermore, as they received permanent visas and entered the stage of having lived most of their lives on St John, even those who expressed the strongest attachment to Nevis and sent the most regular support experienced a gradual distancing from their Nevisian family, especially when their parents died and they lost their main link with the home island. With the death of parents the obligation to send support to Nevis disappeared, especially if any remaining siblings on the island received remittances from their own children abroad. As all the immigrants have become more settled on the island they have begun to merge with the local population to generate a new West Indian community.

### (b) Leeds

The pattern of relocation abroad was much more pronounced in Leeds. This was partly because Nevisians had not experienced the same visa problems in England as they had in the Virgin Islands. Almost all of them had settled in England by 1962, when further immigration from the West Indies was severely restricted. In England, Nevisians found themselves in a completely alien society, which forced them to establish their own, separate, West Indian community.[6]

The Nevisians who emigrated had great expectations of England as the imperial mother country. Going to England meant going to the centre of the old empire. When they found, instead, a racist society on the verge of serious economic depression, offering only menial labour at subsistence wages, they were deeply disappointed and many wished to return to Nevis. But their economic situation and obligations to their families back home prevented them from doing so.

For many of the women, the encounter with the old mother country was a long string of humiliating experiences, as one woman related:

I went to England with my oldest sister, who was 21 and came here to get married. My mother decided that I was to go with her, I was sixteen and a half. ... I was leaving my parents, yet I was glad to go to England. I had gone to an Anglican school, and the minister was a white man, and he used to tell stories about England. ... He used to go to England on holidays, and we would ask him to bring back pictures for us. He then took pictures in parks and other nice areas and showed the slides on a screen. We were very impressed and thought that England was paved with gold, and I day-dreamed under a tree about going to England and seeing the places he had told me about. ...

I didn't like what I saw — I kept seeing chimneys and thought that all the houses were factories ... I cried non stop to go home. I didn't want to stay, and it took me ages before I got used to it.

My first job was in a bread factory. ... Only three blacks worked there ... I was naive, I noticed that I did the dirty work, but didn't realize that we were put to do it. ... Later I did domestic work, but I said to myself: 'Why leave home to do domestic work for others? I will do it for my parents, but not for others.' Then I got a job in a restaurant at £4 a week as a waitress, but I had to leave again as the £4 couldn't even keep me.

We stayed in rooms, where we had to share the kitchen and work in it at the same time. I didn't like that so I waited until late at night. ... My parents had their own house with no one talking, spitting into your pot. I used to cry over it.

I married young and became a mother. I just did the necessary things a wife is supposed to do, stayed at home, looked after the kids, watched telly. I never knew what a pub looked like inside. Never left the kids except in the evening for work.

Despite Nevisian women having associated British culture with respectability, the norms related to female respectability were precisely those that were most offended in England. Women, who were supposed to remain in the domestic sphere or perform light work outside, could only find employment that was physically hard and dirty. Women accustomed to being autonomous in the domestic sphere found themselves confined to rooms in a flat. Not only had their traditional sphere of operation diminished to the point of being 'boxed up in packages', as another woman put it, but even the heart of female family-oriented activities, the kitchen, was intruded by total strangers, men as well as women. To make matters worse, the economic reward for this type of life was extremely poor, making it difficult for the women to fulfil their obligations to their families on Nevis. But despite the initial despair, most of the women not only succeeded in sending support (however small it may have been) to their Nevisian families, but they also managed to regain their respectability. In Leeds this was done largely through marrying and establishing an independent home.

Because of the problems West Indians encountered in England, they tended to settle in their own communities, where they are shielded against such examples of racism as signs indicating that rooms will not be rented to coloured people. However, the difficulties of finding adequate accommodation encouraged some West Indians to speculate in housing in the West Indian areas. In Leeds, West Indians live in Chapeltown, a formerly affluent section of the city with many spacious houses amenable to subdivision and rental at high prices to newcomers with little choice about where to live. Through overcrowding and exploitation the houses deteriorated to the point that many had to be abandoned. While Chapel-town still contains some boarded-up houses, many streets have been subject to urban renewal and today contain modern flats and terraced houses that can be rented or purchased at reasonable rates.

If they were able to afford it Nevisians chose to purchase a house as soon as possible (no matter how run-down it might be) and renovate it on their own, for they realized that only through having their own home could they lead the kind of life they wanted. This required great sacrifices; the husbands often worked overtime while their wives cared for the children during the day and then worked an evening shift. But the reward was, for the men, getting a place, albeit within their home, where they could associate with other West Indians in the way they wanted to — playing calypso, having domino games and drinking. The women were able to reconstruct the domestic space they were used to having as their own. In this way they created their own version of the West Indies in England, as one young woman who was born in England experienced it:

My home has always been West Indian. I live in Britain, but when we are within the four walls of the home we are in the West Indies: the music, the language, the cooking, the atmosphere are West Indian. ... My mom and dad always talk about back home. Outside the home we are black British, at home we are West Indians.

The presence of a distinct West Indian community in Leeds, which, apart from a strong Nevisian presence also has a large number of Kitticians and increasing numbers of Jamaicans, has allowed Nevisian women to form their own ties outside their home island. These provide an important context for their social lives. The West Indian Ladies Association, formed in the late 1970s, is led mainly by Nevisian women, with six of the eight chairpersons in 1987 being Nevisian. The association organizes meetings, outings and dances for its members, thus offering a respectable place for women, otherwise confined to the home, to socialize with one another. Dues are collected every month so that flowers can be sent to members who are in hospital. The association also attempts to collect money to send to the hospital on Nevis. In 1986 the Caribbean Women's Dramatic Society was formed to present plays about the West Indian community. Its first performance was in the summer of 1987 — a play by a Kittician woman about the migration experience from a woman's point of view.

For many of the women the churches provided an important place for social activities, as well as worship. Some attended Methodist and Anglican churches, while others, as on St John, drifted toward the more fundamentalist Baptist and Pentecostal congregations. Church attendance was less regular than it had been on Nevis or St John and seemed to be a less essential aspect of the women's lives.

While the Nevisian women were actively developing a new, respectable West Indian community in Leeds, they were also (over the 30 odd years that many of them have lived in Leeds) gradually developing their own family networks. These local networks have made them less dependent on the male-headed nuclear family, which many of them had established in England. The husband's social independence is offset by the woman's relative economic independence based on wage employment. Some of the women have asserted their newfound independence by refusing to tolerate their husbands' life style, seeing that divorce is a respectable solution to an unhappy marriage in Great Britain:

I made my own life and independence here. I have a right to decide what happens to me. My husband was a Nevisian, and he said to me that if we had lived in Nevis I would not have divorced him. But I replied that we were here, and I would do what the British do. In Nevis a woman wants to be a respectable wife, but then her husband will have other wives as well. My husband had other women, and I didn't want to change him, though I wanted him, if he wanted to change and saw the need to change. Black women get me mad. The husbands run around, and they accept it. I don't see why they should be so unhappy, if they can get peace for themselves.

The Nevisian women have, for such reasons, redefined their cultural values in the new situation of social and economic opportunities in which they have found themselves. In this way they have created a new life in England, which is not easily brought back to Nevis. This emerging sense of alienation from Nevis is reinforced by the fact that many of those from the older generation, who emigrated from Nevis, now have children and even grandchildren in Leeds, who generally speaking do not regard Nevis as their home island and have no desire to move there. At the same time many of the migrants no longer have close relatives on Nevis. While these women still identify themselves as West Indian and feel a close attachment to Nevis, most of them no longer wish to return to the island. Ironically, they have reached this conclusion at the very time that they are actually able to retire, sell their house and move back to Nevis.

I have been to Nevis three times, and the last time was in 1983, when I went back to stay there. When I came there many had left [the island] for work, so many of the people I had known were not there any longer. And those who were there didn't understand what I was talking about, because they had not been in England, and they didn't understand what had happened there.

I returned to England in 1984. The heat almost killed me, and I was homesick for my four daughters and one son in England. I have my own family life in England, they care for me. I have family and grandchildren in Nevis, but didn't know them so well. And the grandchildren didn't like me telling them anything.

## Conclusion

In this study of Nevisian women I have examined what happens when women leave their home community to look for wage employment abroad. While emigration constitutes a break from the domestic sphere, this is not caused by women being confined to the domestic unit on Nevis. Rather the break occurs because, when they emigrate, the women leave the protective sphere of the family network on Nevis, which helped them integrate the ideal of confinement to the domestic sphere with their actual integration into the greater society. The network had provided a flexible context within which they could provide and care for their children without losing respectability. It also provided an important avenue of support which made it possible for women to discharge their duties without the help of a husband. Furthermore, the network enabled women to explore economic opportunities entirely outside the domestic economy both in wage employment on Nevis and work abroad.

With emigration, the Nevisian network lost its importance as a context of every-day life. Nevertheless, being under a strong obligation to provide support for their mothers who had reared them and, in most cases, helped them emigrate, the women remained vital members of the network. In this way, the network, which acted as a centripetal force encouraging women to leave the island to become wage earners in an industrial economy, also locked the women into the Nevisian domestic economy, giving them a form of responsibility that was difficult to reconcile with their new life. Furthermore, while the female networks on Nevis operated within the flexible domestic sphere of the small rural communities of the West Indian island, in the migration destinations they extended to individual women, isolated in the limited private space associated with the domestic sphere of more compartmentalized and complex societies.

The success of the migrant woman therefore depends on the extent to which she can meet the conflicting demands of her obligations to her mother (as a vital person in the maternal network) and the need to develop her own networks at the migration destination. A woman who devoted all her attention to her own family abroad as soon as she emigrated would be berated for having failed in her duty to her mother. But if she remained too closely tied to her family on Nevis she soon found that her new existence abroad was reduced to work alone and that only during her short visits to Nevis did she truly live. Those who managed to lessen their obligations to the Nevis family and to develop new family networks abroad gradually found a new life outside Nevis. The women in Leeds seem to have come furthest in this process, with their obligations to Nevis now partly taken care of by the West Indian Ladies Association. Furthermore, to them migration has become a thing of the past, perhaps to be written about in plays.

The migration situation reveals how the twin poles of the Afro-Caribbean female-centred family ideal work together to create a contradictory situation in which a woman is forced to leave home in order to maintain its ideals. Immigration has enabled some of them to realize the ideal of the nuclear family (and even the status of divorcee which is predicated upon it), but the network nevertheless maintains its importance. The Afro-Caribbean family form can thus be seen to persist, even where its outward manifestation has changed. It remains, therefore, both as an ideal and as a highly concrete socio-economic reality, a vital link to the Caribbean and its cultural heritage.

## Notes

1  Further documentation and analysis of the Caribbean diaspora can be found, for example, in Thomas-Hope (1978, 1986), Marshall (1983) and Chaney (1985).
2  Barry Higman's study of slave populations in the British Caribbean shows that toward the end of slavery, the island's population was below present levels. In 1822 a total population of 9274 was registered on Nevis (Higman 1984: 413).
3  Some women place their children in other households if they have difficulty maintaining them on their own. These households are commonly those of the children's grandparents, childless relatives, or, more rarely, strangers (see, for example, Sanford 1975; Goossen 1972; Olwig 1985). The importance of child fostering in migration is analysed by Soto (1987).
4  Philpott (1968: 468-9) makes a similar point in his discussion about migration from Montserrat.
5  For a discussion of the migration regulations in effect in the US Virgin Islands, see Committee on the Judiciary (1975). A briefer and more up-to-date summary of the migration situation in the Virgin Islands is found in Miller and Boyer (1982).
6  Various aspects of the West Indian migration experience in Great Britain are discussed in Philpott (1973), Lamur and Speckman (1975), Foner (1979), Brock (1986), Carter (1986) and Gilroy (1987).

## References

Abrahams, Roger D. (1983) *The Man-of-Words in the West Indies*. Baltimore: The Johns Hopkins University Press

Brana-Shute, Gary (1976) 'Drinking Shops and Social Structure: Some Ideas on Lower-Class West Indian Male Behaviour'. *Urban Anthropology* 5 (1) 53-68

Brock, Colin (ed.) (1986) *The Caribbean in Europe: Aspects of the West Indian Experience in Britain, France and The Netherlands*. London: Frank Cass

Brown, Susan E. (1977) 'Love Unites Them and Hunger Separates Them: Poor Women in the Dominican Republic'. In R.R. Reiter (ed.) *Towards an Anthropology of Women*, New York: Monthly Review Press, 322-32

Carter, Trevor (1986) *Shattering Illusions: West Indians in British Politics*. London: Lawrence & Wishart

Chaney, Elsa M. (1985) *Migration from the Caribbean Region: Determinants and Effects of Current Movements*. Washington DC: Centre for Immigration Policy and Refugee Assistance, Georgetown University, Hemispheric Migration Project, Occasional Paper Series

Committee on the Judiciary (1975) *Non-immigrant Alien Labour Programme on the Virgin Islands of the United States*. House of Representatives, 94th Congress, Washington DC: US Government Printing Office

Edwards, Elkanah D. (n.d.) *Socioeconomic Factors Contributing to Learning Difficulties among Primary School Children in Nevis*. Report, Charlestown, Nevis: Public Library

Foner, Nancy (1979) *Jamaica Farewell: Jamaican Migrants in London*. London: Routledge & Kegan Paul

Frucht, Richard (1972) 'Migration and the Receipt of Remittances'. In *Resource Development in the Caribbean*, Montreal: Centre for Developing-Area Studies, 275-81

Gilroy, Paul (1987) *'There Ain't No Black in the Union Jack'. The Cultural Policies of Race and Nation*. London: Hutchinson

Gonzalez, Nancie L. Solien (1970) 'Towards a Definition of Matrifocality'. In N.E. Whitten and J.F. Szwed (eds) *Afro-American Anthropology*, New York: The Free Press, 231-44

Goossen, Jean (1972) 'Child Sharing and Foster Parenthood in the French West Indies'. Paper presented at the American Anthropological Association, New York City

Gussler, Judith D. (1980) 'Adaptive Strategies and Social Networks of Women in St Kitts'. In E. Bourguignon (ed.) *A World of Women*, New York: Praeger, 185-209

Higman, B.W. (1984) *Slave Populations of the British Caribbean 1807-1834*. Baltimore: The Johns Hopkins University Press

Lamur, Humphrey and John D. Speckman (eds) (1975) *Adaptation of Migrants from the Caribbean in the European and American Metropolis*. Amsterdam: Department of Anthropology & Non-Western Sociology, University of Amsterdam/ Leiden: Department of Caribbean Studies, Royal Institute of Linguistics & Anthropology

Liburd, Carolyn G. (1984) 'Migration from Nevis since 1950'. BA thesis, University of the West Indies, Jamaica

Lieber, Michael (1976) '"Liming" and Other Concerns: The Style of Street Embedments in Port of Spain, Trinidad'. *Urban Anthropology*, 5 (4) 319-34

Marshall, Dawn (1983) 'Toward an Understanding of Caribbean Migration'. In *US Immigration and Refugee Policy: Global and Domestic Issues*, Lexington, Mass: Lexington Books, 113-21

Miller, Mark J. and William W. Boyer (1982) 'Foreign Workers in the USVI: History of a Dilemma'. *Caribbean Review*, 11 (1) 48-51

Olwig, Karen Fog (1985) *Cultural Adaptation and Resistance on St John: Three Centuries of Afro-Caribbean Life*. Gainesville: University of Florida Press

—— (1987) 'Children's Attitudes to the Island Community: The Aftermath of Out-migration on Nevis'. In J. Besson and J. Momsen (eds) *Land and Development in the Caribbean*, London: Macmillan Caribbean for Warwick University Caribbean Studies, 153-70

—— (1989) 'The Struggle for Respectability: Methodist Missionary Activity on Nevis'. Paper presented at the 14th Annual Conference of the Society for Caribbean Studies, High Leigh Conference Centre, Hoddesdon, Hertfordshire, England, 4-6 July

Philpott, Stuart B. (1968) 'Remittance Obligations, Social Networks and Choice among Montserratian Migrants in Britain'. *Man*, 3 (3) 465-76

—— (1973) *West Indian Migration: The Montserrat Case*. London School of Economics, Monographs on Social Anthropology No. 47, London: The Athlone Press

Population Census of the Commonwealth Caribbean (1980-81) St Christopher/Nevis, 3 vols

Richardson, Bonham C. (1983) *Caribbean Migrants*. Knoxville: The University of Tennessee Press

Sahlins, Marshall (1972) *Stone Age Economics*. Chicago: Aldine

Sanford, Margaret (1975) 'To Be Treated as a Child of the Home: Black Carib Child Landing in a British West Indian Society'. In T.R. Williams (ed.) *Socialization and Communication in Primary Groups*, The Hague: Mouton Publishers, 159-81

Smith, M.G. (1966) 'Introduction'. In Edith Clarke, *My Mother who Fathered Me*, London: George Allen & Unwin

Smith, R.T. (1956) *The Negro Family in British Guiana: Family Structure and Social Status in the Villages*. London: Routledge & Kegan Paul

—— (1973) 'The Matrifocal Family'. In J. Goody (ed.) *The Character of Kinship*, Cambridge: Cambridge University Press, 121-44

—— (1987) 'Hierarchy and the Dual Marriage System in West Indian Society'. In J.F. Collier and S.J. Yanagisako, (eds) *Gender and Kinship: Essays toward a Unified Analysis*, Stanford: Stanford University Press, 165-96

Soto, Isa Maria (1987) 'West Indian Child Fostering: Its Role in Migrant Exchanges'. In C.R. Sutton and E.M. Chaney (eds) *Caribbean Life in New York City: Sociocultural Dimensions*, New York: Centre for Migration Studies of New York, 131-49

Sutton, Constance and Susan Makiesky-Barrow (1977) 'Social Inequality and
      Sexual Status in Barbados'. In A. Schlegel (ed.) *Sexual Stratification: A Cross-
      Cultural View*, New York: Columbia University Press, 292-325
Sutton, Joyah Junella (1986) 'Culturama: An Analysis of a Nevisian Festival'. BA
      thesis, University of the West Indies, Cave Hill, Barbados
Thomas-Hope, Elizabeth M. (1978) 'The Establishment of a Migration Tradition:
      British West Indian Movements to the Hispanic Caribbean in the Century after
      Emancipation'. In C.G. Clarke (ed.) *Caribbean Social Relations*, Liverpool; Centre
      for Latin American Studies, 66-81
——— (1986) 'Caribbean Diaspora, the Inheritance of Slavery: Migration from the
      Commonwealth Caribbean'. In C. Brock (ed.) *The Caribbean in Europe,* London:
      Frank Cass, 15-35
Tobias, Peter M. (1975) '"How you Gonna Keep em Down in the Tropics Once
      They've Dreamed New York?": Some Aspects of Grenadian Migration'. Ph.D.
      dissertation, Rice University, University Microfilms, Ann Arbor
Wilson, Peter J. (1969) 'Reputation and Respectability: A Suggestion for Caribbean
      Ethnology'. *Man* 4 (1) 70-84
——— (1971) 'Caribbean Crews: Peer Groups and Male Society'. *Caribbean Studies*,
      10 (4) 18-41

# X Migration, Development & the Gender Division of Labour: Puerto Rico & Margarita Island, Venezuela

JANICE MONK with the late CHARLES S. ALEXANDER[*]

The literature on migration has begun to pay attention to gender differences in the composition of migration streams from the Caribbean, but few studies attempt to analyse these differences in any detail or to link them to other changes underway in the region. This chapter draws together the findings of two studies previously published separately (Monk 1981; Monk and Alexander 1986) in order to examine how gender differences in patterns of migration are related to different modes of development. It focuses on the ways that the gender division of labour is implicated in development processes, contrasting the case of western Puerto Rico, where rural industrialization was introduced to an agricultural region, with Margarita Island, Venezuela, which has been transformed from an agricultural and fishing economy to one dependent on free port shopping and tourism. In making the comparisons, we examine differences among women and men as well as between them.

In a review of research on Caribbean migration, Elsa Chaney (1985) draws attention to several ways in which gender is salient to the process and its effects. She notes that prior to 1950, emigrants from an array of islands were predominantly men, but that since the 1960s migration has been much less sex selective; she cites a number of cases in the 1970s where women predominated among migrants from Caribbean islands including Jamaica (54.4 per cent female), Grenada (51 per cent female) and Trinidad and Tobago (55.6 per cent female). She alludes to age differences between the migrant populations and those who remain, in particular noting that women in the 20 to 34 year-old groups are over represented among those remaining in a number of Caribbean areas. She suggests that female migration streams are dominated by younger women and those over 45. In addressing differentials among migrants on the basis of education, socio-economic status or rural versus urban origins, she does not, however, disaggregate the data by sex. Concluding her review, Chaney urges scholars to move the research efforts towards the study of migration and, for example, studies of migration and smallholder agriculture, migration and the balance of payments, migration and labour markets, migration and the incidence of female-headed households, and so on.

A major collection edited by Pastor (1985), *Migration and Development in the Caribbean: The Unexplored Connection*, also recognizes the need to examine migration in association with other phenomena. Yet the contributors leave unexplored

* This chapter was conceived by both authors and completed by Monk. It is dedicated to Professor Alexander's memory and to our enjoyable field collaboration in the Caribbean. Support for the research was provided by the University of Arizona, the US Agency for International Development, an Agency Title XII Strengthening Grant, the Tinker Foundation, the University of Illinois at Urbana-Champaign, the Centre for Latin American and Caribbean Studies, the Graduate College Research Board, and the Centre for International Comparative Studies.

the connection between gender and migration, and implicitly assume a continuance of male labour migration and the prevalence of female-headed households in the Caribbean, dependent on remittances for their economic support. This is not to say that women migrants from the Caribbean have been totally neglected in the literature, indeed a considerable number of studies focus on them. But these tend to concentrate on North American, British and French experiences (Foner 1976, 1986; Gonzalez 1976; Goossen 1976; Mortimer and Bryce-Laporte 1981; Prieto 1986; Stone 1983) and pay less attention to the Caribbean experiences that foster women's migration or to the differences between the women who migrate and those who stay behind. From this literature, however, we do learn that emigrating women represent both working and professional classes and that women's desire to leave is affected by the changing opportunities for work in the Caribbean (Gordon 1981; Bolles 1981).

The growing literature on women and migration, addressing international and rural to urban movements around the world, stresses the importance of studying women as migrants and reveals that gender differences in migration patterns reflect complex economic and cultural factors. Important among these are national immigration policies, structural differences in the labour markets, ideologies about male and female roles in society, and changes in the nature of both household and paid work. This literature, represented by several important works (Fawcett et al. 1984; International Migration Review 1984; Phizacklea 1983; Simon and Brettell 1986; Youssef et al. 1979), provides one frame of reference for a Caribbean analysis. A second frame of reference comes from the extensive literature on women and development (including Beneria 1982; Boserup 1970; Dauber and Cain 1981; Rogers 1980; Nash and Fernandez-Kelly 1983), which shows that development programmes have often had negative consequences for women's well being. This research also identifies how a variety of development projects have failed because of their lack of attention to women's roles in production and reproduction.

The literature on women and work, which recognizes the rapid increases in female labour force participation in many countries, provides a third frame of reference. Here the limitations of research and statistics focusing solely on full-time work in formal labour markets are identified and the attention is shifted to the informal sector, part-time work, unpaid work, and the combination of work inside and outside the home. The research shows how gender divisions of labour persist in both paid and unpaid work and that what is women's work in some regions is men's work in others (see Bunster and Chaney 1985; Dixon 1981; Young et al. 1984).

This study is informed by how each of these literatures (on migration, development and work) relates to gender distinctions. The choice of Puerto Rico and Margarita Island as case studies was somewhat fortuitous — our interest in Puerto Rico arose during a teaching assignment there; Margarita was selected primarily because one of us (Alexander) had done detailed fieldwork on the island prior to the creation of the free port. Nevertheless, the comparison has advantages. Both islands are part of the Spanish-speaking Caribbean; government policies have promoted distinctive development policies; in each case we had pre-development data available to us; on each island political circumstances allowed for the unrestricted movement of people to the mainland (the US in the case of Puerto Rico and Venezuela in the case of Margarita). The disadvantages of the comparison are that the two islands differ in scale (Puerto Rico is larger in population and area than Margarita) and that they had somewhat different pre-development economic and social patterns.

## Local Contexts

Geographers Jones and Pico (1955) and anthropologist Julian Steward (1956) describe life in western Puerto Rico around 1950, when the development programme known as Operation Bootstrap was just getting underway. Alexander's (1958) research does the same for Margarita and, in addition, incorporates a focus on migration (Alexander 1961). The area studied in Puerto Rica was in the hills of the western part of the island near the city of Mayaguez. The region had long been devoted to coffee and sugar-cane cultivation carried out on large holdings by wage labourers, predominantly men, with some fruit and vegetable cultivation on small owner-operated farms. Women had few opportunities for earning income other than by doing contract needlework at home for low pay. A dispersed settlement pattern, poor roads and little transport kept rural people, especially women, relatively isolated. Faced with a declining agricultural economy and low living standards on the island, at the end of the 1940s the government began to promote development programmes to improve the economy, health, education and public services. The economic initiatives relied chiefly on attracting manufacturing industries to Puerto Rico by means of tax concessions and other benefits, including low cost and increasingly better educated labour. Plants were opened in rural as well as urban areas. The main employer in the region we studied in the late 1970s was a North American company manufacturing plastic containers for hospital supplies, but nearby were also garment manufacturing and food processing plants. Agriculture had been virtually abandoned by the·time of our research, but roads, water supplies and electricity had been extended to rural areas and people had access to education and health services (Monk and Alexander 1979; 1985).

On Margarita, agriculture had almost disappeared by the time of our fieldwork in 1982. Traditionally the population there had supported itself by subsistence agriculture, fishing and craft work, with some additional income from contraband trade. The gender division of labour was slightly different from Puerto Rico and probably less marked. Men worked in the fields, selling part of their maize or bitter manioc crops to local processors of *arepa* or *casabi* (types of bread). Women cultivated yard gardens for family use and sold surplus produce in town. Both women and men combined various forms of economic activities. Fishing was important in some communities — men did the fishing and wholesaling but women were involved in smoking fish and also sometimes in selling it. Some forms of craft production were important for generating income and these activities were mostly, though not entirely, carried out by women (Alexander 1958). The migration of men to work in the oilfields on the mainland of Venezuela was common and, though some women did migrate, women substantially outnumbered men on the island in the 1940s and 1950s. In 1950 there were only 66 men for every 100 women in the 20-49 age group on Margarita. Under these conditions the women appear to have exercised a fair degree of autonomy over their lives and having children by men other than an absent husband seemed acceptable.

Agriculture on Margarita declined to some extent following the passage of the 1948 Reforestation Act, which suppressed cultivation in the highlands, but the greatest changes resulted from the development of a free port established by the Venezuelan government in 1967. By 1982 the government had issued over 2000 licences for the operation of duty-free shops, selling mainly clothing and household items for everyday use. Though the free port was expected to stimulate international tourism, especially visits by cruise ships, this had not materialized at the time of our fieldwork. No suitable port facilities were available and travel to the island was normally via the mainland, rather than directly from North America or Europe. Hotel building expanded to cater for the duty-free shoppers and beach holiday makers, who were mostly middle-class people who came from Caracas by ferry or plane. The number of available rooms increased from 219 in 1966 to over 3000 by 1980, by which time over a million people a year arrived by ferry and more than 20 flights a day were landing on the island. Shoppers thronged the streets of Porlamar throughout the year, but other tourists mainly came at Christmas, Easter and during school holidays. Like the Puerto Rican government, the Venezuelan government also funded new public services. The quality of roads on Margarita was vastly improved, water was piped from the mainland assuring regular supplies, and the education system was expanded to provide not only primary and secondary schools but also a two-year branch university campus (Monk and Alexander 1986).

## Employment & Migration

To examine how the development programmes had affected employment and migration we conducted survey research in rural communities. In Puerto Rico interviews were carried out by Monk in 1977 in Maricao and Las Marias in a randomly chosen set of households in the two villages and in the surrounding countryside of the *municipios*. Householders were asked about the migration behaviour of their children aged over 15 years and some information was also collected on the parents. In all, information was gathered on 420 adult sons and daughters. In Margarita, Monk and Alexander replicated the Puerto Rican survey in a random sample of households in seven villages in the Gomez district on the north of the island, about 30 to 45 minutes driving time from the free port centre of Porlamar and close to the secondary centre of Juan Griego. Here we decided to analyse occupational data on the householders as well as on their children; the sample includes 175 adults in the households and 315 of their children over age 15.

On the basis of these interviews it is possible to create profiles of male and female patterns of employment and to compare people who have remained in the local communities with those who have left. In Puerto Rico the likelihood was high that neither sons nor daughters would be living in their home communities — 65 per cent of the sons had left and 63 per cent of the daughters. About one-fifth of these had left prior to 1960, and this group included more males than females; since then women and men have been almost equally represented in the migrant group and, for the whole period, rates of migration do not differ significantly by sex. Patterns of initial destinations are quite different for sons and daughters, however, with sons more likely to have left the island (70 per cent) primarily to go to the US. This was also the main destination for daughters (43 per cent), but they also moved to the nearby city of Mayaguez (where a variety of jobs was available in factories and services) and to other areas on the island, including villages and the countryside in western Puerto Rico. Migrants of both sexes were more likely to come from large, poor families than were the people who remained. Indeed, 70 per cent of the migrants were from families receiving some form of US government welfare payment, primarily food stamps, compared with only 30 per cent of the non-migrants. Since families were usually large, the effects of low incomes were heightened and clearly related to the incidence of migration — 83 per cent of the migrants came from families with five or more children and 36 per cent of the total from families with nine or more children.

Differences between the male and female migrants were pronounced, however, in their levels of education. The men who left were more likely to have completed high school than the women, whereas the women were more likely to have only elementary education. By contrast, the men who stayed were more likely than the remaining women to have only elementary education, but higher proportions of the women who stayed had completed high school. Differences were most marked at the upper and lower ends of these educational scales (0-4 years and 9-12 years of schooling) and were not significant for those who had completed 5-8 years. Most of the migrants were young when they left. By the age of 25, 81 per cent of the male migrants and 78 per cent of the female ones had departed. The only statistically significant sex difference in age at the time of migration occurred in the over 40 age group, in which women leaving outnumbered men.

These patterns can throw some light on the impact of the industrial development strategy. For a start, the high numbers leaving indicate that the strategy did not bring enough employment to rural areas to counteract the declining opportunities in agriculture. Though we can also see the effects of the employers' preference for hiring young women at low wages, they none the less sought a 'quality' labour force and recruited the better educated young women. Educated men had few good employment prospects in the area and hence were over-represented among those who left. Of the sons who remained in the area 40 per cent were either unemployed or unemployable at the time of the field research, 10 per cent worked as farm labourers, and 10 per cent had other unskilled jobs, with both types of work likely to be intermittent. The less well educated women could not find local employment as readily as those who were better educated. Not only were the factory jobs for the better educated, but clerical jobs in health, education and other social services, which had expanded as a result of government programmes, were also mainly open to educated women.

For the best educated (post secondary or college level) there were no significant differences in male and female propensities to migrate, though gender distinctions appeared here in the greater likelihood that men would earn college degrees. Almost all the men and women with post-secondary education had left the area. Other women who remained were able to fill roles as housewives, but did not have many other employment options. Older women who needed to support themselves were probably shut out of factory employment, a pattern noted by Helen Safa (1981) in her study of nearby Mayaguez. They had fewer choices and usually had to depend on welfare support or help from their families. This may explain the greater incidence of migration among women over 40 than of comparably aged men.

As noted above, migrants of both sexes were likely to come from poor families. The study did not reveal any significant social class distinctions among women and men migrants on the basis of their families of origin, other than a slight tendency for daughters whose fathers were craftsmen or factory workers to be more likely to leave than these men's sons. Perhaps sons from these 'middle' classes were more able to find employment in their fathers' trades or through their connections than were sons of labouring class men, whereas these families (or the daughters themselves) may have had aspirations for their daughters that could not be met locally. To gain an understanding of this pattern would have required more detailed investigation of motivations than we carried out.

Overall, the Puerto Rican case reveals the effects of the gender division of labour, especially as it is constructed by the industrial demand for young women workers and the expansion of government social services. Of the daughters who had remained in the area 35 per cent were working in the factories. The development

strategy has not created a significant number of jobs for men, whatever their level
of education, or for the least educated women. When these programmes were
instituted, the Puerto Rican government was apparently unaware that these effects
would be experienced, though today we know more about the recruiting patterns
of such companies. By the early 1970s, however, the government instituted
policies to attract petro-chemical industries to the island. This was partly because
it was thought that these would lead to the development of related industries and
partly because jobs in these industries would mostly employ men, which, it was
argued, was necessary in a society with a patriarchal tradition (Commonwealth of
Puerto Rico 1971).[1]

We did not explore how Puerto Rican households in the area managed their
reproductive work, though we learned that married women in their early thirties
were employed in the factories. Since the factories in the area operate on shift
work, with one shift leaving work in the mid-afternoon, it is likely that married
women arranged their domestic work around their job schedule. We did not
encounter many women engaging in informal sector work to survive. We suspect
that the Puerto Rican government's social service programmes and the availability
of US food stamps made life at a subsistence level at least possible.[2]

The Margarita Island case also reveals how the effects of the free port development have been mediated by the gender division of labour. The household
surveys showed that with only 6 per cent of the male and 1 per cent of the female
householders engaged in farming or fishing, virtually no-one remained in traditional occupations. Neither were women continuing to cultivate household
gardens to any significant extent, for less than a third of the households had any
type of fruit or vegetable garden. Most food was imported and sold by salesmen
who drove trucks to the villages or at small roadside stands and stores operated
by both men and women.[3] Many new jobs had opened up for men, though
primarily in the building industry or in driving taxis or small passenger vans.
Almost 60 per cent of the men in the households we studied were employed in
one or other of these jobs. If the men who were too old or ill for employment are
excluded from the data, the percentage would be even higher. About 40 per cent
of the householders' sons who remained on the island were also in these occupations. Though the men's jobs reflect the advent of the free port and the tourist
industry, drivers are also needed to transport the islanders, for there is no bus
service and in the new commercial economy people need to travel to the urban
centres for many of their needs. Unemployment among men of the householder
generation was low, with only a little over 2 per cent identifying themselves as
unemployed, though another 15 per cent were sick, disabled or retired.
Unemployment was higher among the sons who remained in Margarita (12 per
cent). Nevertheless, these employment figures should not be interpreted as
evidence that rural men were earning good incomes, for it was our impression
that men in construction were underemployed; they reported intermittent work
and often local employment, rather than regular employment on the large
commercial construction projects.

With respect to employment linked to the free port, Margaritan women were in a
rather different position to the men. Though one might have expected the hotels
and duty-free shops to provide many jobs for them, the women from these rural
communities were not in fact thus employed, even though the distance to town
was not great. About half the women of the householder generation were housewives and reported no employment or informal sector work. Almost 20 per cent of
the adult daughters were similarly situated. A number of other women (20 per
cent of the householder sample) combined housework with informal sector activi-

ties — being self-employed in sales, service or production, or a combination of these. Sales work often involved operating a small store (*bodega*) in or attached to their own home, or simply selling soft drinks from a home refrigerator to neighbours. Production included food processing, such as grinding corn for making *arepa*, or raising chickens or rabbits to sell, or piecework, particularly making parts of shoes. Services included letting out space in one's home, baby-sitting, laundering and mending clothes. Operating a *bodega*, which required capital, was more common among married women, whereas production and services were more often carried out by women in female-headed households. With the exception of one cottage industry in a village where a high proportion of women and men engaged in making a modern, low-cost, rubber-soled fabric shoe, craft activities had almost entirely disappeared, whether for home use or for sale. Half a dozen women continued to make pottery or weave hammocks, which were among the few local items produced for sale to tourists.

For the women householders the free port had thus generated little direct or indirect employment. Although 7 per cent identified themselves as sales workers, they were not working in the duty-free shops. Rather they were older women, occupied as *revendedores*, buying free port goods and reselling them as street vendors on the island or on the mainland. Slightly over 10 per cent of the women householders were service workers, but they were employed as school cooks, seamstresses and janitors, with only a couple working as maids.

Among the adult daughters who remained on the island, the employment patterns were different from those of their mothers. Unemployment was high, with about 30 per cent being neither housewives nor employed.[4] While 19 per cent were housewives, they did not report supplementary activities to create income. Another 17 per cent were still students. Among those who were employed — clerical (13 per cent) or professional and technical (9 per cent) — jobs were more common than any work connected with the free port or hotels. Only one daughter was employed in a free port shop. Basically, however, these women's jobs were in 'female' occupations.

The new economic situation on the island has been associated with a significant change in the patterns of migration.[5] Overall the extent of migration was lower than in the Puerto Rican case. About one third of the householders' children had left the island, and of these, 56 per cent were male and 44 per cent female. But the former predominance of women on the island has been reversed and, by 1981, the sex ratio on the island was 101 men to every 100 women. One reason for the change is that men had ceased to leave Margarita at the rate they did formerly. The data on the householders' adult children indicate that among those who left 20 or more years ago, sons outnumbered daughters by 214:100. Among those who left in the last ten years, there were only 83 sons leaving for each 100 daughters. Men have also returned to the island at a higher rate than women. Over 40 per cent of the sons who moved from the island at some point were living on the island at the time of the survey, compared with only 21 per cent of the daughters.

The data also reveal class differences intersecting with gender differences within the migrant group. Daughters from the more affluent families were leaving the island at a higher rate than sons. Among the daughters who had left, 26 per cent were members of families in which the father had a professional or technical occupation, compared with only 15 per cent of the migrant sons. Only 7 per cent of daughters from these families remained on the island, compared with 11 per cent of the sons. More daughters of craftsmen, skilled labourers and transport workers had also left than sons (32 per cent of the migrant daughters were from such households compared to 23 per cent of the sons). The migrant sons were more likely to be from labouring families or to have fathers who were farmers or small shop owners. The daughters had left to seek education and had not returned. Daughters who remained on the island were slightly more likely to be from lower-class families than those who left (27 per cent were the daughters of labourers, and 27 per cent the daughters of farmers or small shopkeepers) and it is they who were likely to be the unemployed.

Migration brought some advancement for both sons and daughters who remained away from Margarita. For a start, they were better educated — 43 per cent of the sons and 27 per cent of the daughters had acquired some post-secondary education, compared with only 16 per cent and 14 per cent respectively of those who stayed in Margarita. Occupationally, they were far more likely to be engaged in professional and technical occupations than the non-migrants (20 per cent of the migrant sons and 17 per cent of the migrant daughters held profes-sional or technical employment compared with 2 per cent of the sons and 9 per cent of the daughters who remained on the island).

Margarita Island's economy has clearly changed radically since the development of the free port, but the consequences have been very different for men and women and for women of different social classes. Despite a large number of jobs having been created in the hotels and shops, the women from the villages we studied had not taken them up, even though spatially they were relatively close. The reasons seem partly to lie in an imbalance between the cost of the journey to work and the wages earned in town. At the time of our survey, sales clerks in free port shops were paid about 900 bolivars a month. Daily transport to town cost 360 bolivars a month and the women mentioned other costs of working, including having to buy lunches and suitable clothes. It is also likely that employers, at least in the shops, did not want to hire less educated village women to sell to their customers from Caracas. But young women from middle-class families presum-ably saw better opportunities on the mainland, for they too did not take these jobs. Our impression, based on informal inquiries, is that the employees in the shops and hotels were coming to the island from elsewhere. Shop owners were also often reported to be outsiders.

## Migration, Development & the Gender Division of Labour

Taken together, the Puerto Rican and Venezuelan cases show that major economic changes have occurred since the development programmes were intro-duced and that these have affected rural women and men very differently. The gender division of labour, which is manipulated by employers and shapes people's ideas about what kinds of work they can do, lies at the heart of these differences. Factory work in Puerto Rico has no gender specific requirements, but employer prejudice and cultural tradition dictate that women are hired for these low-paid and repetitive jobs. Likewise, the predominance of men in transport and construction on Margarita is the reflection of a cultural view about what work is suitable for men rather than women. On both islands, migration is the main option for those who do not find employment in these sectors; otherwise their fate is likely to be unemployment.

Ideologies about gender roles make some kinds of work available to women and other kinds to men, though these vary between cultures. Policy makers and professionals in the development field rarely take these distinctions into account. It is, however, more important to discover how or even whether these gender distinctions can be modified to allow for a more equitable development within societies. Why, for example, is it more appropriate for Puerto Rican women than men to work in factories, or for Margaritan men rather than women to drive taxis? Why cannot Margaritan women work in the construction industry?

These cases also reveal distinctions *among* men and women, not only *between* them. They also show that development programmes may benefit some women or men more than others — a point seldom stressed in the literature on the negative effects of development on women, though the best studies do examine diversity among women. Still, in the cases we describe, it is sometimes difficult to decide what constitutes an improvement in life for the people in question. Are high school educated women in Puerto Rico over qualified for low-paid factory jobs?[6] Would they be better off if, like the Margaritan women with education, they left the island to further their education and employment elsewhere? And what about the women and men who have come to Margarita from the outside to take employment generated by the free port? At a macro-level, the project might be identified as successful, given the growth in Margarita's trade and population. At the micro-level of the rural communities, the results are mixed, with fewer benefits and more costs to women than to men.

We paid only passing attention to household work and social reproduction in comparing the Puerto Rican and Venezuelan cases. Nevertheless, it is clear that rural Puerto Rican households were heavily dependent on government aid for survival. Venezuelan households had no such support. Married women needing supplementary income usually turned to informal sector activities; for women heads of households this was sometimes their only means of support. It is less clear from these cases how changes in reproductive work (such as the reduction in women's household gardens) are connected to migration, but, as Kate Young (1982) suggests, more inquiries should take up this question. The life stage of women and men, but especially of women, also needs to be taken into account. The Puerto Rican case suggests its relevance as do the numerous reports of the employment of young single women by transnational companies around the globe.

The gender differences that emerge in migration because of the specific nature of development programmes are also likely to have unforeseen social consequences. For example, how are social relations affected when the men in a community are mainly poorly educated and/or unemployed and the women are better educated and employed? Is the division of domestic work changing? How have the self-images and sexual attitudes of Margaritan women changed now that they are no longer the majority population on the island, are more likely to be economically dependent on men than in the past, and live with a more marked gender division of labour than before the advent of the free port economy?[7]

Finally, can we fully understand gender differentiated movements if we look at them only in the local context? Changes in national policies and the decisions of international businesses to move their investments have ramifications at local, regional and international levels that are often different for women and men. Both cases illustrate this point. Situations in which migration is constrained by national boundaries, as in much of the rest of the Caribbean, may create different patterns from those we studied. Formulating development and population theories and policies are difficult tasks, but they become increasingly complex when we begin to take gender into account in a systematic way. Only through such efforts, however, can we begin to create equitable programmes and adequate theories.

## Notes

1  Such industries are capital rather than labour intensive and do not create a comparable number of jobs for the investment involved.
2  This situation is subject to changes in government support policies.
3  Women are still an important component of the sellers in the food markets of Porlamar, but this does not involve people we interviewed.
4  We have been asked whether prostitution might be an unreported occupation of these young village women. We saw or heard no evidence to support this conclusion.
5  Migration of non-Margaritans to the island has obviously occurred. The population increased from 75,899 in 1950 to 196,911 in 1980 (Monk and Alexander 1986). The nature of this movement also warrants investigation.
6  A growing literature on women's factory employment by transnational corporations points to the many exploitative and hazardous aspects of this work, which are negative for any employees, regardless of their level of education.
7  Alexander's impression was that the unemployed young Margaritan women were less confident and assertive than the women he knew on the island in the 1950s and certainly than many of the older women we interviewed.

## References

Alexander, Charles S. (1958) *The Geography of Margarita and Adjacent Islands, Venezuela*. Berkeley: University of California Publications in Geography, No. 12
——  (1961) 'Margarita Island: Exporter of People.' *Journal of Inter-American Studies*, 3 (4) 549-57

Beneria, Lourdes (ed.) (1982) *Women and Development: The Sexual Division of Labour in Rural Societies*. New York: Praeger

Bolles, A. Lynn (1981) 'Goin' Abroad: Working-class Jamaican Women and Migration.' In Delores M. Mortimer and Roy S. Bryce-Laporte (eds) *Female Immigrants to the United States: Caribbean, Latin American and African Experiences*, Washington: Smithsonian Institution

Boserup, Esther (1970) *Women's Role in Economic Development*. London: George Allen & Unwin

Bunster, Ximena B. and Elsa M. Chaney (1985) *Sellers and Servants: Working Women in Lima, Peru*. New York: Praeger

Chaney, Elsa M. (1985) *Migration from the Caribbean Region: Determinants and Effects of Current Movements*. Washington: Georgetown University Centre for Immigration Policy and Refugee Assistance

Commonwealth of Puerto Rico, Economic Development Administration (1971) *Economic Development in Puerto Rico during the Last Twenty Years*. San Juan: Evaluation and Programming Section, General Economic Division, Office of Economic Research, mimeographed

Dauber, R. and M.L. Cain (eds) (1981) *Women and Technological Change in Developing Countries*. Boulder: Westview Press

Dixon, Ruth (1981) 'Jobs for Women in Rural Industry and Services.' In B.C. Lewis (ed.) *Invisible Farmers: Women and the Crisis in Agriculture*, Washington: Agency for International Development, 271-328

Fawcett, James, Siew-an Khoo and Peter C. Smith (eds) (1984) *Women in the Cities of Asia*. Boulder: Westview Press

Foner, Nancy (1976) 'Male and Female: Jamaican Migrants in London.' *Anthropological Quarterly*, 49 (1) 28-35
——  (1986) 'Sex Roles and Sensibilities: Jamaican Women in New York and London.' In Rita J. Simon and Caroline B. Brettell (eds) *International Migration: The Female Experience*, Totowa: Rowman & Allenheld

Gonzalez, Nancy L. (1976) 'Multiple Migratory Experiences of Dominican Women.' *Anthropological Quarterly*, 49 (1) 35-44

Goossen, Jean (1976) 'The Migration of French West Indian Women to Metropolitan France.' *Anthropological Quarterly*, 49 (1) 45-52

Gordon, Monica (1981) 'Caribbean Migration: A Perspective on Women.' In Delores M. Mortimer and Roy S. Bryce-Laporte (eds) *Female Immigrants to the United States: Caribbean, Latin American and African Experiences*, Washington: Smithsonian Institution

*International Migration Review* (1984) 'Special Issue on Women in Migration.' 18 (4)

Jones, Clarence F. and Rafael Pico (eds) (1955) *Symposium on the Geography of Puerto Rico*. Rio Piedras: University of Puerto Rico Press

Monk, Janice (1981) 'Social Change and Sexual Differences in Puerto Rican Rural Migration.' In O. Horst (ed.) *Papers in Latin American Geography in Honour of Lucia Harrison*, Conference of Latin Americanist Geographers

Monk, Janice and Charles S. Alexander (1979) 'Modernization and Rural Population Movements: Western Puerto Rico.' *Journal of Inter-American Studies and World Affairs*, 21 (4) 523-50

—— (1985) 'Land Abandonment in Western Puerto Rico.' *Caribbean Geography*, (2) 1-15

—— (1986) 'Freeport Fall Out: Gender, Employment and Migration, Margarita Island.' *Annals of Tourism Research*, 13 (3) 393-413

Mortimer, Delores M. and Roy S. Bryce-Laporte (1981) *Female Immigrants to the United States: Caribbean, Latin American and African Experiences*. Washington: Smithsonian Institution

Nash, June and Maria Patricia Fernandez-Kelly (eds) (1983) *Women, Men, and the International Division of Labour*. Albany: State University of New York Press

Pastor, Robert A. (ed.) (1985) *Migration and Development in the Caribbean: The Unexplored Connection*. Boulder: Westview Press

Phizacklea, Annie (ed.) (1983) *One Way Ticket: Migration and Female Labour*. London: Routledge & Kegan Paul

Prieto, Yolanda (1986) 'Cuban Women and Work in the United States: A New Jersey Case Study.' In Rita J. Simon and Caroline B. Brettell (eds) *International Migration: The Female Experience*, Totowa: Rowman & Allenheld

Rogers, B. (1980) *The Domestication of Women*. London: Tavistock

Safa, Helen (1981) 'Runaway Shops and Female Employment: The Search for Cheap Labour.' *Signs*, (7) 418-34

Simon, Rita J. and C. Brettell (1986) *International Migration: The Female Experience*. Totowa: Rowman & Allenheld

Steward, Julian H. (1956) *The Peoples of Puerto Rico*. Urbana: University of Illinois Press

Stone, Karen (1983) 'Motherhood and Waged Work: West Indian, Asian and White Mothers Compared.' In Annie Phizacklea (ed.) *One Way Tickets: Migration and Female Labour*, London: Routledge & Kegan Paul

Young, Kate (1982) 'The Creation of a Relative Surplus Population: A Case Study from Mexico.' In Lourdes Beneria (ed.) *Women and Development: The Sexual Division of Labour in Rural Societies*, New York: Praeger, 149-78

Young, Kate, Carol Wolkowitz and Roslyn McCullugh (1984) *Of Marriage and the Market: Women's Subordination Internationally and its Lessons*. London: Routledge & Kegan Paul

Youssef, Nadia, Mayra Buvinic, Ayse Kudat, Jennifer Sebstad and Barbara Von Elm (1979) *Women in Migration: A Third World Focus*. Washington: Office of Women in Development, Agency for International Development

# SECTION TWO

## Economic Roles of Caribbean Women

---

# PART 1

## Rural Employment

---

Amerindian women played a major role in the region's agriculture and under slavery women worked side by side with men in the fields of the plantations. Even today the Caribbean is seen as a region of female farming. Over one-third of small farms in the Eastern Caribbean are operated by women. In 1961 women provided more than half the paid agricultural labour force in many Caribbean territories and, though the number of women agricultural workers has declined more quickly than that of male workers, it is still the most common source of off-farm employment for rural women in the smaller islands.

Women work as hired labourers on farms, as family helpers or operators on their own farms, and as traders in farm produce. Farms operated by women tend to be smaller than those operated by men and are more likely to be freehold. Land use on female-operated farms is distinctive in that it is usually dominated by food crops for local use, such as vegetables and ground provisions, rather than by export crops like sugar or bananas. Women farmers rear mostly small stock such as pigs, which can be fed on scraps and seen as part of housework.

There is also a marked gender division of labour in Caribbean agriculture. This varies according to crop and livestock sector, size of farm and level of technology. Divisions of labour appear to be most flexible among the more educated and technically sophisticated farmers. The age of rural women also affects the role they play on the farm. In many areas women farmers are younger than male farmers and less likely to have spent time overseas. Women cultivate to feed their children and in old age depend on remittances from their offspring.

# XI Small Farm Food Production & Gender in Barbados

CHRISTINE BARROW

Afro-Caribbean rural women have had a hard time emerging from invisibility or from Eurocentric stereotypes in research and policy-making. Researchers, often in the absence of any contradictory evidence, tend to follow the lead given by Boserup and classify the Caribbean, along with Latin America, as characterized by 'male farming systems' (an exception is Henshall 1984: 173-4). Such systems are to be found in the context of population pressure and plough cultivation, where males undertake the bulk of agricultural labour with assistance from hired hands drawn from among the landless, while women devote themselves to work in the home (Boserup 1970: 15-35). The impact of colonial capitalism, whereby women are 'marginalized' through being confined to subsistence food production with traditional methods and tools, while men take over land and move into high technology and cash crop production (Boserup 1970: 53-63), is also assumed to be universal in Third World countries.

Within the Caribbean, women in agriculture have rarely been identified as a group to be given special attention, either by researchers or planners. In the historical and social science literature gender distinctions remain overshadowed by class and race considerations. The dominant plantation model, for example, contrasts plantation and peasant with reference to resource base and policy concerns and the term 'peasant' is essentially male.[1] Even at the level of family and household the reality of women's lives is blurred by ethnocentric stereotypes. The anthropology conducted in the Caribbean during the 1950s and 1960s created images, which survive to the present, of women who are expected to be modest and obedient and to exhibit proper standards of sexual fidelity and morality (Clarke 1957: 91; Rodman 1971: 61). Their daily routines are taken up with household chores and they 'spend a greater part of their time within their own house and yard' (Greenfield 1966: 106) while their husbands as household heads are responsible for providing economic support (Smith 1956: 76).

Recent feminist scholarship has done much to correct these biases from a historical perspective (Beckles 1988; Brereton 1988; Reddock 1984) by emphasizing socio-demographically women's continuous involvement in the labour force (Massiah 1984) and by stressing their central breadwinner roles and strategies for family survival (Sutton and Makiesky-Barrow 1981; Barrow 1986). Only a few, however, have focused specifically on gender distinctions in agricultural activities and the contribution of women as small farmers (Henshall 1981; Knudson and Yates 1981).

The objective of this study is simply to continue this work of placing Caribbean rural women on the map. We do so by examining women as small-scale farmers in Barbados, focusing, in both historical and contemporary perspective, on two main dimensions, namely gender distinctions in resource allocation and the division of labour by gender.

## The Plantation Legacy

### (a) Resource Allocation

The image of agriculture that comes to mind for Barbados and the wider
Caribbean is a plantation heritage of mono-crop production for export and the
neglect of food production for subsistence and local markets; land consolidation
into large-scale plantation units and small farmers, deprived of resources, strug-
gling to survive. The argument that 'peasant' development in Caribbean countries
has been stifled by the dominant plantation sectors is central to Beckford's (1972;
1974; 1975) plantation model. In the competition for resources, small farmers, male
and female, have always been severely disadvantaged by the plantation
stronghold over land, labour, credit and other essential inputs. Mass alienation
from the land has resulted in large numbers of farmers on plots too small and
infertile to support viable peasant farming or, indeed, to absorb the labour available in the peasant sector. Compounding the situation is the ever-increasing
pressure on scarce land by expanding rural populations. With few alternative
employment opportunities to absorb the excess manpower, plantations have been
able to secure sufficient labour at relatively low wage rates. In the competition for
labour with the peasant sector, plantations already have the advantage of comparatively high wages and more regular employment. Resources and infrastructural
requirements such as capital and credit, technology and knowledge, processing
and marketing have all been heavily concentrated in export crop (mainly sugar)
production. Although Beckford's analysis has been subject to criticism (Benn 1974:
258; Bernal et al. 1984: 79), the image of Caribbean small farmers lacking viability
as independent economic units persists in the literature. Caribbean peasantries are
seen to survive as subordinate sectors deprived of resources.

The legacy of unequal allocation of land is nowhere more apparent than in
Barbados. At the top of the scale the plantation sector controls 64,413 acres, or 87
per cent of the total acreage, which is consolidated into 1.0 per cent of the total
number of holdings. Small farms, i.e. under ten acres, cover only 9582 acres, or 13
per cent of the total acreage, which is spread between 99 per cent of the total
number of holdings (Barbados Agricultural Census 1971). Unfortunately, no
information is available on gender and ownership in relation to these holdings.
The customary pattern whereby land holdings are subdivided equally among all
children has generally ensured that women are not discriminated against in land
tenure arrangements. However, it has also given rise to further fragmentation and
to farming on decreasing acreages of marginal land.

Correlating with this continuing stranglehold on land, we find the slow growth
followed by a recent decline in the number of small farms and farmers. Post-
emancipation small farm development was stunted and it was not until the crisis
in sugar and bankruptcy of many plantations at the end of the nineteenth century,
coupled with remittances from migrants in Panama and elsewhere in the early
twentieth century, that a small proprietor sector began to expand (Marshall et al.
1974). By 1946 there were 30,752 such holdings (i.e. of under 10 acres) occupying
17,238 acres of a total arable acreage of 93,346 acres (Halcrow and Cave 1947: 2).
Since then, however, small farming has declined. The most recent agricultural
census reports 12,629 smallholdings occupying, as mentioned, 9582 acres. This
represents a decline of nearly 50 per cent. Further pressure on scarce land
resources is indicated by the existence of 13,519 'holdings without land'. This
represents the large number of livestock farmers who, in the absence of available
land for rental or purchase, graze their animals on nearby vacant lots. A total of
10,000 small farmers was reported for 1971, though this figure was not disaggre-

gated by gender. A rough estimate for the contemporary situation puts the total at 5000 male and 4000 female farmers.

### (b) Labour and Gender

The foundation for women's involvement in agricultural labour in the Caribbean was laid during the days of slavery when women toiled alongside their menfolk both in the cane fields and on small allotments. We examine their involvement in these activities in turn.

In the plantation labour force women and men alike worked throughout the year from six in the morning to six at night with a midday break of two hours, six days a week, with days off on Sundays, Christmas and Easter. In the interest of maximizing sugar production and profitability the slave system minimized gender distinctions, reducing both male and female slaves to productive machines as far as was possible. Even where these distinctions could not be totally elimi-nated, for example, when women had to be given time off for child bearing, this was reduced to two weeks and planters required the women to work even harder on their return to the fields to compensate for their absenteeism (Mair 1987: 6).

Though there are many gaps in our historical knowledge, it is implied that children and domestic chores were the responsibility of women. For Barbados, it was reported that small children were taken into the fields by their mothers and carried on their backs as they continued their 'painful stooping' work (Ligon 1657: 48). From the historical record it appears that mothers took full charge of their children until they were six years old, when it was time for them to enter the Third Gang, and that fathers had very little to do with them; neither did the plantation administration.

Women were also involved in farming the small allotments allocated to slaves for subsistence cultivation. Variations in the emphasis placed on slave provision grounds are reported for the Caribbean. In the self-feeding territories, Jamaica, for example, planters had sufficient land in mountainous areas to give a half acre provision lot to each slave couple. In Barbados there was no such land and the bulk of foodstuffs was imported, for planters were reluctant to withdraw resources from profitable sugar production. It was only with the pressures the amelioration now placed on the slave system and the fear of recurrence of the devastating famine of the late 1700s, which occurred as a result of disrupted trade, that Barbadian planters began to provide slaves with allotments. It has been estimated that by the late 1700s planters on the larger plantations were allocating an average of between four and ten perches of land and, occasionally, though rarely, up to a quarter acre to 'each adult Negro' (Dickson 1814: 149).

It is unclear whether female slaves as well as males were allocated land. Patter-son strongly implies that this was so for Jamaica, though Mintz and Price were unable to find evidence of grants of provisions ground to women (Patterson 1967: 169; Mintz and Price 1976: 38). On the Codrington Estates in Barbados the decision was made to allocate allotment land by house rather than by person, so that the 100 square feet allotted to each hut was shared among household members (Bennett 1958). Given the strong patriarchal assumptions underlying planter culture, we might well assume that, since it was they who organized allotment allocation, male slaves benefited. However, while this may be the case it is also possible that the African heritage of female, or at least joint, control over the land in practice modified these Eurocentred cultural prescriptions so that the allocation of land by planters did not necessarily preclude female control.

The labour of all able household and family members was used on these allot-ments, but the position as regards a division of labour by gender is obscure. While we know that women in Africa played major roles in subsistence agriculture in terms of labour, decision-making and control over land and income generated from the sale of produce, the extent to which this was 'carried over' to allotment cultivation in the Caribbean is not clear. Available historical evidence strongly implies that child care and domestic duties were the responsibility of women, but it is not known what, if any, part men played in these duties of social reproduction. How the labour and authority in relation to farming the allotment were divided, in particular what time and energy women had left from field work and domestic and child care duties, remains undocumented, as do gender distinctions in relation to marketing and control over income from sales. Descriptions of Sunday markets in Barbados suggest that they were dominated by women (Thome and Kimball 1838: 66), though men were also involved in selling produce. Mintz and Price, however, note the absence of descriptions of independent market women in pre-emancipation Jamaica and refer to accounts of single males and family groups. The puzzling and still unanswered question is why it was that after emancipation women came to dominate trading as they did in Africa and men took over agricultural production (Mintz and Price 1976: 40-1).

In summary, the plantation slave legacy has bequeathed a number of characteristics. Firstly, virtually all land and other resources were incorporated into plantation sugar. The corollary was mass alienation from the land. Pre-emancipation 'proto-peasantries', to use the term adopted by Mintz, have been identified for some Caribbean territories, but for Barbados the slave population was denied access to land. What little evidence there is of the origins of small farming suggests that women were very much involved in both production and marketing.

Second, women were fully incorporated into the labour force and expected to perform at a level equal to men. In other words, the argument that the impact of capitalist production on traditional agriculture had the effect of reducing the status of women relative to men is not applicable here. Capitalism, in the form of plantation slave economies did not 'marginalize' black women and demean their status by confining them to domesticity and subsistence production. Quite the contrary, the system demanded that their agriculturally productive roles in the cane fields took priority over biological and social reproduction. The pattern continued after emancipation as women acquired land and cultivated food crops for sale in the informal internal marketing systems which they created and controlled.

Thirdly, women were also required to take on the tasks of social reproduction, which included not only child care and domestic chores, but also mini-scale food production on allotments, and to combine this additional burden with work in the cane fields and planter households. Thus, while the slave plantation system and stranglehold on resources constituted perhaps the most severe form of exploitation and dispossession ever to have existed, at the same time for black women it resulted in a remarkable degree of personal autonomy and equality in relation to their menfolk. It is with this heritage in mind that we now examine and compare male and female small farmers in the contemporary Caribbean context.

## Contemporary Small Farmers in Barbados: Male and Female

The account which follows is based on the results of a questionnaire survey conducted in Barbados of a sample of 111 small farmers (56 males and 55 females) and follow-up, in depth interviews and observation. Following the format outlined earlier, we examine gender distinctions in relation first, to resources and second, to the division of labour.

## (a) Resource Allocation

### Land

In relation to land the plantation system continues to be reflected in the minuscule acreages controlled by small farmers in the sample. A total of 41 per cent of them control under one acre and only 15 per cent over five acres. Female farmers control somewhat less land than the males with an average of 1.98 acres compared to a male average of 2.95 acres. Although acreages are small, tenure is reasonably secure. The majority of the plots are owner-operated and ownership among female-controlled plots is somewhat higher (73 per cent) than among male (60 per cent). Among the remaining plots most are rented, but only 19 per cent of these are covered by a written agreement, all but one of these being farmed by men. Thus, though gender distinctions are not marked, there is evidence that women are at some disadvantage concerning the size of their holdings, though in a more favourable position concerning security of tenure.

In contrast to men, the image of women using farming as a way of making use of a resource that has become available to them (such as poor quality, inherited land) is to some extent applicable. Henshall, for example, reported in an earlier survey that females in Barbados, along with those in other Anglophone Caribbean territories, farm poorer quality, more isolated, inherited land. There is little discrimination, by law or custom, against women having access to land in Barbados, either through inheritance or purchase. A total of 65 per cent of the plots owned and farmed by women were inherited, compared with a corresponding figure for men of 41 per cent. However, though it was beyond the resources of the project to conduct soil quality tests and impractical because of variations on any one plot, farmer perceptions indicated general satisfaction, with 78 per cent of males and females rating their soil quality as 'fair to good' or 'very good'.

Farm fragmentation and the distance between residence and farm land has also been identified as a characteristic of small farming in the Caribbean. This phenomenon has been attributed to pressure on land and the consequent scarcity of land for expansion near to the farmer's residence or other farm parcels. While it may be true that fragmentation spreads risks, this 'advantage' is far outweighed by the time and effort spent travelling from home to each parcel and by the crop thefts, which occur as a result of the farmer's inability to supervise a number of distant parcels. In our sample 85 per cent of females and 77 per cent of males cultivate only one parcel. In addition, virtually all parcels (82 per cent) are located adjacent to the farmer's residence or within a few yards of it.

The question of land hunger among Caribbean small farmers has been the subject of recent debate with the view expressed that the demand for land exhibited from the post-emancipation days is no longer a major issue. As the argument runs, economic modernization has created alternative occupational opportunities in tourism, manufacturing and the public service sectors and the stigma of agricultural work, together with heavy migration to urban centres, has relieved pressure on agricultural land. This may be so but the existence of about a quarter of the farmers in our sample who do not own the land they cultivate, 80 per cent of whom would wish to own it, is indicative of significant and persistent land hunger. Though the majority (57 per cent of males and 64 per cent of females) expressed satisfaction with the amount of land they controlled, this was frequently elaborated with comments such as: 'If I had more land I would have to plant it, and then I would have to sell the crops and I can't even sell what I have now.' In other words, land hunger may be disguised by a system of inadequate infrastructural supports for farm expansion in areas such as marketing and distribution.

Although female farmers seemed to be somewhat more content with farm size, this does not mean, as we saw, that they farm more land or that they obtain land more easily than their male counterparts. According to the majority of respondents, male and female, landowners prefer to sell to men who are perceived as stronger, 'more serious' farmers and as having more success in loan applications for land purchase.

If we turn to the other side of the picture, we find little evidence of idle land within our sample. Only 14 per cent of the farmers are responsible for additional plots of land that lie idle[2] and, of these, more than half are less than an acre in size. The acreage is fully utilized on 70 per cent of all the cultivated plots. In the cases of both uncultivated plots and idle land on cultivated plots, the farmers generally referred to the temporary nature of its non-use; either the land was fallow, required clearing and/or was intended for use in the near future. Only in a few cases was the land idle because of a farmer's inability to cultivate through poor health or other commitments. Interestingly, women have a somewhat better record of land utilization than men. Land is fully utilized on 74 per cent of total plots under their control, compared with 64 per cent of those farmed by men.

## Crops

All the farmers in the sample are crop producers, except that is for the five who concentrate solely on livestock production, and the majority practice mixed cropping. The most common crops are vegetables, grown by 76 per cent of the males and 60 per cent of the females, and ground provision (root crops), grown by 46 per cent of the males and 40 per cent of the females. Less common are tree crops, which are cultivated by 22 per cent of the males and 36 per cent of the females. Most significant here is the low proportion of farmers who grow sugar cane, 26 per cent of the males and 33 per cent of the females. It is clear that females show some preference for the less labour-intensive tree crops and sugar cane and also that much diversification of production has occurred since the earlier half of the century when farmers were devoted to sugar production and characterized as having a 'sugar cane sense' (Skeete 1930: 13).[3]

## Labour

In the competition for labour small farmers have always been at a disadvantage when compared with the plantations, where more advanced techniques and a greater volume of work make it economic to offer higher wage rates (Beckford 1974: 212). The small farmers' wage bills have been estimated as high as 75 per cent of total expenses (Halcrow and Cave 1947: 22). They are rarely able to employ people regularly and establish a dependable source of labour. The following statement made over 50 years ago (Skeete 1930: 10-11) still applies: 'With few exceptions, agricultural labourers employed by peasant proprietors are more expensive than plantations. Labourers demand higher rates of pay when working on smallholdings. They work shorter hours than plantation labourers, and the character of their work is often moderate or poor.'

With the modernization of the economy and the opening up of more attractive employment opportunities in sectors such as construction, tourism and manufacturing, plantations were faced with severe labour shortages. As this became a problem for planters, it reached crisis proportions for small farmers. All the farmers in the sample, female and male, utilize labour to assist on their farms.

However, female farmers show a higher level of dependence on unpaid, family members. In addition, they find the acquisition of labour to be more problematic, with 34 per cent mentioning scarcity and 49 per cent high costs as major problems, compared with 30 per cent and 39 per cent respectively of the males. Male labour, in particular, is beyond the means of the majority of female farmers. It is also difficult to find since for a man to work for a woman farmer is considered to be a job of the lowest status (Henshall 1981: 49).

Farmers bemoan the passing of the 'old days' when family members, especially children, were required to assist with simple farm tasks and informal cooperative groups of neighbouring farmers would work on each other's land. This exchange labour arrangement, believed to be of African origin and variously known as 'morning sport', 'day for day', or 'coup de main' (St Lucian Creole), was widespread throughout the Caribbean until the last generation or so. It involved the movement of a group of farmers to work on each other's land in turn, the farmer whose turn it was for that day providing the food and drink for the group.

The farmers in the sample receive remarkably little assistance from their children and grandchildren. For the male farmers overall, only 47 per cent of their resident children and grandchildren assist with farm work, while for the females the proportion at 43 per cent, is even lower. In more general terms only 21 per cent of the farmers, twice as many males as females, argued that Barbadian small farmers help each other without payment and then mainly by lending tools and giving advice rather than with labour. In this respect farmers of both genders agreed that assistance between men is more common than between women mainly because, as one female respondent put it: 'Like me now, there isn't much I can do. I have my housework. But if a man ... he can help because he don't have to come home and cook. They have more time, women have more responsibility.'

The decline in informal cooperation among farmers has not been replaced to any significant extent by increased membership in formal agricultural associations, as might be expected as farming becomes modernized. Only 18 per cent of the farmers in the sample (12 males and 8 females) are members of a farmer's organization, the majority of these belonging to the Barbados Agricultural Society (BAS). Total membership of the BAS is approximately 800 farmers, only about 5 per cent of these being female. However, an estimated further 5 per cent are male members who represent a woman, usually a wife or common law partner, who is responsible for the farm work. Services offered by the Society include credit, marketing facilities for food crops and pigs, and advice through demonstrations, newsletters and radio programmes. All small-scale sugar producers belong to the Barbados Sugar Industries Limited (BSIL), which provides a subsidized fertilizer and cultivation service and handles the marketing and factory processing of cane.[4]

*Credit*
The BAS provides loans up to a maximum of $12,000. The terms and conditions for these loans are relatively easily met by small farmers. Rather than requiring collateral in the form, for example, of title deeds, as do the Barbados National Bank (Agricultural Loan Section) and other commercial banks, the BAS ensures repayment by marketing the farmer's produce and deducting regular instalments. In spite of this only approximately 30 members of the BAS have loans from that institution.

In the absence of information from the BAS and other funding agencies concerning gender distinctions in loan applications and acquisitions, information in this respect is somewhat vague. Henshall reports that most women in her sample indicated that the absence of credit was not a major problem. Compared with their male counterparts the women farmers had lower levels of financial investment, but this was not generally due to loan refusals. They were less motivated to expand and improve their farming and had therefore not found it necessary to apply for credit (Henshall 1981: 51). Within the sample the scarcity of credit was mentioned as a problem by 19 per cent of the farmers with no significant gender distinction in this respect. One must not, however, conclude from this that the remaining farmers have successfully applied for loans, rather that such applications are deterred by predictions of bureaucratic delays and arduous repayment conditions.

*Technology*
As Caribbean agriculture has moved from a situation of abundant, free (or at least cheap) labour to one in which labour has become scarce and more highly priced, the importance of technology has increased. As labour became attracted to modern sector opportunities and therefore less available to agriculture, the plantation sector moved to mechanize the sugar industry.

Agricultural research and development in Barbados has focused almost entirely on large-scale sugar production. The small farmers remain neglected, despite their labour problems being even more critical than those of the plantations, and their need for technological assistance is evident. Hoes and cutlasses continue to be their main tools, though several have invested in back-pack spraying equipment and one or two in small hand ploughs. Irrigation, however, is a major problem, the equipment available being beyond the means of most small farmers. The need for inexpensive and appropriate technology for small farming is clearly evident.

From a gender perspective distinctions with reference to technology are not marked. Although the tasks of ploughing and spraying, for example, are generally perceived as 'man's work', women often own and operate the necessary machinery, particularly in the absence of a male presence on the farm. Overall, it should be noted that 'there is no evidence that women farm less efficiently in terms of techniques employed or use fewer modern inputs than male farmers' (Henshall 1981: 51).

*Marketing*
Farmers in Barbados produce for sale and many experience problems with marketing and prices. Interestingly, males find these more problematic with 41 per cent mentioning them as problems compared with 16 per cent of the females, a distinction which probably had its roots in the Caribbean female experience with and dominance over the internal marketing of food crops which, as we indicated earlier, dates back to pre-emancipation days. A clear majority of the farmers (79.3 per cent) are involved in marketing their own crops, not delegating this task to anyone else and more often than not managing without assistance. However, marketing is uncertain and time consuming, many farmers having to allocate one day a week for this. Less than a quarter of both males and females are able to rely on one marketing outlet and must therefore move from one location to another as they attempt to dispose of their produce. Most farmers utilize the services of hawkers which, although carrying the advantage of direct and immediate remuneration at the farm gate, considerably reduces the farmers' profit. Farmers are generally highly resentful, asserting that hawkers claim the financial rewards while they (the farmers) do all the work. It was generally agreed by both farmers and agricultural officials that the hawkers' price mark-up is often over 100 per cent. Farmers also believe that hawkers are mainly responsible for the high levels of praedial larceny of crops. According to one farmer, 'they [the hawkers] come in

the day to buy and they see what you got and where it is and they know when it will be ready. So they come back in the night and t'ief'.

Contacts between farmers and the more institutionalized marketing outlets in the modern sector are not common. For example, only 6.5 per cent (6 per cent female and 7 per cent male) sell to hotels and guest houses and although 39 per cent (40 per cent female and 38 per cent male) dispose of their produce to local super-markets, in both cases this is a hit or miss operation with no agreements for regular quantities at stipulated prices. Only 11.5 per cent (8 per cent female and 15 per cent male) of the farmers utilize the marketing facilities provided by govern-ment through the Barbados Marketing Corporation or by the BAS.

It is clear that the plan for intersectoral linkages between agriculture and the tourist sector, the agro-processing industry and modern supermarkets has not materialized to any significant extent as far as small farmers are concerned. Although sugar cane farmers continue to be provided with a guaranteed market through the BSIL, the price is low and unprofitable. As one agricultural official put it, 'only the farmer who does not keep accounts will grow cane'.

In summary, it is evident that gender distinctions do exist within the sample of small-scale farmers. This conclusion, however, requires some qualification. First, dissimilarities between male and female small farmers are overshadowed and appear much less significant when examined in the wider framework of planta-tion/small farm disparities, where the plantation monopoly over resources and small farm deprivation persists. Small farmers, male and female, continue to be locked out of the system in terms of land, credit, technology and access to markets in the modern sectors of the economy. Their low membership in farmer's organi-zations indicates that these are not viewed as providing much in the way of assis-tance in these respects. Secondly, it is clear that female small farmers are not a homogeneous group. While the sample shows that there are some women who farm minuscule lots of inherited land with no inclination to expand and with unpaid family labour, no credit and minimal technology, this is not true of all and, indeed, is seen also to be the case with some male farmers.

*(b) The Division of Labour by Gender*
Small farmers in Barbados have survived as part-time cultivators. This is hardly surprising given their lack of resources and infra-structural supports necessary for a more full-time commitment. In the sample 56 per cent of the women work a four or more hour day on their farms, compared with 71 per cent of the men.

Labour on the farm is traditionally allocated according to gender, though with considerable overlap. Thus, forking the ground and spraying crops are jobs for men and sowing seeds for women, but most other tasks such as reaping, weeding and watering are not gender specific. Even the traditional allocation of selling crops to females and butchering livestock to males is less marked today. Roles are often reassigned in order to get the job done. This is particularly true of women who in the absence of male partners or labourers undertake the tasks of forking, ploughing, or even butchering. Although the majority of respondents, 78 per cent of the females and 84 per cent of the males, identified the slaughter of livestock as 'man's work', some noted a change: 'In all my years I see men do butchering, but as I say things are balancing. Men do and soon women will do too.' Women are fully involved in decision-making and in the control of farm finances. In fact they have a reputation for careful saving and budgeting. According to one woman who farms in partnership with her husband, 'You know how it is with men — they spend money on foolishness. So I handle the money. Sometimes he [husband] would joke and ask "Where's my pay?".'

The corollary of an inadequate resource base for small farmers and the part-time nature of their involvement in farm work is the need to secure additional income from other employment. This, however, is more apparent among male than female farmers. The majority of women (73 per cent) reported no additional gainful employment, compared with 52 per cent of the men.

Two major reasons are advanced to explain this distinction. First, adult working members of the household and family are expected to contribute financially and it is to the women, as mothers, aunts or grandmothers, that these contributions are made. Within the sample 64 per cent of the female farmers receive such support compared with only 23 per cent of the males. Their need for income from additional employment is likely therefore to be less urgent than for their male counterparts.

The second reason requires more elaboration. It concerns the involvement of women in the duties of social reproduction which, when combined with farming, leaves them little time or indeed energy for additional income-generating activities. Child care and domestic tasks are 'woman's work' and men do not generally become involved except temporarily in emergency situations.

Among the sample, 91 per cent of the women are involved to a greater or lesser degree in housework and child care. In other words, very few manage to relieve themselves of these tasks completely by delegation to another female household member, so that they can spend more time on their farms.

It is here then, in the perception of priorities and the allocation of time and energy, rather than in relation to resource allocation, that gender distinctions become more apparent. For the men, farming is their major role in life and it performs an essentially economically productive function. Within the multiplex roles of women, on the other hand, the familial role complex of mother/wife/kinswoman is central and farming is part of the duties of social reproduction. This is not said to demean women's farming — not to imply that women fit in a little time for cultivation after child care and domestic duties have been completed or that they are limited to subsistence production. Clearly this is not so. In the Afro-Caribbean context the economic support of the family is perceived as the joint responsibility of both conjugal partners and *women's social reproduction is defined to incorporate productive money-making work*, be this in agriculture or another sector of the economy. Income generation is an essential component of being a mother, grandmother, wife or daughter. In this respect the Caribbean woman has much in common with her traditional African counterpart. As Sudarkasa (1981: 54) argues: 'To be a good wife and mother a woman had not only to cook and attend her husband and children, but she had also to farm, trade or otherwise contribute to her household's livelihood.'

In the minds of Barbadian women farmers, just as there is no demarcation of their lives into two spheres defined as 'domestic' and 'public', so also there is no separation into two roles, one familial and the other productive. There is also little conflict between the two. Only 22 per cent of the women in the Barbados sample said that they found difficulty combining child care and domestic duties with farming, and this was generally either because of an additional job or the presence of small children. Though they feel the heavy load of what in the literature has been referred to as a 'double burden', for them it is one single role.

## Conclusion

Even this preliminary account, limited though it is to small farm women and to the Barbados context, is sufficient to raise serious questions concerning the images we have of rural agricultural women in the Caribbean. The women in the sample are not involved in 'male farming systems' and have not been reduced to subsistence cultivation in contrast with men by the impact of capitalist development. Neither are they confined to the domestic/private sphere, preoccupied with child care and domestic duties.

The legacy of the slave plantation system survives to the present and it is not only apparent in the asymmetrical distribution of agricultural resources between plantation and small farm sectors. The heritage also left a cultural system of values and behaviour, which prescribed the full involvement of Afro-Caribbean women in the economy, in agricultural or other income-generating pursuits. The corollary of this is a remarkable degree of equality between men and women in access to land and other resources. While it is clear that differences do exist, for example, female farmers control somewhat less land, are perhaps more reluctant to apply for loans and have greater difficulty acquiring labour, the general pattern has survived to the present and we must look elsewhere for gender distinctions. It is in relation to the fundamental *raison d'être* of their involvement that differences become clear. For women, farming is an integral part of social reproduction, part of being a mother or a wife; for many men it functions primarily as economically productive labour.

But the picture is incomplete. More ethnographic evidence extending gender across national, racial and class boundaries is required against which to test the statements presented here and with which to make Caribbean agricultural women visible as women. In addition, even within the group selected here as the main focus of interest (Afro-Caribbean small-scale women farmers in Barbados), there are significant variations. They must not be assumed to constitute a homogeneous group. Two important variables, age and stage in the life cycle and the presence or absence of a resident adult male, for example, a conjugal partner or a son, are likely to have a significant effect on a woman's involvement in farming, what motivates her to farm and at what level of intensity. A single younger woman with no children may be more commercially-oriented than one with a farmer husband and several young children, while those women who head households and are in their child-bearing years may need to emphasize the commercial farming component of their social reproduction, but have less time and resources to do so. For male farming also we may find similar distinctions. Thus older men may be less oriented to commercial expansion and more towards the economic maintenance of their household (supplementing their pensions).

Finally, at the level of official policy, what little exists in the way of small farm programmes in Barbados has yet to recognize gender distinctions and to acknowledge the importance of farming as an extension of social reproduction, i.e. its role in improving family nutrition and welfare. What exists in the way of policy for small farmers continues to direct attention and resources towards the enterprising, expanding farmers, in other words, mainly males.

## Notes

1   The applicability of the concept 'peasant' to the Caribbean has been questioned (Mintz 1971; and Marshall et al. 1974). I prefer to use the term 'small farmers', thereby avoiding connotations such as viability, independence and long enduring ties to the land.

2  None of the farmers in the sample rented out agricultural land to others.
3  A 1946 survey estimated that 79 per cent of all smallholdings produced sugar (Halcrow and Cave 1947: 10).
4  Information on the BAS was provided by the President, Mr Haynesley Benn, and on the BSIL by the Manager, Field Division, Mr Trevor Rudder. Both are gratefully acknowledged.

## References

Barbados (1971) *Agricultural Census*. Bridgetown

Barrow, C. (1986) 'Finding the Support: A Study of Strategies for Survival'. *Social and Economic Studies*, 35 (2) 131-76

Beckford, G. (1972) *Persistant Poverty*. London: Oxford University Press

——  1974) *Aspects of the Present Conflict between the Plantation and the Peasantry in the West Indies*. Geneva: Librairie Droz

——  1975) 'Caribbean Rival Economy'. In G. Beckford (ed.) *Caribbean Economy: Dependence and Backwardness*. Jamaica: University of the West Indies, ISER

Beckles, H. (1988) *Afro-Caribbean Women and Resistance to Slavery in Barbados*. London: Karnak House

Benn, D. (1974) 'The Theory of Plantation Economy and Society: A Methodological Critique'. *The Journal of Commonwealth and Comparative Politics*, 12 (3) 249-60

Bennett, J. (1958) *Bondsmen and Bishops: Slavery and Apprenticeship on the Codrington Plantations of Barbados, 1710-1838*. Berkeley: University of California Press

Bernal, R., M. Figueroa and M. Witter (1984) 'Caribbean Economic Thought: The Critical Tradition'. *Social and Economic Studies*, 33 (2) 5-96

Boserup, E. (1970) *Women's Role in Economic Development*. London: George Allen & Unwin

Brereton, B. (1988) 'General Problems and Issues in Studying the History of Women'. In P. Mohammed and C. Shepherd (eds) *Gender in Caribbean Development*. University of the West Indies: Women and Development Studies Project

Clarke, E. (1957) *My Mother who Fathered Me: A Study of the Family in Three Selected Communities in Jamaica*. London: Allen & Unwin

Dickson, W. (1814) *Mitigation of Slavery*. London: Longman, Hurst, Orme & Brown. Reprinted in 1970. Westport, Connecticut: Negro Universities Press

Greenfield, S.M. (1966) *English Rustics in Black Skin: A Study of Modern Family Forms in a Pre-Industrialized Society*. New Haven, Connecticut: College & University Publishers

Halcrow, M. and J.M. Cave (1947) *Peasant Agriculture in Barbados*. Bridgetown, Barbados: Department of Science and Agriculture, Bulletin No.11.

Henshall, J.D. (1981) 'Women and Small-Scale Farming in the Caribbean'. In O. Horst (ed.) *Papers in Latin American Geography in Honor of Lucia C. Harrison*. Muncie, Indiana: Conference of Latin American Geographers, 44-56

——  (1984) 'Gender versus Ethnic Pluralism in Caribbean Agriculture'. In C. Clarke, C. Leys and C. Peach (eds) *Geography and Ethnic Pluralism*, London: Allen & Unwin

Knudson, B. and B. Yates (1981) *The Economic Role of Women in Small-Scale Agriculture in the Eastern Caribbean: St Lucia*. Barbados: University of the West Indies, Women and Development Unit

Ligon, R. (1657) *A True and Exact History of the Island of Barbados*. London

Mair, L. (1987) *Women Field Workers in Jamaica during Slavery*. Mona, Jamaica: Department of History, University of the West Indies

Marshall, W. et al. (1974) 'The Establishment of a Peasantry in Barbados'. In *Social Groups and Institutions in the History of the Caribbean*. Papers presented to the 6th Annual Conference of Caribbean Historians, Puerto Rico 4-9 April, 84-104.

Massiah, J. (1984) *Employed Women in Barbados: A Demographic Profile 1946-1980*. Barbados: ISER, University of the West Indies

Mintz, S. (1971) 'Men, Women and Trade'. *Comparative Studies in Society and History*, 13 (3) 247-69

Mintz, S. and R. Price (1976) *An Anthropological Approach to the Afro-American Past: A Caribbean Perspective*. Philadelphia: Institute for the Study of Human Issues

Patterson, O. (1967) *The Sociology of Slavery*. London: MacGibbon & Kee

Reddock, R. (1984) 'Women, Labour and Struggle in Twentieth Century Trinidad and Tobago, 1891-1960'. Doctoral thesis, University of Amsterdam

Rodman, H. (1971) *Lower Class Families: The Culture of Poverty in Negro Trinidad*. London: Oxford University Press

Skeete, C. (1930) *The Condition of Peasant Agriculture in Barbados*. Bridgetown: Department of Science & Agriculture

Smith, R.T. (1956) *The Negro Family in British Guiana: Family Structure and Social Status in the Villages*. New York: Routledge & Kegan Paul Ltd

Sudarkasa, N. (1981) 'Female Employment and Family Organization in West Africa'. In F.C. Steady (ed.) *The Black Woman Cross-Culturally*, Cambridge, Mass: Schenkman Publishing Company Inc., 49-63

Sutton, C. and S. Makiesky-Barrow (1981) 'Social Inequality and Sexual Status in Barbados'. In F.C. Steady (ed.) *The Black Woman Cross-Culturally*. Cambridge, Mass: Schenkman Publishing Company Inc., 469-98

Thome, J. and J. Kimball (1838) *Emancipation in the West Indies: A Six Month's Tour in Antigua, Barbados and Jamaica in the Year 1837*. New York: The American Anti-Slavery Society

# XII  A Profile of Grenadian Women Small Farmers

JOHN S. BRIERLEY

The character and traditions of West Indian small-scale agriculture are inexorably linked to the role of women in the region's economy. Since pre-Columban times, women have been associated with supplying the subsistence needs of their households. This fundamental activity for human survival has largely gone unheralded in the region's economic history which has focused principally on the development of natural resources and the production of export crops, both male-dominated activities. In the latter half of the twentieth century the economic virtues of food self-sufficiency have been repeatedly extolled for the island nations of the Caribbean. To this end, attention has been directed to the small farm sector as a potential source of increased food production. By rights, the role of women should be of paramount importance in this regard, yet few studies have singled out women farmers for discrete investigation.

Since the 1960s small farmers in Grenada have been the subject of several studies (Brierley 1974; Ifill 1979; CARDI 1980; LeFranc 1980). While they refer to the fact that women head one in five small farm households, not one of these studies singled out the female component to determine what distinctive characteristics their farms possessed. It was assumed that their farms were essentially the same as all small farms in terms of production, organization and management since the variable of gender did not emerge as statistically significant in any of the analyses. Certainly, this was the explanation in my own case after conducting a variety of principal component and factor analyses on small farm data (Brierley 1974). Yet the contributions of women farmers to social and economic development in Grenada are unquestionable and indispensable but, like those of women in other Third World nations, they have too readily been taken for granted.

This essay presents four aspects of female small farmers. First, it reviews facets of their social history and household composition. It follows with brief accounts of the women farmers' means of acquiring farming knowledge and their inputs of farm labour. The third consideration is that of the farm unit, with attention being focused on farm size, structure and production system. It concludes with a summary of their agrarian problems. When and where appropriate, comparisons are made with their male counterparts.

## The Sample

This study is extracted from a 5 per cent random sample of Grenadian small farmers who were surveyed in 1982. For the purposes of the questionnaire survey, a small farmer was defined as a head of household who occupied at least 0.4 hectares but less that six hectares of land, irrespective of its type of tenure. A head of household conforms to M.G. Smith's (1962: 15) definition as being, 'that person whom the community as well as the household members regard as the head of the domestic group. In addition, the head tends to assert headship whenever necessary. Domestic units based on cohabitation may have female heads if the male partner is ill, incapacitated, or otherwise dependent, socially and economically on the woman.'

From a total of 186 sampled farmers, there were 38 women farm operators. This proportion, 20.4 per cent, is consistent with the 20.7 per cent found in my own 1969 survey (Brierley 1974) and with those of other similar surveys for Grenada. For example, Ifill (1979: 3) had 19 per cent and CARDI (1980: 55) 22 per cent. According to Momsen (1988: 88) other surveys in the Eastern Caribbean have recorded proportions of women farmers varying from a low of 23.0 in St Lucia to a high of 53.1 per cent in Barbados.[1] It is on the sample of 38 women that the following profile is based.

### Social History & Household Structure

Table 12.1 reveals the preponderance of elderly women in the sample. Twenty-four (63 per cent) are over 55 years of age. Their mean age exceeds that of their male counterparts by 3.4 years, a difference which is related to women's longer life expectancy. This point is reinforced by Table 12.2, which shows that widows make up 37 per cent of the sample. Old age and its associated deterioration in physical and mental abilities goes a long way to explain the level of active participation and interest these women have in agriculture.

**Table 12.1: Age Distribution of Women Farmers**

| Age Group | Number | % |
| --- | --- | --- |
| Less than 35 years | 2 | 5 |
| 35-44 years | 3 | 8 |
| 45-54 | 9 | 24 |
| 55-64 | 10 | 26 |
| 65-74 | 10 | 26 |
| Over 75 years | 4 | 11 |
| TOTAL | 38 | 100 |

Data on marital status denote a pattern consistent with other studies. The majority (68 per cent) were or had been married. Widows had usually assumed the role of household head on the death of their spouse and thereby become small farmers. Those who were married yet were deemed to be in charge of the domestic unit, had husbands who were either working abroad on a permanent basis or were too incapacitated to run the household. Single women farmers often were daughters attending to the needs of an aged and infirm mother and/or father to the extent that they had become *de facto* the principal decision maker for the household. Other single women either lived alone or acknowledged they had 'no man in the house'. Female-headed households had an average size of 4.1 persons as against 5.4 for male-headed farm households. They contained fewer children than households headed by men (Table 12.3) but most of the women farmers had children living overseas, especially in the United States and the United Kingdom (Table 12.4).

**Table 12.2: Marital Status of Women Small Farmers**

| Status | Number | % |
| --- | --- | --- |
| Single | 10 | 26 |
| Common-law | 2 | 5 |
| Married | 6 | 16 |
| Widowed | 14 | 37 |
| Divorced or separated | 6 | 16 |
| TOTAL | 38 | 100 |

Unlike women in other Third World nations who have had to sacrifice their own schooling in order to assist their parents with chores and so allow their brother(s) to gain an education, Grenadian women have not been so deprived. As noted in CARDI's study (1980: 55), a relatively high level of literacy prevails amongst small farmers. In this study all but five women were able to read and write, while 61 per cent had successfully completed the final grade of primary school or better. The mean standard of attainment at 4.8 years of schooling was the same for both men and women farmers. It had been thought that older women might possibly have had lower achievement levels owing to the economically depressed times Grenada experienced prior to the Second World War (HMSO 1945), but the data provided no support for this contention.

**Table 12.3: Gender Differences in Household Size and Composition**

| Age Group | | Mean Household Size | |
| --- | --- | --- | --- |
| | | Female-Headed | Male-Headed |
| Children: | Under 5 years | 0.29 | 0.56 |
| | 5-15 years | 0.89 | 1.17 |
| Adults: | Head and spouse | 1.15* | 1.73 |
| | Others | 1.76 | 1.92 |
| | Mean total | 4.09 | 5.38 |

\* Includes husbands employed overseas or sick

At an earlier period in their lives, off-farm employment would temporarily or regularly have been undertaken by most of these Grenadian rural women. One-third of the sample had previously worked as labourers on estates, while two of the better-educated had taught in primary schools. At the time of the survey, however, only four women (11 per cent) worked off the farm: two as unskilled labourers on neighbouring estates, one as a village shop owner-operator and the other as a home-based seamstress. Herein lies a major difference between the women and the men farmers. Of the males, 57 per cent had off-farm employment thereby ensuring greater financial security given the vulnerabilities of farm production and the externally controlled price fluctuations of export-crop commodities.

A distinguishing feature of female as compared to male small farmers is the strength of the former's ties to Grenada and its rural environment. Of the sample, only three had lived or worked overseas (in Aruba, the United Kingdom and

Venezuela) and in all cases for less than nine years. Another four women had resided and worked for relatively short periods of their lives in one of Grenada's two main towns, St George's or Grenville. Consequently, with a mean age of 59.2 years, these women have deep roots in the countryside — a connection that is far greater than for male farmers, the majority of whom have been migrants, either within Grenada or overseas, at some point in their lifetime. This attachment of women to Grenada's rural setting has provided them with the opportunity to build up a detailed knowledge of local events, customs and practices, which contributes to the preservation of traditional beliefs and values.

**Table 12.4: Location of Migrant Children of Women Small Farmers**

| Location | Number | % |
| --- | --- | --- |
| US | 24 | 36 |
| UK | 23 | 35 |
| Trinidad | 8 | 12 |
| Canada | 7 | 11 |
| Other | 4 | 6 |
| TOTAL | 66 | 100 |

By the time children reach their late teenage years, mothers or grandmothers have transferred, through example and discourse, the basis of their traditional farming knowledge. This includes the widespread belief in the influence of the lunar cycle on the rhythm of specific agricultural activities (Clarke 1957: 18). Knowledge derived principally from women during a child's formative years often forms the basis of any farming activities an individual may subsequently undertake.

Other sources of a woman's farming knowledge tend to be of secondary importance. These include formal sources, namely primary schools and the nation's extension service. For the most part, agriculture is given low priority in the school curriculum and, if instruction is provided via demonstrations in a school garden, it inevitably involves Eurocentric planting techniques of crops in rows and pure stands. Such instruction not only undermines lessons learned in the home garden but also often fails to be convincing because crop growth is poorer than in family kitchen gardens owing to the inadequate attention and interest bestowed on the school plot. Extension personnel too have had limited impact on women farmers. In general, extension officers seek to give advice to the small farmers with the most land, usually men. However, as one-third of the women farmers had been employed on estates producing the island's main export crops, they had knowledge of the particular requirements and diseases of these crops. Those lacking such experience were more likely to seek aid from knowledgeable friends and respected neighbours than from extension officers. For the most part, female small farmers exhibited an independent spirit and trusted to their long experience in farming to cope with any exigency.

## Labour Inputs

Not surprisingly, in the light of the sample's variations in social history and household composition, there is a marked divergence in the time devoted to farm work. At one extreme are the seven women who admitted to spending no time, either working or supervising the labour of others, on their land. All were elderly women over 60 years of age who had given responsibility for farm work to other household members. Nevertheless, they maintained their position as head of the household.[2]

Another group of nine women regularly supervised the work of family members and/or hired hands for an average of two hours per morning. This supervision would entail visiting the individual parcels of land where the work was being performed if the woman was physically fit enough to do so. If she was not able to go into the field then instructions were given at home each day. Within this group are five widows whose husbands had had social standing in the local community because they had been school teachers, clergymen or civil servants. As such, these men had considered it socially inappropriate for their wives to dirty their hands, except for tending to a flower garden. This observation accords with other West Indian studies which have shown that the nature and input of women's work on the farm varies with the socio-economic status of the male partner (Momsen 1988: 90).

At the other extreme, there was one 48-year-old woman who worked a regular eight-hour day, five days a week throughout the year on her 4.5 hectare holding. She stated that she enjoyed the physical demands and challenges of cultivating a range of tree crops and vegetables. As a result, her holding was amongst the best maintained in the survey. Her other domestic responsibilities, such as preparing meals, washing clothes, sweeping the house and caring for two small children, had been delegated to her 26-year-old daughter who lived with her.

**Table 12.5: Gender Differences in Mean Farm Labour Input**

| Labour Input | Female | Male |
| --- | --- | --- |
| Mean hours per day spent on farm work | 3.37 | 4.79 |
| Mean days worked per week | 3.13 | 4.10 |
| Mean number of regular hired workers | 0.57 | 0.75 |
| Mean number of seasonal hired workers | 1.16 | 1.24 |
| Mean number of children who regularly assist | 0.53 | 0.57 |
| Mean number of other household members who assist | 0.03 | 0.05 |

In the whole sample, only nine women (24 per cent) worked 20 hours or more per week on their holdings. The average labour input, involving either working or organizing others, amounted to 3.4 hours per day for 3.1 days per week, for a mean weekly input of 10.5 hours (Table 12.5). Much of this work was undertaken during the morning prior to the temperature reaching the daily maximum. At the busier times of the farm calendar, when land is being prepared and crops planted, the weekly average labour input for women increased to 14.4 hours. These hours may be compared with those of the men farmers who worked, on average, 4.8 hours per day, 4.1 days a week for a total of 19.7 hours, which increased to a weekly total of 23.8 hours during the busy season. Other sources of labour input on female-operated farms, such as hired help and assistance from unpaid family members, were all less than those associated with male small farmers (Table 12.5).

As in other societies, gender is the basis for a division of labour on the farm. Activities that are thought to be particularly physically demanding and which might affect a woman's health and childbearing ability are left to men. Consequently, in the Grenadian context, this implies that women hardly ever perform the spade or fork work associated with preparing the soil for planting, do not undertake the cutlassing (cutting) of dense bush, or carry especially heavy loads such as 50 kilogram stems of bananas, or move fully grown cattle from one tethering site to another. In most other agricultural activities women participate when physically fit. Women play the dominant role in managing the kitchen garden even when a man heads the household. Once the ground has been prepared, then the planting and subsequent cultivation of crops in this garden is often left entirely to women.

If production of food crops is on a commercial scale, then their sale, whether to an itinerant vendor or in the local market will be negotiated by women. In general, Grenadian women are considered to possess a better developed sense of business acumen than their men, so inevitably it is the woman's finger that monitors the economic pulse of the household.

## The Farming Unit

Smallholdings occupied by women farmers are only slightly smaller and less fragmented than those of men (Table 12.6). This similarity is, in large part, attributable to the parameters used in defining a small farmer. When consideration is taken of the farm's pattern of tenure then substantial differences between the genders are evident. Female farmers claim ownership to 48 per cent of their holdings and have a similar proportion of rent free land. This latter is usually land which they are taking care of for a relative who is overseas, or undivided family land for which they were responsible at the time of the survey. Only a very small proportion of land is rented by women. These data contrast sharply with those for male farmers (Table 12.6).

**Table 12.6: Gender Differences in Farm Structure**

| Parameter | Female | Male |
|---|---|---|
| Mean farm size (hectares) | 2.00 | 2.03 |
| Mean fragments of land per farm | 2.63 | 2.78 |
| Mean % of holdings owned | 48.00 | 61.80 |
| Mean % of holdings rent free or family land | 49.80 | 19.50 |
| Mean % of holdings rented | 1.60 | 16.00 |
| Mean % of holdings sharecropped | 0.50 | 2.60 |
| Mean % of holdings uncultivated | 33.00 | 36.00 |

Explanations for these differences are complex. It may be the case that because the sampled women had rarely left Grenada, they were regarded by their relatives as being permanent residents of the nation and so were considered to be suitable custodians of any land that had been inherited or purchased. However, knowing that women farmers had freehold title to a comparatively small acreage may have encouraged their relatives to give them usufruct to land so that they might increase their farm income. In some cases, in partial exchange for the care of a child, usually a grandchild, nephew or niece whose parents were overseas, the woman farmer gained the right to use and harvest any crops on land these children's parents owned. The child itself would often assist the grandmother or aunt with farm chores.

Individuals who aspire to become independent farmers but lack the capital with which to purchase land may opt to rent instead. However, only one woman rented land, probably because women do not generally perceive of farming as a vocation. Most of the sample, 90 per cent, had become farmers by default through the death or incapacitation of their male household head. Under such circumstances renting of land has no place.

A surprising feature of the farms operated by women is the degree to which their land is utilized. Table 12.6 shows that their holdings have a slightly lower proportion of idle land than those managed and worked by men, as noted by Barrow for Barbados (Chapter 11). With the knowledge that women farmers are older, spend less time working on their farms and occupy more rent-free land, this statistic is unexpected. Given the small size of the sample of women farmers too much significance should not be attached to this finding.[3]

## The Farming System

Grenadian small farms have two production thrusts, subsistence and cash cropping, either or both of which may be present on a given holding to varying degrees. Subsistence crops are grown in the kitchen garden and/or on a provision ground which is a piece of land away from the house. If production from these areas unexpectedly exceeds household needs, then the surplus is either given away to less fortunate friends and relatives or sold. The majority of Grenadian small farmers also grow export-oriented crops, notably bananas, cocoa and nutmeg, while a few specialize in the production of food crops for the local market. As a result of the widespread practices of inter-cropping and inter-culture, subsistence and cash crop production frequently coexist on the same piece of land. Although livestock are found on many smallholdings they are not a major component of the small farming system.

By combining considerations of the aforementioned crop emphasis with the economic importance of agriculture, a classification of the sub-groups within the female farming system is obtained (Table 12.7). The distinction between semi-commercial and commercial is made on the basis that the former household derives less than half its earned income from farming. Semi-commercial farmers either had non-farm employment and/or derived income from their male partner or other relative who sent remittances to support the family. While Table 12.7 reveals the importance of export-crop production for women farmers, it also provides a comparison with the men. Two noteworthy differences are apparent: first is the higher proportion of subsistence farmers amongst women; second is the lack of women specializing in commercial food-crop production. Both characteristics are attributable to the age factor. All four subsistence farmers are over 60 years of age and three are over 70. Commercial food-crop production is a labour intensive activity and women neither had the time nor were able to supply the necessary labour.

Table 12.8 also indicates the lack of interest in commercial food-crop production among women farmers. The two women who were market gardeners were both relatively young, under 44 years, and worked land in parts of the island noted for supplying St George's town with vegetables and ground provisions. Women farmers who had livestock exhibited a preference for smaller animals, whereas younger men kept more cattle because of the physical strength needed to handle them.

## Table 12.7: Gender Differences in Farming Systems

| Economic Class | CASH CROP EMPHASIS | | | Total | |
| | Domestic food crops | Export crops | Mixed* production | No. | % |
|---|---|---|---|---|---|
| *Female Farmers* | | | | | |
| Subsistence | - | - | - | 4 | 10.5 |
| Semi-commercial | 1 | 6 | 3 | 10 | 26.3 |
| Commercial under 4 ha | 1 | 16 | 5 | 22 | 57.9 |
| Commercial over 4 ha | - | 2 | - | 2 | 5.3 |
| TOTAL No. | 2 | 24 | 8 | 38 | - |
| % | 5.9 | 70.6 | 23.5 | - | 100.0 |
| *Male Farmers* | | | | | |
| Subsistence | - | - | - | 2 | 1.4 |
| Semi-commercial | 7 | 32 | 2 | 41 | 28.1 |
| Commercial under 4 ha | 16 | 66 | 13 | 95 | 65.0 |
| Commercial over 4 ha | 1 | 8 | 1 | 10 | 6.5 |
| TOTAL No. | 24 | 106 | 16 | 148 | - |
| % | 16.2 | 72.6 | 11.0 | - | 100.0 |

* Defined as having a combination of both food crops and export crops in the farmers' list of three principal cash crops

## Table 12.8: Principal Cash Crops of Women Farmers

| First Crop | Number of Farms | % |
|---|---|---|
| Nutmeg | 13 | 38.2 |
| Cocoa | 9 | 26.5 |
| Banana | 5 | 14.7 |
| Coconut | 2 | 5.9 |
| Ground provisions (dasheen, yam, sweet potato) | 2 | 5.9 |
| Others | 3 | 8.8 |
| TOTAL | 34 | 100.0 |

| Second Crop | | |
|---|---|---|
| Cocoa | 8 | 26.7 |
| Nutmeg | 8 | 26.7 |
| Banana | 5 | 16.7 |
| Pigeon pea | 3 | 10.0 |
| Ground provisions | 2 | 6.6 |
| Others | 4 | 13.3 |
| TOTAL | 30 | 100.0 |

Table 12.9: Agricultural Problems of Women Small Farmers

| Problem | % of Total Reporting Problem |
|---|---|
| Crop pests and diseases | 76 |
| Difficulty hiring reliable labour | 74 |
| Praedial larceny (theft of crops) | 66 |
| Cost of fertilizer | 61 |
| Poor water supply for irrigation | 37 |
| Transport problems — poor roads | 37 |
| Lack of farm credit facilities | 21 |
| Soil erosion | 18 |
| Marketing arrangements and facilities | 13 |
| Inadequate agricultural extension services | 13 |

Consideration of the three main cash crops for each farm, ranked in order of their economic importance, provides an insight into the land use associated with these farming systems. The results reveal the dominance of Grenada's three main export crops, bananas, cocoa and nutmeg (Table 12.8). While these findings are broadly in line with those of other studies of the nation's small farmers (Brierley 1974; 1985 and Ifill 1979), women farmers are less likely than men to grow bananas. Harvesting of this crop, as noted previously, is physically demanding and not work normally associated with women or even men in late middle age. Consequently, it is women with young men in their households or with hired help who are prepared to cut and carry stems of bananas, who cultivate this crop. In contrast, the tending and harvesting of cocoa and nutmeg orchards is less arduous and can be undertaken by a broad cross-section of the farm population. These tree-crop holdings were characterized by old stands of cocoa and nutmeg which were past peak production. In general, the women's holdings were in no worse condition than those associated with older male farmers.

## Agrarian Problems Perceived by Sampled Farmers

When asked to identify the range of problems affecting their farming operation, farmers provide insights into their concerns and perceptions. These, in turn, are deemed to influence their attitudes and behaviour and will vary with the nature and scale of the farming system and the farmer's age and aspirations. On the whole, the problems identified by women (Table 12.9) mirror those of small farmers in general, namely that their land fails to realize its full productive capacity. This failure is due, on the one hand, to a set of infrastructural deficiencies, notably the inadequacy of government to provide plant protection services, policing to prevent praedial larceny and subsidies to reduce fertilizer prices. On the other hand, there was the labour shortage problem, in particular the difficulty of securing and retaining hired hands who were reliable and diligent. This was a complaint made by three-quarters of the women farmers but only half of the men (see also Chapter 11). Such a difference is not unexpected in view of the previously noted gender differences in age and household composition. Women did, however, consider inadequacies in the supply of water and the network of feeder roads to be less of a problem than did the men — a difference that may be attributed to women having less direct involvement and spending less time on the land. Thus Table 12.9 conveys women's perspective on farming problems dominated by difficulties in pest control and labour supply.

## Conclusion

This profile of Grenadian women farmers has shown that the majority are overseeing the final stages in the life cycle of a small farm. During their lifetime the land they own has been acquired through inheritance, either on the death of their own parents or of their spouse, who may have both inherited and bought land for farming. Ultimately, the death of these female heads of household will terminate the existence of their smallholdings. Owing to the prevalent practice of joint inheritance, the farm unit will be subdivided so that, in principle, children associated with the couple who built up the farm will receive equal shares. The resulting small units of land can be seen as the embryonic stage in the development of a new small-farm enterprise. Should this be the case, then in all likelihood the initial undertaking will be to establish a kitchen garden which will be generally tended by women.

Women have a permanency of place in rural Grenada which is reassuring for their children. In due course, these children may assist their mother and/or grandmother by sending her remittances, or allowing her to use land they own rent free. Such assistance undoubtedly helps many women small farmers cope with the hardships wrought by old age. Thus small farms play a pivotal role in the life cycle of rural women in Grenada.

## Notes

1 The definition used in most of the sample surveys quoted differs from that used by Brierley. In Momsen's work, women were considered to be farmers if they were the major decision maker on the family farm, even if they were not the household head. Only in a small minority of households are these roles separated but this minority is significant enough to explain, at least in part, the higher figures for the other territories.
2 Lydia Pulsipher in Chapter 4 notes a similar situation in Montserrat where family support enables elderly women to maintain a position as head of the household.
3 Elsewhere in the region, farms run by women tend to have more uncultivated land than those run by men (Henshall 1981). On the other hand, these figures for Barbados and Grenada may represent a real intensification of production by women subsistence farmers in the face of the inflation of the 1980s.

## References

Brierley, J.S. (1974) *Small Farming in Grenada, West Indies*. Winnipeg: Manitoba Geographical Studies, No. 4

—— (1985) 'West Indian Kitchen Gardens: An Historical Perspective with Current Insights from Grenada'. *Food and Nutrition Bulletin*, 7 (3) 52-60

CARDI (1980) *A Profile of Small Farming in Antigua, Montserrat and Grenada*. St Augustine, Trinidad: University of the West Indies

Clarke, Edith (1957) *My Mother who Fathered Me: A Study of the Family in Three Selected Communities in Jamaica*. London: Allen & Unwin

Henshall, J.D. (1981) 'Women and Small-scale Farming in the Caribbean'. In Oscar Horst (ed.) *Papers in Latin American Geography in Honor of Lucia C. Harrison*, Muncie Indiana: CLAG, 28-43

HMSO (1945) *West Indian Royal Commission Report 1938-39*. London: Cmd 6607

Ifill, M.B. (1979) *Report on a Farm Survey Conducted in Grenada*. Port of Spain, Trinidad: Economic Commission for Latin America

LeFranc, E.R. (1980) 'Grenada'. In *Small Farming in the Less Developed Countries of the Commonwealth Caribbean*. Barbados: Caribbean Development Bank, 2-57

Momsen, J.H. (1988) 'Changing Gender Roles in Caribbean Peasant Agriculture'. In J.S. Brierley and H. Rubenstein (eds) *Small Farming and Peasant Resources in the Caribbean*, Winnipeg: Manitoba Geographical Studies (10), 83-100

Smith, M.G. (1962) *West Indian Family Structure*. Seattle: University of Washington Press

# XIII  Women in Agriculture in Trinidad: An Overview

INDRA S. HARRY

This chapter[1] looks at the work and daily life of women who farm in Trinidad and emphasizes their contribution to agricultural production on the island. Women's work is examined in relation to six crop and/or animal farm types. Comparisons are made with the role of their male counterparts and inputs by children and hired help are identified. The underlying hypothesis presented here is that, on average, women work as many hours per day and days per year on family farms as their spouses but gender differences in labour inputs can be identified when individual products and their modes of production are examined. Generally there is a direct correlation between the number of tasks associated with the production of a crop and the involvement of family members.

Women have always been involved in agriculture in the Caribbean and these roles have been continuously modified by colonization, plantations, new crop introduction, education, technology, migration, tourism and industrialization. However, it has only been in the past decade that several gender related studies have been conducted in the region to identify and quantify the inputs made by women in food production. Trinidad produces a diversity of crops grown both for domestic consumption and export and women play major roles in the cultivation of these crops. However, little attention is paid to the female component of the agricultural labour force and to the stabilizing role women can continue to play in a declining industry.

In order to provide a profile of women farmers in Trinidad, several aspects of the social environment of agriculture are considered. These include household structure and the age and education of farmers in each farming sector. Central to the types of crops cultivated is the land tenure system. Land ownership is integral to both the type of cropping system used and to whether or not that land stays productive. Emphasis is on the production of an agricultural commodity and the numbers and attitudes of the family and hired workers involved in the crop cycle.

## Historical Background

Trinidad is the most southerly member of the Lesser Antillean island chain (Figure 13.1). It lies close to the estuary of the Orinoco River about seven miles from Venezuela and has an area of 4827 square kilometres. Topographically, only a small percentage of land is suitable for agriculture. Like other islands in the region, Trinidad had a local Amerindian population before European colonization and crop cultivation was apparently introduced in about 300 BC from Venezuela. Shifting agriculture was practised with men doing the land clearing and women the planting, weeding and harvesting. By the fifteenth century many root crops

**Figure 13.1: Map of Trinidad**

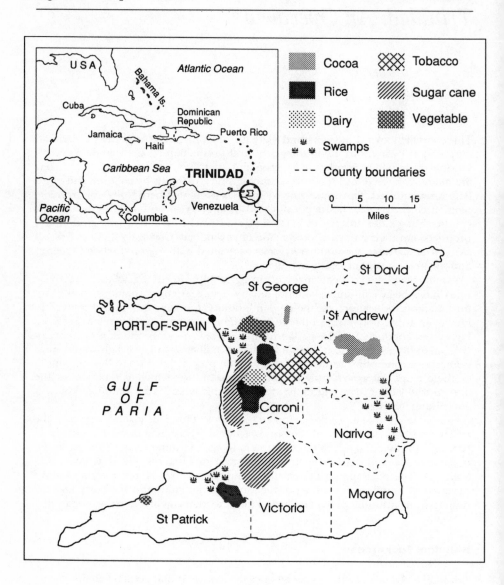

like manioc, sweet potato, yam and peanut were cultivated along with other crops such as maize, pineapple and cotton. Women were instrumental in food production and this role 'not only increased the status of a woman in society, but her greater ties to the land and to other female members of the extended family through cooperation in agricultural activities made her continued presence in her native group after marriage desirable (Newson 1976: 63).

After 1492 the indigenous population declined substantially and 'discovery' was followed by waves of European settlers, slaves and plantations. That year also marked the beginning of intensive commercial agriculture on the island with the introduction of cocoa and tobacco growing. Men cleared the land but in the crop-specific skilled tasks in tobacco like picking, sorting, drying and packing of tobacco leaves, both men and women were involved. Women played secondary roles in the cocoa industry helping mainly at harvest times. The change to cash cropping meant that shifting practices had to be curtailed as these new crops occupied most of the arable land and available labour. Women grew all the food for domestic consumption and there was a dietary switch from root crops to maize (Newson 1976) which may have been related to the extra demands of cash crops on women's time and labour.

By 1797 sugar cane, coffee and cocoa were being widely cultivated using slave labour and later indentured labour from India. Information on the prevailing sexual division of labour is limited but most likely women worked alongside their male counterparts. Momsen (1986) points out that the majority of slave women worked in the fields under harsh conditions and were subject to the same physical punishment as men. This was also the case with indentured women and an article published in the journal, *All Trinidad Sugar Estates and Factory Workers Trade Union*, from interviews with three ex-indentured women, reputedly aged 109, 118 and 127 years, confirms this fact. They indicated (*Battlefront*, 19 May 1978: 7) that:

In the cultivation, you will find women dominated the gangs. They were out early in the fields performing hazardous duties like dropping lime and phosphate of ammonia, planting foods on the estates, that is vegetable crops and ground provisions, heading [sic] manures, cutlassing, weeding, cutting cane, loading them on carts and most of the time carrying the cane on their heads.

After emancipation, many liberated slaves became subsistence farmers or small traders (Wood 1968: 68). Following indentureship, many East Indians were given Crown Land and became small-scale sugar and cocoa growers, rice producers or market gardeners (Tikasingh 1973).

An experimental dairy sector was established by the Ministry of Agriculture in 1964. Few of these state farmers were experienced dairy farmers, but those selected were given a primary herd, sufficient land for pasture and a permanent home. Farmers were able to purchase additional infrastructure and animals with capital borrowed at low interest rates with long-term guarantees from the Agricultural Development Bank (Trinidad & Tobago 1978) In post-colonial Trinidad, the East Indian population became the backbone of agriculture and labour patterns found on farms were largely a combination of traditional systems brought from India and those acquired during the colonial indentureship period.

## The Field Survey

Information for this chapter was obtained from a questionnaire survey conducted in 1979. Initially, the objective was to obtain as many interviews as possible using a random sample. However, this approach was later changed to a stratified survey based on the dominant crop cultivated. Interviews were conducted with small-scale growers and dairy farmers and their spouses in various agricultural communities on the island. Considerable emphasis was placed on the cultivation of major crops like tobacco, cocoa, sugar cane, rice and vegetables and respondents were asked questions relating to the production of these crops and to family participation in the various processes involved in the crop cycle. The roles of children and of hired workers were also ascertained.

Altogether 130 households were sampled. Of these 14 were in the tobacco sector, 41 in cocoa, 15 in sugar cane, 16 in rice, 28 in market gardening and 16 in dairying. The choice of these sectors was based on both economic importance and accessibility. It included extensively and intensively cultivated crops as well as those grown for domestic use and those for export. Unlike other West Indian islands (see Momsen 1986) migration did not influence gender roles in Trinidad, but rather the type of crop dictated the extent to which various family members were incorporated into production.

## Farm Household Structure & Social Environment

Because of the history of the island, most of the farmers surveyed were of East Indian origin, with about 62 per cent being Hindu and 11 per cent Muslim. They dominate all sectors especially sugar cane, rice and vegetable production. The next largest group (18.5 per cent) consisted of Afro-Caribbean farmers who managed one-quarter of both the cocoa and dairy farms investigated. Unlike many other parts of the Caribbean, farms were within easy reach of schools, drinking water and medical facilities. Most of the homes were built of concrete, had two-storeys, running water and electricity and almost all had adjacent flower and vegetable gardens.

The average family size on the farms surveyed was 6.7 persons of which 2.3 were adult men, 2.2 adult women and 1.2 boys and 1.0 girls under 15 years. The sugar cane sector had the biggest families and cocoa the smallest. As shown in Figure 13.2 the largest percentage of male farmers was in the age group 41-50 years while women farmers were mostly in the 31-40 age group. Of the total male respondents, 26.3 per cent were under 40 years, 52.7 per cent between 41 and 60 years and 21 per cent over 61 years of age. Among the women respondents 42.7 per cent were under 40 years, 49.2 per cent between 41 and 60 years and only 8.1 per cent older. The cocoa, sugar cane and rice farmers were the oldest and tobacco, vegetable and dairy producers the youngest.

In general, women were less educated than men with only 3.9 years of schooling, while men had an average of 5.3 years. The only exception was found in the dairy sector where the farmers were younger and women had had more years of schooling (5.6) than their spouses (4.7). When all sectors were combined, 30 per cent of the men and 42 per cent of the women farmers had had no education. The cocoa, sugar cane and dairy sectors had the least educated males and sugar and rice the least educated females. Since most farm families are following national trends and are educating both sons and daughters for a 'better life', these respondents probably represent the last generation with such a disparity in education.

## Land Tenure

Land ownership is central to farming in Trinidad and to a large extent determines what crops will be planted. When land is owned, it passes from one generation to another thereby ensuring a continuation of farming. Land on farms surveyed was either owned through purchase or inheritance, or was rented or leased from government sources. Perennial or tree crops were usually grown on freehold land and short-term produce was on rented or leased land. Although most respondents indicated a desire to own land, only 47.7 per cent (62 farmers) actually did. Most proprietors were in the cocoa, sugar and rice sectors: of these 22.6 per cent (14 farmers) were male and 25.8 per cent (16 farmers) were female while the remainder reported joint ownership by both spouses. Owned land was purchased by 36 farmers and inherited by 26 farmers. Female land owners inherited land from their late spouses and although it was possible for women to buy or lease land in Trinidad, none of the women interviewed actually had done so.

**Figure 13.2: Gender Distribution of Age of Farmers by Product Sector**

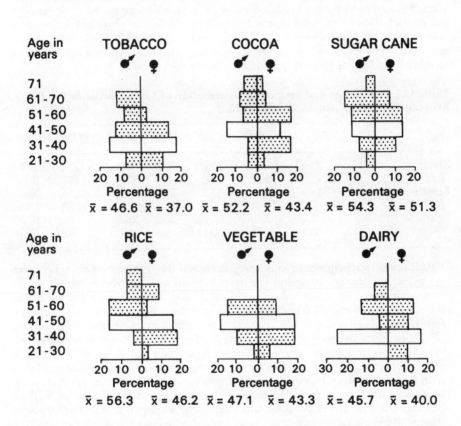

The extent of cultivated area was related to the crop grown. Extensively cultivated crops such as cocoa and sugar cane average 16.9 and 22.4 acres while intensive crops such as tobacco and vegetables occupied an average of 9.3 and 3.0 acres respectively. Cocoa farmers owned and farmed the most land and vegetable farmers owned and cultivated the smallest acreages. Of the farms managed by women, half were smaller than nine acres and most were in one parcel. Of the female-headed farms, 17 were not fragmented, six were divided into two parcels and three into three parcels. In addition, 93 per cent of the female-owned and managed farms were within walking distance of the family home. Unlike other parts of the Caribbean where a scarcity of good land exists, crops in Trinidad were generally grown on appropriate soil types and women farmers were not relegated to marginal land.

## Responsibility for the Farm & Crops

Not surprisingly, this variable was difficult to ascertain. The strategy employed here was to select three areas of responsibility, namely the ultimate responsibility for the farm, for the major and for the secondary or minor crops cultivated and for crop selection. Overall responsibility for the farm could therefore be attributed to the male spouse, the female spouse, or both jointly. As was expected in an Indian dominated farming community, male spouses managed or were responsible for the family farm in most cases. Off-farm employment did not affect this arrangement. Altogether 64 per cent of farms surveyed had male management, 20 per cent female and 16 per cent joint (Table 13.1). Of the 26 female-managed farms, five were purchased, six inherited and eleven rented or leased. Most of the female managers were widowed or separated from their spouses but had continued to farm with the help of hired help and other family members.

**Table 13.1: Percentage and Frequency Distribution of Male, Female or Joint Responsibility for Farm, by Product Sector**

| Sex | Tobacco | Cocoa | Cane | Rice | Veg. | Dairy | Total |
|---|---|---|---|---|---|---|---|
| Male | 78.6 | 61.0 | 75.0 | 50.0 | 53.6 | 75.0 | 63.8 |
| f | (11) | (25) | (12) | (8) | (15) | (12) | (83) |
| Female | 14.3 | 22.0 | 13.3 | 25.0 | 17.9 | 25.0 | 20.0 |
| f | (2) | (9) | (2) | (4) | (5) | (4) | (26) |
| Joint | 7.1 | 17.1 | 6.7 | 25.0 | 28.6 | 0.0 | 16.2 |
| f | (1) | (7) | (1) | (4) | (8) | (0) | (21) |

On all farms, the primary or major crop occupied the highest percentage of land and in most instances provided the most farm income. However, minor crops were interspersed or alternated with the major crop. Responsibility for the major crop varied but overall 51.5 per cent of all respondents reported that both spouses were responsible for the major crop. This was not surprising and reflected the interdependency between spouses on farms. However, on closer examination of individual sectors, sugar cane was found to be dominated by male decision makers, whereas cocoa and vegetable farms were generally jointly managed. Even when the male spouse had off-farm employment, these major crop patterns were the same. Minor crops included tobacco, sugar, rice and vegetables as well as bananas, oranges, sweet potatoes and maize. For example, commercial tobacco farmers also grew sweet potatoes, maize and other vegetables; cocoa farmers had coffee, bananas and oranges interplanted with their crop; sugar farmers had rice and vegetables. Vegetable farmers grew three crops per year and as a result did not have minor crops. Again, most respondents indicated that responsibility for care was usually joint, reflecting the cooperative nature of most farming units in Trinidad. Men were also involved in the selection of secondary crops and roughly half of all respondents (49.2 per cent) indicated that the male spouse selected the crops which were to be grown; the other two categories of decision making were of equal importance.

## Crop Cultivation

Many variables are involved in crop cultivation and to a large extent the greater the intensity of production, the greater is the family involvement. Cultural practices dictated what kind of equipment, chemical inputs and skills were needed. Most farms had the usual complement of hand tools like cutlasses, rakes and hoes. Pest control sprayers were owned by 69 per cent of farmers interviewed and almost all farmers in the tobacco, vegetable and dairy sectors had one. Vehicles were also owned by 38 per cent of all respondents with the largest proportion of owners being in the same three sectors. Tractors were, however, only owned by 15.4 per cent of the farmers surveyed and most farmers rented tractors when necessary. Carts drawn by animals were owned by about 12 per cent of farmers and were used mainly for hauling sugar cane. Men were the primary users for most of the equipment (except for manual tools) and only 6.9 per cent of female farmers used sprayers or drove vehicles. However, there is a tendency for younger women on the island to acquire driving skills and this trend will in the future lessen their dependency on their spouses for transport.

Fields were either manually watered using buckets or mechanically irrigated using a pump. Of the total farms surveyed, 41 (31.5 per cent) were irrigated manually, while 25 (19.2 per cent) used pumps, particularly in the tobacco and vegetable sectors. Of those respondents who used manual irrigation 19 were male and 22 female. Not surprisingly, of those farmers using mechanical irrigation 17 were male and only 8 female. In Trinidad, as in many other parts of the developing world, women did not use new technology.

The use of fertilizer was a more common cultural practice and men, women and children were involved in fertilizer application. Of the 96 farmers who used insecticides, males performed the task on 77 farms and both spouses did it on ten farms. Only five women, all of whom owned their own farms, sprayed their own crops. In general, women were afraid to spray and complained that it was dangerous for their health. Several male farmers also had health concerns about pesticide usage but indicated that they had no choice but to use it. On female-operated farms, pest control was delegated to hired hands and to male family members.

## Crop Production Cycles & Labour Patterns

Unlike other surveys of gender and agriculture in the Caribbean, this study emphasized the agricultural rather than the social aspects. Environmental conditions and history dictated what types of crops could be cultivated and these in turn influenced labour inputs. The steps associated with the production of each agricultural commodity were isolated. This kind of dissection was necessary to identify the complementary roles of men, women, children and hired help. A practical aspect of this approach was that male farmers could relate more easily to 'work' and to crops, rather than to a discussion on labour patterns. It was only through long interviews with both spouses that current trends in the gender division of labour could be determined. In all instances crop production revolved around certain tasks like land preparation, nursery establishment and maintenance, field planting, fertilizer application, pest control, harvesting, transporting and marketing. Some crops had more tasks associated with their production while others had less.

**Figure 13.3: Cultivation Cycle for Tobacco, Illustrating Labour Output**

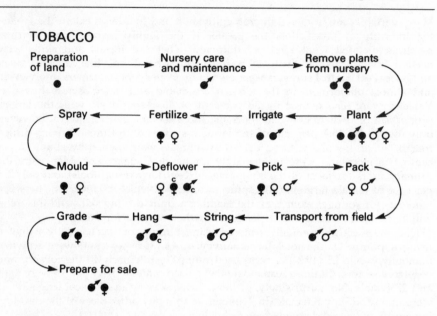

TOBACCO

Tobacco and vegetable cultivation are synonymous with intensive, high labour demand production cycles and, as a result, the whole farm family was involved. The average tobacco farm in Trinidad was about 9.5 acres and employed an average of 3.6 men and 4.8 women during the growing and harvesting seasons. The season began with land preparation (done mechanically) and the generation of seedlings for later planting in the field. As indicated in Figure 13.3, subsequent tasks included seedling removal and planting, irrigation, weeding, fertilizing and harvesting. Among these, male tasks included nursery care, spraying, stringing leaves (on stakes) and hanging tobacco leaves for curing. Fertilizing, caring for young plants in the field, excising unwanted flower buds, and picking were usually done by women. Both spouses were involved with the preparation of nursery stock, planting, grading and preparation of leaves for sale. Children (especially boys) helped with the removal of flower buds and the hanging of leaves for drying. Workers of both sexes were hired during the busy periods.

Similarly, vegetables like tomatoes, lettuces, eggplants and cucumbers require intensive labour from the time of seedling preparation to marketing. Again, as illustrated in Figure 13.4, care and maintenance of the nursery and spraying were male tasks, while female tasks included fertilizing, weeding and tying plants to stakes. Planting, irrigation and harvesting were done jointly. Children helped whenever possible with tasks like irrigation, harvesting and preparation of the produce for sale. Also any additional tasks required after a crop was harvested (for example, the ripening of tomatoes) were usually done by women. It is apparent from Figure 13.4 that the cultivation of vegetables in Trinidad is a multi-step process and all family members are involved at some stage.

Extensively cultivated crops like cocoa and sugar cane, where farms were an average size of 16.9 and 22.4 acres respectively, usually involved fewer tasks. Since cocoa is a tree crop, it requires only periodic attention with the heaviest labour demands occurring during the harvest and post-harvest periods. The production cycle, as shown in Figure 13.5, indicates that most field activities like excavating drains for proper drainage, cutlassing to remove weeds, pruning of trees, spraying, picking fruit, cracking pods and transporting were generally male tasks; women and children helped with the collection of fruit after picking, removal of seeds from cracked pods, walking on seeds to remove external pulp, drying the beans in special houses on the roadside near the home and preparing the seeds for sale. Both sexes were involved in cocoa production, but there was a distinct gender division of labour in this sector.

**Figure 13.4: Cultivation Cycle for Vegetables, Illustrating Labour Input**

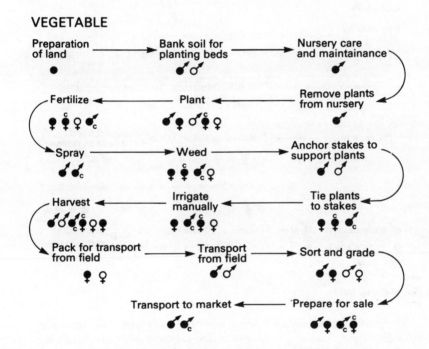

Sugar can be classified as a male dominated crop for most of the work is done by male spouses or by hired workers. The average farm was 22.4 acres and during the season 3.7 male and 1.3 female workers were employed. Although this crop required periodic attention and had fewer activities associated with its cultivation, harvesting was a very strenuous activity. Female labourers were hired for planting (which occurs every ten years) and during the harvest period. They helped with soil preparation, planting and harvesting and loading cut canes for transporting to selling points. By choice, few female spouses were involved and their activities were usually restricted to fertilizing. Typical masculine tasks included spraying for weeds, burning cane before harvesting, cutting and transport from the fields.

Rice production is truly a joint effort (see Figure 13.6). There are basically two active periods in the rice production cycle: the planting period from June to July and the harvesting period in October. The average size of the fields on surveyed farms was 6.7 acres and during the busy periods 3.9 men and 4.5 women workers were employed. Although rice fields are mechanically prepared, embankments had to be constructed to hold moisture for wet-land cultivation. This is usually done by the husband, who also prepares the nursery stock for later planting. Other male activities involve transport of the matured stalks from the field and sale of the product. Many tasks like planting, weeding and harvesting are done jointly by hired men and women. Exclusively female tasks like drying and winnowing the grain are done near the farm house. In general, wherever possible, both male and female agricultural workers are hired to do strenuous tasks like harvesting and transporting cut stalks from the field.

**Figure 13.5: Cultivation Cycle for Cocoa, Illustrating Labour Input**

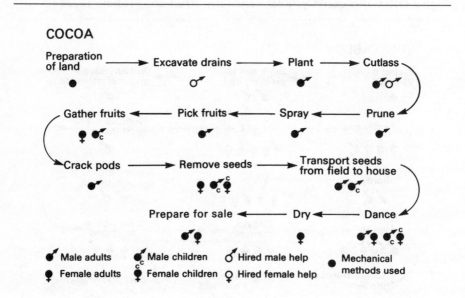

## Animal Care

Most farmers keep animals for home use or for sale and their care seems to be predominantly a female responsibility. Of 114 non-dairy farms, 33 kept dairy cows, 8 had beef cattle, 24 reared goats, 3 had pigs, 13 had mules or donkeys and 25 kept chickens. Women were generally involved in the rearing of most of these animals but men cared for larger animals, cows and equine stock. The time involved for caring for these animals did not seem to be a factor, since cows, goats, chickens and equines took less than two hours per day. Pigs, which were kept by three female farmers, demanded the most time, usually a total of three hours a day for feeding and cleaning out. Keeping small manageable animals was seen as an extension of 'housework' for most women. These animals were reared close to the farmhouse, fed at least partly on scraps and were used either for food or sold for additional income.

On dairy farms, some goats, pigs and poultry were also kept and in all cases women were responsible for the care and maintenance of these animals. Furthermore, two tasks were usually undertaken on dairy farms: caring for cows and cultivation of pasture. Milking, feeding and cleaning are carried out twice daily. These tasks are performed jointly in the morning but are done exclusively by women and children in the afternoon. Animal spraying for insects and other pests is usually done by men, but the application of de-worming medication is a joint responsibility. Land preparation for pasture is done mechanically but planting and fertilizing were shared by family members. On an average day, dairy farm women worked as many as 13 hours on housework, child care and animal maintenance, while their spouses only worked eight hours on the farm.

**Figure 13.6: Cultivation Cycle for Rice, Illustrating Labour Input**

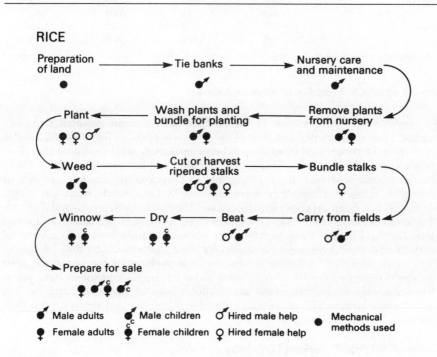

## Marketing

Transport and the time required for selling determined who sold the produce of the farm. In general, major crops are sold by men, minor crops by either men or women. Tobacco is sold to a private company, cocoa to a middleman or a marketing board, sugar to a processing plant and vegetables to retailers. Table 13.2 shows the gender division of labour for crop sales on farms surveyed by major farm sector. Most vendors were male. The selling of tobacco required 12 hours per week, cocoa 7, sugar cane 30, rice 5 and vegetables a minimum of 15 hours per week during the harvesting period. When transport was needed, milk was sold by male farmers. However, women also sold products like milk and smaller animals at the farm gate and invariably retained this income for home use. Both men and women participated in the sale of minor crops.

Some distinction was discerned in the sale of animals. In most cases women sold smaller animals like pigs, goats and poultry from the farm gate, whereas men sold beef calves and milk to processors. If the husband had off-farm employment, this pattern remained the same. However, if women managed their own farms, they sold beef animals as well as other animals.

**Table 13.2: Percentage and Frequency Distribution of Major Crop Vendor, by Product Sector**

| Vendor | Tobacco | Cocoa | Cane | Rice | Veg. |
|--------|---------|-------|------|------|------|
| Male   | 85.7    | 72.5  | 100.0 | 100.0 | 53.6 |
| f      | (12)    | (29)  | (15)  | (11)  | (15) |
| Female | 00      | 20.0  | 00    | 00    | 21.4 |
| f      | (00)    | (8)   | (00)  | (00)  | (6)  |
| Joint  | 14.3    | 7.5   | 00    | 00    | 25.0 |
| f      | (2)     | (3)   | (00)  | (00)  | (7)  |

## Work Patterns & Attitudes of Women Farmers

An analysis of work patterns of Trinidadian farm women revealed that they worked 12 to 15 hours per day. Half of this time was spent in the field and the rest on household chores and child care. When questioned, most indicated that their spouse's non-farming time was spent on 'drinking and having a good time'. Many women interviewed said that their parents had worked on cocoa, sugar, rice or vegetable farms and that they were exposed to farm work at an early age. Marriages had been arranged for them when they were between 12 and 15 years of age, to husbands aged 12 to 17 who belonged to the same economic and social class. As child brides, these women were viewed by their in-laws as additional workers and their lives were controlled by their mothers-in-law and husbands. They were expected to labour in the fields as well as in the home for their husband's extended family. Usually after about ten frugal and subservient years, they were able to purchase land and build houses of their own and become independent farmers. These women raised large families and worked with their husbands in all aspects of production.

**Table 13.3: Typical Working Day, Tobacco Farmer**

| Time of Day | Activity |
|-------------|----------|
| 03.00 - 07.00 hrs | Prepare and serve family breakfast; clean house; prepare children for school |
| 07.00 - 12.00 hrs | Work in vegetable or tobacco fields |
| 12.00 - 13.00 hrs | Lunch and rest |
| 13.00 - 15.00 hrs | Sell in markets |
| 15.00 - 18.00 hrs | Prepare produce for sale the next day |

The typical vegetable farmer in the survey started her day at 5.00 a.m. Since the fields are relatively close to the farmhouse, she was able to return home for a rest and to do tasks like laundry and then go back to the fields later to help her sons and husband. A tobacco farmer's day was even more demanding and, since the income from tobacco was lower than from vegetables, she had the additional task of trying to sell vegetables in the local market. Most of the housework was done by daughters, but during the hectic tobacco season the whole family shared the farm work. The farmer whose schedule is shown in Table 13.3, had been married at 13 and had eight children. However, as a hired labourer, she learnt how to grow tobacco and later obtained a growing contract with the West Indian Tobacco Company. Her main goals in life were to own her own land and to educate her children. Dairy farmers also work excessively long hours on the farm. Most of them also came from farming backgrounds and many were forced to work as farm labourers to help support the family. Since many spouses had off-farm jobs, most of the work associated with the dairy industry was done by women. Their days began at about 4.30 a.m. (Table 13.4) and revolved around the milking schedule for the dairy herd and providing for family needs.

**Table 13.4: Typical Working Day, Dairy Farmer**

| Time of Day | Activity |
| --- | --- |
| 04.30 - 05.30 hrs | Prepare family breakfast ingredients |
| 05.30 - 07.00 hrs | Milk cows |
| 07.00 - 08.00 hrs | Cook and serve breakfast and send children to school |
| 08.00 - 12.00 hrs | Clean animal pens; feed calves and tie goats; weed section of pasture |
| 12.00 - 14.00 hrs | Lunch and rest |
| 14.00 - 16.00 hrs | Wash churns; milk cows; clean pens |
| 16.00 - 18.00 hrs | Prepare and serve evening family meal |

Respondents had definite ideas about their lives and roles. Some were analytical, while others had never critically analysed their lifestyles. In most cases, farm women focused their attention on feeding their families and on maintaining their households. They were subservient to their husbands and felt that their own needs were of minor importance. Over four-fifths felt that they played a major role in agriculture while the remainder felt that this role was diminishing. The tobacco, vegetable and rice farmers were particularly adamant about the crucial roles they played on their farms. When asked whether they were treated fairly only 23 per cent answered in the affirmative while others were uncertain. Again, when asked whether they were satisfied with their roles as workers, mothers and wives, 40 per cent were positive, 26 per cent said no and 34 per cent said it was 'God's wish'. About 91 per cent expressed a wish for smaller families, while only 46 per cent were teaching their children about agriculture. In general, however, most parents did not want their children to become full-time farmers, but for financial security wanted them to own land.

## Conclusion

Gasson (1981) identified three roles for farm women in the south of England. The first was the farm housewife who did not work regularly on the farm nor was she responsible for any farm enterprise. The second category, the working farmwife, spent part of each day working on the farm but was rarely in charge of the farm enterprise. The third group, women farmers, had some responsibility for the farm and spent much of their working time on the farm.

To some extent these categories can also be applied to farm women in Trinidad. Clearly, sugar cane is a male dominated crop and most women in this sector were satisfied to be farm housewives. However, in the cocoa, rice, tobacco, vegetable and dairy sectors, women worked as many days per week (4.8) as their male counterparts (4.9) and, based solely on this fact, they should be classified as women farmers and not as working farmwives. This is especially true for the tobacco, vegetable and dairy sectors which are labour intensive and where men usually had off-farm employment.

To a large extent, women farm out of necessity in Trinidad. Unlike Guyanese women (Odie-Ali 1986) and Vincentians (Glesne 1986), few respondents had a great love for this occupation. Since most farm families wanted their children in other jobs, the future for agriculture in Trinidad looks dismal. State farms have not lived up to their predicted potential and therefore cannot be used to buoy up the industry. The most lucrative is the vegetable sector and this trend will undoubtedly continue for the foreseeable future. The tobacco, rice and cocoa areas are shrinking rapidly due to lack of profitability, shortage of labour and larceny. Nationally there are no legal hindrances to women who wish to continue in agriculture. They can lease land, rent equipment, and obtain loans and technical advice when needed. However, the problems facing the whole industry affect them as well and unless they can join cooperatives or other support organizations, the number of women in agriculture will continue to decline substantially in the future.

## Note

1   Originally presented as a paper at the Commonwealth Geographical Bureau workshop on Women and Development held at Newcastle upon Tyne University, April 1989.

## References

*Battlefront* (Trinidad) (1978) 'Indentured Labour'. 19 May, p. 7, col. 2.

Gasson, Ruth (1981) 'Roles of Women on Farms: A Pilot Study'. *Journal of Agricultural Economics*, 31 (1) 11-20

Glesne, C. (1986) 'Inclusion and Incorporation in Agricultural Production: The Case of Young Vincentians'. Paper presented at the Conference on Gender Issues in Farming Systems, Research and Extension, University of Florida, February

Momsen, J. (1986) 'Gender Roles in Caribbean Small-scale Agriculture'. Paper presented at the Conference on Gender Issues in Farming Systems, Research and Extension. University of Florida, Gainesville, February

Newson, L.A. (1976) *Aboriginal and Spanish Colonial Trinidad*. New York: Academic Press

Odie-Ali, S. (1986) 'Women in Agriculture: The Case of Guyana'. *Social and Economic Studies*, 35 (2) 241-90

Tikasingh, G. (1973) 'The Establishment of the Indians in Trinidad, 1870-1900'. University of the West Indies, Ph.D. dissertation

Trinidad & Tobago (1978) *White Paper on Agriculture*. Trinidad: Ministry of Agriculture, Lands and Fisheries

Wood, D. (1968) *Trinidad in Transition*. London: Oxford University Press

# XIV  Women & Cuban Smallholder Agriculture in Transition

JEAN STUBBS

The 1990s opened with the Cuban government declaring a 'special period' in which food self-sufficiency was to be crucial. Export crop (especially sugar) lands were to be turned over to domestic production and there was to be a return to the plough. For a country that had, for three decades, followed an increasingly technically oriented, agriculturally based, export led development model, this was a dramatic shift. It came as a two-pronged response to both a stepping-up of the threat from the United States and to the speed of events in Eastern Europe, which had resulted in the breakdown of established trading patterns.[1] If carried through, the 'special period' could have some highly significant ramifications for agricultural policy and agrarian relations, not least in smallholder agriculture.

Currently facing one of its toughest periods since the 1959 revolution and having embarked on a 'rectification' process heading in a diametrically opposite direction from that of Eastern bloc market reforms (Mesa Lago 1988; Roca 1988; Zimbalist 1989; Deere and Meurs 1990), Cuba is under more pressure than ever before to re-evaluate smallholder production and the centrality of women to that production. External events have only compounded significant internal factors that had already occasioned considerable rethinking along these lines.

This chapter takes a new look at some of these factors.[2] It draws extensively on an earlier study of cooperatives to explore linkages between gender, household and agrarian policy. In the context of a national women's movement centred on the Federation of Cuban Women (FMC), which has taken up women and development issues (Larguia and DuMoulin 1986) and is now focusing more closely on gender and patriarchy within the socialist development experience (Pereira 1989; FMC 1990), it suggests the existence of a gender-sensitized, pre-collective voice among Cuba's women farmers.[3]

## Rethinking Smallholder Agriculture

Cuba was an anomaly among the post-Second World War wave of Third World 'peripheral' countries embarked on socialist transformation, in that collective forms of agriculture quickly came to predominate over private. In addition, there continued to be an explicit preference for large state farms, even after the recognition in the mid-1970s that agricultural production cooperatives were a transitional form (Acosta 1972 and 1973; McEwan 1979; Lehmann 1982; Rodriguez 1987).

The reason for this lay primarily in Cuba's pre-revolutionary agro-exporting economy with foreign and local capital investment. The 1959 and 1963 land reforms placed 70 per cent of farm land in state hands (Acosta 1972 and 1973; Rodriguez 1987). Formerly private US and Cuban-owned sugar estates were to become the technologically advanced state farms of socialist agriculture (Pollitt

1981 and 1983). United States reprisals in the form of a trade embargo were met with a 1963 Soviet-Cuban trade agreement whereby the USSR would replace the US as Cuba's major sugar market. This was seen by many as the 'new dependency' (Pollitt 1985).

Throughout the 1960s, state enterprises were similarly promoted in cattle, dairy, poultry, citrus, banana, plantain and other areas of production. In the 1970s, these were fostered in conjunction with 'technification', integral development plans and schools in the countryside that could provide labour. The external link came from relatively favourable trading with the West (the US excluded) and increasing integration into the Eastern European trading bloc.

Given the predominance of large-scale agriculture, a commonly held myth about Cuban smallholder agriculture is that it was insignificant, both before and after the revolution. The disruption of traditional farming was argued to have generated a surplus of rural labour and to have kept subsistence farming to a minimum. However, agricultural modernization also strengthened archaic forms of production, as capital accumulation was sought through credit, buying and land-leasing operations. Large-scale modern farming units coexisted with small-scale tenant and subtenant farms and sharecropped holdings.

The smallholder sector was actually strengthened under the 1959 agrarian reform through land entitlement (Martinez-Alier 1970; Lehmann 1981). The sector has declined since, both in terms of the number of smallholders and as a proportion of total agricultural land. In the late 1960s, when there were 400,000 state farm workers, there were 250,000 farmers in the National Association of Small Farmers (ANAP) on some 30 per cent of the agricultural land. By the mid-1980s, comparable figures were 600,000 state farm workers but only 180,000 ANAP farmers on 15 per cent of the land. However, among the crops produced by this sector were important export items, especially tobacco which continues to be 75 per cent non-state produced, and a significant proportion of food crops for domestic consumption including 32 per cent of the bean crop, 66 per cent of vegetables, 54 per cent of coffee, 53 per cent of fruit and 34 per cent of tubers. This in itself proved reason enough for greater attention to be paid to smallholder production.

Since 1970, there have been four turning points in attitudes to smallholders. The first came after the 1971 Congress of the National Association of Small Farmers (ANAP), which resulted in a revitalization of the small farming sector. It occurred in the wake of the disastrous effects of the all-out drive by the state for the 10 million ton sugar harvest, which had led to the halving of output of other export crops such as tobacco and a critical shortfall in production for domestic consumption (McEwan 1979; Lehmann 1981; Martin 1987). The second was in 1977, when the ANAP Congress endorsed an agrarian policy favouring a voluntary, autonomous cooperative movement within the small farm sector. The aim was to encourage smallholders already grouped together in credit and service cooperatives (CCSs) or peasant associations (ACs) to pool their land and other means of production to form agricultural production cooperatives (CPAs). It was hoped that these would boost agricultural output and generate resources for cooperative village services and amenities, thereby attracting people, especially the young, to stay on the land (Peek 1984; Trinchet Vera 1984; Kay 1987; Stubbs and Alvarez 1987).

The third occurred in 1985, after the Second National Meeting of Cooperative Farmers, with the closing down of the farmers' market and the tightening up of the smallholder, cooperative and state agricultural sectors. These measures were a response to tense agrarian relations because of the enrichment of the middle-sized farmers from the market and a fall in domestic production to meet export commitments, especially sugar (Meurs 1990; Stubbs 1989).

The fourth turning point came in 1990, with the call for intensified food production, involving switching some sugar lands back into domestic food crop production in the state, cooperative and smallholder sectors. This development also involves increased irrigation and streamlining of the food distribution network (Deere and Meurs 1990).

## Women in Smallholder Agriculture

Closely tied in with the view that Cuban smallholder agriculture has been insignificant is the notion that there was a low involvement of women in the pre-revolutionary period. This was supported by the disaggregated figure for women in the 1959 agricultural census, which indicated that they comprised only 1.5 per cent of the economically active agricultural population. The figure in the 1953 census was similar at 2 per cent. There was little change in the post-revolutionary period. By the 1930s women made up less than 10 per cent of the economically active agricultural population.

The figures reflect statistical information gathering and notions of what is defined as economically active rather than the realities of women's agricultural labour (Deere and Leon 1980). In the Cuban case there was a school of thought that saw pre-1939 capitalist development as having created a large class of landless labourers (Martinez-Alier 1970). Another view (Nelson 1950; Pollitt 1977 and 1980) pointed to the prevalence of small tenant and subtenant farms and sharecropped holdings, which supported a large semi-peasantry/semi-proletariat that paid rent in kind (a quarter to half the crop) and was highly dependent on family labour and forced at different times of year to employ or sell labour. Neither approach took into account the fact that visible exploitation of male labour in male-headed households was accompanied by intensified child and female participation in seasonal harvesting and in the subsistence production and family reproduction crucial to survival.

After the revolution, child labour virtually ceased and there was a certain withdrawal of women's labour.[4] In the state farm sector, increasing 'technification' and mechanization demanded new skills that for social reasons were not always easy for women to acquire. An initial separation of agricultural work from the domestic unit posed the classical break between work and home. Improved rural living standards, as a result of overall development policy and changing family structures (Alvarez 1983; Rojas et al. 1988; Cruz n.d.), often meant less economic pressure on women to supplement family income and when women did choose to work, openings in such expanding non-agricultural spheres as health and education often proved far more attractive. As a result, in agriculture proper, women were to be found mostly in the unremunerated casual and seasonal workforce, the often unremunerated volunteer brigades organized by ANAP and the Federation of Cuban Women (FMC) and as an integral part of unremunerated small farm family labour (Stubbs and Alvarez 1987).

Some of these points began to be highlighted when women in smallholder agriculture proved to be strong supporters of Cuba's agricultural cooperative movement of the late 1970s. Whereas men expressed doubts about giving up their private plot of land and having to adapt to working with others, women liked working in the fields collectively as opposed to individually, economic independence from fathers and husbands through paid labour, and the new cooperative amenities.

Under the 1959 land entitlement programme, land security had been given to male heads of households for the most part, reflecting an agrarian pattern more characteristic of contemporary Hispanic America than that of the Caribbean. Some female heads of household had been granted land titles but they were the exception rather than the rule. Even when a woman secured a land title, a man in the family would, in most cases, take on farm production responsibilities.

For the first time in Cuban agrarian history, with the cooperatives (CPAs) women were encouraged to become farmers in their own right, on an equal basis with men. The result of a concerted mobilization effort was that in 1979 over a third of the cooperative farmers were women (Deere 1985; Stubbs and Alvarez 1987). This sudden 'visibility' of women in the CPAs had fast outstripped the state agricultural sector, where in 1981 women accounted for only 14 per cent of that sector's work force and 6 per cent of the executive posts.

In 1983, a peak year for the cooperative movement in many respects, the indicators for women went into reverse. They made up only 23 per cent of total cooperative farmers, although in absolute terms they had more than quadrupled in number. In 1985, when CPA figures in general were worsening, women represented 25 per cent of cooperative members and 12 per cent of cooperative executive committees. A concerted effort to consolidate the cooperative farm movement as of 1986 has so far failed to stem the downward trend, including that of women. In 1987 the figure stood at 22 per cent when 81 per cent of women were considered fit for work. That same year, women accounted for only 13 per cent of executive committee members and there were only six women presidents as opposed to 12 in 1983. When the 1987 work figures are broken down further, women accounted for less than 12 per cent of the total work time. Partly because women on the whole worked shorter hours but also because they often did different kinds of work, average daily pay for women was $4.87, whilst for men it was $5.75 (Alvarez and Perez 1989). In effect, a withdrawal of women from field labour was taking place, similar to that which had occurred in the 1960s on the state farms. We shall now turn to consideration of some of the factors involved in one particular case study.

## Cooperative Smallholder Tobacco

A study of women in tobacco cooperatives (Stubbs 1987) was conducted in 1984 to collect some local disaggregated data on what was at the time seen as a national success story. The indicators for both women and cooperative farming were, as it transpired, just beginning to change and the gender approach to the study illuminated some of the problem areas.

Tobacco was chosen on the strength of prior historical knowledge of the sector (Stubbs 1985) and because it continued to be a crop characterized by smallholders, women's labour and a burgeoning cooperative movement. The two areas of study — San Luis (Vuelta Abajo) in western Pinar del Rio province and Cabaiguan (Vuelta Arriba) in central Sancti Spiritus, formerly part of Las Villas province — were both famed for their tobacco but differed as to the kind of tobacco grown, land tenancy and several other variables, which could then be seen in relation to gender patterns. A 1940s to 1980s time span was taken to see points of continuity and rupture over pre- and post-revolutionary periods within the life experience of farm people.

On 1945 agricultural census figures, San Luis farms were smaller, more intensely sharecropped and more lucrative than those of Cabaiguan. High yields and the superior quality of its export cigar wrapper tobacco gave San Luis farms double the value and income of those in Cabaiguan, where, in terms of income, cattle and sugar were more important. The largest proportion of unpaid labour was in San Luis, where there was much greater crop specialization and an influential agrarian bourgeoisie in tobacco. Fertile company land was worked on a waged labour, tenanted and sharecropped basis, through a patriarchal system of local benefits, calling on family labour for services and operating local stores on credits and chits. Owners and managers bore little of the risk of what was a highly delicate and seasonal crop and, since little else was grown, tobacco families were particularly susceptible to market changes, using cheap migrant labour from surrounding areas at peak harvest time. In Cabaiguan many landowners were absentee or managed far removed parts of their cattle estates and let or sharecropped out the tobacco land. There was a greater chance of other agricultural and non-agricultural work but the area as a whole was less prosperous.

The revolutionary land reforms wrought significantly different changes in the two regions. In each they provided security for smallholders. In San Luis, however, an effort was made to keep a substantial part of former company land under state control and tenants and smallholders were encouraged to become part of new state farms that proved to be successful in growing quality tobacco but less so at being cost-effective ventures. In Cabaiguan, the tobacco that fell into state hands from the large estates, often by default, was much more dispersed. Cabaiguan growers became smallholders and state farms were left to grow tobacco with less experienced labour. Although various state farms grew tobacco over the years, it was never very successful and in 1983 was turned over entirely to the smallholder sector.

As prime smallholder beneficiaries of land redistribution, tobacco growers were pioneers in grouping together farmers for the collective use of curing sheds, irrigation and machinery, credit and supplies, such that tobacco ACs and CCSs numbered over 1000 by 1971. If they suffered from the emphasis on sugar in the late 1960s, they benefited from the 'tobacco recuperation' period of 1971-5, with special emphasis on crop costing and pricing and tobacco agro-technology. Strong support for the cooperative movement of the late 1970s came from the tobacco sector, but tobacco cooperatives were also among the first to run into difficulties.

Major CPA stumbling blocks detected in the 1984 study concerned economies of scale, costing and profits. In line with the cooperative movement in general, mergers caused the number of tobacco CPAs to start declining in 1983. Membership dropped back that same year after new social security laws provided retirement pensions for cooperative farmers, a good many of whom were already of an eligible age. This compounded an already observable pattern of increasing CPA land size, such that by 1985 land area had more than quadrupled in contrast to only a doubling of the number of farmers. The resulting structural strains and financial losses in labour-intensive tobacco were such that, by 1985, almost a third of tobacco CPAs, a good many of them in San Luis where farms were the most tobacco-intensive, recorded net losses.

Tobacco CPAs, like state farms, reported that their principle outlays were labour costs, fertilizers, pesticides and (if growing shade tobacco) cheese-cloth, in that order. The labour costs included bringing in temporary labour from other areas and other sectors, paying the often considerably higher salaries that labour would earn otherwise, and also providing transport, accommodation and food. The shortage of agricultural labour was rooted in the rapid development of other sectors of the economy which competed too favourably for an increasingly educated work force. It was also, however, related to the transition to collective farming systems (whether state or cooperative) from smallholder farming with its high family labour component.


## Gender & Household in Tobacco

Prior to 1959, according to the life stories of San Luis and Cabaiguan farm families, it is clear that the gender division of labour was such that men were broadly responsible for agricultural production but rarely undertook domestic chores, whether washing clothes, cooking, cleaning, caring for the children, fetching and carrying water, picking tubers, grinding corn or feeding the chickens and pigs. The pattern was for boys and girls to be working by the age of seven: the boys in the fields with their fathers and the girls around the farmhouse with their mothers. At the height of the harvest, when extra labour was essential, girls' and women's work also involved cooking for the field hands. The poorer the tobacco family, the greater the need to fall back on family labour and in this situation women and girls would also be out in the fields planting, weeding, pruning and harvesting the tobacco.

The type of tobacco determined to a large extent the kind and amount of work the women did (see also Chapter 13). The cigar wrapper tobacco of San Luis was traditionally harvested by leaf in baskets and the leaves were then threaded together to be strung on poles to dry. This was seen almost exclusively as women's work, done in the shade, with needle and thread. The dark filler tobacco of Cabaiguan was tougher and stickier because of the black resin it contained. It was traditionally harvested by knife in stalks of four leaves at a time, hung over the outstretched arm and then transferred to poles. Heavy work such as this, and field labour in general, were traditionally considered unsuitable for women. The Cabaiguan tobacco did not need to be threaded, as it was hung straight onto poles in the barns.

There were also variations in the seasonal sorting of tobacco in the initial months after harvesting, during which both municipalities provided temporary employment for thousands of women. The better quality wrapper tobacco of San Luis demanded greater classification into grades and therefore more skilled and better paid personnel; on average 100-300 people were employed in each sorting shed in peak periods. The more select the farm, the better the pay and conditions in this, one of the few forms of paid labour available to rural women. But there were many sorting sheds where the economic necessity of tobacco families was such that women and girls from the age of ten would accept pittance rates for long hours of work. In Cabaiguan, conditions and pay in the sorting sheds were on the whole worse and, given the lower intensity of tobacco growing and the concentration in towns of large sorting sheds employing up to 1000 workers, considerable distances had to be travelled to reach the work.

With the agrarian reform and rural development, the land peasant families worked was made their own, the family wage was effectively raised, children were sent to school and, as tobacco production fell in the 1960s, less labour was needed in the fields and sheds. However, the 'tobacco recuperation' of the 1970s involved women in FMC-ANAP brigades doing regular salaried work in harvesting and sorting. A more stable labour market was created, organized at first through CUBATABACO, the umbrella state tobacco-handling enterprise and later by the production cooperatives.

Tobacco areas were among those to show higher percentages of women cooperative farmers but again San Luis and Cabaiguan differed quite markedly. In San
Luis women comprised 24 per cent of the membership in CPAs and 1.6 per cent in
the CCSs; in Cabaiguan, the figures were 38 per cent and 25 per cent respectively.
Membership criteria could differ enormously from one CPA to another. At one of
the older cooperatives in Cabaiguan, it was found that both men and women were
automatically made members on pooling their land and membership numbers
were fairly equal for the sexes. In San Luis, on the other hand, no women were
listed as land contributors and strict rules regarding stability in agriculture often
worked against them. In all cooperatives, there were active and non-active members of both sexes. Given the ageing demographic structure of tobacco growers,
many of the 'non-active' had retired. This was especially true for women. Also
among the women, there would be 'land-contributory' members who neither
worked in the fields nor were active in cooperative business, and also women who
did substantial work in agricultural production but had not contributed land and
whose membership had not been recognized.

The lower proportion of women cooperative members in San Luis may also be
explained by the small town location which offered a greater variety of job
opportunities. One cooperative found no women who would join except a young
graduate accountant. Wives of male cooperative farmers were already on the
CUBATABACO pay-roll as salaried workers and would be hired back by the
cooperative during harvest time. Other women were older or had young children
and only worked during peak harvest periods. Grown daughters were often
working for the state sector in education or health, at least until marriage and
children interrupted work. Even then San Luis differed from Cabaiguan in that it
offered more accessible child care facilities.

Women's work on the cooperative varied considerably. In the dark filler tobacco
area of Cabaiguan, where women had traditionally been less involved in tobacco,
they were often organized into non-tobacco agricultural work, producing root
crops and vegetables for local consumption and sale to the state, though this division of labour was by no means obligatory and some women took pride in working the tobacco. This pattern was less marked in San Luis, where other crops were
produced less frequently and women had traditionally done more work in tobacco. When Cabaiguan cooperatives experimented with Burley tobacco, the
women were particularly pleased to be able to pick and thread the leaves. One cooperative took the tobacco to the women in their homes to be threaded on their
front porches. Women who had retired from the fields or who had other family
commitments were able to help out and earn some money. In both areas, women
predominated in cultivating produce and tending livestock for family consumption, organized either collectively (when it was recognized as cooperative labour)
or around the individual household (when it was not).

Household servicing was only dimly perceived as part of the collective process of
accumulation of wealth, over issues such as meals. Few cooperatives organized
collective lunch for their members and then only for outside seasonal workers.
Cooking lunch for outside workers was recognized as paid labour, cooking for
family members was not. One male accountant ventured to say that collective
lunch facilities were 'costly' to the cooperative, while at the same time he lamented
that women's responsibilities in the home worked against their stability in field
labour. At that cooperative, half the members were women, of whom only 19 per
cent actually worked in the fields and only 7 per cent worked regularly. Women
accounted for only 11 per cent of the total number of days worked during the year
and took a corresponding 11 per cent of the profits.

Another cooperative reported only 15 per cent of members were women but almost all worked on a regular basis and took a more proportionate share of annual profits. None the less, the general comment was that women much preferred not to have to do the hot and hard field work. In the Cabaiguan area there were women who took in home sewing from a nearby garment factory as a softer option.

The marked increase in the visibility of women had produced a generally heightened awareness of women's role in production. Neither men nor women expressed the view that women should stay at home and not work for the cooperative, but rather saw women's domestic responsibilities as an obstacle to their increased participation. This was reflected in the high number of women in casual and seasonal work and the poor representation of women at the executive level of the cooperative.

In the Cabaiguan area, men complained about women members because they worked less than men in the fields and took less of an interest in day-to-day cooperative business. Women had their own complaint: they wanted the men to change and begin to carry their weight around the home so that women could participate more in the cooperative.

Generational change was very marked and talked about. *Machismo* was very much a topic of conversation. Older women felt that things were a lot easier than previously and that new doors were opening for younger women, even if it was too late for them. Younger women schooled away from home returned challenging taboos.

The mother-in-law of one cooperative president, retired and in her sixties, remembered how from her early teens she had had to help her mother carry food to the field hands and fetch and carry water. Later, she worked in the tobacco sorting sheds while also taking in washing and ironing. She was at the time virtually running her own household as well as that of her daughter next door. Her daughter, who worked in the cooperative store, grew up in the early years of the revolution. Quite restricted as a girl, she married at 17. The granddaughters had had opportunities denied their mother. The son, unlike the daughter, had been allowed to go away and study. He was a school teacher but had come back to live with his mother in the village. He was one of the few men who did housework, even after marrying. In contrast, the daughter's husband, as president of the cooperative, had little or no time for the home. The granddaughters expressed a certain resentment at being expected to help at home much more than their brother. The eldest granddaughter, in particular, was critical of old-fashioned small community gossip which restricted the freedom of girls.

Few of the men did much around the house, but the women making the greatest demands on them tended to be those who were working, gaining confidence in themselves and questioning established mores such as the gender division of labour, male authority and dual sexual standards. Women expressed a lot of resentment that men still thought they had the right to have affairs but that their women did not. When the men in question held posts of authority, this could be cause for collective action. In the case of one married couple, both on the executive committee, when the husband had an affair with a younger cooperative member, the situation was judged to be such an embarrassment for the wife and other committee women that the man was suspended from his duties.

## Cooperative & Gender Challenges for the 1990s

By definition, cooperatives are socio-economic units in which individual well-being depends on collective success. In the San Luis and Cabaiguan tobacco areas, by the mid-1980s economic success was in doubt and several policy imperatives were proposed. One was land consolidation. In San Luis, in particular, the haphazard way in which land tenure patterns had changed had created a veritable mosaic of state, cooperative and smallholder farms. A second proposal was to break up the biggest and most unwieldy of the cooperatives into more manageable plots and, in some instances, to dismantle them as cooperatives *per se* by introducing a system of piece-rate labour. A third option, given the ample profit margins on tobacco manufacture and trade compared to losses in cultivation, was a revision of crop pricing. A fourth was to review the labour question in gender terms.

Bank statistics for the 1983-4 tobacco harvest showed a much lower positive end-of-year balance on credits for the cooperative than for the smallholder farmer (140 pesos against 1510 on average, a ratio of less than 1:10). As an approximate comparative indicator, this figure is highly misleading, precisely because it conceals real distribution of income. For the smallholder sector, all income is registered under the farm owner or representative and the work of family members and others in the production process is not taken into account. In the case of the cooperative, the farmer's income from work done individually is supplemented by advance daily pay, social security, paid maternity leave for women, and sickness and other related benefits. In addition, some families may have more than one cooperative farmer. Cooperatives in Cabaiguan were more profitable than in San Luis because they were both less dependent on tobacco and had income from cattle and sugar.

Figures for cooperative and individual farmer incomes were much closer for sugar (734 pesos against 835, a ratio of 9:10), which is much less of a small farm crop, has a lower female labour input and admits mechanization and economies of scale. In coffee, which is more like tobacco, the statistics were again uneven (40 pesos against 512, a ratio of less than 1:12). Coffee has the added dimension of being grown in mountain areas which had seen an exodus of population to lowland development zones. Special measures were taken *vis-à-vis* this crop in the late 1980s, with debt cancellation, crop price increases and the organization of special work brigades. The area was also helped by the creation of a special mountain infrastructure including village mini-dams and solar energy plants, road and home building efforts and the first family doctor programmes.

Since 1984, awareness of the complexities of the rural household in transition and of the life cycle and generational factors in accounting for women's labour input has been significantly heightened. As household economic pressures eased, women in many of the farm households joining the cooperatives, especially older women and women with small children, found it a great relief to be able to give up field labour, but by so doing they jeopardized the successful running of the cooperative. Cooperatives needed women's involvement if they were to succeed. But for this to happen, attitudinal changes were needed among men and women and men needed to become more involved in the household.

By the late 1980s, women made up over a third of all extension workers in the cooperatives and frequently reported encountering incomprehension from male farmers. In company with women doctors, nurses and farmers on the cooperatives, they began to be more vocal within the cooperative movement. In 1988, a first National Women Farmers' Meeting was held with 300 delegates drawn from all levels of agriculture. The meeting raised a new voice within the farm movement, challenging the overwhelmingly male face of ANAP and calling for a re-evaluation of the role of women farmers.

They were arguing not to turn the clock back but to overcome newfound obstacles. As women, they wanted to strengthen the cooperatives with more training and job possibilities and less job segregation. They wanted a break with traditional canons of women's work, especially with a view to attracting and keeping young women coming out of agricultural schools and institutes. While the urban-rural gap had narrowed considerably and the rural population in general, including women, had benefited from many of the revolutionary state's development initiatives, certain gender patterns had emerged. Rural women had lower educational and work attainments, higher rates of fertility, earlier marriages, multiple teenage pregnancies and larger families than urban women. As the rural household was perceived less as an economic than as a social unit, so it had in some ways been reinforced as the woman's 'domain', especially given the relative lack of change in gender relations in rural areas and the concomitant lack of socialized facilities such as rural day-care centres and dining rooms. The women demanded priority for such facilities, along with the schools and doctor/nurse clinics, whose proximity has particular ramifications where the gender division of labour is concerned.

Their demands were in tune with the wider societal concerns raised in the post-1985 national campaign of 'rectification' endorsed by ANAP and the FMC, for, despite the still telling slogan of *atención al hombre* (literally: attention to men), rectification looked to less economic and more socio-political concerns, a return to a more collective approach rather than the individual enrichment and the free marketing solutions that had been under experimentation.

As Cuba moves into the 1990s, cooperatives will have to prove themselves from both a productive and a social point of view. The post-1985 effort to consolidate them has so far only been tentative. There would seem little incentive for remaining smallholders to pool their land on straight economic grounds, since their overall productivity and profit margins continue to surpass those of the cooperatives (Deere and Meurs 1990). Socially, the response of smallholders remains to be seen as the ageing individual smallholder is not being replaced and women are questioning their subordinate role in this sector.

However, success at this juncture arguably lies less with internal than with external factors. When the cooperative movement started Cuba had favourable trade relations with both West and East. In the early 1990s the tide in the West turned with the collapse of prices for Cuba's major exports and rising interest rates, which caused Cuba to default on its foreign debt repayments. The buffer was trade with Eastern Europe and with the Soviet Union in particular. When economic restructuring (*perestroika*) began in the Eastern bloc in the mid-1980s, the Cuban government had embarked on its 'rectification' in a radically different direction. The drawbacks of the 'new dependency' on Eastern bloc models, whether pre- or post-*perestroika*, became more obvious.

Cuba has found itself having to administer its own 'structural adjustment' and attempt more autochtonous, cost effective, less technical, basic needs approaches in its 'special period'. This has involved mass labour mobilizations in the state sector. Greater strain has also been placed on the already more labour-intensive, non-state, cooperative and individual smallholder sector, with new pressures on the rural household. Yet, out of an overall panorama that is currently bleak, could come something positive. If handled well, the emphasis on food self-sufficiency has the potential of rendering the domestic table less bare. And there would seem to be women ready to try to shape things to come in ways that will further, not hinder their own as well as their families' position.

## Notes

1   The 'special period' was announced in spring 1990, in the wake of aggressive US policy in the area: military invasion of Panama, drug enforcement policies in Colombia, electoral policies in Nicaragua, attack on a Cuban merchant vessel, large-scale naval exercises in the Gulf of Mexico and increased troop presence on the US Guantanamo naval base in south-eastern Cuba. It outlined absolute priorities in industry and agriculture in the worst possible scenario of invasion and total blockade. The US continues to operate its trade embargo with Cuba and this single factor is considered Cuba's major development obstacle, perhaps more so than ever before given present levels of global integration. US pressures on other advanced Western countries to follow suit also take their toll. In the rest of the Western hemisphere, trading with Latin American countries is slowly on the increase but there is little with the Caribbean area, except for Guyana. The Third World as a whole accounts for less than 10 per cent of Cuba's overseas trade. Major uncertainties lie with the Eastern bloc. Trade with countries like Hungary and Czechoslovakia was drastically affected, and the collapse of the Soviet Union, with whom 70 per cent of Cuba's total overseas trade was index-linked on terms highly advantageous to Cuba, spelled major dislocation throughout 1991 and 1992. In the former Soviet bloc, there is a body of opinion to the effect that trading is as important to the Soviet bloc as it is to Cuba, and the 1990 Russia-Cuba trade agreement even exceeded that of previous years. However, there have since been dramatic shortfalls, not least of the oil that used to drive the Cuban energy system, factory and farm equipment included.
2   This is a revised and updated version of earlier articles based on research conducted by the author in conjunction with Mavis Alvarez, agricultural economist of the National Association of Small Farmers of Cuba (Stubbs and Alvarez 1987; Stubbs 1987). Field research was facilitated by a post-doctoral award from the Committee on Latin American Studies of the Social Science Research Council, the American Council of Learned Societies and a Nuffield Foundation Small Grant.
3   Over its 30-year history, the FMC has been active at a national policy-making as well as grassroots level, rural areas included. However, issues of gender and patriarchy tended to be subsumed under assumed benefits for women of overall socialist development, and relatively little attention was paid to farm women per se.
4   Historical parallels might be drawn between women's withdrawal from field labour in the aftermath of slavery in the late nineteenth century, in the state farm sector in the early revolutionary period and on the cooperatives in the 1980s.

## References

Acosta, José (1972) 'La Estructura Agraria y el Sector Agropecuario al Triunfo de la Revolución'. Economía y Desarrollo, 9, 50-83

—— (1973) 'La Revolución Agraria en Cuba y el Desarrollo Económico'. Economía y Desarrollo, 17, 136-63

Alvarez, Mavis (1983) 'Experiencia Cubana en la Promoción del Rol de la Mujer en la Economía Campesina'. Paper presented to the FAO/ECLA Panel on Peasant Economic Strategies: The Role of Women, Bogota

Alvarez, Mavis and Niurka Perez (1989) 'La Mujer Campesina en Cuba: Respuesta a las Estrategias de Nairobi: Avances, Obstáculos y Recomendaciones.' Mimeo

Cruz, Lidia Elizabeth (n.d.) 'Composición de la Familia Rural Cubana'. Unpublished dissertation, Centro de Estudios Demograficos, Universidad de La Habana

Deere, Carmen Diana (1985) 'Rural Women and Agrarian Reform in Peru, Chile and Cuba'. In June Nash and Helen Safa (eds) Women and Change in Latin America. South Hadley: Bergin & Garvey

Deere, Carmen Diana and Magdalena Leon de Leal (1980) 'Medición del Trabajo de la Mujer Rural y su Posición de Clase.' Estudios de Población, 5, January-June, 63-9

Deere, Carmen Diana and Mieke Meurs (1990) 'Markets, Markets Everywhere? Understanding the Cuban Anomaly'. Paper prepared for the Conference on

*Perestroika* of Agrarian Production in the USSR: Problems and Perspectives, National Academy of Sciences, Moscow

FMC (Federation of Cuban Women) (1990) *Proyecto de Tesis*, 5th Congreso, Havana

Kay, Cristobal (1987) *New Developments in Cuban Agriculture: Economic Reforms and Collectivization*. University of Glasgow, Centre for Development Studies, Occasional Paper No. 1

Larguia, Isabel and John DuMoulin (1986) 'Women's Equality and the Cuba Revolution'. In June Nash and Helen Safa (eds) *Women and Change in Latin America*, South Hadley: Bergin & Garvey

Lehmann, David (1981) 'Smallholder Agriculture in Revolutionary Cuba: A Case of Under-Exploitation?' *Development and Change*, 16, 251-70

—— (1982) 'Agrarian Structure, Migration and the State in Cuba'. In P. Peek and G. Standing (eds) *State Policies and Migration in Latin America and the Caribbean*, London: Croom Helm

Martin, Adolfo (1987) *La ANAP: 25 Años de Trabajo*. Havana: Editora Politica

Martinez-Alier, Juan (1970) 'The Peasantry and the Cuban Revolution from the Spring of 1959 to the End of 1960', in Raymond Carr (ed.) *Latin American Affairs*. Oxford: Oxford University Press, 137-57

McEwan, Arthur (1979) 'Cuban Agriculture and Development: Contradictions and Progress'. In D. Ghai, A.R. Khan, E. Lee and S. Radwan (eds) *Agrarian Systems and Rural Development*, London: Macmillan for ILO

Mesa Lago, Carmelo (1988) 'Cuba's Counter Reform (Rectification): Causes, Policies and Effects'. In Sergio Roca (ed.) *q.v.*

Meurs, Mieke (1990) 'Agricultural Production Socialism: New Approaches to Agricultural Development'. In Sandor Malebsky and John Kirk (eds) *Transformation and Struggle: Cuba Faces the 1990s*, New York: Praeger

Nelson, Lowry (1950) *Rural Cuba*. Minneapolis: University of Minnesota Press

Peek, Peter (1984) *Collectivizing the Peasantry: The Cuban Experience*. Geneva: ILO

Pereira, Rita (1989) 'La Mujer en Cuba: Realidades y Desafios'. Paper presented at Conference on Thirty Years of the Cuban Revolution: An Assessment, Halifax, NS, November

Pollitt, Brian (1977) 'Some Problems in Enumerating the "Peasantry" in Cuba'. *Journal of Peasant Studies*, 4 (2), 162-80

—— (1980) *Agrarian Reform and the Agricultural Proletariat in Cuba, 1958-66. Further Notes and Some Second Thoughts*. University of Glasgow, Institute of Latin American Studies, Occasional Paper No. 30

—— (1981) *Revolution and the Mode of Production in the Sugar Cane Sector of the Cuban Economy, 1959-80: Some Preliminary Findings*. University of Glasgow, Institute of Latin American Studies, Occasional Paper No. 35

—— (1983) 'The Transition to Socialist Agriculture in Cuba: Some Salient Features.' *IDS Bulletin*, No. 13

—— (1985) *Sugar 'Dependency' and the Cuban Revolution*. University of Glasgow, Institute of Latin American Studies, Occasional Paper No. 43

Roca, Sergio (ed.) (1988) *Socialist Cuba: Past Interpretations and Future Challenges*. Boulder, Colorado: Westview Press

Rodriguez, José Luis (1987) 'Agricultural Policy and Development in Cuba'. *World Development*, 15 (1), 41-66. Also in A. Zimbalist (ed.) *Cuba's Socialist Economy Toward the 1990s*, Boulder and London: Westview Press

Rojas, Iliana, Mariana Ravenet and Jorge Hernandez (1988) 'Desarrollo y Relaciones de Clases en la Estructura Agraria en Cuba'. *Estudios sobre la Estructura de Clases y el Desarrollo Rural en Cuba*, Havana: Universidad de La Habana

Stubbs, Jean (1985) *Tobacco on the Periphery: A Case Study in Labour History, 1869-1950.* Cambridge: Cambridge University Press

—— (1987) 'Gender Issues in Contemporary Cuban Tobacco Farming'. *World Development*, 15 (1). Also in A. Zimbalist (ed.) *Cuba's Socialist Economy Toward the 1990s*, Boulder and London: Westview Press

—— (1989) *Cuba: The Test of Time.* London: Latin American Bureau/New York: Monthly Review Press

Stubbs, Jean and Mavis Alvarez (1987) 'Women on the Agenda: The Cooperative Movement in Rural Cuba'. In Carmen Diana Deere and Magdalena Leon (eds) *Rural Women and State Policy: Feminist Perspectives on Latin American Agricultural Development.* Boulder and London: Westview Press

Trinchet Vera, Oscar (1984) *La Cooperativa e la Tierra en el Agro Cubano.* Havana: Editora Politica

Zimbalist, Andrew and Claes Brundenius (1989) *The Cuban Economy: Measurement and Analysis of Socialist Performance.* Baltimore: Johns Hopkins University Press

# XV Development & Gender Divisions of Labour in the Rural Eastern Caribbean

JANET HENSHALL MOMSEN

Women in the Caribbean exhibit higher levels of labour force participation than in most parts of the Third World and indeed these levels are often above those of many industrialized nations. Economic activity rates are highest in the French islands of Martinique and Guadeloupe and lowest in the Hispanic Caribbean (see Table 1.1, p.12). Within the Anglophone Caribbean, proportions are lower in Trinidad and Guyana where there are many people of Indo-Caribbean heritage. The last two decades have seen not only an increase in the proportion of women in the region's labour force but also a marked movement of women out of agriculture and into the service sector.

This high level of economic activity reflects a tradition of economic autonomy among Afro-Caribbean women which may be attributed to four historical factors. First, under slavery women were expected to perform much of the heaviest field labour and, second, after emancipation, male out-migration left many women alone to carry the burden of supporting their children (Momsen 1988). The restrictions on marriage enforced by slave owners weakened the conjugal ties while often leaving the mother-child bond intact, though recent research suggests that these effects may not have been as widespread as previously thought (Higman 1984). Sex-specific migration further encouraged the development of female-headed households. In the Eastern Caribbean, on average, 35 per cent of households are headed by women (CARICOM n.d.: Vols 1 and 3).

A third factor was access to land which enabled many female-headed households to survive economically because they had the resources for subsistence production. In the Eastern Caribbean women inherited land in their own right or were able to cultivate land belonging to migrant male relatives. Fourth, education, which has been widely available for the last century, has come to be seen by women as their main source of security.[1] In many cases where men have sought economic opportunity through migration, women have achieved it through education.

In this chapter I focus on the role that development level and structural adjustment play in determining women's participation in the labour force. In particular, I look at women's transition from small-scale agriculture to participation in the formal economy. Variation with levels of development will be demonstrated by using comparative data from the lesser and more developed islands of the Eastern Caribbean and by considering time series data for specific islands wherever possible.

Demas redefined development in the Caribbean as requiring both the capacity for self-sustaining growth and structural transformation of the economy. Sir Arthur Lewis in his dual economy model hoped that this transformation could be achieved through labour intensive 'industrialization by invitation', which would allow a capitalist sector to absorb the excess labour released from the subsistence sector. Lewis was one of the few Caribbean economists to consider the impact of development on women (Massiah 1990). He realized that the policy he proposed would have a very specific gender effect in the Caribbean as women moved from small-scale agriculture and other home-based work to factory work (see Chapter 17). The young women in the export-oriented factories of the free trade zones of Jamaica (Bolles 1983) and St Lucia (Kelly 1987) are contemporary examples of this phenomenon.

**Table 15.1: Social Benefits, Women's Economic Activity & Participation in Agriculture, 1980s**

| Territory | % women over 15 & economi- cally active | Women as % of agri- cultural workers | % of women in selected occupations | | | Government social benefit expenditure as % of GDP |
|---|---|---|---|---|---|---|
| | | | (A) | (B) | (C) | |
| Antigua & Barbuda* | 36.3 | 25.3 | 50.40 | 62.70 | 8.44 | n/a |
| Bahamas | 34.0 | n/a | 46.69* | 61.71* | 11.17* | 0.5 |
| Barbados | 60.4 | 41.7 | 48.96 | 60.55 | 26.65 | 0.9 |
| Belize | n/a | n/a | 53.63* | 46.30* | 9.65* | n/a |
| Cuba | 33.8 | 13.1 | n/a | n/a | n/a | 7.1 |
| Dominican Republic | 13.5 | 2.1 | 47.37* | 37.26* | 21.54* | 0.5 |
| Guyana | 27.7 | 10.3 | n/a | n/a | n/a | 0.8 |
| Haiti | 58.1 | 36.7 | 40.13 | 47.56 | 14.22 | 0.1 |
| Jamaica | 66.1 | 36.4 | n/a | n/a | n/a | 0.3 |
| Martinique | 50.0 | 27.8 | 57.68* | 72.95* | 10.26* | n/a |
| Montserrat | 47.7 | 22.0 | 49.20 | 65.79 | 14.28 | n/a |
| Netherlands Antilles | n/a | n/a | 42.84* | 52.13* | 10.41* | n/a |
| Puerto Rico | 26.2 | 2.6 | 52.70 | 52.98 | 20.95 | n/a |
| St Vincent | 41.2 | 41.0 | n/a | n/a | n/a | n/a |
| Suriname | 28.9 | 28.6 | n/a | n/a | n/a | 0.6 |
| Trinidad & Tobago | 33.4 | 17.5 | 49.61 | 53.49 | 11.74 | 0.3 |
| France | 44.2 | 33.5 | 41.40 | 62.06 | 15.58 | 18.6 |
| Netherlands | 30.8 | 15.6 | 38.84 | 53.17 | 7.51 | 21.7 |
| United Kingdom | 52.1 | 20.2 | 38.30 | 60.04 | 17.07 | 10.6 |
| United States | 50.2 | 19.9 | 48.90 | 64.87 | 18.51 | 7.0 |
| USSR | 61.3 | 52.0 | n/a | n/a | n/a | 13.7 |

* 1970 data; (A) Professional/administrative; (B) Clerical/sales/services; (C) Production/transport/labourers. *Sources*: United Nations (1989); Government of Montserrat (1984); Momsen (1988a: 88); Statistical Institute of Jamaica (1985).

Rising costs and resource depletion have made both agriculture and off-shore industrialization increasingly uncompetitive. Today many Caribbean countries see tourism as offering the only hope for the future. All these changes have affected women. In the light of the growing multipolarity of the world economy, McIntyre (1989: 8) states that: 'The large majority of Caribbean countries have to transform their patterns of development from one centred around the utilization of natural resources to one relying upon the utilization and upgrading of their human resources.' Yet in the 1980s many of the region's states were affected by the debt crisis and structural adjustment which made sustainable economic transformation difficult to achieve.

Girvan (1988: 18) calls structural adjustment 'the most influential development strategy in the English speaking Caribbean today'. Structural adjustment policies have led to cutbacks in government services which are both staffed by and utilized by women to a major extent (Antrobus 1989). Growing unemployment, rising prices for food and a reduction of social services have forced women into the 'invisible structural adjustment' (United Nations 1989) of coping strategies to protect their families.

Despite a commonality based on a long history of colonialism and a location on the periphery of the world economy, Caribbean states have different levels of wealth and nutrition (Table 1.1), and of social benefits (Table 15.1). Population size and fertility rates vary (Table 1.1) as does the relative importance of different sectors of the economy (Table 15.1). All these factors influence the economic role of women. By considering a small subset of Caribbean states in the Eastern Caribbean I hope to show the affect of economic development on gendered patterns of employment.

## Production & Reproduction

Women's work is not adequately represented in official statistics for a variety of reasons clearly delineated by Lourdes Beneria (1982). The Women in the Caribbean Project (WICP) showed that women themselves considered that work involved 'those activities which are necessary to the daily survival of themselves and their households, as well as those which earn an income' (Massiah 1986: 227). Many of the officially non-working women in Barbados and St Vincent in 1970 engaged in short-term income earning activity, usually small-scale agriculture or home craft working. Massiah calculates that if home production was taken into account it would raise the general worker rates of women in the WICP sample from 44.2 to 53.9 in Barbados, 48.3 to 62.6 in Antigua and from 32.6 to 48.6 in St Vincent (Massiah 1986: 230). Clearly this under-representation of women's economic role is most severe in St Vincent, the least developed of the three islands sampled, and least important in Barbados where the formal economy offers more opportunities (Table 15.1). Massiah (1986: 226) finds that work is considered by Caribbean women as a valued activity 'which not only has a positive impact on a women's sense of self but also makes a positive contribution to their societies'. The WICP also found that women valued work as a source of economic independence, a view echoed in Skelton's (1989) work in Montserrat.

Under slavery, economic activity rates for men and women were at the maximum. Slave women formed a majority in the field labour force on plantations towards the end of slavery but it was only after 1780, with technical and organizational changes in the sugar industry, that gender divisions of labour became marked (Morrissey 1989: 75). Women worked provision grounds in their own right and dominated the local trade in fresh produce. With emancipation and the introduction of choice, women were the first to leave the work-force but male migration and the growth of female-headed households led to a resurgence of high economic activity rates for women. According to the Census of 1891 between 57 and 78 per cent of British Caribbean women were gainfully employed. Between 1911 and 1921 in Barbados, during a period of high male migration to Cuba and Panama, women constituted over 61 per cent of the island's paid labour force.

The closure of many migration outlets, coupled with economic recession, forced women and men into direct competition for jobs. The economic discontent of the 1930s and the resultant labour riots led to the rise of trade unionism and eventually to a fundamental reorganization of the labour market. Wages determined by collective bargaining became the main regulator of the system and women were marginalized both in the unions and the labour force (see Chapter 16). This situation, as in post-war Britain, was accompanied by social pressures for women's role to be reinterpreted as centred on the home and children. W.A. Lewis notes this in his seminal article, 'The Industrialization of the British West Indies', in which he concludes that 'what has happened in the islands is that, as the population has grown, the number of jobs has failed to keep pace with it, and women have been forced to retire from industry in favour of men' (Lewis 1950: 4).

**Table 15.2: Barbados Labour Force Participation Rate**

| Year | Males | | Females | |
|------|-------|------|---------|------|
| 1891 | 55.0 |        | 58.8 |        |
| 1911 | 54.5 |        | 60.8 |        |
| 1921 | 57.4 |        | 62.1 |        |
| 1946 | 58.1 |        | 38.8 |        |
| 1960 | 47.6 |        | 27.5 |        |
| 1970 | 46.2 | (49.3) | 26.4 | (29.3) |
| 1980 | 48.1 | (51.6) | 32.2 | (37.5) |
| 1987 |      | (51.9) |      | (42.6) |

*Sources*: Adapted from Massiah (1984); CARICOM (n.d.: Vol. 3); and *Encyclopaedia Britannica* (1990). Early figures are based on the employed population over 15 years; figures in brackets utilize the economically active population over 15 years of age.

It is often suggested that female economic activity rates follow a 'U'-shaped curve along the trajectory from pre-industrial to post-industrial society. Consideration of the historical data from Barbados provides evidence of a possible 'U'-shaped curve of female economic activity, though the upturn of the curve has only occurred since 1970 after a 50 year decline (Table 15.2). Divergence between male and female rates of economic activity became apparent in 1946 and the first sign of a reversal of this trend came in the 1980 Census figures. Figures from the later part of the decade indicate an acceleration in this trend.

Massiah (1984) links these changes to the island's transition from an agricultural economy to one with a much more diversified base. The increase in economic activity for both sexes in 1980 reflects the growth in the proportion of the population of working age. The ratio of women to men workers is the highest recorded since 1921. The increase in economic activity was greater during the 1970s and 1980s for women than for men as a result of improved female education levels and an economy in which employment opportunities for women, especially in light industry and tourism, were expanding. Fertility rates also influence the extent of withdrawal from the labour market during the child-bearing years, emphasizing the importance of the intersection of women's reproductive and productive roles. There is some evidence that similar trends are found in other Eastern Caribbean territories, but their time series data are generally less complete than in Barbados.

Within each island there are spatial differences in female activity rates. In Barbados, the most urbanized parish (St Michael) does not exhibit the highest female employment rates. In 1960 the highest levels (averaging 50.2) were found in the northern parishes, i.e. in the most rural ones. By 1970 the highest rates were found in the southern parishes surrounding the city and were probably associated with employment in tourism. In 1980 the link with tourism was confirmed, for the highest female economic activity rates were recorded for the parishes of St James and Christchurch, which contained the main concentrations of tourist accommodation. This is quite different from the pattern found in Jamaica, where female employment decreases with distance away from major urban areas. The smaller size of Barbados and ease of communication, as well as the greater importance of urban-based industry and services as employers of women in the Jamaican economy may explain these differences. The spatial change in Barbados between 1960 and 1980 reflects the transfer of labour from agriculture into tourism.

## The Labour Market

The dual labour market theory has been used to explain why gender divisions of labour continue to exist. The formal/informal sector dualism developed by Hart (1973) provides a framework within which the many small-scale activities of Third World women can be fitted. However, in applying the dualist scheme to the Caribbean, Anderson and Gordon (1989) found that a tripartite model was necessary to describe the range of economic activity in the region. In particular they found that primary sector capital intensive industries in the Caribbean, such as the garment and electronics industries, which employ so many women, did not offer 'good' jobs. They propose a segmentation into primary and secondary formal sectors, differentiated by the skill level required, and an informal sector. Plantation agriculture is grouped with the secondary formal sector and small-scale agriculture with the informal sector.

Lynch (1989) suggests that the dependent nature of Caribbean labour markets means that explanations have to be sought outside the region in the working of the global economic system and the new international division of labour. This is undoubtedly true at the macro level but comparative studies of local labour markets can illuminate regional level explanations.

## Gender Divisions of Labour in Barbados & Montserrat

Data from more developed Barbados and less developed Montserrat will be utilized to examine the response of gender divisions of labour to changes in the structure of these island economies. Although official statistics offer only a partial picture of women's work, Massiah found that conventional census data do provide a valid reflection of the circumstances prevailing among women in the formal sector of the region's economies. She concludes that official data indicate that the incipient shift in the distribution of occupation categories among workers does parallel the industrial transformation of these economies (Massiah 1986: 228).

Montserrat and Barbados were selected for closer study because of the distinctiveness of their patterns of development and the availability of both census and field survey data. Both islands have moved from a dependence on agriculture, in which men and women were equally involved, to an expansion of light industry and a growing service sector dominated by health, education and tourism, all of which employ relatively high proportions of women. As Table 15.3 shows, the transformation in Montserrat occurred approximately a decade later than in Barbados.

**Table 15.3: Gender Division of Labour in Barbados and Montserrat by Occupation & Percentage of Labour Force**

| | BARBADOS | | | | | | | |
|---|---|---|---|---|---|---|---|---|
| | 1946 | | 1960 | | 1970 | | 1980 | |
| | M | F | M | F | M | F | M | F |
| Agriculture | 31.2 | 27.4 | 26.4 | 26.4 | 17.4 | 15.9 | 11.1 | 9.0 |
| Mining | 0.8 | 0.0 | 0.9 | 0.2 | 0.6 | 0.1 | 0.5 | 0.0 |
| Manufacturing | 21.4 | 17.8 | 17.9 | 11.5 | 16.0 | 14.0 | 12.0 | 20.4 |
| Construction | 15.4 | 0.8 | 17.4 | 0.7 | 21.3 | 0.9 | 16.5 | 0.8 |
| Electricity/ water | 0.7 | 0.6 | 1.5 | 0.1 | 2.1 | 0.3 | 2.0 | 0.2 |
| Commerce | 10.8 | 17.1 | 13.9 | 22.2 | 12.5 | 19.2 | 11.9 | 15.6 |
| Transport/com-munications | 6.3 | 0.2 | 8.2 | 0.8 | 8.4 | 1.8 | 10.0 | 3.4 |
| Services | 13.5 | 36.6 | 13.9 | 38.1 | 21.7 | 47.8 | 35.0 | 50.6 |
| *Index of Dissimilarity* | 29.6 | | 32.7 | | 32.8 | | 26.7 | |

| | MONTSERRAT | | | |
|---|---|---|---|---|
| | 1970 | | 1980 | |
| | M | F | M | F |
| Agriculture and Fishing | 20.1 | 20.7 | 12.6 | 7.2 |
| Mining and Quarrying | 0.6 | 0.0 | 0.3 | 0.0 |
| Manufacturing | 5.8 | 4.4 | 8.2 | 13.1 |
| Electricity/water | 2.0 | 0.5 | 2.6 | 1.0 |
| Construction | 34.1 | 2.1 | 25.3 | 0.8 |
| Commerce | 8.7 | 16.9 | 9.3 | 19.3 |
| Transport/communications | 7.2 | 2.2 | 6.6 | 2.7 |
| Services | 21.5 | 53.2 | 35.0 | 55.9 |
| *Index of Dissimilarity* | 40.5 | | 35.6 | |

*Sources*: Massiah (1984) and Government of Montserrat (1984)

In Barbados in 1946 the main economic activity for men was agriculture, followed by manufacturing, while for women service employment was more common than agricultural employment. By 1980 agriculture was of minor importance for both men and women, while service employment had become dominant for both sexes. As the nature of manufacturing has changed so have gender roles. In 1946 most men in this sector were employed by the sugar industry, while women worked mainly as dressmakers or seamstresses. By 1980 this sector had become relatively more important for women workers than for men because light assembly industry employing women replaced sugar manufacturing. The biggest changes occurred during the 1960s, when both sexes moved rapidly out of agriculture and into the service sector following the growth of tourism and the expansion of government jobs in the newly-independent nation. Modernization of the economy also created more jobs in the utilities and transport and communications industries. Commerce increased as an employer in the immediate post-war years for both sexes but declined relatively after 1960, though it remains the third largest sector for women workers. Construction reached a peak in 1970, reflecting the demand at that time for new facilities for Barbadians and tourists and the availability of former agricultural workers, but it has remained dominated by men.

In Montserrat, where a high proportion of men left the island in the 1950s and early 1960s, women became numerically dominant throughout the civil service, in teaching and in the financial sector. In a 1972 survey it was found that women operated 44 per cent of the small farms but this proportion had fallen to 32 per cent in 1983, after much male return migration (Momsen 1988: 88). There was an increase in the proportion of the adult population recorded as economically active from 57.5 per cent in 1970 to 63.6 per cent in 1980 (Government of Montserrat 1984). This change was the result of higher participation rates for women which rose from 37.4 per cent in 1970 to 50.3 per cent in 1980 while rates for men fell from 82.2 per cent in 1970 to 78.3 per cent in 1980. Between 1970 and 1980 employment in agriculture almost halved while employment in services trebled and industrial jobs increased by one-fifth. Montserratian women were quick to seize the opportunity offered by these new jobs and many moved into the formal economy for the first time. Consequently the number of women officially recording home duties as their main occupation fell from 43 per cent to 26 per cent of adult women over the inter-censal period.

## Economic Activity & Fertility

The movement of women out of small-scale agriculture and into the formal economy has gone hand in hand with the fertility transition (see Table 1.1). In his study of Barbados, Handwerker (1989) feels that the fertility transition there has been a function of the increasing proportions of women who view childbearing as entailing consumption expenditures. This, in turn, is related to the changes in the workings of the labour market with the opening of new and competitive access channels. These changes have enabled women to perceive themselves differently. Prior to 1960 women could improve their access to resources only by bearing children. Women hoped that their children's fathers would provide support and that eventually the children themselves would be the financial providers for their mothers (see Chapter 6). Now, with improved educational and economic opportunities, women have become 'agents, who can chart their own course in life' (Handwerker 1989: 121). However, Handwerker notes that it is crucial to distinguish fertility declines that result from fluctuations in economic conditions from fertility declines that result from the social conditions that bring about the fertility transition.

In Montserrat, the increase in the female participation rate was a response to deliberate government policy in the 1970s, when it was realized that there was a need to make young female workers available in order to attract footloose assembly industries. This was done by providing day care centres for the children of single mothers and nursery facilities for all children between the ages of three and five (Skelton 1989). It was found that employers preferred women workers as they felt them to be 'more stable in this society, [for] they have to take care of families and [so] they tend to be much more reliable' (Skelton 1989: 215). Thus in Montserrat the opportunity costs of children for working women have been reduced. In Barbados child care facilities are less widely available and are spatially concentrated in Bridgetown, but Hall (1987) found that half of all women interviewed would use nurseries if these were available.

Skelton's survey of employed women in Montserrat (Skelton 1989) found that only one-third had grown up in households with both parents, and most were now limiting their own fertility. However, women in rural areas who were not in paid employment were less likely to use contraception. Many still held the traditional view that women are born with a fixed number of children they have to bear and that having children is part of the rite of passage to full womanhood. Recent increases in fertility rates in Montserrat (Government of Montserrat 1984) probably reflect improvements in the economic situation on the island and a more equal sex ratio rather than the major social change that Handwerker feels is necessary for the fertility transition to occur.

## Female Labour Mobility

Anderson and Gordon (1989), in their study of labour market mobility in Jamaica, found a high degree of stability with 80 per cent of their sample being immobile between sectors over the period 1979-1984. They also found that stability was greatest in the central government sector, the secondary formal sector and in agriculture. Women were less mobile than men except in the informal sector. It might be expected that studies over a longer time period, especially one which incorporated rapid structural transformation of the local economy, might reveal different patterns of mobility. Time series data from Barbados and Montserrat are used to test this.

In Montserrat women workers moved out of agriculture faster than men in the 1970s and are now concentrated in the service sector, commerce and manufacturing, while men are mainly employed in services and construction. Male return migrants tend to invest in small businesses, employ other former migrants and produce for export (Jones 1988). A useful summary of sex segregation in the workforce is the Index of Dissimilarity, derived from the positive percentage point difference between the male and female occupational distributions. This index gives us the proportion of one sex that would have to move out of its present occupation in order for the distribution to be gender neutral. In analysing Jamaican data, Gordon (1989) found very little change between 1943 and 1984, but in Barbados inter-censal change is very noticeable. Table 15.3 shows that dissimilarity in the Barbadian labour force increased up to 1970 but fell rapidly in the next decade as the proportion of women in the work-force increased. In like fashion, for Montserrat the Index of Dissimilarity declined between 1970 and 1980 indicating a decrease in occupational segregation as the female labour force expanded.[2]

Despite this very rapid response to the transformation of the island's economy by Montserratian women, a 1987 survey (Skelton 1989) showed that 46 per cent of women interviewed had had stable careers. Not unexpectedly, those jobs that demanded high levels of training, such as teaching and nursing, were the most stable, while the new recruits to manufacturing had either been unemployed or had come from domestic or service work. In the sample only two agricultural workers had moved into agri-industry, weaving the sea island cotton grown on

Montserrat. The most unstable occupations were clerical and service jobs. On the whole, as W.A. Lewis had predicted, the new jobs in garment manufacturing and data entry firms were filled by women who had previously been unemployed or in temporary or part-time jobs.

Various attempts have been made to establish if development changes society's attitudes to the suitability of certain types of jobs for women or if the traditional view is retained in which women's productive jobs in the labour force are seen as extensions of their reproductive work. Skelton (1989) found that 53 per cent of the women she interviewed would like to change their job while a further 17 per cent would like to remain in the same economic sector but with a different job. Health care, mainly nursing, was the main field that women would have liked to move into and, even here, only one woman wanted to be a doctor. The second most popular field, computing and accounting, was less traditional. On the other hand, many of the women working in the data-entry firms wished to become secretaries.[3] The fourth most popular option, especially for women in the civil service and banking, was to start their own business. There is some indication that among the more successful women non-traditional jobs are being considered.

Surveys of children's aspirations were carried out in both Montserrat and Nevis. In Montserrat almost half the girls interviewed wanted to be teachers, while the next most popular occupations were nursing, secretarial work and accounting (Skelton 1989). It was felt that these girls were strongly influenced by the existing role models on the island. Olwig (1987) found a less realistic view of job possibilities in terms of the likelihood of obtaining the necessary training among children on Nevis. However, career aims were still largely on traditional lines even though most Nevisian children expected to have to go overseas because of the lack of local opportunities on this largely agricultural island. Clearly, despite female sex ratios in most of the region (Table 1.1) gender divisions of labour are firmly established in society.

## Divisions of Labour in Small-Scale Agriculture

To understand the changes in reproductive work, which are occurring at the same time as the changes in the paid labour force in these small transitional economies, the focus will now narrow down to small-scale farmers in St Vincent, Nevis, Montserrat and Barbados. As Table 1.1 shows, St Vincent is the poorest island in the Eastern Caribbean while Barbados has the highest per capita Gross Domestic Product. The percentage of women small farmers ranges from 46 per cent in St Vincent to 26 per cent in Barbados (Table 15.4).

On these small islands the separate identity of rural and urban areas is much less marked than in most parts of the world. Farm families are often involved in urban employment even while they continue to cultivate the land. Women on these farms may have several occupations in addition to their domestic duties: they may be the decision maker on the farm or they may assist the farm operator by providing labour, they may sell farm produce or they may work in a non-farm job in order to support the household. Individuals may fulfil all these roles during their lifetime, but they are more likely to do so sequentially than simultaneously. Occupational multiplicity is far less common among women farmers than among men. In both Nevis and Trinidad one-sixth of women small farmers were found to have off-farm jobs (Henshall 1984), whereas in the 1987 Barbados survey 28 per cent of women farmers, virtually the same proportion as in 1963 (Aspinall and Momsen 1987), worked off the farm mainly in clerical, banking, hotel or domestic jobs. These figures are considerably higher (as are the figures noted by Brierley for Grenada in Chapter 12) than those found in the WICP, where only between 4 and 6 per cent were recorded as having more than one job.

**Table 15.4: Women Small Farmers in the Eastern Caribbean**

| Island | Year of Survey | Sample Size | % of Women Farmers |
|---|---|---|---|
| Barbados | 1963 | 207 | 53.1 |
| Barbados | 1987 | 126 | 25.8 |
| Grenada | 1969 | 256 | 20.7 |
| Grenada | 1982 | 186 | 20.4 |
| Martinique | 1964 | 203 | 35.5 |
| Martinique | 1981 | 17919 | 20.0 |
| Montserrat | 1972 | 527 | 44.2 |
| Montserrat | 1985 | 136 | 27.9 |
| Nevis | 1950 | 205 | 29.2 |
| Nevis | 1979 | 91 | 30.8 |
| Nevis | 1985 | 407 | 39.3 |
| St Lucia | 1964 | 187 | 42.8 |
| St Lucia | 1980/81 | 7520 | 23.0 |
| St Vincent | 1972 | 6862 | 46.2 |
| Trinidad | 1979 | 80 | 28.8 |

*Sources*: Momsen (1988a: 83-100) and Brierley, Chapter 12 of this book.

The distinctiveness of this small-farm subset of working women can be seen most clearly when the results of the two surveys in Barbados are compared. Despite the 24 year gap during which the island's economy had been transformed, the 1987 survey, which was designed to replicate the earlier one, showed that not only were the same proportion of women farmers working off the farm but the jobs they did had not changed very much. Work as a sugar plantation labourer was still the single most common job, though its overall dominance had declined somewhat. In general, the pattern of social class among small farmers, as reflected in employment, had remained surprisingly static with one-fifth of farmers surveyed in both years holding permanent, pensionable professional or civil service jobs (Aspinall and Momsen 1987). On the other hand, women farmers are still more likely than men to depend for a large proportion of their income on remittances, usually from family members working abroad (Momsen 1986).

In St Vincent and Nevis, two of the least developed islands, fewer women than men have skilled off-farm jobs, but in more developed Barbados there is little gender difference in skill levels of employment. Recent changes in the economy of Montserrat do not appear to have effected the small farming sector and the women entering these new jobs no longer farm even part time. Farming in the poor islands of Nevis and St Vincent is important for both family subsistence and a cash income and so is attractive to young people, especially men (Byron 1987; Glesne 1986). In Barbados there is an expanding hobby farming sector which allows those with full-time off-farm jobs to enjoy their own fresh produce. Montserrat appears to be transitional between these two groups of islands.

## Gender Divisions of Labour Time

The local context, household structure and stage in the family cycle are all determinants of gender divisions of hours worked. However, there is considerable evidence that women have less leisure, greater intensity and fragmentation of work, and more frequent recourse to multiple simultaneous occupations than men. Women small farmers often work a 16-hour day starting well before sunrise. Work occupies some 80 per cent of their waking hours and many feel they have no leisure time at all.

### Table 15.5: Weekly Hours Worked On & Off Small Farms by Farm Operators

BARBADOS

| Age | Male N=34 | | | | Female N=12 | | | |
|---|---|---|---|---|---|---|---|---|
| | Farm Peak | Work Low | Off-farm Work | Peak Total | Farm Peak | Work Low | Off-farm Work | Peak Total |
| 20-34 | 25 | 25 | 34 | 59 | 10 | 8 | 45 | 55 |
| 35-49 | 10 | 6 | 45 | 55 | 17 | 13 | 26 | 43 |
| 50-64 | 31 | 18 | 32 | 63 | 51 | 33 | 16 | 67 |
| 65+ | 22 | 16 | 4 | 26 | 17 | 14 | 0 | 17 |

NEVIS

| Age | Male N=71 | | | | | Female N=28 | | | | |
|---|---|---|---|---|---|---|---|---|---|---|
| | Farm Peak | Work Low | Off Work | Mark-eting | Peak Total | Farm Peak | Work Low | Off Work | Mark-eting | Peak Total |
| 20-34 | 46 | 39 | 4.7 | 0.3 | 51 | 31 | 19 | 3 | 0.6 | 34.6 |
| 35-49 | 54 | 43 | 5.8 | 0.8 | 60.6 | 33 | 20 | 3.3 | 5.1 | 41.4 |
| 50-64 | 37 | 26 | 18.4 | 2.4 | 57.8 | 25 | 16 | 1.3 | 4.6 | 30.9 |
| 65+ | 37 | 31 | 3.3 | 1.6 | 41.9 | 27 | 22 | 1.8 | 4.9 | 30.7 |

Sources: Barbados fieldwork 1987; Nevis fieldwork 1979.

Time is the scarcest resource for most Third World women (Momsen 1988). The CAFRA Women in Caribbean Agriculture Project found that, in addition to agricultural labour, farm women in St Vincent spent between five and ten hours a day on domestic work, 65 per cent of which was child care, while in Dominica women spent between three and ten hours a day, of which 38 per cent was child care (French 1989/90: 12). Where there were young children in the household the daily hours spent on domestic tasks were at the higher end of the spectrum. There was evidence of a relationship between the age of the children and the ability to carry out farm work, with land left uncultivated because of the time demands of young children. Dominica has a better provision of basic facilities and larger households than St Vincent and it was felt that these factors played an important role in determining the average burden of domestic work in rural households. In the survey it was noted that the maximum assistance with housework provided by men amounted to an average of 24 minutes a day. Thus, individual women may have benefited in the extended households, which made up 35 per cent of those surveyed in Dominica, where the household chores could be shared between several adult women, whereas in St Vincent only 18 per cent of households were extended.[4]

These relationships should be kept in mind when Table 15.5, which shows hours spent on farm and off-farm work, is considered. For agricultural work, the relative time input of men and women varies with the economic status of the farmer, the type of farming, seasonality of labour demand, the amount of off-farm employment and the sex of the farm operator. The population described in Table 15.5 has little internal differentiation in terms of economic status or type of farming, but the other variables are taken into account. Because of the small sample size in Barbados too much reliance should not be put on the data for that island, but when considered in tandem with the other tables, Table 15.5 does provide a broad understanding of the situation.

In both islands mean hours of farm work recorded for men are greater than those for women but most women would spend an additional four to eight hours a day on child care, meal preparation and housework. Time spent on household duties is less in Barbados because of the smaller number of children in the family (one child on average per Barbadian family compared to a mean number of 2.3 in the Nevisian families surveyed) and the much wider availability of piped water and electricity in Barbadian homes. It is believed that this accounts for the difference between the average 35 hours a week women in Nevis spent on farm work and the 46 hours spent by Barbadian women. The CAFRA project also found that in St Vincent, where the burden of domestic tasks was greatest, women spent fewer hours than men on farm work, while in Dominica they spent as long or longer than men in the fields. Differential domestic loads also account for the gender differences in Barbados and Nevis in hours spent in farm work and paid employment: men in Barbados work only four hours more than women but in Nevis male work hours exceed those of women by an average of 12 hours a week. Clearly the time demands of household chores have a direct affect on the amount of work women are able to do on Caribbean small farms.

The use of female labour as a reserve work-force to cope with peak demand is shown by the much greater seasonal decline in hours worked on the farm for women than for men: low season hours for women in Barbados are 70 per cent of peak compared to 77 per cent of peak for men, and in Nevis low season hours for women are 66 per cent of peak versus 81 per cent of peak for men. Brierley found similar patterns in Grenada (see Chapter 12) with women's low season hours being 73 per cent and men's 83 per cent of peak hours.

## Conclusion

Development in the Caribbean is accompanied by the increased economic activity of women. Higher levels of education, declining fertility rates, improvements in household facilities and structural transformation of economies are facilitating women's access to paid work. There is some evidence that the rapid growth of women in the work-force is resulting in a less rigid gender division of labour. However, domestic responsibilities remain a heavy burden for women. Recent structural adjustment policies have resulted in high female unemployment rates and may lead to renewed 'housewifization' (Reddock 1989) and re-feminization of small-scale agriculture (Momsen 1987) as women search for new survival strategies for their families. The traditional economic autonomy of Caribbean women makes the dual burden of reproductive and productive work ever more onerous in the face of economic uncertainty.[5]

## Notes

1   In Montserrat, in 1980, a higher proportion of women than men under 34 had completed secondary
    education (CARICOM n.d.: Vol. 1, 70). In Barbados, in 1980, 14.5 per cent of adult women but only 12.2
    per cent of men, as compared to 6.3 per cent of women and 7.0 per cent of men in 1970, had passed
    some secondary school leaving examinations. It is also noticeable that although there are more adult
    men than women with university degrees in the Barbadian population, for the cohort aged 15 to 24 in
    1980, there are more women than men with a university education (CARICOM n.d.: Vol. 3, 30-1).
2   In Chapter 6 Dagenais shows that female occupational segregation, although decreasing in Guade-
    loupe, is still much greater there than in metropolitan France.
3   In her work in Jamaica, Pearson (Chapter 19) found a similar aspiration pattern.
4   Sylvia Chant (1987) also noticed this beneficial effect of extended families on the time demands of
    housework in her study of Queretaro in Mexico.
5   I would like to thank the second year geography students of Newcastle University who helped with
    data collection in Barbados in 1987. Fieldwork in Nevis was funded by the Social Sciences and
    Humanities Research Council of Canada and in Montserrat and Nevis by the Nuffield Foundation.

## References

Anderson, P. and D. Gordon (1989) 'Labour Mobility Patterns: The Impact of the
    Crisis'. In G. Beckford and N. Girvan, *Development in Suspense*, Jamaica:
    Friedrich Ebert Stiftung, 174-97

Antrobus, Peggy (1989) 'Gender Implications of the Development Crisis'. In G.
    Beckford and N. Girvan (eds) *Development in Suspense*, Jamaica: Friedrich Ebert
    Stiftung, 145-60

Aspinall, R.J. and J.D. Momsen (1987) 'Small-Scale Agriculture in Barbados 1987'.
    Seminar Paper No. 52, Department of Geography, University of Newcastle
    upon Tyne

Beneria, Lourdes (ed.) (1982) *Women and Development: The Sexual Division of Labour
    in Rural Societies*. New York: Praeger

Bolles, A. Lynn (1983) 'Kitchens Hit by Priorities: Employed Working-Class
    Jamaican Women Confront the IMF'. In June Nash and M. Patricia Fernandez-
    Kelly (eds), *Women, Men and the International Division of Labour*, Albany: State
    University of New York Press, 138-60

Byron, Margaret (1987) 'Vegetable Production in Nevis'. Unpublished B.A. disser-
    tation, Plymouth Polytechnic, England

CARICOM (n.d.) *1980-1981 Population Census of the Commonwealth Caribbean.
    Montserrat, Vol. 1*. Kingston: Statistical Institute of Jamaica

——— (n.d.) *1980-1981 Population Census of the Commonwealth Caribbean. Barbados,
    Vol. 3*. Kingston: Statistical Institute of Jamaica

Chant, Sylvia (1987) 'Family Structure and Female Labour in Queretaro, Mexico'.
    In J.H. Momsen and J.G. Townsend, *Geography of Gender in the Third World*,
    London: Hutchinson, 177-93

*Encyclopaedia Britannica* (1990) *Britannica Yearbook*. Chicago: Encyclopaedia Britan-
    nica Inc.

French, Joan (1989/90) 'The Women in Caribbean Agriculture Project'. *CAFRA
    News*, 3 (4) 4-28

Girvan, Norman P. (1988) 'Notes on the Meaning and Significance of Develop-
    ment'. In Patricia Mohammed and Catherine Shepherd (eds) *Gender in
    Caribbean Development*, 10-20

Glesne, Corrine (1986) 'Inclusion and Incorporation in Agricultural Production:
    The Case of Young Vincentians'. Paper presented at the Conference on Gender
    Issues in Farming Systems, Research and Extension, University of Florida,
    Gainesville, February

Gordon, Derek (1989) 'Women, Work and Social Mobility in Post-War Jamaica'. In Keith Hart (ed.), *q.v.*, 67-80

Government of Montserrat (1984) *9th Statistical Digest 1984*. Montserrat: Statistics Office

Hall, Lisa (1987) 'Women Farmers in Barbados'. Undergraduate dissertation, Department of Geography, University of Newcastle upon Tyne

Handwerker, W. Penn (1989) *Women's Power and Social Revolution: Fertility Transition in the West Indies*. London: Sage Publications.

Hart, J.K. (1973) 'Informal Income Opportunities and Urban Employment in Ghana'. *Journal of Modern African Studies*, 11 (3) 61-89

Hart, Keith (ed.) (1989) *Women and the Sexual Division of Labour in the Caribbean*. Kingston, Jamaica: The Consortium Graduate School of Social Sciences

Henshall (Momsen), Janet (1984) 'Gender versus Ethnic Pluralism in Caribbean Agriculture'. In C. Clarke, D. Ley and C. Peach (eds) *Geography and Ethnic Pluralism*. London: George Allen & Unwin, 173-92

Higman, Barry W. (1984) *Slave Populations of the British Caribbean, 1807-1804*. Baltimore: Johns Hopkins University Press

Jones, Lewis W. (1988) 'The Impact of Return Migration on the Economic Development of a Small Caribbean Island: The Case of Montserrat'. Undergraduate dissertation, Department of Geography, University of Newcastle upon Tyne

Kelly, Deidre (1987) *Hard Work, Hard Choices: A Survey of Women in St Lucia's Export-Oriented Electronics Factories*. Barbados, Occasional Paper No. 20. Institute of Social and Economic Research, University of the West Indies

Lewis, W. Arthur (1950) 'The Industrialization of the British West Indies'. *Caribbean Economic Review*, 2 (1) 1-51

Lynch, Roslyn (1989) 'Gender and Labour Market Theories: A Review'. In Keith Hart (ed.) *q.v.*, 29-46

Massiah, Joycelin (1984) *Employed Women in Barbados: A Demographic Profile, 1946-1970*. Occasional Paper No. 8, Institute of Social and Economic Studies, University of the West Indies, Barbados

—— (1986) 'Work in the Lives of Caribbean Women'. *Social and Economic Studies*, 35 (2) 177-240

—— (1990) 'Defining Women's Work in the Caribbean'. In Irene Tinker (ed.) *Persistent Inequalities*, Oxford: Oxford University Press, 223-38

McIntyre, Alister (1989) 'The International Economic Situation: Elements for a Policy Agenda'. In G. Beckford and N. Girvan (eds) *Development in Suspense*, Jamaica: Friedrich Ebert Stiftung, 1-10

Momsen, Janet (1986) 'Migration and Rural Development in the Caribbean'. *Tijdschrift voor Economische en Sociale Geografie*, 77 (1), 50-8

—— (1987) 'The Feminization of Agriculture in the Caribbean'. In J.H. Momsen and J.G. Townsend (eds) *Geography of Gender in the Third World*, London: Hutchinson, 344-7

—— (1988) 'Gender Roles in Caribbean Agricultural Labour'. In M. Cross and G. Heuman (eds) *Labour in the Caribbean*, London: Macmillan, 141-58

—— (1988a) 'Changing Gender Roles in Caribbean Peasant Agriculture'. In J.S. Brierley and H. Rubenstein (eds) *Small Farming and Peasant Resources in the Caribbean*, Winnipeg: Department of Geography, University of Manitoba

Morrissey, Marietta (1989) *Slave Women in the New World*. Lawrence: University Press of Kansas

Olwig, Karen Fog (1987) 'Children's Attitudes to the Island Community: The Aftermath of Out-migration on Nevis'. In J. Besson and J. Momsen (eds) *Land and Development in the Caribbean*, London: Macmillan, 153-72

Reddock, Rhoda (1989) 'Historical and Contemporary Perspectives: The Case of Trinidad and Tobago'. In Keith Hart (ed.) *q.v.*, 47-66

Skelton, Tracey (1989) 'Women, Men and Power: Gender Relations in Montserrat'. Unpublished Ph.D. thesis, University of Newcastle upon Tyne

Statistical Institute of Jamaica (1985) *The Labour Force 1984*. Kingston: The Statistical Institute of Jamaica

United Nations (1989) *1989 World Survey on the Role of Women in Development*. New York: United Nations

# PART 2
# Urban Employment

Even before the ending of slavery women workers outnumbered men in many Caribbean towns although they were concentrated in a very narrow range of occupations, as domestic servants or vendors. They have continued to take advantage of urban employment opportunities and in post-war years have moved out of agriculture faster than men. Today women workers dominate in the fastest growing sectors of manufacturing and services and in the informal economy. However, the recession of the last decade has led to the loss of formal sector jobs accompanied by higher unemployment rates for women than for men. Throughout the Caribbean, many women have turned to the informal sector for survival, particularly to such occupations as petty trading and prostitution.

Female economic activity rates, which as late as 1921 were higher than male rates fell rapidly until around 1960. This may be seen as related to the 'housewifization' process identified in most industrial capitalist societies. However, recent Census statistics show a marked decline in those women who are recorded as being employed only in home duties.

Even when women take leading roles in fighting for their rights as workers, men usually come to occupy the senior positions in labour organizations. Patriarchal attitudes in society make it difficult for women to achieve managerial positions or to seek jobs outside the accepted stereotypes and this situation is little affected by differences in ethnicity or nationality between employers and workers. Women are still concentrated in job ghettoes of occupations considered suitable such as teaching, nursing and other services or assembly-line manufacturing in export processing zones. As argued by Pearson, changing this gender division of labour will not be easy.

# XVI Transformation in the Needle Trades: Women in Garment & Textile Production in Early Twentieth-Century Trinidad

RHODA REDDOCK

The predominance of females was one of the most striking characteristics of the urban areas of early twentieth-century Trinidad and Tobago. In the Victorian era, when middle-class women were expected to stay at home and be seen and not heard, the working-class women of Trinidad and Tobago were able to exercise relative freedom. And these women played an important role in political action and revolt during this period.

According to de Verteuil (1884: 169-70), the higher ratio of females to males was evident in urban areas as early as 1851, when 'the proportion was in the towns, 100 females to about 74 males; and in the rural districts, 100 males to about 75 females'. In 1884 he described a situation in which there were 106 females to 100 males in Port of Spain and San Fernando, but only 76 females to 100 males in the rural areas. He sought an explanation (de Verteuil 1884: 170) in the gender division of labour. 'The gathering of females in towns may be explained by the following considerations: females are customarily more employed as household servants than males. ... There is, in addition to this, a very large proportion of washerwomen, seamstresses, hucksters, cigar makers and petty traffickers who more than compensate for the number of tailors, shoemakers and other artisans of the male sex.'

This chapter[1] is about one group of these working women, namely the seamstresses or dressmakers. The participation of women in garment and textile production must be a central feature in any reconstruction of the history of women's labour and struggles. As the historian of women's labour history, Ivy Pinchbeck (1981: 111) notes: 'From the earliest times the productive work of women has been of greater importance in the textile industries than in any other trade.' The textile and garment industry has, with few exceptions, been the most consistently 'feminized' of all industries. In this process of feminization the value of labour power is cheapened. This situation was recognized as early as the nineteenth century in England where male workers, through their trade unions, sought to stop women from taking over their jobs and thus lowering the wages of the entire industry. A high degree of female participation in a particular occupation has this effect because women have a subordinate position on the labour market, for their wages are assumed to be supplementary to those of male bread-winners.

Garment production, however, is affected by additional factors. Most young girls are trained in the skills of needlework at home or at school, so a constant pool of skilled and semi-skilled labour is always available. This fact is not usually recognized and garment and textile production is often viewed as a low or unskilled occupation and the skills needed seen as merely natural manual dexterity. Another characteristic of the garment industry is its high labour intensity.

According to Safa (1981: 420) 'Cheap labour is essential for labour-intensive industries because they are highly competitive.' The garment industry is, of course, one of the most competitive, for its comparatively simple technology, low capital investment and pre-trained staff facilitates the relatively easy entry of new firms. Competition within the industry is also reinforced by the nature of the products. This is because garments, particular women's garments, have a high turnover rate as a result of changes in fashion and demand from one period to another.

But the factors mentioned above also mean that firms can leave the industry as easily as they can enter it. The 'dispensability' of the female labour force is thus another important factor. This flexibility now inherent in the nature of female wage labour has been determined by women's relationship to the family and her reproductive role, which is seen as her primary occupation. Any other occupation carried out in addition to this is seen as secondary. As a result, unemployed women can disappear into the family and not even appear in the unemployment statistics.

## Dressmaking 1900-31

During the late nineteenth and early twentieth centuries, garment production was totally in the hands of petty commodity producers. J.N. Brierley, writing in 1912 about Trinidad, mentions the existing industries as comprising the production of Angostura Bitters, carriage building, cigar and cigarette making, furniture, match and soap making, a tannery, a brewery and an electric printery, but no mention is made of a garment industry. Similarly in the *Trinidad & Tobago Blue Books* of 1903-4, 1914-15, 1921 and 1937 no mention is made of the existence of a garment industry.[2] Yet, according to Jack Harewood (1975: 143), during this period dressmaking was the occupation of 95 per cent of the skilled female workers in Trinidad and 84 per cent of the combined group of skilled and semi-skilled employed women. In 1891 a total of 9000 dressmakers was recorded and this number rose to over 10,000 in 1901 and over 13,000 in 1911.

**Table 16.1: Estimated Expenditure per Fortnight of a Family (US$)**

|                   | 1914   | 1920    |
|-------------------|--------|---------|
| Food              | $4.98  | $10.51  |
| House Rent        | .46    | .46     |
| Clothes           | .68    | 1.99    |
| Medicines         | .04    | .10     |
| Tools             | .27    | .11     |
| Furniture         | .07    | .19     |
| Fuel, lights etc. | .47    | .90     |
| TOTAL             | $6.81  | $14.42  |

In such a situation, the control that dressmakers had over the production of garments was very real. As Table 16.1 indicates, the Wages Commission report of 1920 showed that after food, clothes were the second most expensive item on the budget of a working-class family, defined as a man, a wife and three children.[3]

But among the middle and upper classes a market also existed to supplement clothes imported from France and Britain. The society in the towns then as now was extremely fashion conscious and the skilful production of garments was very important. At this period it should be noted that even undergarments were not factory produced.

As a rule dressmakers worked in their own homes. In some instances clients would visit them there but in the majority of cases dressmakers first went to the home of the client (middle and upper class) and there took measurements and discussed the work and the price. After having cut and possibly stitched the cloth the dressmaker then walked again to the house of the client for a fitting. When the garment was completed, it would be delivered to the customer. According to a contemporary of this period (de Boissière 1982):

> They charged in accordance with the means of the customer and their own social station. If a dressmaker lived in a room in a yard she would charge perhaps 60 cents to make a dress. If in a house she might charge $1.20, $1.80, $2.40, $3.00 depending on the type of dress and the days spent on it. If it took five days the charge might be $2.40, if two days perhaps $1.80.

In some cases payment was not instant. The dressmakers would often have to wait months before being paid and consequently were often in a precarious financial situation.

**Table 16.2: Trends in Occupations of Females Aged 10 Years & Over, 1891-1946**

| Occupations | 1891 | 1901 | 1911 | 1921 | 1931 | 1946 |
|---|---|---|---|---|---|---|
| Agricultural labourers | 22,651 | 24,172 | 28,425 | 29,292 | 18,722 | 8,131 |
| General labourers | 4,510 | 4,565 | 4,915 | 6,672 | 3,146 | 1,353 |
| Dressmakers/seamstresses | 9,177 | 10,601 | 13,156 | 13,109 | 8,774 | 8,917 |
| Total skilled crafts | 9,577 | 10,917 | 13,407 | 13,110 | 9,364 | 9,317 |
| Personal service | 14,849 | 19,900 | 21,295 | 25,348 | 21,511 | 17,525 |
| Professional service | 745 | 976 | 1,405 | 1,105 | 2,189 | 3,077 |
| Clerical workers | 18 | 76 | 170 | 121 | 805 | 3,263 |
| Sales workers | 2,452 | 2,888 | 3,568 | 5,317 | 4,448 | 4,689 |
| Population gainfully occupied | 56,716 | 65,814 | 77,210 | 85,565 | 63,750 | 52,956 |

*Source:* Report on the Manpower Situation in Trinidad and Tobago No. 1, Ministry of Labour, 1959

Unfortunately little information exists on labour organizations during this period. It is known that dressmakers, along with hundreds of other urban women, participated in the water riots of 1903 and the 1919 labour disturbances and that one of the 11 women wounded and admitted to hospital in 1903 was Benita Hernandez, a 27 year-old seamstress of 51 Prince Street, Port of Spain. In addition, the Trinidad Workingmen's Association (TWA) organized after 1919 had a seamstress section.[4] Other sections included waterfront workers, porters, shipwrights, iron workers, domestic servants, clerical workers, clerks and agricultural workers. In addition there were at one point three women's branches.

Between 1921 and 1931 the number of dressmakers in Trinidad fell from over 13,000 to less than 9000 (Table 16.2) and this decline largely accounts for the reversal of the earlier expansion of female employment in manufacturing. It should also be noted that the majority of these urban seamstresses were of African descent.

Most Indians at this period lived in rural areas and agriculture was the main
occupation of Indian women. This distinction is illustrated in Table 16.3. In 1931,
however, despite the overall decline in employed women, the total number of
women in the towns still exceeded that of men, possibly because domestic service
continued to occupy large numbers of women.

**Table 16.3: East Indian Population: Gender Differences in Selected
Occupations, 1931**

| Occupations | Male | Female | Total |
|---|---|---|---|
| Agricultural labourers | 24,638 | 11,326 | 35,964 |
| Domestic servants | 304 | 949 | 1,253 |
| Laundresses | - | 32 | 32 |
| Seamstresses | - | 274 | 274 |

The reasons for the decline in female employment after 1912 are not openly
apparent, but the answer could lie in the effects of the post-war depression on the
country and the decline in agriculture. There was a fall in the general level of
employment but, as today, women were the worst affected. This led to a high rate
of emigration of women, mainly to the United States, in the early 1920s. *The Labour
Leader*, the newspaper of the Trinidad Workingmen's Association, noted in 1923
that 'a review of the passenger lists for the last six months showed that 90 per cent
were women'.[5] The paper called on the Trinidad government to remedy the situation by providing adequate means for women to earn a living and also asked the
Colonial Office to send a Royal Commission to investigate the situation.

### The Transition to Factory Production

This was the period when in Trinidad and Tobago, using local capital and
entrepreneurship, the process of industrialization of garment production began.
The manufacture of shirts was the first type of garment production to be taken
over by small factories. The first known shirt factory, Copeland's, was started in
the early 1930s. The development of this factory illustrates very clearly the process
of transformation from independent petty-commodity production to factory
production. Nick Copeland, who was of Syrian origin and had previous knowledge of shirt-making, started operations in the store of his friend Mr Antonio in
Park Street, Port of Spain. He took cloth on consignment from the big stores of the
time, such as Stephens & Todd and Millers, and used a counter in Mr Antonio's
store as a cutting table. After being cut, the shirts were taken to the homes of
dressmakers to be stitched. As business developed some women began to bring
their personal sewing machines to the shop so that they could sew there. After a
while Copeland leased a property at the corner of Park and Pembroke Streets,
bought his own machines and material and employed more workers. At first only
shirts were produced. They were made of fine cotton, had removable collars and
sold for six cents each. Originally each worker sewed an entire shirt but eventually
there was a change to piecework and the firm diversified into pyjama production.

This initial enterprise of Nick Copeland was the seed from which the local
industry developed. It led to his sister, Philippa Jean Mahanna Haddaway,
coming to Trinidad and starting the Renown shirt and pyjama factory.[6] Similarly

Matthew Reynold Gonzalves, who later became president of the Trinidad and Tobago Garment Manufacturers' Association, came from St Vincent to Trinidad in 1940 to work at the Copeland garment factory as a cutter. After one year, he started his own business it is said 'with two girls under his house and using a bicycle to deliver his goods'.[7] By the end of the 1930s there were four small plants employing 50 to 100 predominantly female workers each, in addition to 'homeworkers' producing for the factories, giving a total of 642 women working from 8.00 a.m. to 5.00 p.m. for 60 cents a week (Lowe 1977: 2; *The Empire* 1939: 152; *The People* 1939: 2; Calder-Marshall 1939: 39).

**Table 16.4: Production Processes**

| | |
|---|---|
| 1 | stitching on labels |
| 2 | putting on yokes |
| 3 | sewing the yokes to the back of the shirts |
| 4 | sewing the back to the front of the shirt |
| 5 | addition of the pockets |
| 6 | addition of the shoulders |
| 7 | putting on the sleeve piece and the sleeves |
| 8 | closing the sides |
| 9 | putting on cuffs |
| 10 | putting on collars |
| 11 | hemming |
| 12 | trimming |
| 13 | pressing |

The 1940s saw the consolidation of factory production and a further decline in the number of self-employed seamstresses. In 1944-5 the Copeland garment factory ceased operations and was purchased by a consortium of Haddaway, Sampson and Sabga and was then known as Premier Garments Ltd. Other factories also developed with larger buildings and more modern machinery. The Second World War acted as a boost to production. Jang Bahadoorsingh, for example, is known to have supplied the local contingent of the US army with military uniforms. In 1948 the Shirt Manufacturers' Association was founded with the aim of procuring advantages for the members through bulk purchasing of raw materials and to gain tariff protection for the industry (Lowe 1977: 2).

Over this period wages had increased from six cents a shirt in the early 1930s to 60-72 cents per week in 1939. Although the labour force was predominantly female, the sexual division of labour in the factory was such that certain jobs, those of layers, cutters and draughtsmen, were done by men. An ideology developed, which was occasionally challenged by women, that only men could do those 'skilled tasks', which received higher wages. In the production of garments the above piecework process took place (Table 16.4) and workers were paid per dozen units. At each stage the work was checked by supervisors; most of whom were women. Only the men were given training for their 'skilled' jobs.[8]

Little information on the conditions of work or even on the wages of shirt and garment workers at this time can be found. Even today the conditions of work in the garment industry are worse than in many other industries. Contemporary government reports, such as the Trinidad and Tobago Annual Report or the Administrative Report of the Industrial Adviser, give details of wages and conditions in the sugar and oil industries and in government employment, but little or nothing on the predominantly female shirt and garment industry.

One factor that must be noted in this discussion is the racial characterization of the industry. The factory owners, with few exceptions, came from the group of Jews and Syrian-Lebanese who entered the country in the pre- and post-war period and took over local entrepreneurial leadership. The period around 1930 was one of heightened racial consciousness among people of African descent in Trinidad and Tobago, fuelled by the Italian invasion of Ethiopia. The majority of garment workers apart from those in the Jang Bahardoorsingh factories were of African origin and the combination of poor working conditions and racial opposition to the foreign factory owners led to great militancy on the part of the garment workers during this period.

## Organization & Struggle

As noted earlier in this chapter and elsewhere (Reddock 1980), women of Trinidad and Tobago have always participated in socio-economic and political struggles on their own behalf and on behalf of their society. So too in the garment industry this was no exception. Unfortunately the struggles of the garment workers in 1939, for example, have received no previous attention from labour historians. This is even more surprising as this was one of the first real industrial trade union struggles in the country involving a number of factories.

In this particular case the strike began on 20 June 1939 at the Renown shirt factory. It occurred after a breakdown in negotiations between the owner Mahanna Haddaway and the Shop Assistants' and Clerks' Union. According to one source (*The Empire*, October 1939: 152) she resisted the union's modified demands of a 12 per cent increase for piece rate and part-time workers. After seven days the workers of other factories (Sabga's, Briks & Chizer and Straumwasser shirt factories) came out on strike in sympathy with their sisters at Renown. But, in addition to this, the owner's maid and cook also walked off their jobs in solidarity with the striking garment workers. Page 3 of *The People* of Saturday 1 July described the situation in these words:

SHIRT FACTORY WORKERS GO ON STRIKE: Maid and Cook Join in Walk Out
Up to yesterday the workers at Renown Shirt Factory were still on strike. While the employers of the other two above-mentioned factories showed a conciliatory disposition, it is alleged that the attitude of the management of the Renown factory is far from encouraging. The maid and cook of Mrs Mahanna Haddaway, proprietress, walked out on Thursday morning to show their solidarity with the garment workers.
On Wednesday afternoon the girls paraded the streets of Port of Spain displaying posters. They were cheered by onlookers. Their claim is for increases ranging from six to twelve cents per dozen for shirts and of five cents per dozen for pyjamas.
An officer of the union told *The People* yesterday morning that the girls were determined to hold out to the bitter end.

This strike became the centre of paternalistic attention from local trade union leaders and colonial officials interested in instituting 'trade unionism' in the colonies. This is of course not to underestimate the great strength and militancy of 'the girls', as they were referred to, which apparently surprised their male colleagues. Thus *The People* of 8 July 1939 was headlined 'RENOWN SHIRT FACTORY TO BE BOYCOTTED: Industrial Adviser's Effort at Conciliation Fails: Captain Cipriani Fails' and added: 'All the trade unions have pledged assistance and until the management of Renown factory agree to a satisfactory arrangement all products of the factory will be boycotted and all stores displaying Renown-made garments will be boycotted.' The article went on to state that at a crowded meeting on Wednesday 5 July, leading trade unionists including Messrs O'Connor, Arneaud and Duprey of the Shop Assistants' and Clerks' Union, Jack of the Public Works and Public Service Workers' Union, Harper of the Seamen's Union and Clement Payne of the United Workers' Freedom Committee were 'making strong appeals to the audience to continue to give *the girls* their support. All labour leaders except Cipriani were helpful and fully supported the strike. On Wednesday and Thursday attempts were made to break the strike by police accompanying strike breakers' (my emphasis). One poster read 'Labour must be Paid, Before Large Profits Made' and they sang *Follow* [sic] *Christian Brothers*.

On the request of the United Workers' Freedom Committee, John Jager MP[9] raised issues related to the strike in the British Parliament and in October that year, *The Empire*, official journal of the Fabian Colonial Bureau, carried a report of the strike headlined 'TRINIDAD: FIRST STRIKE OF WOMEN WORKERS: Victory After 14 Days':

> The victory was due to the significant and unexpected courage of the striking *girls* and the support both of the public and of the trade unions. Membership of the union, which caters for the distributive trades, has been increasing by leaps and bounds as a result of the strike, which focused the attention of all classes of workers on the benefits of trade unionism. A salutary effect has also been noticed on unionism throughout the Colony generally. .... It is highly significant that young women who have had drilled into them the idea that demonstrations are unseemly should have had the courage to man the picket lines. Instead of losing caste they have won the admiration of their fellow workers in other lines who regard them as having proved themselves to be true trade unionists.

(emphasis added)

It is interesting to note that in the recording of this event the names of countless men who supported the struggle have been mentioned but no mention has been made of any woman save *the girls*. By their struggle they were able to gain 12 per cent increase in wages; an eight hour day; two weeks annual holiday after one year; protective clothing for pressers supplied by the employer and the establishment of a system of shop floor representation.

During the strike Quintin O'Connor, general secretary of the Shop Assistants' and Clerks' Union, lost his job as a hardware clerk for, among other reasons, having been on the picket line at the Renown garment factory. After this he joined the Federated Workers Trade Union (FWTU), which had been formed in 1937 and the former union was made a branch of the latter. In the late 1940s and early 1950s, therefore, the majority of garment workers were represented by the FWTU.

## Post-War Industrialization 1947-60

The post-war period 1947-60 saw the initiation and establishment of the programme of import-substitutive industrialization or 'industrialization by invitation' in Trinidad and Tobago. Although W.A. Lewis published his famous essay 'The Industrialization of the British West Indies' in May 1950, activities leading in this direction had begun earlier. For example, as early as 1941 a local industries committee had been established and, years later in 1947, the then governor Sir John Shaw set up a committee under his chairmanship 'to survey the fields of finance, economics, production and development of local industry' (Armstrong 1960: 17). The interim report of this committee submitted in 1948 recommended the establishment of an industrial board with the following functions (Armstrong 1960: 17):

(a) To explore the possibility of establishing new industries;

(b) to examine applications for assistance from private enterprise wishing to expand or

(c) to advance such funds as are available to approved applicants.

These recommendations reinforced the pre-1950 industrialization attempts described in the preceding section which had been largely undertaken by resident entrepreneurs dependent on locally raised capital. To a large extent these attempts fitted in with the positions taken by the Fabian socialist-oriented British Labour Party of the post-war period. Within the Colonial Development and Welfare Programme operational during this period 'the development of local manufactures on an economic basis' (West Indian Royal Commission 1945: 64) was a long term activity aimed at shifting dependence from agricultural production. As one writer (Brailsford 1945: 27) put it:

> In both cases we realize that the first remedy is to acclimatize here, preferably in the villages, suitable industries which will employ the surplus labour now squandered in uneconomic methods of cultivation. Fewer hands in India must raise more wheat; those released from useless toil in the fields must build houses and weave cloth. This argument is equally applicable to Africa. The first enterprises to encourage are obviously processing industries based on the local crops, spinning and weaving of cotton and the making of pottery and furniture.

Thus between 1947 and 1950 legislation was passed aimed at supporting local manufacturing. These laws included the Income Tax (in aid of Industry) Ordinance of 1947 and 1950 and in March 1950 the enactment of the Aid to Pioneer Industries Ordinance, No. 13 of 1950. This ordinance among other things provided for an income-tax holiday for five years, exemption of taxes on dividends to shareholders for seven years and exemption from customs duty on building materials and equipment for five years.

The industrialization by invitation programme advocated by W.A. Lewis (himself a Fabian) in 1950 introduced much more forcefully the question of the use of foreign capital. This model was based on the Puerto Rican model of industrialization. In his justification of this model of industrialization for the region, Lewis used the drastic decline in the participation of the Caribbean female population in wage employment. He noted (Lewis 1950: 3-4):

> In the first place, women have retired from employment into the home. Thus, in Jamaica, the ratio of gainfully occupied women to total number of women between the ages of 15 and 60 has declined from 78 per cent in 1911 to 50 per cent in 1943. The same thing has happened elsewhere, for example in the Leeward Islands, where the proportion of gainfully occupied women to women of 10 years and over declined from 73 per cent in 1891 to 48 per cent in 1946. ... Actually we can see from the Census that much of this female retirement from industry is not voluntary but compulsory. ... What has happened in the islands is that, as the population has grown, the number of jobs has failed to keep pace with it, and women have been forced to retire from industry in favour of men.

In his recommendations of industries to be initially established, Lewis used the following criteria listed in order of importance: ratio of wages to gross output; indices of fuel consumption; horse power and average size of establishment. Using these criteria, his stated concern about women's employment and his own stated recognition that 'women's wages are lower than men's' (Lewis 1950: 20) it is no surprise therefore that textile and garment-related industries comprised a large section of those industries recommended by him as *most favourable*. They included the production of hosiery, lace, textile packing, tailoring, mackintoshes, aprons, corsets, shirts, millinery and hats (Lewis 1950: 26). Further down in his list under *medium favourable*, he included weaving, textile finishing and the production of wool, silk and linen. In his further explanation of this list he goes on to stress that, of the 42 favourable industries recommended, those that offered the greatest opportunities were hosiery, leather, the garment industries, footwear, china, the paper trades, glass, building materials, canning and the textile industries. Thus in this period the Trinidad garment industry, which had been founded in the previous decade, received its political and economic justification, leading to an even greater degree of mass production in the country.

**Table 16.5: Real Output in Value Terms of Production in Textiles, Clothing & Other Consumer Goods (TT$m.)**

| 1951 | 8.5 | 1956 | 16.2 |
|------|------|------|------|
| 1952 | 9.8 | 1957 | 18.8 |
| 1953 | 12.2 | 1958 | 21.2 |
| 1954 | 12.4 | 1959 | 23.1 |
| 1955 | 13.6 | 1960 | 22.4 |
| | | 1961 | 25.3 |

*Source:* Rampersad (1964: 33)

It is ironic that this strategy had the opposite effect with regard to the employment of women. The period 1946-60 saw a further overall drop in the female participation rate in manufacturing from 11,358 in 1946 to 9899 in 1960 (Harewood 1960a: 149), from 21.7 per cent of the female working population in 1946 to 14.3 per cent in 1960. There was an increase in the total number of male and female paid employees. But for women the subsequent decrease in the number of 'own account' (self-employed) workers and the increase in 'unpaid family workers' was much more significant (Harewood 1975: 146). Thus in the industrialization process in this period, despite Lewis's initial concern, the most adversely affected were the women workers. The changes in the relations of production within the garment industry contributed greatly to this situation, which was described by Jack Harewood (1975: 150) in these words:

It has been pointed out that the decline in female employment in manufacturing is more than accounted for by the fall in employment in dressmaking. Thus while the industry group sustained a fall of 1500 in female employment, the decline in dressmaking was 4200 (from 8800 to 4600). Also while male employment in manufacturing increased there was a significant fall in employment in the clothing industry while the two most important industries — sugar refining and petroleum refining — both had significant increases in employment.

Under these conditions it is not surprising that garment and textile manufacture expanded greatly during this period. According to one source, production in this group (along with other consumer goods) between 1951 and 1961 showed 'a very high and sustained rate of growth' (Rampersad 1964: 33) with an average annual rate of 10.4 per cent which was significantly higher than that of the rest of manufacturing industry (see Table 16.5). In addition to an increase in the number of wage-employing establishments, this period also saw greater diversification in the types of garments produced, as illustrated in Table 16.6.

As would be expected 90 per cent of the workers in the garment industry continued to be women with the exception of small numbers of men employed as cutters, particularly in firms producing men's clothes. The majority of women were in the age group 15-45 years and they operated a highly developed piecework system. In 1948, the Factories Ordinance (Ch. 30 No. 2 of 1948) was passed

**Table 16.6: Employment, Wages & Salaries in the Trinidad Garment Industry in 1953 (TT$)**

*Tailoring & Dressmaking*

| | | |
|---|---:|---|
| Number of establishments | 18 | |
| Number of working proprietors | 21 | |
| Number of administrative, technical and clerical staff | 47 | TE* $ 77,000 |
| All other employees | 257 | TE* $173,000 |
| Number of wage and salary earners engaged | 304 | |
| Total wages and salaries paid ($) | 250,000 | |
| Average earnings per person engaged ($) | 821 | |
| Payments to Employers Pension & Provident Fund ($) | 1,000 | |
| Gross output ($) | 1,022,000 | |
| Net output ($) | 597,000 | |

*Manufacture of Shirts & Pyjamas*

| | | |
|---|---:|---|
| Number of establishments | 14 | |
| Number of working proprietors | 16 | |
| Number of administrative, technical and clerical staff | 45 | TE* $ 68,000 |
| All other employees | 601 | TE* $276,000 |
| Number of wage and salary earners engaged | 646 | |
| Total wages and salaries paid ($) | 343,000 | |
| Average earnings per person engaged ($) | 530 | |
| Payments to Employers Pension & Provident Fund ($) | nil | |
| Gross output ($) | 2,337,000 | |
| Net output ($) | 844,000 | |

*Manufacture of Other Wearing Apparel*

| | | |
|---|---:|---|
| Number of establishments | 6 | |
| Number of working proprietors | 6 | |
| Number of administrative, technical and clerical staff | 23 | TE* $ 41,000 |
| All other employees | 390 | TE* $214,000 |
| Number of wage and salary earners engaged | 413 | |
| Total wages and salaries paid ($) | 255,000 | |
| Average earnings per person engaged ($) | 618 | |
| Payments to Employers Pension & Provident Fund ($) | n.k. | |
| Gross output ($) | 1,823,000 | |
| Net output ($) | 937,000 | |

*Source:* Trinidad & Tobago Central Statistical Office (1957: 53). TE* = Total Earnings

setting down standards of working conditions and of facilities for clothing, washing, sanitation and first aid.[10] However, these have seldom functioned in the interests of the workers. The Annual Statistical Report of 1957 shows that with the exception of the copra industry, which had average annual earnings of $472, the garment industry had the lowest average earnings at $821, $530 and $618, when the general average for all industries was $1269 per annum (Table 16.6). In fact in 1958 Jack Harewood noted that the workers with the lowest average earnings in non-agricultural firms were in the service sector, including commerce at $632 per year and in the manufacture of wearing apparel at $641 per year (1960a: 116). In another publication (Harewood 1960) he supported this by stating that in 1957 there were very few female workers earning $600 and over. This low level of earnings must also be examined in relation to the high rate of growth experienced by the industry during this period.

## Organization & Struggle

Numerous efforts were made to organize the garment workers during the period 1947-60. One of the earliest of these attempts was made by Quintin O'Connor, then of the Shop Assistants' and Clerks' Union. The name of O'Connor is almost synonymous with the organization of garment workers, for it is well documented that he was fired from his job as a sales clerk after joining the picket lines at the Renown garment factory in 1939. The period of the late 1940s and 1950s saw an increase in the number of unionized garment workers, but, despite their low wages and poor working conditions, many did not join unions. The Safie textile mills of Arima (later Texstyle Mills),[11] a North American firm enjoying 'pioneer status', was one of the worst examples of a non-unionized work place.

In the early 1950s, wages councils (on the earlier instigation of Cipriani and the TLP) were established to deal with problems of extremely low wages. According to one respondent, this criterion was linked to those areas of work where predominantly female workers were employed.[12] Some unions regarded these as a threat to union organization, but the FWTU participated in this as a means of 'seek[ing] relief for women in the garment and laundry industry', one real problem being the fact that low-waged workers were unable to pay the union dues. The joint wages councils were empowered to fix minimum wages and conditions of work that were statutory. Over and above this, unions could still bargain and negotiate wages and conditions. The minimal character of the wages and condi-tions laid down by the joint wages councils was such that garment and textile workers continued to suffer some of the worst conditions of all workers in the country. The women workers in many instances struggled to improve their situ-ation by going on strike. This happened in another strike at the Renown factory, as a result of which it ceased operations, at the Elite shirt factory and, in 1952, at the Safie textile mills in Arima. During this period the state, by means of the police, brutally crushed the workers' strike action.

The strike at the Safie textile mills, possibly the first in Arima, was notable in that it started without a union. At a public meeting under a shop opposite the Arima market, the predominantly female workers from this factory agreed to go on strike to protest against their low wages and poor working conditions, including high dust levels. The way in which the situation unfolded was characteristic of the majority of struggles in which women workers predominated. Rather than organize themselves, they turned to experienced politicians and trade unionists, such as John La Rose of the Workers' Freedom Movement, to lead their struggle. In discussing this experience La Rose recalled that he led the march singing the traditional 'Solidarity forever [three times], the union makes us strong'. However, during the march itself the women changed the words to 'Safie underpaying workers [three times], Safie must pay'. The manager refused to meet a delegation and at that point a union, the FWTU, was introduced. The strike brought a few gains, but very little improvement in overall conditions. As in 1939, the names of the men leading the strike were recorded in the newspapers of the day, but there was no mention of specific women.

In 1953, under pressure from the British Trades Union Congress, mainly through the second visit of F.W. Dalley (Brereton 1981: 229), unionization expanded. The FWTU affiliated to the ICFTU and, with this, came affiliation to the International

Ladies Garment Workers' Union (IGLWU), which at this time supported the US garment manufacturers' investment in low-wage Caribbean countries as a means to union solidarity.[13]

Because of its 'orthodox' trade union methods, during the late 1950s and 1960s the FWTU lost its membership, first to W.W. Sutton's Amalgamated Workers' Union (AWU) and, later, to Vas Sanford's Union of Commercial and Industrial Workers (UCIW).[14] The UCIW first organized the workers at the Maidenform factory, which produced almost entirely for export. It then went on to reorganize factories formerly organized by the AWU and FWTU (including the Elite shirt factory and the MICO and Premier garment factories) and thus became the main union for the organization of garment workers in the country. In 1960 the UCIW's membership fee was $TT3.00 and its union dues were 25 cents a week. In addition to the larger unionized establishments, however, there were also smaller non-unionized ones employing workers under even worse conditions.

## Conclusion

A study of the period 1900-60 shows the transformation in the social relations of production from independent petty commodity production, to small local factory production and, finally, to large-scale mass production for export. Throughout the entire period independent dressmakers or seamstresses continued to exist, though in varying numbers. Today all three forms of production coexist and women still comprise the majority of the work-force. One difference in the current situation, however, is that more women are now accepting or demanding leading positions in their own struggles, as in the case of Gertrude Philips, president of the Texstyle branch of the All Trinidad Sugar and General Workers' Trade Union, which staged the longest strike in the history of Trinidad and Tobago (from 1979 to 1982).

Despite the struggles that have been fought and continue to be fought, and despite the fact that many firms in the 1980s were operating under the US '807' programme,[15] the predominantly female garment and textile industry continues to offer low wages and poor working conditions. Although similar situations occur elsewhere in the world (see Gomez and Reddock 1987), the history of women workers has attracted surprisingly little attention and generated very little data.

Another familiar pattern is that in which women are lauded for their militancy, yet allow the leadership of their struggles to be taken over by men. By properly identifying what factors reproduce this situation, future struggles could bring about more fundamental changes.

## Notes

1  An expanded version of this chapter was published under the title 'Women and Garment Production in Trinidad and Tobago 1900-1960', *Social and Economic Studies*, 39 (1) 89-125, March 1990.
2  Catherine Lowe (1977) notes that in the 1930s there were three small plants employing around 50 employees each. No specific date of inception was given.
3  We see here the analysis of the Trinidad and Tobago working class in terms of the colonial stereotype of the conjugal nuclear family. They, however, go on to assume the employment of both women and children in the estimation of a minimum wage (p. 7).
4  The Trinidad Workingmen's Association (TWA) was originally formed in the 1890s from among artisans and labourers. After the 1919 strike some of its leading members were deported and Captain A.A. Cipriani became president. It was a workers' organization and never a trade union, though around 1935 two of its sections came to be referred to as unions. Its name was eventually changed to the Trinidad Labour Party (TLP).

5 'The Exodus from Trinidad: Women Leading the Way', *Labour Leader*, 12 May 1923: 2; 'The Exodus from Trinidad: Again They Go', *Labour Leader*, 26 May 1923: 12.
6 Interview with close associate of Mr Copeland who prefers to remain anonymous, 29 October 1981.
7 Interview with Marjorie Wilson, then trade union organizing officer UCIW.
8 Interview with Babsie Craigwell, garment worker for over 30 years, 13 August 1981.
9 John Jager was a former member of the Arbitration Tribunal into wages in the oil industry in December 1938 and January 1939. While there he met trade union leaders and activists including those of the Shop Assistants' and Clerks' Union.
10 Interview with Joseph Grannum, former member of the Federated Workers' Trade Union, 10 November 1981.
11 Ibid.
12 Ibid.
13 Ibid.
14 Interview with Marjorie Wilson, Grievance and Organizing Officer of the UCIW.
15 Under the '807' programme, cut garments are exported from the US for stitching and finishing in the Caribbean and then re-exported to the US.

## References

Armstrong, W.E. (1960) 'The Impact of Industry Development on the Economy of Trinidad and Tobago'. *ISS Research Paper*, 8 E-P

Brailsford, H.N. (1945) 'Socialists and the Empire'. In Rita Hinden (ed.) *Fabian Colonial Essays*, London: George Allen & Unwin

Brereton, Bridget (1981) *A History of Modern Trinidad 1783-1962*. London: Heinemann

Brierley, J.N. (1912) *Trinidad: Then and Now*. Trinidad: Franklin's Electric Printery

Calder-Marshall, A. (1939) *Glory Dead*. London: Michael Joseph Ltd

de Boissière, Ralph (1982) Personal communication, 24 May

de Verteuil, L.A.A. (1884) *Trinidad: Its Geography, Natural Resources, Administration, Present Condition and Prospects*. London: Cassell & Company (2nd ed.)

*Empire, The* (1939) 'First Strike of Women Workers: Victory after 14 Days'. October

Gomez, Ofelia and Rhoda Reddock (1987) 'New Trends in the Internationalization of Production: Implications for Female Workers'. In Rosalind Boyd, Robin Cohen and Peter Gutkind, *International Labour and the Third World: The Making of a New Working Class*, Aldershot: Avebury/Gower Publishing Group

Harewood, Jack (1960) *Employment in Trinidad and Tobago 1960*. Institute of Social and Economic Research, Population Census Research Programme Publication, 5, Kingston

—— (1960a) 'Overpopulation and Underemployment in the West Indies'. *International Labour Review*, 82 (2), 1-32, August

—— (1975) *The Population of Trinidad and Tobago*. CICRED Series for World Population Year 1974, Trinidad

Lewis, W.A. (1950) *Industrial Development in the Caribbean*. Caribbean Commission, Port of Spain

Lowe, Catherine (1977) 'The Growth of the Garment Industry in Trinidad and Tobago'. Caribbean Studies thesis, University of the West Indies, St Augustine

*People, The* (1939) newspaper, 1 July 1939 and 8 July 1939 issues

Pinchbeck, Ivy (1981) *Women Workers and the Industrial Revolution 1750-1850*. London: Virago Press

Rampersad, Frank (1964) *Growth and Structural Change in the Economy of Trinidad and Tobago 1951-1961*. Kingston: Institute for Social and Economic Research

Reddock, Rhoda (1980) 'Industrialization and the Rise of the Petty Bourgeoisie in Trinidad and Tobago'. Unpublished master's thesis, ISS, The Hague

Safa, Helen I. (1981) 'Runaway Shops and Female Employment: The Search for Cheap Labour'. *Signs*, 7 (2) 413-33

*Trinidad & Tobago Blue Books* (1903-4; 1914-15; 1921, 1937). London: Colonial Office
Trinidad & Tobago Central Statistical Office (1957) *Annual Statistical Digest*, 7
West Indian Royal Commission 1938-39 (1945) *Statement of Action Taken on the
Recommendations*. London: HMSO, Cmd 6656

# XVII  Gender & Ethnicity at Work in a Trinidadian Factory

KEVIN A. YELVINGTON

Learn that the world is waiting to drag you down. 'Woman luck de a dungle heap', they say, 'fowl come scratch it up'. But you save yourself lest you turn woman before your time, before the wrong fowl scratch your luck.

—Erna Brodber
*Jane and Louisa Will Soon Come Home*

The conjunction of ethnicity, class and gender is a part of everyday life in Trinidad. It permeates every social situation and depends on day-to-day activity for its social existence and meaning.[1] In this chapter I focus on three aspects of gender and ethnicity in social relations in a factory in Trinidad. These are the composition and structural positions of the members of the work-force; the role and forms of supervision supporting the organization's economic imperatives; and social relations between the workers. Sociological analyses of female workplace behaviour have often failed to consider the nature and implications of sexual divisions in industry (Brown 1976: 39). Here I intend to redress that imbalance by suggesting the existence of an interplay between structural and symbolic properties.

## The Factory & its Setting

This chapter is based on a year's participant observation in Trinidad, from July 1986 to July 1987.[2] During that period I worked (without pay) alongside the factory workers described below and generally tried to immerse myself in their extra-factory lives. I thus studied not only their workplace behaviour, but also their various 'survival strategies'.

Essential Utensils Ltd (EUL)[3] was established in 1972 by Nigel Tiexiera, a white Portuguese Creole with a master's degree from a Canadian university and his wife Jane, who comes from a well-known and wealthy French Creole family. Since the introduction of the Aid to Pioneer Industries Ordinance in 1950, industrialization in Trinidad and Tobago has been mainly the province of the Industrial Development Corporation (IDC). The Tiexieras applied to the IDC for a factory building and were allocated one on the Diego Martin Industrial Estate.

When a subcontracting agreement with a US multinational ended, Essential began to produce similar items under its own brand name. At that time (1980) it was one of the few locally-owned firms to be exporting its products and, in the early 1980s, it won the Prime Minister's Export Award. The firm began by exporting to the Caribbean Economic Community (CARICOM), but during the 1980s expanded into Central and South America. By 1986 it was exporting its products to 24 countries.

Diego Martin is a district north-west of the capital, Port of Spain, and its bound-aries extend from Four Roads to the north coast. The area can now be considered a suburb of Port of Spain: every working day commuters into 'town' must leave by 6.30 a.m. to avoid the rush hour traffic jam, which is reminiscent of major North American cities. It is an area of wide income disparities, with modern air-condi-tioned houses with high fences and guard dogs existing alongside 'board houses' (dwellings built on wooden stilts and made from plywood, two-by-fours or pine planks). A Caribbean Conference of Churches report (1986: 81) identified 'pockets of poverty' in the area. Ethnically, the area has been predominantly Creole (see Table 17.1), but the proportion of East Indians is increasing. It includes several churches of various denominations, including Spiritual Baptist and Orisha places of worship, one or two mosques and, in recent years, a Hindu temple has been built.

**Table 17.1: Ethnic Breakdown for Diego Martin & Trinidad & Tobago**

| Ethnic Group | Diego Martin | Trinidad & Tobago |
| --- | --- | --- |
| Black | 53.0% | 40.8% |
| East Indian | 11.6 | 40.7 |
| Mixed | 27.5 | 16.3 |
| White | 4.5 | 1.0 |
| Chinese | 1.4 | .5 |
| Other/not stated | 1.6 | .6 |
| Syrian/Lebanese | .4 | .1 |
|  | 100.0 | 100.0 |

Source: Compiled from the 1980 census report

The industrial estate is the site of the area's only manufacturing industry. Besides Essential there are factories manufacturing car batteries, nylon stockings, kitchen appliances, plastic signs and ice cream cones. In addition, there are three garment manufacturers. These factories are similar to Essential in that most of the work-force is female and lives nearby.

## Workforce Characteristics

Until it began to break down at the turn of the century, Trinidad had a long history of an ethnic division of labour (Yelvington 1985). The ethnic composition of the work-force at Essential is anachronistic and somewhat reminiscent of Edgar Mittelholzer's (1950) *A Morning at the Office*. The owners are white, most of the office workers are white, Chinese or 'high brown', the accountant is East Indian, most of the floor supervisors are white and the line workers are black or East Indian.

There is, of course, a sexual division of labour. The majority of Essential's line workers are female. As can be seen in Table 17.2, 52 of the 63 line workers (or 82.5 per cent) are females with ages ranging from late teens to mid-forties. The remainder are young men in their late teens and early twenties. There is one 35-year-old male toolmaker with a 20-year-old male assistant, who are both East Indian. The floor supervisors are all males aged between about 30 and 50. Among the female workers, 71 per cent are black and 25 per cent are East Indian. There are five East Indian and six black male line workers. Three of the eight floor supervisors are East Indian, the rest are white. One supervisor is Dutch and one is a white Jamaican, the rest were born in Trinidad.

**Table 17.2: Age, Sex & Ethnicity of Factory Line Workers**

| Age | Sex | Black | East Indian | Mixed | Totals |
|-----|-----|-------|-------------|-------|--------|
| 16-25 | M | 6 | 4 | 0 | 10 |
|       | F | 17 | 9 | 2 | 28 |
| 26-35 | M | 0 | 1 | 0 | 1 |
|       | F | 6 | 2 | 0 | 7 |
| 36-50 | M | 0 | 0 | 0 | 0 |
|       | F | 15 | 2 | 0 | 17 |
| Totals | M | 6 | 5 | 0 | 11 |
|        | F | 37 | 13 | 2 | 52 |

The workers all come from urban working backgrounds, but differ in their 'life situations' and personal circumstances. Only a few of the supervisors have had any formal technical training. Ruud, for instance, who trained as an engineer in the Dutch Navy, is responsible for keeping complex machinery in working order. And Vishnu, the toolmaker, can be described as a highly-skilled worker. The others merely seem to have acquired general mechanical skills from having worked on cars, which they apply to some of the less complex, relatively antiquated machinery in the factory. All the male line workers, except one, live in households with a parent and other extended kin. These young men have completed at least some secondary schooling, but only Terry, a 20-year-old, has any 'O' levels. A few are taking night courses at the John Donaldson technical training college in Port of Spain, including Ben, the assistant toolmaker.

The women's educational and skill backgrounds are different from those of their supervisors. Only two of the female workers over 26 have any secondary school education. None have any technical training as such, but several have completed courses in crafts such as dressmaking and cake-icing. It should be said, though, that some of the more experienced female workers are expected to maintain and know how to repair the machines with which they work and in this area they tend to be more skilled than their supervisors.

Of the younger women, more than half have some secondary school experience. A few have taken craft courses, while others are involved in technical and commercial training. For example, during the period of my fieldwork, Imogen, 19, was completing an electrician's course in Laventille at a Catholic organization, Servol, which specializes in vocational training. Many of these workers were far better placed than their mothers, who were often domestic servants and, in having continuous employment, some had even improved on the positions their fathers had held at corresponding periods of their lives.

Most of the women over 30 are in residential mating relationships, i.e. consensual cohabitation or legal marriage. About 95 per cent of the female workers over 25 have children. Some of the female workers are the main breadwinners of the household, as some of their menfolk have been retrenched recently due to the wider economic crisis in the country, the 'recession', as Trinidadians call it: the country was 20 per cent poorer in 1986 than in 1982. The pattern is for younger women, even if they have children, to live in the same household as their older kin. Table 17.3 shows the position of the labour force in 1986. Between 1970 and

1984, female participation in the labour force increased by 3.5 per cent, compared to a 1 per cent decrease for men during the same period (Trinidad & Tobago 1987: 49), although by 1977 women's median monthly income was only 65 per cent of men's (Hyacinth 1979: 16-17).[4]

**Table 17.3: Population, Labour Force & Employment Estimates, 1986**

|  | (Thousands) | | |
|  | Both Sexes | Male | Female |
| --- | --- | --- | --- |
| Total population | 1199.2 | 600.2 | 599.0 |
| Non-institutional population | 1195.2 | 598.0 | 597.5 |
| Population under 15 years | 398.5 | 202.6 | 195.9 |
| Population 65 years and over | 66.8 | 30.4 | 36.4 |
| Dependency ratio (%) | 63.0 | | |
| Non-institutional population 15 years and over | 795.2 | 394.6 | 400.6 |
| Labour force | 471.2 | 316.3 | 154.9 |
| Labour force participation (%) | 59.0 | 80.0 | 39.0 |
| Employment | 393.2 | 265.9 | 127.3 |
| Unemployed | 78.0 | 50.3 | 27.7 |
| Unemployment rate (%) | 16.6 | 15.9 | 17.9 |

*Source*: Trinidad & Tobago 1987b (Review of the Economy 1986 and appendix 16)

It is difficult to say what will happen as the recession deepens. The government, which directly employs between 40 and 50 per cent of the country's work-force, is beginning to reduce the number of its employees. If this is done on the basis of seniority, we can assume that most of those affected will be women. On the other hand, during the later years of the 1980s the government enacted policies which seemed to favour the more traditional of the industrial employers of women. While overall unemployment in garment, textile and footwear production went from 8 to 25 per cent between 1985 and 1986, local garment manufacturers increased their work-force from 2500 in November 1987 to 5000 in November 1988. This was due to new duty-free concessions, a ban on foreign clothes and a task force created to clamp down on the illegal import of goods. One manufacturer is quoted as saying (*Trinidad Guardian*, 21 December 1988: 3): 'This is a phenomenal turn around in an industry once considered dead. It is probably the most vibrant industry in the economy today.'

## Gender at Work

To understand why this particular work-force is employed we need to look not only at structural factors, but also at the average worker's options. Unemployment among young women is the highest of any group: there are few options open to young women who have left school without educational qualifications, so employment in a factory that favours their group seems relatively attractive. In practice, marriage is not seen as an alternative to wage labour.

New workers are often the kin of people already working in the factory and almost all had heard about the vacancy from a friend on the inside. Tiexiera said he preferred younger female workers. 'The older girls with families aren't as dependable. They're late, they're always having babies, they have to take time off when their children are sick. Nah. I definitely prefer to hire young girls.' Apart from the obviously offensive way in which he refers to women as 'older girls', he has no real grounds for assuming that women with family responsibilities who depend on their salaries for their children's as well as their own survival, should be less valuable to the firm. For a start, as I discuss later, because 'respectable' behaviour at work enhances prestige, the older women do not participate in the horseplay and flirting engaged in by the younger workers.

**Table 17.4: Examples of 1986 Wages for EUL Line Workers, in TT$**

| *Temporary* | | *1 Year's Service* | |
|---|---|---|---|
| Weekly wage | 110.00 | Weekly wage | 160.00 |
| Hourly rate | ($2.75) | Hourly rate | ($4.00) |
| NIS* | 3.50 | NIS* | 4.50 |
| Health Charge | 8.25 | Health Charge | 8.25 |
| Take Home Pay | 98.25 | Take Home Pay | 147.25 |
| | | | |
| *Permanent* | | *2 Years' Service* | |
| Weekly wage | 130.00 | Weekly wage | 180.00 |
| Hourly wage | ($3.25) | Hourly wage | ($4.50) |
| NIS* | 3.50 | NIS* | 5.75 |
| Health Charge | 8.25 | Health Charge | 8.25 |
| Take Home Pay | 118.25 | PAYE** | 3.00 |
| | | Take Home Pay | 163.00 |

\*   National Insurance Scheme; **Pay as You Earn income tax scheme. *Note*: At the time of the fieldwork, the exchange rate was as follows: TT$3.60=US$1.00; TT$5.28=£1.00

What Tiexiera does not say is that the younger workers are more docile and can be paid less. New workers are categorized as 'temporary' and required to serve a six-month probationary period during which they can be fired without warning and are paid at a lower rate. This cannot justifiably be called a training period because almost all the jobs can be learned in less than half an hour and a new worker with average ability can become as productive as experienced ones in a matter of days. If their performance is satisfactory at the end of the six-month probationary period, the workers are made 'permanent' and receive a small pay rise. Sometimes this is withheld as a disciplinary procedure. Wages at Essential are lower than at other similar firms. Figures compiled for November 1986 within the industry group, not differentiated by sex, indicate that the average minimum wage was TT$10.34 an hour for an assembler, $7.99 an hour for a machine operator and $9.72 an hour for a labourer (Trinidad & Tobago 1987a: 35). The examples of wages given in Table 17.4 show that wages at Essential lag far behind. The wages at Essential are similar to those in the garment industry, the traditional employer of female manufacturing workers (see Chapter 16), which averaged $214.82 a week in 1986 (Trinidad & Tobago 1987a: 41).

Jobs in the factory are allocated by gender. The women are involved in jobs like soldering wires, testing electrical components, glueing labels and other tedious tasks that require patience and concentration. They are machine operators and they are sedentary. On the other hand, the men are given jobs that require and allow time for mobility within the factory. In fact they seem to take much pleasure in taking the risks associated with leaving their posts and walking around the factory. Some operate machines, but they are mainly responsible for assisting the supervisors by moving boxes of finished products and retrieving materials from the storeroom. On the whole, they are not in jobs where it could be said that a male was necessary because of the physical strength needed. The workers have an idea about what are appropriate women's and men's jobs. Vishnu teased Jeremy, who was temporarily assigned to operate a machine all day, in the following manner: 'I didn't know it didn't have enough girls to work here'.

### Table 17.5: Educational Attainment for Trinidad & Tobago 1980, (Ages 15+)

| Level | Male (%) | Female (%) |
|---|---|---|
| No education | 3.4 | 6.4 |
| Primary | 60.8 | 56.6 |
| Secondary | 31.1 | 33.8 |
| University | 2.9 | 1.5 |
| Other/unstated | 1.8 | 1.7 |
| Totals | 100.0 | 100.0 |

Source: Trinidad & Tobago 1980 Census report

Female workers are seen as less likely to want to join a union and Tiexiera often said that if a union came to Essential he would close the factory down. Two years before my fieldwork he had apparently fired 20 workers who were secretly trying to gain union recognition. In addition, Tiexiera was constantly reminding the workers about the state of the country's economy. 'He using this recession as a excuse' said Cheryl, who then *steupsed* (sucked her teeth loudly in disapproval — called *churi* in Suriname and *chups* in other parts of the Caribbean — see Chapter 8).

Actual recruitment practices seem to contradict the 'dual market' theory of female labour, which holds that women are excluded from the productivity-enhancing jobs that would enable them to increase their wages and, hence, their status. However, this view assumes that the market operates impersonally. As Humphrey (1985: 219) shows from studies of Brazilian industry, 'the supposedly objective economic laws of market competition work through and within gendered structures. The market does not value male and female labour independently of gender.' Likewise, from her studies of women's work in Morocco, Joekes (1985: 189) inverts the presumed causation and argues that women's lower pay is not mainly a reflection of their relative lack of education: 'If it is a fact that women can be paid less than men, then by the same token women will be placed in jobs with a low grade rating'. In fact, Table 17.5 illustrates that in Trinidad and Tobago a higher percentage of women than men have secondary education. Table 17.6 provides information on the enrolment in some selected courses in the country's technical and vocational institutions. What this points out is the extent to which young women and men are still channelled into 'traditional' (though not necessarily so for Trinidad and Tobago) occupations.

Trinidadians saw food prices and the general cost of living double during the 1980s.[5] Typical responses to such pressures are to find additional sources of income and to develop 'support networks' (Gussler 1980). Comitas (1973) points out the prevalence of occupational multiplicity in the rural Caribbean, but I see this pattern as applying fairly generally to the working class. Many (supervisors included) have supplementary ways of earning money, such as growing and selling fruit and vegetables, dressmaking, minding children, making stuffed animals, installing car stereos and catering for parties and weddings. Some engage in unpaid work on tracts of land owned by kin in the rural areas (cf. Momsen 1987).

**Table 17.6: Enrolment in Technical & Vocational Schools, Final Term 1983/4**

| Course | No. of Students (full and part-time) | |
|---|---|---|
| | Male | Female |
| Accounting technicians | 47 | 125 |
| Auto and diesel mechanics | 115 | 7 |
| Business management | 86 | 152 |
| Construction carpentry | 53 | 4 |
| Commercial art | 24 | 11 |
| Computer programming | 81 | 64 |
| Domestic electronics service | 92 | 1 |
| Dressmaking and design | - | 54 |
| Electrical/electronics engineering | 88 | 7 |
| Electrical installation | 171 | 6 |
| Mechanical engineering | 138 | 5 |
| Plumbing | 45 | 7 |
| Practical cafeteria management | 3 | 12 |
| Shorthand/typing | - | 96 |
| Welding | 106 | 5 |

*Source:* Compiled from Trinidad & Tobago 1987c (Annual Statistical Digest 1985, Tables 66a and 66b)

The informal internal economy at Essential is almost identical to the one Cuales (1980: 81-3) describes in her study of female workers in a factory in Curaçao. Brian, 21, is training to be a Spiritual Baptist pastor and he sells sweet bread, *aloo* pies and soft drinks at the factory. His godmother makes the sweet bread and he makes the pies; he gives her some of the profits. He is part of a fairly extensive internal informal economy. Myra, who bakes sweet bread and cakes for sale, is Brian's friendly competitor and her profits are reported to be around $40 a week. Denise roasts peanuts, puts them in bags and brings them to work to sell. Tia's aunt, who works in a garment factory on the same estate, often goes to Margarita, a free port island off Venezuela (see Chapter 8) and brings back items of clothing, which Tia sells at the factory. Trinidadians are known for their preference for foreign goods and the items usually attract attention. However, when their quality is judged to be poor, the customers charge that the aunt is merely supplying goods that are produced in the factory where she works. All entrepreneurs grant credit to other workers and usually there is a scramble to collect what is owed after pay packets are passed out on Friday.

The emphasis on entrepreneurship is indicative of an individualistic ethos, which is found throughout the Caribbean. When asked about the types of jobs they would like, almost all the workers indicated that they would like to open up their own businesses.

## Supervision & Resistance

In Trinidad there is much talk of the presence of a so-called 'Carnival mentality' and its effect on industrial productivity. The notion derives from a local stereotype of blacks as unserious, fun loving and lazy. East Indians, on the other hand, are considered more industrious. But, despite numerous meetings and government and academic inquiries into productivity in the recent past, no clear-cut solutions to the problem have emerged (cf. Nunes 1987; Williams 1987; Ryan 1982). Some scholars have recently started to explain worker apathy and lack of productivity in terms of management practices, particularly the 'driver style' of supervision which is seen as a legacy of slavery. Tiexiera and the supervisors basically adhere to McGregor's (1960) 'theory X', which holds that people naturally dislike working and so have to be forced to do so. But the theory of a 'Carnival mentality' is, in my view, invalidated by the fact that so many of the workers are engaged in multiple occupations and generally exhibit a strong desire for material possessions.

There is no doubt, however, that a powerful workplace norm operates against being seen to be working hard. At Essential workers of all ages are adept at go-slows and other such delaying tactics, though the older workers are less obvious about it. For example, one of the groups assigned to making a particular product, in which all the workers were under 25, had its daily quota calculated at 200 products. The workers said they did not feel they could make that many and every day made 150. The workers kept a close count on the number produced and, usually, would have almost reached their targets at about 4.00 p.m. Between 4.00 and 4.30 p.m., which was when work stopped, only about three items would be produced. They reasoned, correctly, that if Tiexiera knew they were capable of making 200, he would set the quota at 225. Instead, through their collective action, they were able to alter the formal production schedule. If someone was thought to be working too hard, the usual barb was 'Tiexiera your father or what?'

There was a different atmosphere when Tiexiera came out of his office onto the adjacent factory floor. All pretence of not working hard was forgotten and managers and workers alike put their heads down and concentrated on their work: Tiexiera has a bad temper and the supervisors were often insulted (*buffed up*) in front of the workers. On a few occasions during my fieldwork year, Tiexiera caught workers idling and suspended them right then and there. Temporary workers were occasionally fired on the spot.

Though some interpreted Tiexiera's behaviour as 'racial', others put it down to bad temper and greed. But, since there was always a danger that Tiexiera would walk out of his office door, the workers were taking a considerable risk in being idle. Because of short-staffing, the line supervisors were expected to fill in and therefore could not always keep a watchful eye on the workers. At around 4.00 p.m. the supervisors would often go down into the stores office on the factory floor. The workers would then ease up. I do not believe this is collusion between the supervisors and workers against the owners; I see it rather as the supervisors' acceptance of a situation.

On Fridays work stopped at 4.00 p.m. and the workers would crowd around the stores office to wait for the personnel manager to hand out their pay packets. Though notices are posted on the bulletin board telling workers to go back to work after having been paid, these are always ignored. On pay day, besides paying off accounts for food purchased during the week, the *sou-sou* 'captains' take their deposits. (*Sou-sou* is based on a West African rotating credit system: such groups are called *meeting turns* in Jamaica, *partners* in the Eastern Caribbean and *sam* in Curaçao.) In a group of say five people, individuals may put in $50 a week. Each week it would be someone's turn to get his or her 'hand' of $250 until the cycle was complete. The captains are the people who run the *sou-sou* and in Trinidad they are almost always women. Women, it was explained to me, could be trusted with money, whereas men could not.

Social distance between supervisors and work-force along ethnic and gender lines seems to have been cultivated by Tiexiera as a factor in the production process. He once told me that 'there was a time when we used to look at race, ... race was important in hiring, but not any more'. By this he meant not only the hiring of supervisors, but also that East Indians were preferred as line workers. This conformed to old Trinidadian stereotypes. Though Tiexiera claimed to have abandoned this approach, during the period of my fieldwork a Portuguese Creole supervisor was replaced first by a white man and later by an East Indian man. So, to echo Humphrey (1985), the market does not value labour independently of gender *and* ethnicity.

Older workers told me that there had once been a black supervisor who 'stood up' to Tiexiera and argued for more money for them, but that he eventually became disillusioned and left. Some felt that ethnicity had something to do with the supervisor taking up the workers' complaints. But what the workers call selective hiring is not confined to a particular ethnic group. As Martha put it: 'Everybody want to push he race to the top. If you go to a Indian place, it only have Indians working there. Negroes, we would do the same. It *natural* to help you own people'. This, I think, is evidence of the 'culture of ethnicity' in Trinidad.

The day-to-day activities of the supervisors seem to have immediate effects on the workers. What one notices is the amount of sexual horseplay and the way the supervisors flirt with the workers. This was encouraged by the spatial situation at the factory where men and women spend eight hours a day in close proximity. Outside the factory, they operate in relatively separate domains. This horseplay and flirting only occurred among the younger workers. Once, during a break, Lloyd was standing at the front of the factory when Patricia walked by. Patricia, an East Indian, had only been working there for about three months, but from the beginning Lloyd had started to flirt with her in an increasingly licentious way, to which she often responded in kind. It was known that Lloyd, who was divorced, had several outside economic activities and a cabin cruiser moored at the Trinidad Yacht Club, so it is possible that Patricia was trying to use her flirting instrumentally. Henry and Wilson (1975: 178) note that the exploitative nature of Caribbean male-female relationships had necessitated women's 'employment of certain manipulative techniques and rationalizations in order to attain, or convince themselves they have attained, it would seem, the kind of relationship they desire'.

On this occasion, after commenting to another supervisor about her propensity to wear tight jeans, he said in an audible voice as she turned the corner, walking past, 'Ooh, I would love to fuck she'. This was a version of the 'dropping words' technique,[6] used here by Lloyd to make his intentions explicit. Weeks later they came to the wedding of one of the workers together, but Lloyd got drunk and they apparently had an argument. Back at the factory Lloyd was rather tentative in his subsequent forays and if any sexual relationship ever developed I was unaware of it. I was not aware of any sexual activities within the factory of the kind Roy (1974) documents in his study of an American factory.

Whitehead (1976: 177-9) shows how joking abuse is used by men to control women. Likewise, at Essential, we can say that flirting has the unintended consequence of controlling the workers. Their resultant alienation may explain their apparent lack of interest in trade unions, which they may see as primarily benefiting men.[7] Sexual harassment in Trinidad and Tobago is a much talked-about problem, and I consider the supervisor-worker relationships described above to be examples. In 1987, Singing Sandra won the Calypso Queen title with a song called 'Die With My Dignity':

Yuh want to help to mind you family
Yuh want to help yuh man financially
But nowadays it really very hard
To get a job as a girl in Trinidad
Yuh looking now to find something to do
Yuh meet a bossman who promise to help you
But when the man lay down the condition
Is nothing else but humiliation
They want to see yuh whole anatomy
They want to see what yuh doctor never see
They want to do what yuh husband never do
Still don't know if the scamps will hire you
Well if is all this humiliation
To get ah job these days as a woman
They will keep their money
I will keep my honey
And die with my dignity

*Trinidad Express,*
(19 February 1987: 19)

## Factory Social Relations

Social relationships in the factory fell into four groups. Women over 30 tended to establish peer group relationships among themselves while younger women formed separate social links. Young male peer groups were differentiated along ethnic lines while supervisors rarely associated with workers. Although I share some of Besson's (Chapter 2) reservations about Wilson's 'reputation and respectability' model in accounting for female behaviour, in the factory older women are accorded prestige for acting 'respectable'. 'Proper' behaviour for an older woman is constrained in its scope.

Those who do not conform often pay the price in moral sanctions. For example, 45-year-old Vera had never married and had no children. She was seen by the workers as spreading gossip and was ostracized by many of the older women. She was also ridiculed behind her back for spending most of her time in conversation with the two youngest women in her department. One 26-year-old worker, herself the mother of three children, said 'no wonder she crazy. It not natural to have no child. If I was she, I'd be crazy too'. In Vera's case, I could not tell whether she had resorted to associating with younger workers because she was isolated, or whether she was being ridiculed as a result of spending time with younger workers. Either way, it seems she had little control over her failure to live up to the other workers' expectations.

Denise, 35, was a somewhat different example. She had two teenage children and was divorced. She worked in a department away from the main shop floor and was also regarded by most of the workers as a gossip. Her network consisted almost wholly of younger workers. She often went to parties with the younger workers and flirted with the men. 'I find for a big woman she fast [bold and wild]', said Terry, a young man with whom she did not flirt.

The shop floor culture reflects these divisions. The peer groups of the younger female workers are pervaded by an emphasis on romance: they bring to work and share magazines named *Photoromance* and *Kiss*, which are produced in Italy and contain pictures of glamorous white models. Pollert (1981: 137) writes about similar behaviour among the younger workers in an English factory and puts it down to the fact that they are cushioned from domestic responsibilities. The workers at Essential, however, are not exempted from domestic duties: indeed, 12 of the 28 females under 25 have children of their own. The workers' responsibilities include contributing to the household income. Some hand over up to half their weekly pay to elder kin. Irene, for example, was 24 and the mother of twin boys, aged 7. Her starting take-home pay was $98 a week and after the six-month probationary period she was made 'permanent' and her take-home pay increased to $118. She lived with her mother, step-father, step-sister, step-brother and her two children. She contributed $20 to the household and undertook various household chores, mainly child care.

While the older women workers talk about home and church, as well as their work, male peer groups are generally cut off from each other by ethnicity and their conversation focuses on women, soccer, cars and music. Meeting points between the younger men and women workers mainly consist of flirting. In these relationships, the flirting is initiated by both sides and is part of a general pattern of constant horseplay among the younger women workers, who are mostly confined to one particular department. The men use their mobility within the factory to play the so-called 'sex-fame game', the essential element of which is to 'sweet-talk' a woman in order to make a sexual conquest. This raises the question of whether flirting relationships may be regarded as joking relationships. Radcliffe-Brown (1952: 100) points out that joking relationships obtain between those who may marry and avoidance between those who may not. In a study of joking relationships in a Glasgow factory, however, Sykes (1966: 192-3) shows that relations between younger workers, who were potential sexual partners, were characterized by modesty, while gross obscenity prevailed between those older workers who were not potential sex partners.

At Essential, while black men flirt with black and East Indian young women, East Indian men generally only flirt with East Indian women. This was explained to me by Carla, an East Indian, who said: 'You kidding? A black man would love to marry a Indian woman. She will cook for he and keep he house clean and look after the chirren. A black woman, he couldn't keep she at home'. This statement is further illuminating on at least two counts: first, while there are few instances of long-term domestic relationships between blacks and East Indians, when they do occur they seem to be between black men and East Indian women. Secondly it suggests that women see themselves through the eyes of men and at times define themselves in terms of what is useful to men. The flirting relationships, then, seem to conform to Radcliffe-Brown's usage, and the ones between supervisors and workers tend to reproduce a system whereby white men had sexual access to black and East Indian women under slavery and indenture.

However, it is a mistake to assume that, in themselves, factory relationships can fully explain factory behaviour. I therefore also examined the 'networks of support' (cf. Wellman 1981) of a selected group of workers. In this context 'support' is taken to mean the exchange of emotional, financial and informational assistance to help each other 'mek do'. It was noticeable that goods and services were exchanged across ethnic lines much more frequently among women than men, among whom this sort of activity was almost non-existent. Bourdieu (1977: 62) suggests that women are less sensitive to 'symbolic profits' and that lending between women is the antithesis of the exchange of honour among men: 'The urge to calculate, repressed in men, finds more overt expression in women, who are structurally predisposed to be less concerned with symbolic profits accruing from political unity, and to devote themselves more readily to strictly economic practices.' Similarly, I would not want to explain this sort of activity by saying that women are 'naturally' less ethnocentric than men, but by pointing out that the women in the factory did not lose status through exchange with others beyond their ethnic group and that, given their structural position and their familial responsibilities, they realized that they would have access to a wider range of resources if they were to initiate exchanges beyond their own group.

## Conclusion

In this chapter I have tried to set the patterns of social behaviour in the factory in their historical context and to discuss the cognitive aspects of this behaviour. I have also shown the responses of the workers to the exercise of power and authority and their creative efforts to better their economic circumstances. I want to conclude with two points: one relates to the future of female workers in Trinidad and Tobago and the other concerns the theoretical contributions of the concepts of gender and ethnicity.

### Table 17.7: Monthly Wages in Manufacturing in 1985

| Country | | Monthly Pay (in 1985 US$) |
|---|---|---|
| Canada | | 1429.92 |
| Rep. of Korea | (male) | 398.67 |
| | (female) | 187.01 |
| Singapore | (male) | 345.25 |
| | (female) | 218.98 |
| Costa Rica | | 179.13 |
| St Lucia | | 146.64 |
| Trinidad & Tobago | | 144.44 |
| Philippines | (skilled) | 77.18 |
| | (unskilled) | 60.99 |
| Sri Lanka | (male) | 36.88 |
| | (female) | 25.93 |

Note: These wages are based on an eight-hour working day and a 20 working-day month. Source: Compiled from the International Labour Office, Yearbook of Statistics 1987 and International Monetary Fund, International Statistics Yearbook 1987, various pages

First, as oil revenues decline the government will increasingly look to the opportunities offered by the expansion of foreign capital investment. This move is encouraged by trade agreements with the United States and Canada and by the introduction of free trade zones, both of which tend to foster higher rates of female employment. Success in attracting such employers will depend on keeping local wages down relative to those in other countries (Table 17.7).[8]

As Table 17.7 suggests, while comparing favourably with some countries where 'off-shore' production is located, the wage structures of CARICOM countries and of the Caribbean area in general place these countries at a distinct disadvantage in comparison with the low wage economies of Asia. Therefore, to attract US invest-ment CARICOM governments must be willing to offer additional 'advantages', one of which is cheap female labour.

Secondly, the study suggests that gender and ethnicity are constructed in relation to each other. This argument has also been suggested by Parmar (1982: 258), who has studied women in Britain. She writes that 'Women are defined differently according to their "race".' In addition, I would further argue that gender, ethnicity and class are socially constructed with reference to each other and that a multi-dimensional view must be adopted if one is to understand the complexities of power relations in the factory context.

## Notes

1   Ethnicity is a particular 'involuntary' social identity seen in relation to a socially constructed ultimate ancestral link between an individual and a named group, which have shared an ancestor and a common culture. This subjective identification is not arbitrary nor purely imaginary and is character-ized by what Ching (1985), writing on Trinidad, called the 'social construction of primordiality'. It is here that 'practice' approaches to ethnicity, in their current form or with modifications, are useful (Yelvington 1991). I define gender as a particular sense of the self which is socially constructed in relation to perceived and non-perceptable biological criteria. Since perception here is social in origin, and dependent upon the way individual/society relationships may be interpreted in various contexts, we can say that gender is culturally-specific.
2   An earlier version was presented as a paper to the Society for Caribbean Studies 12th Annual Confer-ence, Hoddesdon, Hertfordshire, England, 12-14 July 1988. I would like to thank a number of people for their comments on earlier versions of this paper, including Clemen Aquino, Nuraddin Auwal, Bridget Brereton, R.W. Connell, Maria Patricia Fernandez-Kelly, John French, Ralph Grillo, David Harrison, Aisha Khan, Janet Momsen, June Nash, Sheila Smith, Steve Vertovec, and Faustina Ward-Osborne. In addition, I have benefited from conversations, correspondence and encouragement from several people in the Caribbean, UK and US, including John Humphrey, Anthony Maingot, Joycelin Massiah, Patricia Mohammed, Ruth Pearson, Dorian Powell, Ann Whitehead, Donald Wood and Annette Ching, to whom I owe a special debt. I would especially like to thank the workers, managers and owners of Essential Utensils Ltd, who must remain anonymous.
3   The specific characteristics of the factory and the individual owners, supervisors and workers have been fictionalized to protect the anonymity of those concerned.
4   Still, this seems an improvement over the recent past. In 1965, the median monthly income of female workers was TT$83.50, while men's income was $146.50. In 1971, the comparison was $93.00 for females, $167.50 for males. In 1977, the comparison was $293.00 for females, $449.50 for males. However, throughout the period, the median monthly income of female government employees approximated that of male government employees.
5   After running in double figures, inflation in 1985 was 7.6 per cent, the lowest since 1971. But subsidies were withdrawn from certain food imports after the preferential exchange rate was changed in February 1987. There followed two rounds of price increases at the end of March 1987, affecting government-controlled basic food items: evaporated milk (up 41 per cent), powdered baby milk (up 29 per cent), cheese (up 32 per cent), potatoes, onions, garlic and tinned sardines. The Economist Intelli-gence Unit (1987/8: 11) predicted that inflation in 1987 would run at between 20 and 30 per cent.
6   'Dropping words' is a technique used in Trinidad when someone wants to shame someone else. For example, when the victim is walking by the aggressor might utter some sensitive secret about the victim in an audible voice, but without looking at the victim and without apparently referring specifi-cally to them. To gain status, the victim must remain 'cool-cool' and pretend not to hear, for if they are provoked their response is taken as proof by the audience that the accusations were in fact true. In Trinidad, a premium is put on decorum in social exchanges.
7   As part of my research I had several conversations with female union officials about female workers. They told me not only of the general unwillingness of male union officials to incorporate females into the power structure, but of how the husbands and boy friends of female members would occasionally disrupt meetings that were held at night and demand that their womenfolk return home.
8   Protests in Trinidad were started in early 1988 by the pressure group, Women Against Free Trade Zones. This was a joint project of women's groups, the Oilfields Workers' Trade Union, which vocifer-ously opposed the zones (cf. Vanguard, 26 March 1988: 3-4) and the Women's Studies Unit at the University of the West Indies. See also Chapter 16 for an earlier example of women's role in Trinidad and Tobago trade unions.

## References

Bourdieu, Pierre (1977) *Outline of a Theory of Practice.* Translated by Richard Nice, Cambridge: Cambridge University Press

Brodber, Erna (1980) *Jane and Louisa Will Soon Come Home.* London: New Beacon Books

Brown, Richard (1976) 'Women as Employees: Some Comments on Research in Industrial Sociology'. In Diana L. Barker and Sheila Allen (eds), *Dependence and Exploitation in Work and Marriage,* London: Longman, 21-46

Caribbean Conference of Churches (1986) *A Social Survey of the Poverty Situation in Trinidad*. Port of Spain: Caribbean Conference of Churches

Ching, Annette M.T. (1985) 'Ethnicity Reconsidered, with Reference to Sugar and Society in Trinidad'. Unpublished D.Phil. thesis, University of Sussex

Comitas, Lambros (1973) 'Occupational Multiplicity in Rural Jamaica'. In Lambros Comitas and David Lowenthal (eds) *Work and Family Life: West Indian Perspectives*, Garden City: Anchor Books, 156-73

Cuales, Sonia (1980) 'Women, Reproduction and Foreign Capital in Curaçao'. *Caraibisch Forum*, 1 (2) 75-86

Economist Intelligence Unit (1987/8) *Country Profile: Trinidad and Tobago*. London: Economist Intelligence Unit

Gussler, Judith D. (1980) 'Adaptive Strategies and Social Networks of Women in St Kitts'. In Erida Bourguignon (ed.) *A World of Women*, New York: Praeger, 185-209

Henry, Frances and Pamela Wilson (1975) 'The Status of Women in the Caribbean: An Overview of their Social, Economic and Sexual Roles'. *Social and Economic Studies*, 24 (2) 165-98

Humphrey, John (1985) 'Gender, Pay and Skill: Manual Workers in Brazilian Industry'. In Haleh Afshar (ed.) *Women, Work and Ideology in the Third World*, London: Tavistock, 214-31

Hyacinth, S. (1979) *Changes in the Status of Women 1900-1977*. Trinidad & Tobago: Central Statistical Office, (mimeo, restricted circulation)

International Labour Office (1987) *Yearbook of Statistics 1987*. Geneva: ILO

International Monetary Fund (1987) *International Statistics Yearbook 1987*. Washington DC: IMF

Joekes, Susan (1985) 'Working for Lipstick? Male and Female in the Clothing Industry in Morocco'. In Haleh Afshar (ed.) *Women, Work and Ideology in the Third World*, London: Tavistock, 183-213

McGregor, Douglas (1960) *The Human Side of Enterprise*. New York: McGraw-Hill

Mittelholzer, Edgar (1950) *A Morning at the Office*. London: Hogarth

Momsen, Janet Henshall (1987) 'The Feminization of Agriculture in the Caribbean'. In Janet H. Momsen and Janet Townsend (eds) *Geography of Gender in the Third World*, London: Hutchinson, 344-7

Nunes, Frederick E. (1987) 'Culture, Motivation and Organizational Performance'. *Asset*, 5 (2) 3-16

Parmar, Pratiba (1982) 'Gender, Race and Class: Asian Women in Resistance'. In Centre for Contemporary Cultural Studies, University of Birmingham, *The Empire Strikes Back*, London: Hutchinson, 237-75

Pollert, Anna (1981) *Girls, Wives, Factory Lives*. London: Macmillan

Radcliffe-Brown, A.R. (1952) *Structure and Function in Primitive Society*. London: Cohen & West

Roy, Donald (1974) 'Sex in the Factory: Informal Heterosexual Relations Between Supervisors and Work Groups'. In Clifton Bryant (ed.) *Deviant Behaviour*, Chicago: Rand McNally, 44-66

Ryan, Selwyn (1982) 'The Role of Management in Productivity'. In Trinidad & Tobago, *National Consultation on Productivity Report*, Ministry of Labour, Social Security and Cooperatives, 41-6

Sykes, A.J.M. (1966) 'Joking Relationships in an Industrial Setting'. *American Anthropologist*, 68 (1) 188-93

Trinidad & Tobago (1980) *Population and Housing Census*, Port of Spain: Government Printing

—— (1987) *Social Indicators Report*. Port of Spain: Central Statistical Office

—— (1987a) *Economic Indicators: October-December 1986*, Port of Spain: Central Statistical Office

—— (1987b) *Review of the Economy 1986*. Port of Spain: Government Printing

—— (1987c) *Annual Statistical Digest 1985*. Port of Spain: Central Statistical Office

*Trinidad Express*, 19 February 1987: 19

*Trinidad Guardian*, 21 December 1988: 3

*Vanguard*. 26 March 1988: 3-4

Wellman, Barry (1981) 'Applying Network Analysis to the Study of Support'. Resource Paper No. 3, Toronto: Centre for Urban and Community Studies, University of Toronto

Whitehead, Ann (1976) 'Sexual Antagonism in Hertfordshire'. In Diana L. Barker and Sheila Allen (eds) *Dependence and Exploitation in Work and Marriage*, London: Longman, 169-203

Williams, Gwendoline A. (1987) 'Management and Development in the Business/Industrial Environment of Trinidad and Tobago: A Focus on Major Socio-Cultural Issues'. *Asset*, 4 (1) 17-33

Yelvington, Kevin A. (1985) 'The Context of Acculturation: The Modernization Process and Occupational Diversification in Trinidad and Tobago 1891-1980'. Unpublished MA thesis, Florida International University

—— (1991) 'Ethnicity as Practice? A Comment on Bentley'. *Comparative Studies in Society and History*, 33 (1) 158-68

# XVIII Women's Contribution to Tourism in Negril, Jamaica

LESLEY McKAY

This chapter[1] provides a case study which serves to show that, despite women being economically active, paid work does not necessarily liberate them from the domestic sphere, but can, paradoxically, tie them even closer to home and the influence of partners and family. Catering for tourists in Negril is predominantly, if not exclusively, a female occupation. Holiday cottages and cafés are generally known by the name of the woman responsible for them, for example *Grandma P's*. Women also play a major role as vendors of souvenirs and other goods to tourists in Negril. It could be hypothesized that tourism should, therefore, benefit women as a group rather than men.

Self-employment has been the source of self-determination for many ethnic or minority groups within and without the Caribbean area (Light 1972). Self-employment allows an individual to cut through discrimination in employment, promotion and wages. Similarly the service industries, which are so central to tourism, have long been a female province. Not only does such service work fit in with ideological expectations of women's role, but it utilizes skills a woman will already have acquired and so she is not hindered by any lack of training. Furthermore, in the Caribbean, women have traditional role models to follow, as higgler (Mintz 1971) and guesthouse landlady (Brodber 1982) when seeking employment in tourism. The recent development of the industry in Negril is further potential encouragement, for there is no established stratification or domination of positions of authority to deter any would-be participant.

However, as the data below show, there are other factors at play which limit female participation and earnings in the industry. Participation is affected by access to capital, family ideology and formal barriers. Women are reluctant to seek loans from a bank, even assuming they have the necessary collateral. Thus, women traditionally must rely on friends or family for initial advances or 'work up', i.e. a small amount of investment capital into which subsequent profits are gradually reinvested. A combination of these two methods is the most usual pattern.

Cultural factors and notions of femininity are a second consideration. The notion of 'respectability' (see Besson in Chapter 2), along with the value attached to motherhood, means that a woman's self-advancement can be restricted because her own needs are put after those of her family or partner. Conversely, of course, the incentive to 'build up' enough money to be able to afford an education and better life for her family can act as a powerful motivating factor. In practical terms 'respectability' bars women from the 'big money' in tourism, which comes from drugs, speculation and enterprises that demand a certain amount of technical know-how (for example, bicycle rentals or water sports). Gender differences are apparent even in the market-place, where women sell food and clothing and men sell black coral jewellery and wood carvings.[2]

The third factor, that of formal barriers, interacts with the other two. By 'formal barriers' I mean the practical problems imposed on small-scale entrepreneurship by, for example, laws, taxes, the regulations of planning authorities, tourist boards and agencies, and the seasonality of tourism. Using the two main spheres of female activity described here as examples, marketing and letting rooms,[3] it will be seen that, partly as a result of these barriers, tourism does not in itself provide an unproblematic means of social mobility.

## Market Women in Negril

There are two official market sites in Negril — one at Rutland Point, strategically situated outside the largest hotel complex, Hedonism II, and one in the town centre, or more accurately across a bridge from the town centre. Both these markets were set up by the vendors themselves, which is a reflection both of the poverty endemic in Jamaica and the strength of will of the women involved. These markets provide a good illustration of the interplay between the formal and informal sectors.

Though Negril has never had a formal market-place (Davenport 1956), the growth in tourism brought large numbers of 'outsiders' into the town to sell.[4] With increased competition, some of the traditional higglers who sold fruit or speculated in small goods began to diversify by investing, first, in basket and straw work and, later, when they had more money, in T-shirts and 'flour sack' clothes. When their rivals began to sell dry goods, some of the women with sufficient funds built 'shops' or 'kitchens' and began to sell cooked food. The roundabout in the centre of Negril became the main location for these activities. It was the bus stop and therefore an access point for tourists, but also convenient for transport for the women and their goods. Although a few sellers were Negrilians, it was the outsiders who dominated the market. They mostly came from areas within a 20-mile radius of Negril, such as Little London, Sheffield or Grange Hill, rather than from Montego Bay.

At its peak in 1980, before the new market was built, the central market had about 50 vendors. It became increasingly permanent in form as stalls, then shops, restaurants and even household accommodation were built. It was an eyesore and a health hazard. Because there was no proper sanitation or drainage, waste and sewage were dumped directly into the river or the sea itself, to be washed up onto the beach some time later.

It was partly on health grounds that the local business community argued for the removal of the market. The higglers took advantage of the bureaucratic confusion that resulted when the owner of the market site, the Negril Area Land Authority (NALA), found that it was not empowered to enforce the squatting laws. Since it was seen to be impossible to move the squatters, the Urban Development Corporation (UDC), which assumed responsibility from NALA in 1980, was forced to create two formal market-places. Lack of funds provided a practical excuse for complying with the wishes of larger investors and limiting the number of vendors. Some 24 stalls were built on a site that was less visible from the new road and therefore less offensive to the eyes of tourists. But the official limitation of numbers has not worked. When vendors moved onto the site and resisted attempts to move them, the UDC had to compromise. By 1985 vendors without an official stall were able to obtain a site in the market-place on which to erect their own stalls at two-thirds of the rent paid for a UDC-provided stall.

This was a case of local adaptation to an imposed situation. First, the vendors took advantage of the arrival of tourists and the lack of an established market-place. Resistance to attempts to limit numbers forced the UDC to accept a dual structure of tenants. Likewise other rules have been reinterpreted. For example, though the UDC forbade the sale of foodstuffs, these are still sold and some families continue to live illegally on the site. Nor is the vetting of potential vendors entirely in the hands of the UDC. Generally, any vendor who ceases to trade passes the stall on to friends or family 'for a consideration', i.e. payment or some favour at a later date. This process reinforces the differences between Negril's two markets. The central market is dominated by women from Little London, Sheffield and areas to the east, whereas the Rutland Point market is dominated by traders from Lucea, Green Island and Orange Point. This is even more striking because of the size of the central market, which is especially homo-geneous in areas of origin and has a much greater percentage of 'old' vendors, i.e. those with over four years' experience.

The historical antecedents of Rutland Point market are somewhat different. It was built at the same time as the central market in anticipation of an increase in market activity with the arrival of Hedonism II and to absorb some of the vendors from the town centre. Yet, because of its isolated position, the market is less popular among the sellers. It depends solely on business from the one hotel and on passing trade in or out of town along the main North Coast road. Though Hedonism II is said to have the best off-season accommodation rates in Jamaica, tourists spend very little at the market because the hotel complex is completely self-contained, with all activities, food and drink included in the package price. Few tourists, apart from those participating in group activities such as cycle tours, venture outside the complex and some do not even have Jamaican money to spend.

Many of the Rutland Point vendors would have preferred to have had a place in the central market had they been able to get one. But most are deterred even from trying by the numerous difficulties and perceived unfriendliness of the other market women and Rastafarians at the central market.

Vendors of both markets are united in their attitudes towards their UDC land-lords. Complaints among vendors include having to keep paying regular rents irrespective of seasonal fluctuations in trade, restrictions on the sale of the cheaper, more easily disposable foodstuffs and produce and lack of UDC action on hustlers and security. In allocating blame to the UDC it should be noted that the problems came from individual employees rather than from the authority itself. In Negril, in particular, the local manager took advantage of the town's distance from the Kingston head office to abuse his position.

Market-place vendors differed from the other vendors in Negril, not so much in geographical area of origin, but in age, religion and length of vending experience. Many of the vendors along the road through the village did not have a pitch in the market because they had come after the available places had been filled. For others it had been because they had failed to raise sufficient capital to invest in non-food-stuffs such as T-shirts. This is often due to lack of selling experience, for experi-enced vendors know how to 'build up' from foodstuffs to the non-perishable crafts and goods stipulated by the UDC. But they were not all poorer than the market women. Some were Negrilians who had chosen what they considered to be better sites on their own, or (more commonly) who had decided to locate on land away from the competition generated by 94 vendors in a confined space.

As the tourist industry grew in Negril more vendors with shops and stalls else-where on the island moved into the area. These women looked down on the poorer women in Negril market and deliberately chose to set up shop away from the people they regarded as 'not presentable'. But not all the women want to sell crafts. Though fruit and vegetables offer less of a profit (100 per cent) than T-shirts and crafts (estimated at between 300 and 400 per cent), they do provide a steadier income throughout the season. Also, some women prefer to sell produce because it is 'what they know' — i.e. it offers them the reassurance of experience.

Higglering outside the market areas is, however, illegal and leaves women open to eviction. Individual women I talked to apparently chose not to think about it. This attitude is understandable in view of the irrationality and arbitrary nature of many local authority actions. None of the women were certain of their rights, or of the particular authorities involved, and some were downright confused. One woman, for example, stated confidently that the UDC had given her permission to open a boutique, whereas the land on which she had her shop in fact belonged to a private owner in Savanna-la-Mar.

Comparison of the two markets showed that the Rutland Point women were, on the whole, younger and more ambitious. Many had worked in hotels before saving the money to set up in the market. Selling is better money than hotel work, but is not the end of their ambitions. Some were saving in order to emigrate. In Negril central market, women's ambitions focused mainly on their children, hoping that they would find work in hotels, banks, or offices. Many showed ambivalence towards their daughters following them into the market.

While there is no hostility between the occupants of UDC stalls and the later arrivals who built their own stalls more cheaply (on the contrary, there was considerable cooperation — 'we all have to make a living'), the Negril market is divided internally. The split is between the women and the Rastafarian men, with many people dubbed Rastafarian because of their dreadlocks rather than their religious beliefs. They were considered to be dirty, violent and untrustworthy. The market women accused them of stealing, taking away their business, smoking ganja and hassling the tourists.

In both markets there was a sense of solidarity among the women, which was reinforced by church sisterhood, the proximity of their homes (they had usually grown up together) and kinship. Though all the vendors spoke of how 'we mek fe weself', with 35 different women linked to the same three families, it was clear that family links were extremely strong and that family ties were an important factor in getting a site. Though each vendor was in effect working for herself, members of the same families did tend to group together in the market. Despite their mothers' ambitions of a better life for them, several daughters had already followed their mothers into selling and kin ties played an important role in child care and in the day-to-day practical matters such as minding the shop or directing potential customers to friends. Networks through friendships are important to the women, but none of the women placed such friendships above family.

Family is important too insofar as a woman's entry into marketing is determined by her domestic status. As I noted above, the initial capital usually comes from family members and rarely from a woman's own savings. Though there was little difference in marital status between market women and vendors outside the market areas, the occupation of a woman's partner appeared to be a key variable. The husbands of central market women are more likely to be in regular employment and many of the women said that they began by borrowing from their partners. Younger unmarried women sometimes used motherhood as a means of raising money to invest, for a child's father would often feel under an obligation to see that the mother was able to provide for the child.

All this casts some doubt on the extent to which these women really are independent. Not only does a lot of their initial money come from male partners, but their actual participation in marketing also often depends on the encouragement or permission of their men. For example, Miss P's husband would not let her do domestic work for anyone else and Miss N saw herself as working for her husband in that she ran the shop he had bought and stocked. In a number of respects, therefore, men directly influence their partner's entry into the labour market.

Male partners also sometimes intervene directly and, in some instances, virtually colonize their women's stalls. One such case concerned a woman from Little London who had set up a shop and house for herself on a vacant piece of land. Then a boyfriend, whom she had met in Negril, moved in to live with her in the room adjoining the shop. In the following months he began to dominate relations with her customers. He set prices, propositioned women tourists, hassled the men and generally ruined what little business there was in the slow season. When I left she was planning to move her shop a couple of miles up the beach. She was not alone in this problem: I met two other women in a similar position.

On the other hand, many market women are proud of their independence. They see the money they make as their own and joke about their husbands having no idea of how much they earn. Although the men set the women up in business with a view to increasing their own incomes, the market women hide their earnings from their husbands and even plan major moves behind their backs. This is an example of the gamesmanship discussed by Henry and Wilson (1975), in which interpersonal relations are mediated through economic considerations, which is hardly surprising given the marginality of so much of Caribbean life.

But such assertions of independence do not really challenge the established status quo. For a start, the women vendors do not question traditional assumptions about a woman's place being with her family and the man being the head of the household. Their secrecy about their earnings is in fact an acknowledgement that the male head of the household is entitled to know what they earn. They are thus manipulating rather than challenging the situation.

Yet one has to recognize the market women's strength in pioneering the internal market system. They may have had the role model of women higglers, but they had no experience of the longer term investment needed in craft work or of selling to tourists. They were marketing in a different context. A couple of women told me that they had to overcome some initial shyness. The fruit vendors too had to operate in a different context. They are not part of the tradition described by Katzin (1960), whereby higglers sell peasant produce they themselves have collected. They are a development of the system first referred to briefly in Davenport (1956), in which women resell supplies that they themselves have bought from the market.

## Landladies in Negril

An unusual feature of tourist accommodation in Negril — which is emphasized in the brochures — is that there is an abundance of cheap accommodation let by the locals themselves. This is usually attached to the Negrilian's own home, with very basic facilities, such as shared outdoor showers and no electric lights. In 1985 such accommodation could be rented for between US$5 and $10 a night, which was cheap for tourist accommodation in Jamaica, but more than one would expect to pay for a three-bedroomed house in a good area of Kingston. The Jamaica Tourist

Board (JTB) formally identified 14 tourist boarding houses, which were advertised by signpost even in the off-season. In addition to these official 'cottages', unofficial rooms are let to tourists on a less formal basis. Guests find out about such accommodation, not from signs or advertisements, but from local children or friends. As one might expect, some of this accommodation is very basic. Mr C, for example, lets rooms that his own family had moved out of years ago; they are without electricity or running water and water for the guests is kept in an outside oil drum, which is filled each morning by two of his granddaughters.

The decision about whether or not to let rooms has quite a lot to do with a person's domestic situation. The data I collected showed that the most successful landladies, i.e. the best known or those with the most imposing buildings, were those who in the 1960s had limited economic alternatives and no young family. Migrant women returning from the UK without their husbands often took advantage of family land and the absence of other family members to let rooms. In only four out of twelve cases was the woman's male partner in permanent residence at the time, though all but two have since settled with a steady male partner. It is possible that migrant remittances in the past had given these women an opportunity to acquire the better rooms that commanded the higher rents. Family size was another important consideration. Those with large families had neither the space nor the time to rent rooms. Others are hindered by their families; one woman told me that her husband would not let her look after a white man, but insisted that she 'sit and look at him'. Families sometimes help women by building rooms for them to rent. Children also help by finding potential guests and looking after them when they arrive. An older son is also sometimes useful for security purposes.

Unlike the market women, these Negril women have had no traditional role models on which to base their behaviour as landladies. They thus tend to model themselves around the stereotypical mother figure (Walton 1978) and, as an extension of a traditional Jamaican practice, are often even addressed as 'mother' by their clients. Again and again landladies would tell me that they did their work 'for love' rather than money. Even if this were untrue, that they felt the need to say so indicates that the women were at least aware of how their role should be presented. In my own and other tourists' experience of landladies there were countless examples of such solicitude. The landladies looked after money, took charge of their guests' welfare (both moral and physical) and even organized their friendships and love lives. And, in a few extreme cases, the guests became 'family' insofar as they paid no rent and had a room permanently kept for their return.

These comments are not, however, intended simply to reinforce the image of the selfless, kindly, soft-hearted soul depicted in early Jamaica Tourist Board brochures (see Perez 1975). As Brodber (1982) notes, these women are often very individualistic and highly authoritarian. They have to be because it is not easy to look after white men in Negril. Landladies report that they cannot take rum or ganja like Jamaicans ('his blood is too cold') and that they mix with low women and Rastas. Guests often leave without paying or without paying in full. These women need to be mentally tough, not only to cope with problems such as these, but to deal with the absence of the kind of social cohesion the market women enjoy. Life during the off-season is isolated and they often find it difficult to adjust to the more confined family environment of small, mainly female personal networks remaining in their yards (see Chapter 4).

As I note briefly above, Jamaican households tend to be characterized by the 'absent man'. Even older men do not stay at home for long, but go out 'sporting' elsewhere. Men never help in the house in any way, so the entire care of the guest rooms falls onto the woman in the family's shoulders. In a country with few washing machines or other household appliances this work is physically demanding. Most of these women have some help with the laundry (in itself an indication of status) and this invariably comes from within the family network.

There are also other reasons why these women need to be so independent. The Jamaica Tourist Board gives them no help at all in advertising their rooms, or even in directing people to Negril and government taxes take no account of seasonality. Recent tourist legislation passed in Jamaica has imposed a tax of J$200 a year on each room, regardless of hotel category. This has directly hit the very small businesses, for which the tax represents a week's rental, rather than the bigger hotels and villas, for which not only is the tax less than a night's rental, but where the rooms are more likely to be filled in the off-season because owners have links with US travel agents. In Negril the new tax has forced Mama H to give up the business she had built up from scratch and run for 15 years.

The maternal role in Negril has been exaggerated into a virtual ethnic stereotype. No doubt this is partly due to the US influence, for, as Hooks (1982) points out, the same sorts of stereotypes pertain to Jamaicans as to the blacks of the American South. As a stereotype, it is sufficiently close to reality, or to how the role of women is perceived, to be more or less acceptable. But because it somehow denotes a lack of respect when it is used by white men, the owners of larger businesses tend to choose impersonal names to avoid the stereotype. If the ethnographic stereotype of young men, so exploited by 'dreads' and Rastas, is one of extreme physical prowess, the maternal role is more demanding in its necessary solicitude for others and does seem to be discouraging younger women from becoming landladies. Even though many middle-class white women own villas and hotels, many Jamaican women feel that it is beneath them to take in guests. Young women with money seem to prefer either to leave Negril altogether or to invest in a more modern, if riskier, business such as water sports. Other women indicated a disinterest in keeping rooms because of the loss of freedom and privacy it entails.

Landladies also seem to have less financial independence than market women. This would not, of course, matter if it did not matter to the women concerned. However, unless the market women of Negril and those studied by Katzin (1960), Yawney (1983) and Brodber (1982) are atypical of the rest of the Caribbean, it does. Landladies are more dependent than market women on their extended families for the land on which to build their guestrooms and have less opportunity to earn money of their own, for so much of what they earn from their guests gets swallowed up in household expenses. A husband can also calculate more accurately how much money is being earned.

I was struck by the extent to which family ties are used to manipulate women into running businesses. An outstanding example of this in Negril was the case of Grandma P. For over 15 years she ran a guest house for her son, who was a pastor and, as such, barred by his church from holding commercial interests. Grandma P (after whom the guesthouse was named) built up the business to over 20 rooms and it became so successful that it featured in a national newspaper article in the *Sunday Gleaner's* magazine, *Flair*. But at that point her son decided that he wanted to run the business himself, which was a bitter blow to Grandma P, especially since he continued to use and profit from her famous name. At Pointcara Mrs D looks after rooms for her daughter who works in Montego Bay. Miss F takes care of Roots Bamboo for her brother. Both women miss Montego Bay and their friends there. They hate the atmosphere of Negril ('wicked and evil') and the locals themselves. Miss F left work in a shop to look after her brother's business, not for money she claims, but because 'family must look after each other'. The ethnic stereotyping of motherhood thus exists not only for the purposes of tourism, but within the family itself.


## Conclusion

There is ample evidence in the Caribbean to support the claim that female subordination is not solely a result of women's exclusion from the labour force and relegation to the domestic sphere. Women in the Caribbean are economically active in a society in which the predominant ideal is for them to be confined to domestic roles. The fact that women who need to work to survive are accorded low status, are thought of as belonging to a lower class and are not regarded as desirable role models makes the situation worse. Even the 'yard' system (see Chapter 4), in which domestic chores are shared between the adjoining households, fails to give women a sense of their own autonomy, for in it they are still confined to the female sphere of responsibility. And this point is accentuated in tourism. In Negril quite substantial amounts of money can be obtained from tourism, yet with their work located in (or seen as an extension of) their domestic role, women's participation in the tourist industry is unlikely to challenge existing gender roles.

Goffee and Scase (1985), who evolved a fourfold typology of female entrepreneurs according to their attachment to entrepreneurial ideals and conventional gender roles, show that female economic activity is neither a necesary indicator of a desire for personal autonomy nor a challenge to the existing status quo between the sexes. According to them, 'conventional' women face potential conflict between the roles expected of them from both entrepreneurial and gender models. Among other categories of female entrepreneurs this conflict is reduced because the women concerned seek to challenge or change the existing status quo in society. They achieve this by lessening their adherence to gender roles (innovative), loosening their attachment to entrepreneurial ideals (domestic), or denying both (radicals).

With the possible exception of some of the American women, such as GR who keeps a Rastafarian 'yard husband', the majority of women entrepreneurs in Negril, Jamaican and foreign, can be categorized as 'conventional' or 'domestic'. Most of the foreign women, it should be noted, despite their unconventional marriages in that they are white women married to black men, are very conventional in subordinating business to domestic life.

One modification here is that the conflict between work and domesticity is reduced in the Caribbean by the tradition of women's economic activity. Caribbean women do not hold to any such Western concept as 'personal autonomy' in their work, but where conflict does exist, it is still resolved at the expense of entrepreneurial rather than gender ideals; a situation aggravated, as noted above, by the centrality of family relations to the business itself.

West Indian women in Negril are unlikely to change their gender roles or the economy. Their businesses are too small to threaten the interests of Negril's large middle-class businessmen. I am not suggesting a dual economy thesis, but rather that these women's small cottages merely operate at the opposite end of a continuum from hotels and guesthouses. Their potential for growth is limited by a lack of investment capital. The constant reinvestment of the money they earn is best seen as an extension of penny capitalism. Unfortunately, to make the kind of breakthrough in investment levels and profitability achieved by foreign entrepreneurs or middle-class Jamaicans requires the sort of money only overseas migrants returning to Negril or lucky speculators have amassed to date. And, despite their labour, Negrilian women are unlikely to succeed in accumulating such sums of money for themselves.

## Notes

1  This paper is based on a chapter in my M.Litt. thesis, 'The Effects of Tourism on Land Tenure: Migrants and Women in Negril, Jamaica', University of Aberdeen, 1989, supervised by Dr Jean Besson. Study for the thesis, including fieldwork in Jamaica from April to August 1985, was financed by a University of Aberdeen Postgraduate Studentship. I thank Dr Besson and Aberdeen University for their assistance. I also wish to acknowledge the help of the Department of Sociology and Social Work, University of the West Indies, Mona, Jamaica and especially the late June Dolly-Besson, during my fieldwork in Jamaica.
2  This is not, of course, an absolute rule; the difference is one of degree, for some women sell jewellery as a sideline even though their sons are often the ones who obtain it for them.
3  In Negril the two main spheres of female employment other than self-employment are in the hotel trade and prostitution. Obviously access to the latter was difficult, whilst any survey of hotel employees was complicated by the need for the employer's permission and the fact that my fieldwork was conducted out of season, when the majority of hotel staff were laid off.
4  There have always been vendors in Negril, the difference now is in their numbers, in the types of goods they sell and in the absence of the personal ties that had previously existed (Davenport 1956).

## References

Brodber, Erna (1982) *Perceptions of Caribbean Women: Towards a Documentation of Stereotypes*. Barbados: University of the West Indies

Davenport, William H. (1956) 'A Comparative Study of Two Jamaican Fishing Communities'. Ph.D. thesis, Yale University

Goffee, Robert and Richard Scase (1985) *Women in Charge: The Experiences of Female Entrepreneurs*. London: George Allen & Unwin

Henry, Frances and Pamela Wilson (1975) 'The Status of Women in the Caribbean: An Overview of their Social, Economic and Sexual Roles'. *Social and Economic Studies*, 24 (2) 165-98

Hooks, Bell (1982) *Ain't I a Woman? Black Women and Feminism*. London: Pluto Press

Katzin, Margaret (1960) 'The Business of Higglering in Jamaica'. *Social and Economic Studies*, 9 (3) 297-331

Light, I. (1972) *Ethnic Enterprise in America*. Berkeley: University of California Press

Mintz, Sidney W. (1971) 'Men, Women and Trade'. *Comparative Studies in Society and History*, 13 (3) 247-69

Perez, Louis A. Jr (1975) 'Tourism in the West Indies'. *Journal of Communication*, 25 (2) Spring

Walton, John K. (1978) *The Blackpool Landlady*. Manchester: Manchester University Press

Yawney, Carole (1983) 'To Grow a Daughter: Cultural Liberation and the Dynamics of Oppression in Jamaica'. In A. Miles and C. Finn (eds) *Feminism in Canada*, Montreal: Black Rose Books

# XIX  Gender & New Technology in the Caribbean: New Work for Women?

RUTH PEARSON

Ultimately, Caribbean society can only respond adequately to the challenges posed by global technological change if it accepts the need to reward innovation and technological effort. This embraces economic and material incentives, and also social recognition and praise. The society will have to become technologically aware and innovation-minded. And *it will need to be 'opened up' with regard to class, ethnicity and gender, in order to tap all the wide range of potential human sources of technological initiative.*

Norman Girvan (1989: 131), emphasis added

No-one can be unaware of the sweeping technical changes that have revolution-ized manufacturing and computer-telecommunications in recent decades. Many observers of the international economy see these changes as providing an oppor-tunity that was unavailable in previous technological eras, namely the oppor-tunity to leapfrog the traditional stages of industrial and technological innovation, thereby allowing relatively backward economies to adopt industrial strategies appropriate to their local conditions. As a result of heavy investments in research and development post-war technology has been able to generate techniques of production which, through large-scale output and extensive standardized markets, can enhance productivity and lower costs. Third World participation in these technological advances has largely been confined to labour intensive production (or parts of production) offering limited value added beyond the employment of local labour. Since the comparative advantage in locating produc-tion within their economies was largely in the cheapness of their labour, the value added was insufficient to provide enough surplus to engage in further capital accumulation or industrial development and innovation.[1]

For a long time the Caribbean has been the site of such internationalization of production, commencing with Operation Bootstrap in Puerto Rico and Intel's early investment in Barbados. In Jamaica and the Dominican Republic the export processing carried out in the free trade zones is an important source of local employment and foreign exchange earnings and there is similar foreign invest-ment in manufacturing in several other smaller Caribbean economies. Part of the rationale for the Caribbean Basin Initiative in 1984 was to encourage production in the Caribbean for export to US markets, apparently favouring the diversification of products away from the traditional textile and garment industry base of previ-ous years (Griffith 1990).

In terms of the international division of labour, developments in sectors other than manufacturing have received less attention. Among the most important developments here have been the changes in telecommunications technology and in the organization and regulation of intranational and international telecommu-nications services, as well as the fusion of office machinery, computer and telecommunications sectors.[2] During the early 1970s there was a significant trend towards the decentralization and suburbanization of what were then called 'back-office' services (Nelson 1986). This meant that companies were able to utilize the increasing flexibility offered by the hybrid of technologies referred to above to decentralize the physical location of labour and space intensive operations, such as invoicing, pay-rolling, stock control, progress chasing, sales records and analysis accounting. These tasks could be moved away to a location where the cost of appropriate labour and office accommodation was considerably lower than at the metropolitan city centre sites of their company headquarters or operational divisions.

New technologies have not only made possible the physical separation of data recording and handling processes from their place of generation and utilization, but they have also created a demand for new types of data based services. The sophistication of computer and office machinery technology has allowed the corporate sector to utilize data in different ways. A good example of this phenomenon is the procedure adopted by airline companies. An airline ticket contains a range of potential information, which is not actualized until the ticket has been used. At the point of sale the ticket issuing agency can record part of the data range, such as method of payment or class of travel, but in the course of using the ticket the passenger generates a series of additional data such as seat number, or stopovers. In order to reassemble this information and to use it to analyse sales and travel trends, consumer preferences and currency movements, the airline needs to centralize all the data for conversion into machine readable form. New technology allows this to be done at a specific location by collecting all the now separated layers of the tickets, endorsed with various pieces of information about dates and flight numbers, as well as boarding cards and sales receipts for in-flight transactions. This information can then be entered by a data entry operator according to a pre-designed structured programme.

Data entry of airline information was one of the first large-scale operations located in the Caribbean. American Airlines set up one such operation in Barbados in 1984 to service its data needs and has now extended this by forming a wholly-owned subsidiary company, Caribbean Data Services, with operations in at least three Caribbean islands. Its function is to provide off-shore processing of data for both American Airlines and other customers.

Another important source of demand for these kinds of services is the retailing and promotion sector. In the increasingly fragmented and 'customized' world of retailing promotion and competition, producers require detailed information about the location, nature and accessibility of their targeted market segment. Thus many kinds of retail promotion, such as discount coupons or customer's enquiries resulting from magazine features or advertisements, generate additional potential data sets which have to be made machine readable and operational. Many of the data entry bureaux in the Caribbean are involved in compiling sales information such as address lists of customers and locations of transactions involving discount coupons to use for future marketing strategies. These lists often have commercial resale value as customer data bases for other enterprises.

The public sector has also generated a growing demand for the services of the data entry sector. Large record-keeping departments such as Health and Social Security have increasingly required the computerization of their existing records and the establishment of systems for ongoing and future records. Specialized companies tender for these services, frequently using cheap off-shore locations to carry out at least the routine data entry operations.

The range of data handling amenable to relocation internationally is wider than that suggested in the examples outlined above. A schematic typology of the different kinds of data already being processed within the Caribbean is given below:

(1) internal company data storage and records creation, including personnel and pay-roll records, stock control, financial data, and management and staff employment records;

(2) inter-firm transactions, including sales records, accounts, orders, services contracted, and bills of lading and handling;

(3) consumer-firm transactions, including promotions, coupons, credit card status records and transactions, financial transfers, customer orders, health insurance records and applications, and other consumer insurance business;

(4) dedicated information services and data bases, including commodities trading, financial stocks and legal data bases;

(5) restructuring, storage and retrieval of existing data sets, including historical archives, library catalogues, social security and health sector records; and

(6) one-off customized services, mainly based on word-processing text, including company reports and documentation, engineering reports and manuscript typesetting.

The use of cheap Third World labour to perform the routine data entry processes associated with these services predates the fusion of telecommunications and office technology. In Jamaica, for instance, at least one firm has been in business since the mid-1960s, when it subcontracted card-punching data storage operations for clients in the US. But, at least in theory, telecommunications open up a new kind of opportunity: advances in international telecommunications systems and the transmission of optical (visual) imagery via these systems makes it technically possible to transmit from the original hard copy, have this made machine readable and re-transmit it to the client without the need physically to transport either hard copy, magnetic tapes or diskettes. Two-way interactive on-line data transmission offers the possibility of accessing cheap labour in Third World countries to carry out time-sensitive data recording functions such as credit card transactions, opening up yet more of this growing and changing market to Caribbean and other locations.

## Women's Employment in Off-shore Production & Services

It is now widely acknowledged that most workers in export processing industries within the manufacturing sector are women. Indeed, the more labour-intensive the production process, the higher the proportion of women workers. It is therefore wholly consistent and unremarkable that up to 98 per cent of those employed as data entry clerks in the Caribbean are women.[3]

On the one hand, this has been explained in terms of the lower wages women command in the labour market. On the other hand, however, it has been seen in terms of gender relations, which construct women as 'cheap' labour by requiring of them skills, speed and accuracy over a variety of labour processes that command no premiums within the labour market because the employers offer no formal training for them. This analysis has been applied to women workers in Third World export processing (Elson and Pearson 1981) and in the data entry sector (Posthuma 1987). But the question I wish to address in this chapter is the extent to which it is useful to apply the same analysis to women employed in the data entry and data processing operations that have been set up in the Caribbean since the mid-1980s.

Though many of the issues raised are common to the rest of the Caribbean (and to other Third World countries where such operations are important economic activities) I shall confine my discussion to the situation in Jamaica. This is not only because my empirical research is largely limited to that country, but also because its industry contains specific historical, political and economic factors, which raise alternative possibilities that could form a basis for policy intervention in the area of women's skills and career development in new technology employment.

## The Jamaican Data Entry/Data Processing Sector[4]

By 1989 there were 25 firms operating in Jamaica, employing a total of about 2500 people, of whom approximately 90 per cent were women, a not inconsiderable number out of a total workforce of about one million. The companies tend to operate two or sometimes three shifts and have between 25 and 100 or more terminals or keyboard stations. Thus, operator employment ranges from 50 to over 300. In addition, a typical company might employ between 10 and 30 administrative and technical personnel and a range of other workers, including couriers, dispatch clerks and general manual workers for cleaning and maintenance. The Jamaican operations are thus considerably smaller than those reported in the Dominican Republic or the Philippines, but similar to those in Barbados (Freeman 1990).

The pattern of ownership is also different from elsewhere in the Caribbean. Only five of the 25 firms are US-owned subsidiaries or US/Jamaican joint ventures; the remaining four-fifths are Jamaican owned. This is quite unlike the situation in the Dominican Republic, Barbados and St Lucia, where almost all data entry operations are foreign owned. Most of the Jamaican-owned companies are owned and managed by a new generation of black entrepreneurs. For the most part these are professionally trained people who had been employed, either in the public sector or in private industry, during the late 1970s or early 1980s when computerization (in the form of mainframes) was being introduced to their places of work. Their training in the new technology was usually acquired out-of-house and supplied by North American computer trainers, either within the Caribbean or in the US or Canada. Their work experience gave them initial training in the fast changing sphere of new office technology and they had acquired some understanding of the growing market for data entry services and the opportunities for off-shore sourcing for this kind of service. These entrepreneurs come neither from the traditional landowning oligarchy nor the capital-owning élite of Jamaican society. They are the upwardly mobile products of the post-independence expansion of technical and professional education amongst the black middle classes who have been mainly educated at the University of the West Indies.

The location of the enterprises is also worth noting. Five companies, of which four are not wholly Jamaican owned, operate in the Montego Bay area on the north coast of the island; the rest are concentrated mainly in the central business district of Kingston, the capital city. Of the Montego Bay companies, three (in mid-1989) were operating from within the Montego Bay free zone; none of the companies on the rest of the island were based in any of the other Jamaican free trade zones. Indeed, despite Kingston's being the largest and longest-established of the free trade zones, no data entry operations were located there. In contrast, it is believed that the majority of the data entry facilities in Barbados and the Dominican Republic are owned by foreign companies operating from within free trade zones.

One explanation for this difference is that many of the government's incentives for this sector are in the form of packages for foreign investors. In Jamaica, only wholly or mainly foreign owned companies are licensed to operate in the free zones and to receive the incentive package. This includes remission of import taxes on capital equipment, tax-free holidays, access to subsidized services and to the Jamaican Digiport, a high-speed data transmission facility located within the Montego Bay free zone. But access to the Digiport has not so far been a critical factor in the Jamaican industry and exclusion from this facility has therefore not served as a major disincentive or obstacle for Jamaican firms (EXIS 1989). More significant, especially in the judgement of the entrepreneurs themselves, are tax incentives, particularly concessions on import duties on capital equipment. As Jamaican owned companies cannot operate from within the free zones, they are excluded from the concessions on taxes and import duties which are regarded as key promotional benefits.

Until 1987 duty-free import of equipment for this sector was allowed on the basis that the whole of the sector's output was contracted to overseas clients and thus it was in effect an export industry. The industry was also seen by the government as an important net earner of foreign exchange, estimated by the industry itself to amount to US$10 million annually. However, a more recent protocol, connected with an IMF loan facility negotiation, rescinded the industry's privileges in this area, leaving the current paradoxical situation that only firms in the free zones, which are foreign-owned by definition, can claim duty remission on imported capital equipment.

This partly explains why local entrepreneurs rather than foreign investors have been responsible for the high rate of growth in this sector since 1984, from 2 to 28 companies (EXIS 1989: 11). The industry has evolved by taking up a range of different market opportunities across quite a wide spectrum of data entry operations. Indeed, Jamaica's data entry sector contains a far wider range of activities than the larger-scale operations in the Dominican Republic and elsewhere in the region and much of this can be ascribed to the type of ownership and management. In addition to a number of firms specializing in the high speed/high volume coupon/record activities (known in Jamaica as the commodity end of the business), several other more highly skilled and specialized activities are also carried out. These include preparing technical and engineering documents, transcribing court records, putting technical journals onto microfiche, creating a Jamaican legal data base, auto-drafting architectural and engineering plans, computerizing the social security system of a smaller Caribbean state and producing high quality lithographic illustrations for up-market art books.

Jamaica had still (in the late 1980s) not started to compete for time-sensitive jobs requiring access to high speed dedicated data transmission systems. Its normal mode of transmission had been entirely physical, using air transport and couriers. However, by 1989 the organized voice of the industry was beginning to demand access to the Digiport facilities on the same basis as foreign companies operating within the free zone. Jamaican companies had been having to rely on the more costly, slower and less reliable JAMITEL international telecommunications system for fax and other data transmission. Many of the contracts carried out by the industry in the 1980s had required only a five to ten-day turnaround but, with increasing competition from other areas both within and outside the region and rising interest from foreign investors with access to the Digiport facilities, the local industry began to feel that future growth depended on competing for time-sensitive operations. The Jamaican-owned companies were arguing that the industry had reached a plateau from which it was poised to recoup the investment in learning and to expand its operations into a new phase of growth and accumulation (EXIS 1989).

## Women Data Entry Workers: Another Cheap Labour Force?

The previous discussion of the growth of data entry operations in Jamaica confirms the view that the industry relies on market trends generated by the new technology adopted by the advanced economies. Jamaican firms compete on the basis of competitive pricing, which inevitably means that it is necessary to minimize unit labour costs through a combination of low wages and high productivity. As in off-shore manufacturing, women workers are the preferred labour force in such a business environment, both because they generally command lower wages than male workers and because they can work to higher levels of productivity. But, instead of being the new 'high tech' skilled workers of the future, the women employed in this sector are merely playing out a variation of an old theme: most of the women employed in the industry are in low-skilled, low-paid, dead-end jobs with no prospects of moving up any promotion or training ladder.

Data entry operators are generally recruited directly from high school with no previous work experience. Some, however, come through private commercial colleges, but this is largely because neither government training centres nor secondary schools have enough equipment or teachers to provide even minimal training in typing. At the point of recruitment, companies usually require a minimum typing speed of 35 to 45 words a minute. Prospective employees are subjected to a series of aptitude tests, which measure not only their potential for high speed keyboard operations but also their work attitudes and facility for dealing with the unfamiliar technology of VDUs and a stressful work environment. Those selected are put through a training programme lasting anything from two weeks to three months, during which they are paid a training allowance to cover travelling and subsistence expenses. On successful completion of training, they are usually made permanent employees and entitled to a varying range of benefits, including health insurance, subsidized meals and transport, pension schemes and, in one case, child-care facilities. It is believed that foreign-owned firms operating within the free zone offer superior worker benefits (Barnes 1989), though, given that there are US-owned firms in downtown Kingston that offer no employee benefits whatsoever, this may be related more to the kind of work undertaken. Although most workers are recruited at the age of 17 or 18, in some of the longer established firms, where wastage of original recruits has been low, there are also employees in their thirties.

Most operators achieve a speed of over 10,000 key strokes an hour, though 'star' performers have recorded speeds greatly in excess of this. Keyboard operators can progress up a very limited promotion structure, from Grade 1 to Grade 3, with minimal increments in pay. Further promotion is usually to the job of 'verifier', which involves monitoring the accuracy of the output of other operators. In some of the larger enterprises a woman might be promoted to the position of line or department supervisor, which is a more significant avenue of promotion involving substantial pay increases.

Payment is generally based on a minimum hourly rate, plus productivity-related incentives which may vary with the nature and difficulty of the particular job in hand. Basic key operators earn between J$2.00 and J$3.00 an hour, whilst supervisors can earn between J$700 and J$1400 a month, with US firms paying at the top end of the range (1989 figures when the exchange rate was between J$6.00 and J$7.00 per US dollar). Although this compares reasonably well with the minimum weekly industrial wage of J$52, the weekly net wage of a basic keyboard operator, after deductions for travel expenses and meals at work, is likely to be lower.

Most keyboard operators tend not to stay in the job for more than two or three years, largely because of the absence of promotion opportunities for all but a very small minority. Although there is no documented evidence in Jamaica, it is believed that eye strain, back injuries and repetitive strain syndrome are major health hazards for women working under the relentless pace and conditions required of keyboard operators in Jamaica, as in other countries (Barnes 1989). It is not possible to estimate the number of women who leave the industry because of occupation-related health problems.

Thus, in terms of pay, conditions of work, opportunities for promotion, security and longevity of employment, this sector does not perform any better than the garment factories in Kingston's free zone. However, it should be noted that the average weekly wage in data entry operations is substantially higher than the J$90 a week net earnings reported for women workers in clothing factories in 1988 (Anderson 1988).

This would tend to confirm Posthuma's conclusion that women workers in off-shore offices are being used 'only as a low wage labour force, acquiring little valuable training or skills and with no opportunity for job advancement in these industries' (Posthuma 1987: 45). But at the risk of sounding unduly optimistic, or of failing to accept the findings of my own research, I would like to argue that this conclusion, though likely, is not inevitable. This means opening up the issue of 'skill', which is not only important to small economies trying to compete in the world market with the new technology and its associated skills, but it also enables one to question the pessimistic conclusions of other commentators who relentlessly paint data entry as a no-hope occupation for the women employed.

First, the specific historical conditions under which Jamaica's industry has developed, particularly the dominance of a new professional, progressive and educated bourgeoisie, have opened up opportunities that are unavailable to other Caribbean data entry firms, particularly in the Dominican Republic and Barbados. This development has fostered a diversity of operations within the Jamaican industry; some of these are even beyond the scope of what is usually meant by data entry and could more properly be described as software design, or professional and information services. Expansion in other Caribbean countries has consisted mainly of large-scale foreign investment, such as CDS's US$10 million investment in a data entry plant employing 1500 people in Barbados (Watson 1990: 22). The scale of this development dwarfs that of the Jamaican firms and is equivalent to 60 per cent of Jamaica's total employment and 10 per cent of Jamaica's total investment in the sector over the 1984-9 period (EXIS 1989). But, given that Jamaican wages are still 25 per cent below those of Barbados and that the political will exists for maintaining a Jamaican industry, the industry could well start to compete on the basis of professional skills and services rather than just low operating costs, cheap labour and swift turnover.

Paradoxically, this is unlikely to happen unless there are significant changes in the way women's skills are evaluated and rewarded in the labour market. There is evidence to suggest that women employed in the industry are attracted to the possibilities of working with new technology and, if given the opportunity, would seek to obtain more training and experience. For example, Karen Street, Quality Control Operator at Punchline Ltd in Kingston 5, wrote in the company's April 1989 newsletter that 'What I like most is the opportunity to get to know the computer. You can try and experiment with the machine and get to know it better.'

Though I came across several women who had been promoted from keyboard operator to supervisory posts and, in one case, to technical manager, Karen Street's situation is more representative. Despite having been nominated 'Operator of the Quarter' she is pursuing a secretarial course at the Jamaica School of Business. Many of the women who leave the industry through fatigue, frustration or a desire to better themselves, take up secretarial posts. This must be a waste of potential skill and technical ability, for, despite being low paid and repetitive, operating keyboards does bring experience with an evolving technology, which is unique within the Jamaican workforce.

In addition to the over 2000 women currently employed as keyboard operators, there are a further 2000 who have previously worked or been trained within the industry, whose experience has been lost to the economy. The experience and potential for further technical training of these women must be considered in the context of an economy that in 1986 had only 600 trained computer technicians (Girvan 1989). This shortage may help to explain why, despite much rhetoric about the new information technology age, few commercial offices in the financial or public sector have been computerized.

It is a damning reflection on the evaluation of women's skills that workers who have been able to adapt to considerable pressures at work, who have shown flexibility of response to frequently changing programmes on an *ad hoc* basis and have organized speedy through-put of data entry at a guaranteed level of accuracy and quality, should be considered no more qualified than school leavers with basic typing skills. Instead of being channelled towards managerial or information technology training courses and employment, both the women themselves and their past and potential employers are content to allow them to proceed to secretarial training and employment, where their skills and talents will remain unrecognized, unrewarded and underutilized.

This poses an important challenge to the universal and fatalistic analyses that cast women's employment in this sector in the same mould as employment in the garment and electronic assembly factories of the free trade zones in the Caribbean and elsewhere. For all the reasons cited for this sector not being located in such zones and not being dominated by foreign capital, it would be possible to implement policies to support the development of a highly skilled, flexible and innovatory information services sector, which could have a role not just within the island but as a centre of technological innovation and development in the Caribbean region as a whole. But to achieve this, the ongoing practice of writing off women's experience in employment as unskilled and unimportant, of denying its currency in the professional labour market and of affording that experience no usefulness as an orientation for technical training, must be reversed. This might prove far more difficult than gaining access to the Montego Bay Digiport.

## Notes

1  See Sklair (1989) chapter 1 for a discussion of a methodology to assess the extent to which export assembly operations can be considered as successful in development terms.
2  For a detailed discussion of these issues within the North-South context, see Pearson (1988).
3  This is corroborated by Posthuma (1987) and Freeman (1990).
4  The data in this section is based on information I collected during a short research visit to Jamaica in 1989, during which I interviewed 15 of the 25 data entry/data processing companies and collected secondary material from a variety of industrial, governmental and other sources.

## References

Anderson, P. (1988) 'Free Zone Workers in the St Peter Cleaver Community'. Kingston, Jamaica, mimeo

Barnes, C. (1989) 'Data Entry Demands'. *Sistren Magazine*, 11 (3) 18-20

Elson, D. and R. Pearson (1981) 'The Subordination of Women and the Internationalization of Factory Production'. In K. Young, C. Wolkowitz and R. McCullagh (eds) *Of Marriage and the Market*, London: Routledge & Kegan Paul, 144-66

EXIS (1989) *Going for the Iceberg: A Blueprint from Growth and Development in the Export of Information Services*. Kingston: Exporters of Information Services (EXIS), a subgroup of the Jamaican Exporter's Association

Freeman, C. (1990) 'High Tech and High Heels: Barbadian Women in the Off-shore Information Industry'. Paper presented to the Fifteenth Annual Conference of the Caribbean Studies Association, Trinidad & Tobago, May

Girvan, Norman (1989) 'Technological Change and the Caribbean: Formulating Strategic Responses'. *Social and Economic Studies*, 38 (2) 111-35

Griffith, W. (1990) 'CARICOM Countries and the Caribbean Basin Initiative'. *Latin American Perspectives*, 17 (1: 64) 33-54

Nelson, K. (1986) 'Labor Demand, Labor Supply and the Suburbanization of Low-Wage Office Work'. In A. Scott and M. Storper (eds) *Work, Production and Territory*, London: Allen & Unwin, 149-71

Pearson, R. (1988) 'Telecommunications Technology: The Basis for a New International Division of Labour'. Research Paper, Development Policy and Planning Unit, Technology Faculty, The Open University, Milton Keynes

Posthuma, A. (1987) *The New Internationalization of Labour*. Report No. 26, SPRU, University of Essex

Sklair, L. (1989) *Assembling for Development: The Maquila Industry in Mexico and the United States*. London: Unwin Hyman

Watson, H. (1990) 'Recent Attempts at Industrial Restructuring in Barbados'. *Latin American Perspectives*, 17 (1: 64) 10-32

# Index